Severin C. Carlson

Foundations of Economic Analysis

*Originally published by Harvard University Press as
Harvard Economic Studies Volume 80*

*The Department of Economics does not assume
responsibility for the views expressed*

Paul Anthony Samuelson

FOUNDATIONS
OF ECONOMIC ANALYSIS

Mathematics is a Language

J. WILLARD GIBBS

Atheneum   *New York*   *1976*

To my parents

FOREWORD

It says something for the economics of publishing and the voracious appetite of the educated public that an advanced book like the present one should be reissued in paperback form. Authors notoriously wish their works to be widely read, and I am no exception. But I must confess that at first I dragged my heels when the publishers suggested the present edition. After all, the book has been continuously available since its publication in 1947 and, for a scholarly work of its kind, has received and continues to receive a gratifying measure of attention from professional economists. My chief fear—let me come out and admit at once—was that people might be tempted to buy the paperback edition out of miscalculation and error, perhaps confusing it with my elementary textbook. (Since the two books came out within a year of each other, this is no empty terror —as may be illustrated by a true story. My friend, Professor J. Kenneth Galbraith of Harvard University, was asked some years ago to recommend a book typical of what was new in postwar economics to his former wartime chief at the Office of Price Administration, Leon Henderson. Galbraith said, "You might as well read Samuelson's textbook." The inevitable happened and the next time they met, Henderson complained, "The subject of economics has certainly become technical since I last studied it!")

Upon further reflection, though, I came to realize that the book carries its own caveats and warnings in the mathematical equations with which almost every page bristles. And evidence mounts that a new generation is growing up with that minimum training in mathematics which opens the door not only to the language of science but also to new realms of aesthetic delight. So, recognizing economic law, I cheerfully gave my assent.

Mathematics as Recreation and Tool

Aside from the student of economics, who will want to read this work for vocational reasons, those interested in general culture may find the book of interest. It used to be that an educated person was supposed to have a knowledge of the classics, in Greek and Latin and in translation.

What Montaigne and Hazlitt knew, *he* knew. The verses of Milton and Pope, which are salted throughout with literary references that are like Choctaw to a modern, narrowly trained scientist, rang little bells in the conscious and subconscious memory of the well-brought-up man of affairs. The body of knowledge that was worth knowing grew only by slow accretion. When T. S. Eliot was told, "We know more than the Ancients," he was able to reply, "Yes, and it is the Ancients that we know."

Nevertheless, after the time of Newton, there had begun a gradual change. The findings of science, and most notably the mathematical language of science, began to be a mandatory part of a proper education. If your finishing school did not enable you to understand the conversations of Voltaire and Madame du Châtelet on the Newtonian system, or the speculations of Buffon concerning the St. Petersburg Paradox (according to which a rational man would refuse to pay a very high price for the privilege of winning a colossal fortune, but with small probability) —well, you simply had not been properly finished. In the last century, this split between the need to know history and the classics and the need to know the language of science has reached crisis proportions. Sir Charles Snow's plea for a uniting of the "two cultures" merely reflects this long developing tension. And the violent reactions to his commonplace observations are indications that the learned man who is innocent of mathematics has for decades now been experiencing all the frustrations habitually associated with minority groups subject to waning prestige and remorseless pressure.

The present book was not written with the purpose of illustrating how mathematics might be interesting in its applications to a social science. It had the more prosaic, workaday purpose of getting on with the internal problems of economic research. Though not avoiding elegance, I did not seek it when it carried a price tag. Though not courting obscurity, I realized that the treatise would become volumes in length if its many parts received the careful exposition that learners need but which my scholarly peers could do without. None the less, as an unintended by-product or bonus, the book may hold some interest for the reader who is curious about the methodology of the social sciences and of applied mathematics generally. In this respect the book might hopefully be classified with A. J. Lotka's *Elements of Physical Biology,* which a non-biologist like me found enormously stimulating at the same time that it represented a serious attack on the professional problems of that subject.

Those concerned with general problems of philosophy of science and its methodology may find modern economics of considerable interest. By this I do not mean that the methodological views of the venerable economist Ludwig von Mises are more interesting than the positivistic views of his deceased brother, Richard von Mises, the distinguished physicist and mathematician. In my view they definitely are not. But economics is by its nature a softer and less exact science than, say, conventional physics. Now in a hard, exact science a practitioner does not really have to know much about methodology. Indeed, even if he is definitely a misguided methodologist, the subject itself has a self-cleansing property which renders harmless his aberrations. By contrast, a scholar in economics who is fundamentally confused concerning the relationship of definition, tautology, logical implication, empirical hypothesis, and factual refutation may spend a lifetime shadow-boxing with reality. In a sense, therefore, in order to earn his daily bread as a fruitful contributor to knowledge, the practitioner of an intermediately hard science like economics must come to terms with methodological problems. I stress the importance of intermediate hardness because when one descends lower still, say to certain areas of sociology that are almost completely without substantive content, it may not matter much one way or the other what truths or errors about scientific method are involved— for the reason that nothing matters.

General Properties of Minimum Systems

There is still another category of reader who might benefit from modern mathematical economics. Precisely because I wanted to find the common, core properties of diverse parts of economic theory, I concentrated on certain general features of economic analysis: on the nature of an equilibrium system; on the general structure of a maximum problem; on the relationship between comparative statics and dynamics; and so forth. Many fields quite removed from economics also have an interest in similar problems. Thus, much of statics and dynamics in physics involves the analysis of maximum, minimum, or extremum problems. Perhaps you might have thought that physicists had already analyzed these questions in a completely abstract way and that an economist in the twentieth century need merely bone up on what have been the completed findings of classical mechanics. If you had thought that, you

would have been wrong. The great mathematical physicists of the past
—notably Euler, Lagrange, Hamilton, Jacobi, Gauss, Helmholtz, Rayleigh, Poincaré, G. D. Birkhoff, Appel, Hamel, Carathéodory—have indeed introduced variational and minimum principles into classical mechanics and thermodynamics. But remarkably little depth of analysis has
gone into the question of just what is the operational significance for
empirical observation of such extremum formulations. I do not say this
by way of reproach. Since mere variational principles and mere counting
of equations and unknowns proved so fruitful in mechanics, and since
there were so many exciting discoveries to be made at the frontier of
the subject, it is understandable that experts did not use their limited
time to examine and exhaust these problems. Therefore, the kind of
analysis of maximum systems that appears in Chapter III needed to be
done by someone, and, in the language of mountain climbing, I tackled
these problems "because they were there."

One illustration will suffice. In thermodynamics there is a vague
notion called Le Chatelier's Principle. Each text words it differently
but all stress the notion that when you do something to an equilibrium
system—such as squeeze a balloon—the system mysteriously acts to
adapt itself to that stress. My old teacher and friend, Edwin Bidwell
Wilson, has been a distinguished mathematician, physicist, statistician,
and social scientist. Since he was one of Willard Gibbs' few students,
his lectures naturally touched on the Le Chatelier Principle. His preg-
nant remark, "As far as I can see, it represents a theorem in mathematics and not merely a law of empirical physics" set me off to enunciate
the precise property of positive-definite matrices which lies at the bottom of the Principle. Once its general nature was elucidated, applications
to economics like the following one became easy. "The demand for a
factor like labor is less elastic in the short run when land cannot be
varied than in the long run when land can be bought at a fixed rental—
and this independently of whether labor and land are *complementary* or
rival factors!"

PAST AS PROLOGUE

In 1947 kind reviewers hailed this book as a culmination of a great
tradition. In the field of, say, music this would be the highest praise.
But in the dynamic field of science the most important goal is to be

seminal and pathbreaking, to look forward boldly even if imperfectly. Perhaps the significant difference between a science and an art resides in the cumulative aspect of scientific knowledge. The best artist today cannot be expected to sculpt better than Michelangelo, or as well. But any schoolboy knows more than Archimedes, even though Archimedes was the greatest genius of ancient times. And most college graduates in physics know more than Isaac Newton: for as Newton himself said, a scientist sees further than his predecessors because he stands on the shoulders of earlier giants. (But do not misinterpret his modesty: bring Isaac Newton back to life today, give him a couple of years of training, and prepare to see how he forges ahead of the pack!) And yet, though it be important in science to codify the past and generalize it elegantly, we must remember that the future is longer than the past.

Thus, the parts of Newton's *Principia* that embalm in chaste geometry his universal law of gravitation are there to be admired. But, as the modern commentator Clifford Truesdell (*American Mathematical Monthly,* 1953) has pointed out, modern historical research has destroyed much of the attribution of originality to them, even though they beautifully synthesize the subject, avoiding all earlier errors and providing completeness for the first time. Yet it is in Book II of the *Principia,* where he has abandoned the axiomatic method, that "Newton's might of intellect is recognized even more clearly" as he sets out imperfectly the foundations of hydrodynamics and poses conjectures for scientists to verify and correct for the next hundred years.

In this connection, I should like to quote the final paragraph from an early review article on my book by Professor Kenneth Boulding. Boulding is one of the finest spirits of our time—economist's economist, poet, mystic, master of all trades in the social sciences, and my old friend.

"The *Foundations* is an important book. It should be studied not only by the mathematically baptized but also by those who, like myself, hang on to *n*-dimensions by the skin of their teeth. No economist who studies it can fail to profit by it. Nevertheless, the present reviewer cannot help feeling a certain sense of rapidly diminishing marginal productivity in the application of mathematics to economics. There is an elusive flavor of John Stuart Mill about the *Foundations* which makes it seem less like a foundation than a coping stone, finishing an edifice which does not have much further to go. It may well be that the slovenly literary borderland between economics and sociology will be the most fruitful building ground during the years to come and that mathematical economics will remain too flawless in its perfection to be very fruitful." (*Journal of Political Economy,* 1948, p. 199)

What has been the verdict of experience in the fifteen years since these thoughtful words were written? Quite apart from the merits or influence of my book, every knowledgeable observer will realize that during these years economics has become mathematical and technical as never before. If you dislike mathematics, there is today scarcely a graduate school in the land that you can flee to. Our learned journals are full of technical symbolism, and even the intermediate textbooks now bristle with econometric tools. Not even the *Congressional Record* has been spared. For better or worse, serious economics has become a mathematical subject, just as physics and engineering had become a century ago.

In connection with this book, it is the development of research which interests me even more than the problems of education. Frankly, back in 1947 I should not myself have predicted the veritable renaissance of economic theory which turned out to be just ahead. In the United States, in France, in Scandinavia and the Netherlands, in Japan—and even in Britain—mathematical economics ceased to be the preoccupation of an *avant garde* and became part of the main stream of creative scholarship. Far from closing out the prewar tradition of Jevons, Edgeworth, Walras, Wicksell, Marshall, Pigou, Frisch, Hotelling, Hicks and Allen, Tinbergen and Leontief, the *Foundations of Economic Analysis* can now be seen as part of the dawn we associate with the postwar names of K. J. Arrow, R. M. Solow, J. Tobin, M. Allais, H. Wold, L. Hurwicz, M. Morishima, F. Hahn, and numerous other economists all over the world. (I desist from naming mathematicians who have labored in adjacent vineyards.)

The law of diminishing returns is a fact of life we do well to remember. But let us not overlook the creative forces of innovation which work against and thwart it. Thanks to the work of that genius, John von Neumann, game theory was already knocking on the door when World War II ended. The fruitful theories of linear and non-linear programming, of George Dantzig and Gale-Kuhn-Tucker, were waiting in the wings. I think the Gibbsian emphasis on inequalities, which pervades the *Foundations,* helped prepare economists for the new revolutions in thought. But comparing it with, say, *Linear Programming and Eco-*

nomic Theory, a book I helped write (with R. F. Dorfman and R. M. Solow) scarcely a decade later, will show the advanced student of economics how far from exhausted at war's end was the vein of fruitful economic theory.

Kenneth Boulding was right, that one cannot usefully say "I love you" in mathematical language. And, as many of his own recent books in economics and the behavioral sciences have so beautifully demonstrated, there is much to be done by scholars who eschew all metric methods. But still it is true that, whether in Washington, Rotterdam, or Moscow, we today live in a golden age for analytical economics: duality, turnpike theorems, stability of dynamic equilibrium—was there ever a time of more fruitful progress in conquering such new frontiers of knowledge? And I who inherit the skin of that intense young man who from 1937 to 1940 spent the most pleasant years imaginable as a Junior Fellow of the Society of Fellows at Harvard am proud to have helped build these foundations.

PAUL A. SAMUELSON

Cambridge, Massachusetts
August, 1964

PREFACE

THE ORIGINAL version of this book submitted to the David A. Wells Prize Committee of Harvard University in 1941 carried the subtitle, "The Operational Significance of Economic Theory." At that time most of the material presented was already several years old, having been conceived and written primarily in 1937. Further delay in publication has been necessary because of the war, and because of the addition of supplementary treatise-like material going beyond the original conception of the work as indicated by its subtitle.

Because of the pressure of war work I have not been able to do full justice to the literature of the last few years, nor even to include all of the developments of my own thinking. Fortunately, the passage of time has dealt kindly with the analysis contained here, and where it abuts upon the topics treated in Professor Hicks's masterly *Value and Capital*, the similarity in point of view has been reassuring.

My greatest debt is to Marion Crawford Samuelson whose contributions have been all too many. The result has been a vast mathematical, economic, and stylistic improvement. Without her collaboration the book would literally not have been written, and no perfunctory uxorial acknowledgment can do justice to her aid. Nor can the quaint modern custom of excluding the value of a wife's services from the national income condone her exclusion from the title page.

My thanks for prolonged stimulation over many years must go out to Professors Schumpeter, Leontief, and E. B. Wilson, while each of a legion of Harvard graduate students has left his mark upon what follows. The reader will note my dependence upon the sterling contribution to Welfare Economics of Professor Abram Bergson. Grateful acknowledgment is made to the Social Science Research Council and to the Society of Fellows of Harvard University for the opportunities they provided for pursuit of independent research, and to the Department of Economics of Harvard University for their courteous acceptance of the wartime delays in publication.

Acknowledgment is made to the editors of *Econometrica* and the *Review of Economic Statistics* for permission to reproduce parts of my previously published articles. Chapters IX and X are taken almost entirely from two articles that appeared in *Econometrica*, while part of Chapter XI appeared in the *Review of Economic Statistics*.

P. A. S.

CAMBRIDGE, MASSACHUSETTS
JANUARY 1945

CONTENTS

PART I

I. INTRODUCTION 3

II. EQUILIBRIUM SYSTEMS AND COMPARATIVE STATICS . 7

Symbolic Formulation 10
Displacement of Equilibrium 12
Illustrative Tax Problem. 14
Illustrative Market Case. 17
Summary 19

III. THE THEORY OF MAXIMIZING BEHAVIOR 21

Three Sources of Meaningful Theorems . . . 21
A Calculus of Qualitative Relations. 23
Maximum Conditions of Equilibrium 29
Displacement of Equilibrium 30
Displacement of Quantity Maximized 34
Auxiliary Constraints and the Generalized Le
Chatelier Principle 36
Economic Illustrations 39
Analysis of Finite Changes 46
Analytic Functions 52
Convertibility into a Maximum Problem . . . 52

IV. A COMPREHENSIVE RESTATEMENT OF THE THEORY OF
COST AND PRODUCTION. 57

Statement of Problems 57
Conditions of Equilibrium 60
Secondary Extremum Conditions 61
Displacement of Equilibrium. 63
Boundary or Corner Minima. 69
Discontinuities in the Production Function . . 70
Conditions of Equilibrium 73
Determinateness of Equilibrium. 75
Maximization of Profit 76
Indeterminacy in Purest Competition? . . . 78

Discontinuous Case 80
External Conditions of Equilibrium. 81
Summary 87

V. THE PURE THEORY OF CONSUMER'S BEHAVIOR . . 90
Evolution of Utility Concept. 90
Progression in Mathematical Thought 92
The Demand Functions as a Goal 96
Conditions of Equilibrium 97
Displacement of Equilibrium. 100
Meaningful Theorems. 107
Conclusion 116
A Note on the Demand for Money 117
Qualifications Introduced by Uncertainty . . . 122

VI. TRANSFORMATIONS, COMPOSITE COMMODITIES, AND RA-
TIONING 125
Logarithmic Transformations and Elasticities . . 125
General Transformation of Independent Variables. 129
Transformation of Dependent Variable. . . . 133
Transformation of Prices 135
Demand for a Group of Commodities 141
The General Problem of Composite or Aggregate
Commodities 144
The Economic Theory of Index Numbers . . . 146
Present Formulations of Index Numbers . . . 156
Pure Theory of Choice under Rationing . . . 163

VII. SOME SPECIAL ASPECTS OF THE THEORY OF CON-
SUMER'S BEHAVIOR 172
The Cardinal Measure of Utility 173
The Assumption of Independent Utilities . . . 174
Complementarity 183
Constancy of the Marginal Utility of Income . . 189
Why Consumer's Surplus is Superfluous . . . 195
The Many Forms of Consumer's Surplus . . . 197

VIII. WELFARE ECONOMICS 203
The Social Welfare Function. 219
Mathematical Analysis 229
Production Conditions 230

Pure Exchange Conditions 236
Interpersonal Optimal Conditions 243
New Versus Old Welfare Economics 249
Conclusion 252

PART II

IX. THE STABILITY OF EQUILIBRIUM: COMPARATIVE STATICS
AND DYNAMICS 257
Introduction 257
Comparative Statics 258
Stability and Dynamics 260
The Stability of Multiple Markets 269
Analysis of the Keynesian System 276

X. THE STABILITY OF EQUILIBRIUM: LINEAR AND NON-
LINEAR SYSTEMS 284
Introduction 284
Functional Equations and Stationary Solutions . 286
Linear and Nonlinear Systems 288
The Nonlinear Differential Equation in One Vari-
able 288
Example: Logistic Law 291
The Problem of Higher-Order Stability. . . 294
An Example of One-sided Stability-Instability:
Malthusian and Optimum Population Theories. 296
Systems of Equations in *"n"* Variables. . . 299
The Stability of a Stationary Position which is also
a Maximum 301
The Difference Equation in One Variable . . 302
Analytic Solution 307
Other Functional Equations 308

XI. SOME FUNDAMENTALS OF DYNAMICAL THEORY . . 311
Statics and Dynamics. 311
Causal Systems 317
Stationary States and their Generalization. . 320
Resolution of the Problem 329
Concepts of Stability 333
Nature of the Business Cycle 335
Endogenous Models 336

Mixed Exogenous-Endogenous Theories . . . 340
Mixed Systems of a Linear Stochastic Type . . 342
Non-Linear Stochastic Systems 344

XII. CONCLUSION. 350

MATHEMATICAL APPENDIX A. 357

MATHEMATICAL APPENDIX B: DIFFERENCE EQUATIONS. . 380

INDEX 441

Part One

CHAPTER I

INTRODUCTION

The existence of analogies between central features of various theories implies the existence of a general theory which underlies the particular theories and unifies them with respect to those central features. This fundamental principle of generalization by abstraction was enunciated by the eminent American mathematician E. H. Moore more than thirty years ago. It is the purpose of the pages that follow to work out its implications for theoretical and applied economics.

An economist of very keen intuition would perhaps have suspected from the beginning that seemingly diverse fields—production economics, consumer's behavior, international trade, public finance, business cycles, income analysis—possess striking formal similarities, and that economy of effort would result from analyzing these common elements.

I can make no claim to such initial insight. Only after laborious work in each of these fields did the realization dawn upon me that essentially the same inequalities and theorems appeared again and again, and that I was simply proving the same theorems a wasteful number of times.

I was aware, of course, that each field involved interdependent unknowns determined by presumably efficacious, independent equilibrium conditions—a fact which has always been generally realized. But, and this leads me to the second fundamental purpose of this work, it had not been pointed out to my knowledge that there exist formally identical *meaningful* theorems in these fields, each derived by an essentially analogous method.

This is not surprising since only the smallest fraction of economic writings, theoretical and applied, has been concerned with the derivation of *operationally meaningful* theorems. In part at least this has been the result of the bad methodological preconceptions that economic laws deduced from *a priori* assumptions possessed rigor and validity independently of any empirical human behavior. But only a very few economists have gone so far as this.

The majority would have been glad to enunciate meaningful theorems if any had occurred to them. In fact, the literature abounds with false generalization.

We do not have to dig deep to find examples. Literally hundreds of learned papers have been written on the subject of utility. Take a little bad psychology, add a dash of bad philosophy and ethics, and liberal quantities of bad logic, and any economist can prove that the demand curve for a commodity is negatively inclined. His instinct is good; the attempt to derive a meaningful useful theorem is commendable—much more so than the innocuous position that utility is always maximized because people do what they do. How refreshing then is a paper like Slutsky's [1] which attempted, with partial success, to deduce once and for all the hypotheses upon price-quantity budget behavior implied in the utility approach.

The economist has consoled himself for his barren results with the thought that he was forging tools which would eventually yield fruit. The promise is always in the future; we are like highly trained athletes who never run a race, and in consequence grow stale. It is still too early to determine whether the innovations in thought of the last decade will have stemmed the unmistakable signs of decadence which were clearly present in economic thought prior to 1930.

By a *meaningful theorem* I mean simply a hypothesis about empirical data which could conceivably be refuted, if only under ideal conditions. A meaningful theorem may be false. It may be valid but of trivial importance. Its validity may be indeterminate, and practically difficult or impossible to determine. Thus, with existing data, it may be impossible to check upon the hypothesis that the demand for salt is of elasticity -1.0. But it is meaningful because under ideal circumstances an experiment could be devised whereby one could hope to refute the hypothesis.

The statement that if demand were inelastic, an increase in price would raise total revenue is not a meaningful theorem in this sense. It implies no hypothesis—certainly not even that a demand exists which is inelastic—and is true simply by definition. It may possibly have had a certain "psychological" usefulness in helping

[1] E. Slutsky, "Sulla teoria del bilancio del consumatore," *Giornale degli Economisti*, LI (1915), 1–26.

economists ask the right questions of the facts, but even here I have some doubts.

In this study I attempt to show that there do exist meaningful theorems in diverse fields of economic affairs. They are not deduced from thin air or from *a priori* propositions of universal truth and vacuous applicability. They proceed almost wholly from two types of very general hypotheses. The first is that the conditions of equilibrium are equivalent to the maximization (minimization) of some magnitude. Part I deals with this phase of the subject in a reasonably exhaustive fashion.

However, when we leave single economic units, the determination of unknowns is found to be unrelated to an extremum position. In even the simplest business cycle theories there is lacking symmetry in the conditions of equilibrium so that there is no possibility of directly reducing the problem to that of a maximum or minimum. Instead the dynamical properties of the system are specified, and the hypothesis is made that the system is in "stable" equilibrium or motion. By means of what I have called the *Correspondence Principle* between comparative statics and dynamics, definite *operationally meaningful* theorems can be derived from so simple a hypothesis. One interested only in fruitful statics must study dynamics.

The empirical validity or fruitfulness of the theorems, of course, cannot surpass that of the original hypothesis. Moreover, the stability hypothesis has no teleological [2] or normative significance; thus, the stable equilibrium might be at fifty per cent unemployment. The plausibility of such a stability hypothesis is suggested by the consideration that positions of unstable equilibrium, even if they exist, are transient, nonpersistent states, and hence on the crudest probability calculation would be observed less frequently than stable states. How many times has the reader seen an egg standing upon its end? From a formal point of view it is often convenient to consider the stability of nonstationary motions.

In a good deal of Part II the dynamical behavior of systems is analyzed for its own sake, regardless of implications for comparative statics. And in the last chapters of Part I, I have gone beyond the original conception of the book to include such subjects as

[2] L. J. Henderson, *The Order of Nature* (Cambridge, Massachusetts: Harvard University Press, 1917).

welfare economics.   Although the logical content of the theorems enunciated here is different, there is an underlying unity of method.

In the beginning it was hoped that the discussion could be made nontechnical.   Very quickly it became apparent that such a procedure, while possible, would involve a manuscript many times the present size.   Moreover, I have come to feel that Marshall's dictum that "it seems doubtful whether any one spends his time well in reading lengthy translations of economic doctrines into mathematics, that have not been made by himself" should be exactly reversed.   The laborious literary working over of essentially simple mathematical concepts such as is characteristic of much of modern economic theory is not only unrewarding from the standpoint of advancing the science, but involves as well mental gymnastics of a peculiarly depraved type.

On the other hand, I have attempted to avoid all mathematical flourish, and the pure mathematician will recognize all too readily the essentially elementary character of the tools used.   My own interest in mathematics has been secondary and subsequent to my interest in economics.   Nevertheless, the reader may find some parts hard going.   To lighten the way I have placed the purely mathematical theorems in two separate appendices, of which the second gives a reasonably self-contained introduction to the theory of difference equations.

CHAPTER II

EQUILIBRIUM SYSTEMS AND COMPARATIVE STATICS

MOST ECONOMIC TREATISES are concerned with either the description of some part of the world of reality or with the elaboration of particular elements abstracted from reality. Implicit in such analyses there are certain recognizable formal uniformities, which are indeed characteristic of all scientific method. It is proposed here to investigate these common features in the hope of demonstrating how it is possible to deduce general principles which can serve to unify large sectors of present day economic theory.

In every problem of economic theory certain variables (quantities, prices, etc.) are designated as unknowns, in whose determination we are interested. Their values emerge as a solution of a specified set of relationships imposed upon the unknowns by assumption or hypothesis. These functional relationships hold as of a given environment and milieu. Of course, to designate this environment completely would require specification of the whole universe; therefore, we assume implicitly a matrix of conditions within which our analysis is to take place.

It is hardly enough, however, to show that under certain conditions we can name enough relations (equations) to determine the values of our unknowns. It is important that our analysis be developed in such terms that we are aided in determining how our variables change qualitatively or quantitatively with changes in explicit data. Thus, we introduce explicitly into our system certain data in the form of parameters, which in changing cause shifts in our functional relations. The usefulness of our theory emerges from the fact that by our analysis we are often able to determine the nature of the changes in our unknown variables resulting from a designated change in one or more parameters. In fact, our theory is meaningless in the operational sense unless it does imply some restrictions upon empirically observable quantities, by which it could conceivably be refuted.

7

This in brief is the method of *comparative statics*, meaning by this the investigation of changes in a system from one position of equilibrium to another without regard to the transitional process involved in the adjustment. By equilibrium is meant here only the values of variables determined by a set of conditions, and no normative connotation attaches to the term. As will be shown later, it is always possible to set up completely trivial equilibrium systems.

This method of comparative statics is but one special application of the more general practice of scientific deduction in which the behavior of a system (possibly through time) is defined in terms of a given set of functional equations and initial conditions. Thus, a good deal of theoretical physics consists of the assumption of second order differential equations sufficient in number to determine the evolution through time of all variables subject to given initial conditions of position and velocity. Similarly, in the field of economics dynamic systems involving the relationship between variables at different points of time (e.g., time derivatives, weighted integrals, lag variables, functionals, etc.) have been suggested for the purpose of determining the evolution of a set of economic variables through time.[1]   At a later stage I deal with these dynamic problems.

The concept of an equilibrium system outlined above is applicable as well to the case of a single variable as to so-called *general equilibrium* involving thousands of variables. Logically the determination of output of a given firm under pure competition is precisely the same as the simultaneous determination of thousands of prices and quantities. In every case *ceteris paribus* assumptions must be made. The only difference lies in the fact that in the general equilibrium analysis of, let us say, Walras, the content of the historical discipline of theoretical economics is practically exhausted. The things which are taken as data for that system happen to be matters which economists have traditionally chosen not to consider as within their province. Among these data may be mentioned tastes, technology, the governmental and institutional framework, and many others.

    [1] R. Frisch, "On the Notion of Equilibrium and Disequilibrium," *Review of Economic Studies*, III (1936), 100–105. J. Tinbergen, Annual Survey: Suggestions on Quantitative Business Cycle Theory, *Econometrica*, III (1935), 241–308.

It is clear, however, that logically there is nothing fundamental about the traditional boundaries of economic science. In fact, a system may be as broad or as narrow as we please depending upon the purpose at hand; and the data of one system may be the variables of a wider system depending upon expediency. The fruitfulness of any theory will hinge upon the degree to which factors relevant to the particular investigation at hand are brought into sharp focus. And if, for the understanding of the business cycle a theory of governmental policy is demanded, the economist can ill afford to neglect this need on the ground that such matters lie outside his province. As for those who argue that special degrees of certainty and empirical validity attach to the relations encompassed within the traditional limits of economic theory, we may leave to them the task of proving their case.

It is not to be thought that the content of systems as described above must be restricted to the variables usually considered in price and value theory. On the contrary, one employs such constructions throughout the whole field of theoretical economics including monetary and business cycle theory, international trade, etc. It goes without saying that the existence of such systems in no way hinges upon the employment of symbolic or mathematical methods. In fact, any sector of economic theory which cannot be cast into the mold of such a system must be regarded with suspicion as suffering from haziness.

Within the framework of any system the relationships between our variables are strictly those of mutual interdependence. It is sterile and misleading to speak of one variable as causing or determining another. Once the conditions of equilibrium are imposed, all variables are simultaneously determined. Indeed, from the standpoint of comparative statics equilibrium is not something which is attained; it is something which, if attained, displays certain properties.

The only sense in which the use of the term causation is admissible is in respect to changes in external data or parameters. As a figure of speech, it may be said that changes in these *cause* changes in the variables of our system. An increase in demand, i.e., a shift in the demand function due to a change in the data, tastes, may be said to cause an increased output to be sold. Even here, when several parameters change simultaneously, it is impossible to speak of causation attributable to each except in respect to limiting rates of change (partial derivatives).

Symbolic Formulation

All of the above may be stated compactly in mathematical form. Given n variables or unknowns $(x_1, \cdots, x_n)$ and m, greater or less than n, parameters $(\alpha_1, \cdots, \alpha_m)$, we assume n independent and consistent functional relationships involving our variables and parameters. These may be written most generally in implicit form, each equation involving all variables and parameters.

$$f^1(x_1, \cdots, x_n, \alpha_1, \cdots, \alpha_m) = 0,$$
$$f^2(x_1, \cdots, x_n, \alpha_1, \cdots, \alpha_m) = 0,$$
$$\cdot$$
$$\cdot \qquad\qquad\qquad\qquad\qquad\qquad (1)$$
$$\cdot$$
$$f^n(x_1, \cdots, x_n, \alpha_1, \cdots, \alpha_m) = 0,$$

or more compactly,

$$f^i(x_1, \cdots, x_n, \alpha_1, \cdots, \alpha_m) = 0. \qquad (i = 1, \cdots, n)$$

Our equations must not be greater than n in number, for if they were, they could not be both consistent and independent; if less, our system will, in general, be under-determined. If our equations possess certain characteristics, to be discussed later, they may be considered to determine a unique set of values of our unknowns $(x_1^0, \cdots, x_n^0)$ corresponding to any preassigned set of parameters $(\alpha_1^0, \cdots, \alpha_m^0)$.

This functional relationship may be expressed mathematically as follows:

$$x_i = \bigg| g^i(\alpha_1, \cdots, \alpha_m). \qquad (i = 1, \cdots, n) \qquad (2)$$

It should be understood that this does not imply that we can express our unknown variables as any elementary functions of the parameters (such as polynomial, trigonometric, or logarithmic functions). On the contrary, our conditions of equilibrium in set (1) will not in general be expressible in terms of a finite number of elementary functions; and even if they were, we should not be sure that they could be solved explicitly in any simple terms. However, this is of no particular importance, for the elementary functions are only special forms which have been of historical interest in the development of mathematical thought and its physical applications. If one were to draw free hand either at random or as a result of a complete set of observations a demand curve relating price and quantity, this could not in general be more than approximately represented by finite combinations of elementary functions. And yet it is a perfectly good functional relationship indicating a certain correspondence between these variables. Furthermore, if there were any practical need for so doing, it could be tabulated once and for all, be named, and ever afterwards be accepted as a member of the family of respectable functions.

It is precisely because theoretical economics does not confine itself to specific narrow types of functions that it is able to achieve wide generality in its initial formulation. Still it is not to be forgotten that the aim of fruitful inference is the explanation of a wide range of phenomena in terms of simple, *restrictive* hypotheses. However, this must be the final result of our research, and there is no point in crippling oneself in setting out upon the journey.

If one were omniscient, i.e., if *all* the implications of any assumptions were intuitively obvious, the equations (2) would be instantly known as soon as the set (1) were given. Short of such powers, they could only be solved for to any required degree of approximation with much effort; but, of course, it could be done, given the requisite time and patience.

Considering the amount of labor involved, one is tempted to question the advantage of starting from our equilibrium equations in (1). Why not begin directly with the equations in (2)? Indeed, it may be pointed out that these resulting functions between unknowns and parameters could have arisen from an infinity of possible alternative sets of original equations. In particular, consider the set of implicit equations

$$g^i(\alpha_1, \cdots, \alpha_m) - x_i = 0. \qquad (i = 1, \cdots, n) \qquad (3)$$

This can be solved by inspection to give the equations of (2), but of course the solution is trivial. It is trivial in the sense that the result is intuitively obvious from the beginning, and not for the reason that (2) says the same thing as (3). For, after all, this equivalence is also true for (1) and (2), but their identity is not trivial in this psychological sense.

It is important not to be confused in these matters, for they lie at the foundations of scientific deduction, and they have been misunderstood particularly often by economists. By deductive reasoning we are enabled only to reveal to ourselves implications already included in our assumptions. We may bring to explicit attention certain formulations of our original assumptions which admit of possible refutation (confirmation) by empirical observation.

This process may best be regarded as a translation of our original hypothesis into a different language; but in so translating— provided, of course, that no error in logic has crept in—we do not change the nature of our original hypothesis, neither adding nor subtracting from its validity and precision.

The usefulness of the formulation of equilibrium conditions from which emerges our solution lies in the fact that by so doing we often gain knowledge concerning possible and necessary responses of our variables to changes in data. Without such restrictions our theories would be meaningless. Merely to state, as was suggested earlier, that there exists a final functional relationship between all variables and parameters (as of an infinity of accompanying circumstances) is bare and formal, containing no hypothesis upon the empirical data.

It is because in a wide variety of cases we can more or less plausibly assume or hypothesize certain properties of our equilibrium equations that we are able to deduce with the same degree of plausibility certain properties of the resulting functions between our unknowns and parameters. For the properties of the functions in (2) are necessarily related to the structural characteristics of the equilibrium set (1). The properties ordinarily discussed in this connection are not specific quantitative restrictions upon the functions (as being polynomials, etc.), but rather consist of assumptions with respect to slope, curvature, monotonicity, etc.; they are the kind implied by the *law of diminishing returns*.

DISPLACEMENT OF EQUILIBRIUM

It is easy to show mathematically how the rates of change of our unknowns with respect to any parameter, say α_1, may be computed from our equilibrium equations. As a matter of notation let

$$\frac{\partial x_i^0}{\partial \alpha_1} = \frac{\partial g^i(\alpha_1^0, \cdots, \alpha_m^0)}{\partial \alpha_1} = g_1^i(\alpha_1^0, \cdots, \alpha_m^0)$$

stand for the rate of change of the ith variable with respect to the parameter α_1, all other parameters being held constant. It is necessary because of the ambiguity of the conventional notation of partial differentiation to make sure which variables are being held constant.

Such partial derivatives must be evaluated as of a given value of the set of parameters, and hence as of a corresponding set of values of our dependent variables. Consider the initial position

$$(\alpha_1^0, \cdots, \alpha_m^0),$$

and the corresponding set of unknowns

$$(x_1^0, \cdots, x_n^0),$$

where of course

$$f^i(x_1^0, \cdots, x_n^0, \alpha_1^0, \cdots, \alpha_m^0) = 0, \qquad (i = 1, \cdots, n) \qquad (4)$$

and

$$x_i^0 = g^i(\alpha_1^0, \cdots, \alpha_m^0), \qquad (i = 1, \cdots, n) \qquad (5)$$

since our unknowns must satisfy the equilibrium conditions. Differentiating each equation of (1) with respect to α_1, remembering that all other parameters are to be held constant, but that all our unknowns are variable, we get [2]

$$f_{x_1}^1 \left(\frac{\partial x_1}{\partial \alpha_1}\right)^0 + f_{x_2}^1 \left(\frac{\partial x_2}{\partial \alpha_1}\right)^0 + \cdots + f_{x_n}^1 \left(\frac{\partial x_n}{\partial \alpha_1}\right)^0 = -f_{\alpha_1}^1,$$

$$f_{x_1}^2 \left(\frac{\partial x_1}{\partial \alpha_1}\right)^0 + f_{x_2}^2 \left(\frac{\partial x_2}{\partial \alpha_1}\right)^0 + \cdots + f_{x_n}^2 \left(\frac{\partial x_n}{\partial \alpha_1}\right)^0 = -f_{\alpha_1}^2,$$

$$\cdot \qquad\qquad \cdot \qquad\qquad\qquad \cdot \qquad\qquad\qquad \cdot \qquad (6)$$

$$f_{x_1}^n \left(\frac{\partial x_1}{\partial \alpha_1}\right)^0 + f_{x_2}^n \left(\frac{\partial x_2}{\partial \alpha_1}\right)^0 + \cdots + f_{x_n}^n \left(\frac{\partial x_n}{\partial \alpha_1}\right)^0 = -f_{\alpha_1}^n,$$

where

$$f_{x_j}^i = \frac{\partial f^i(x_1^0, \cdots, x_n^0, \alpha_1^0, \cdots, \alpha_m^0)}{\partial x_j},$$

with *all* other variables and parameters held constant. Similarly,

$$f_{\alpha_1}^i = \frac{\partial f^i(x_1^0, \cdots, x_n^0, \alpha_1^0, \cdots, \alpha_m^0)}{\partial \alpha_1}.$$

[2] In matrix terms this is $[f_j{}^i][\partial x_j/\partial \alpha_1] = [-f_{\alpha_1}{}^i]$.

Be it noted that the numerical values of these partial derivatives are fully determined at the equilibrium point in question. Thus, we have n linear equations with constant coefficients in n unknowns $[(\partial x_1/\partial\alpha_1)^0, \cdots, \partial x_n/\partial\alpha_1)^0]$. The solution values of these will depend upon the values of the coefficients; thus, the partial derivatives relating our dependent variables and parameters are determined by the structural properties of our equilibrium system.

Since (6) represents linear equations, their solution for non-singular cases may be represented in the familiar determinantal form:

$$\left(\frac{\partial x_k}{\partial\alpha_1}\right)^0 = -\frac{\sum\limits_{1}^{n} f_{\alpha_1}{}^{i}\Delta_{ik}}{\Delta}, \qquad (k = 1, \cdots, n) \tag{7}$$

where

$$\Delta = |f_{x_k}{}^{i}| = \begin{vmatrix} f_{x_1}{}^{1} & f_{x_2}{}^{1} & \cdots & f_{x_n}{}^{1} \\ f_{x_1}{}^{2} & f_{x_2}{}^{2} & \cdots & f_{x_n}{}^{2} \\ \cdot & \cdot & & \cdot \\ \cdot & \cdot & & \cdot \\ \cdot & \cdot & & \cdot \\ f_{x_1}{}^{n} & f_{x_2}{}^{n} & \cdots & f_{x_n}{}^{n} \end{vmatrix}$$

and Δ_{ik} indicates the cofactor of the element of the ith row and the kth column. Or in matrix terms

$$\left[\frac{\partial x_k}{\partial\alpha_1}\right]^0 = -\left[f_m{}^{k}\right]^{-1}\left[f_{\alpha_1}{}^{k}\right]. \tag{8}$$

ILLUSTRATIVE TAX PROBLEM

For concreteness let us apply our analysis to two simple cases. Consider a firm with a given demand curve relating price and output and a given production cost schedule relating total cost and output. Suppose in addition that the output of the firm is subject to a tax of t dollars per unit. The profit of the firm may be written

π = total revenue − total production cost − total tax payment
   = $xp(x) - C(x) - tx$,

where

    $xp(x)$ = total revenue in function of output,
     $C(x)$ = lowest total production cost at which each output can
           be produced,
      tx = total tax payment.

It is clear that for any given tax rate, say t^0, the firm will decide upon some given output to be produced and sold; i.e.,

$$x^0 = g(t^0), \tag{9}$$

where the functional relationship g corresponds to the functions in (2). However, we cannot leave the matter in so indefinite a state. We wish to know more than that there exists an equilibrium output for each tax rate. What is the nature of the dependence of our variable upon the tax rate regarded as a parameter? Will an increased unit tax result in a larger or smaller output? It is a poor theory indeed which will not answer so simple a question. Let us see if we can arrive at an answer to this through the formulation of the conditions of equilibrium.

It is in general assumed that a firm will select that output which will maximize its net revenue. That is to say, our equilibrium value for output will emerge as a solution of a simple maximum problem. Specifically, it is necessary [3] for a regular maximum of profit with respect to x, as of a given tax rate, that

$$\frac{\partial \pi(x, t)}{\partial x} = 0,$$
$$\frac{\partial^2 \pi(x, t)}{\partial x^2} < 0. \tag{10}$$

The first condition merely states that at a maximum the tangential slope of the profit function plotted against output must be horizontal or equal algebraically to zero. The second condition insures that we do not have a minimum.

For the problem at hand our condition of equilibrium may be derived by simple differentiation to become

$$\frac{\partial}{\partial x} [xp(x) - C(x)] - t = 0, \tag{11}$$

where it is assumed for simplicity that the inequality in (10) is realized for all values of the variable concerned. Now equation (11) corresponds to our equilibrium set (1), which in this case contains but one equation due to the fact that we have only the value of one unknown to determine.

[3] See Mathematical Appendix A, sec. I.

For each value of t, there will correspond a root of the resulting equation in x, and this will be our equilibrium value. Thus, the function (9) may be regarded as the explicit solution of this implicit equation.

Now what have we gained by introducing the maximum problem for the firm? Does this enable us to answer our original question as to the nature of the dependence of the output upon the tax rate? Let us apply the general method outlined above to calculate the rate of change of equilibrium output with respect to the parameter t. Differentiating (11) with respect to t, we get

$$\frac{\partial^2}{\partial x^2} [x^0 p(x^0) - C(x^0)] \left(\frac{\partial x}{\partial t}\right)^0 = 1, \tag{12}$$

where

$$\left(\frac{\partial x}{\partial t}\right)^0 = g'(t^0).$$

In this simple case no resort to determinants is necessary in order to achieve a solution, for

$$\left(\frac{\partial x}{\partial t}\right)^0 = \frac{1}{\dfrac{\partial^2}{\partial x^2} [x^0 p(x^0) - C(x^0)]}. \tag{13}$$

But this provides us with the answer for which we have been seeking. For as a sufficient condition for a relative maximum we know that

$$\frac{\partial^2}{\partial x^2} [x^0 p(x^0) - C(x^0)] < 0. \tag{14}$$

Therefore,

$$\left(\frac{\partial x}{\partial t}\right)^0 < 0, \quad \text{or} \quad g'(t^0) < 0, \tag{15}$$

which is what intuition tells us would happen as a result of such a tax. Be it noted in passing that it is assumed that the firm is always in equilibrium before and after the tax is imposed, and that the tax affects the equilibrium only as indicated in equation (11). In any actual case considerable attention must be devoted to the problem of verifying the correctness of these assumptions before any practical application is made of the conclusions reached.

ILLUSTRATIVE MARKET CASE[4]

Let us consider as another example a market for a good or service where the price and quantity are determined by the intersection of hypothetical supply and demand curves. Furthermore, let us introduce a parameter of shift, α, into our demand curve (e.g., tastes, tax, rival price, etc.). Here we have two variables, one parameter, and two equations to define equilibrium values of our variables in terms of the parameter. Mathematically,

$$D(x, \alpha) - p = 0,$$
$$S(x) - p = 0. \tag{16}$$

As a solution we have

$$x^0 = g^1(\alpha^0),$$
$$p^0 = g^2(\alpha^0). \tag{17}$$

How then will our variables change with changes in α assuming that an increase in α shifts the demand curve upwards and to the right? As before, we differentiate our equilibrium relations with respect to the parameter to get two linear equations,

$$\frac{\partial D}{\partial x}\left(\frac{\partial x}{\partial \alpha}\right)^0 - \left(\frac{\partial p}{\partial \alpha}\right)^0 = -\frac{\partial D}{\partial \alpha}.$$
$$S'\left(\frac{\partial x}{\partial \alpha}\right)^0 - \left(\frac{\partial p}{\partial \alpha}\right)^0 = 0. \tag{18}$$

By simple substitution we get

$$\left(\frac{\partial x}{\partial \alpha}\right)^0 = -\frac{\dfrac{\partial D}{\partial \alpha}}{\dfrac{\partial D}{\partial x} - S'},$$

$$\left(\frac{\partial p}{\partial \alpha}\right)^0 = -\frac{S'\dfrac{\partial D}{\partial \alpha}}{\dfrac{\partial D}{\partial x} - S'}. \tag{19}$$

Now we know that $\partial D/\partial \alpha > 0$ by definition of our parameter of shift. Thus, $(\partial x/\partial \alpha)^0 \gtrless 0$ depending upon whether $S' \gtrless \partial D/\partial x$. At first sight this seems merely to put off the dilemma, to replace one equation by another. But if we examine the kind of market

---

[4] This is treated in greater detail in chap. ix below.

under consideration, it will appear that the mere fact that the market is in stable equilibrium in the initial situation will remove all ambiguity. For if the market is the familiar Marshallian consumer's good market, stability of equilibrium by definition requires that the supply curve cut the demand curve from below (even in the case of decreasing cost due to external economies).[5]

Thus,

$$S' > \frac{\partial D}{\partial x}. \tag{20}$$

Therefore,

$$\left(\frac{\partial x}{\partial \alpha}\right)^0 > 0. \tag{21}$$

However, the algebraic sign of the price change will hinge upon whether there is a positively or negatively inclined supply curve. For

$$\left(\frac{\partial p}{\partial \alpha}\right)^0 = S' \left(\frac{\partial x}{\partial \alpha}\right)^0. \tag{22}$$

Thus, since $(\partial x / \partial \alpha)^0$ is positive from (21), $(\partial p / \partial \alpha)^0$ and S' must be of the same sign, or

$$\left(\frac{\partial p}{\partial \alpha}\right)^0 S' > 0. \tag{23}$$

It is impossible in the price case to get rid of the final ambiguity.

Suppose, however, that this were a market for a factor of production. Here the conditions for stable equilibrium are familiarly defined to be either a positively sloping supply curve with a negatively sloping demand curve; or if the supply curve is negatively inclined, it must be backward rising and steeper than the demand curve.[6] Mathematically, our stability conditions may be expressed

$$\frac{S'}{\dfrac{\partial D}{\partial x} - S'} < 0. \tag{24}$$

For this case, therefore, the sign of the price change is known, while the quantity change is ambiguous, depending upon the algebraic

[5] A. Marshall, *Principles of Economics* (8th edition), p. 346, n. 1, p. 806, n. 1.

[6] J. R. Hicks, *Value and Capital* (Oxford, 1939), chap v.

sign of the slope of the supply curve. In brief,

$$\left(\frac{\partial p}{\partial \alpha}\right)^0 > 0,$$

$$\left(\frac{\partial x}{\partial \alpha}\right)^0 S' > 0. \tag{25}$$

Innumerable other examples could be cited. In general, we should not expect to be able to determine the signs of the rates of change of our variables upon the basis of simple *a priori* qualitative restrictions on our equilibrium equations. This is not because of the difficulty and complexity of solving a large number of equations; for these could be solved if sufficient were known about the particular empirical values of our conditions of equilibrium. It is rather that the restrictions imposed by our hypotheses on our equilibrium equations (stability and maximum conditions, etc.) are not always sufficient to indicate *definite* restrictions as to algebraic sign of the rates of change of our variables with respect to any parameter.

Only imagine a change in a parameter which enters into all of a large number of equilibrium equations causing them simultaneously to shift. The resulting net effect upon our variables could only be calculated as a result of balancing the separate effects (regarded as limiting rates of change), and for this purpose detailed quantitative values for all the coefficients involved would have to be known.

Summary

Before going on in the next section of our work to indicate how the economist is enabled to deduce significant results in a wide category of cases, it will be well to summarize the thread of the argument thus far.

a. For theoretical purposes an economic system consists of a designated set of unknowns which are constrained as a condition of equilibrium to satisfy an equal number of consistent and independent equations (see equation 1). These are implicitly assumed to hold within a certain environment and as of certain data. Some parts of these data are introduced as explicit parameters; and, as a result of our equilibrium conditions, our unknown variables may be expressed in function of these parameters (see equation 2).

b. The method of *comparative statics* consists of the study of the responses of our equilibrium unknowns to designated changes in parameters; i.e., we wish to know the properties of the functions in (2). In the absence of complete quantitative information concerning our equilibrium equations, it is hoped to be able to formulate qualitative restrictions on slopes, curvatures, etc., of our equilibrium equations so as to be able to derive definite qualitative restrictions upon the responses of our system to changes in certain parameters. It is the primary purpose of this work to indicate how this is possible in a wide range of economic problems.

CHAPTER III

THE THEORY OF MAXIMIZING BEHAVIOR

THREE SOURCES OF MEANINGFUL THEOREMS

IT WILL be remembered that in the case of a unit tax on a firm's output it was possible to state unambiguously the direction of change of output with respect to a change in the tax rate. This was so because of the fact that the equilibrium output for each tax rate was derived from the condition that profit must be at a maximum.

As will become evident in the course of our exposition, this is by no means an accidental, isolated case; it is merely an application of a very general principle of economic method, which lies at the bottom of much of economic theory. In fact, aside from those parts of economic doctrine whose results are inconclusive—and the most ardent advocates of economic theory will admit that this includes a large part of accepted analysis—there is not much which cannot be brought under this heading.[1]

The general method involved may be very simply stated. *In cases where the equilibrium values of our variables can be regarded as the solutions of an extremum (maximum or minimum) problem, it is often possible regardless of the number of variables involved to determine unambiguously the qualitative behavior of our solution values in respect to changes of parameters.*[2]

It so happens that in a wide number of economic problems it is admissible and even mandatory to regard our equilibrium equations as maximizing (minimizing) conditions. A large part of entrepreneurial behavior is directed towards maximization of profits with certain implications for minimization of expenditure, etc.

---

[1] The reader may verify this result by paging through any good economics textbook, such as Marshall's *Principles*, and analyzing the derivation of various theorems stated.

[2] It may be pointed out that this is essentially the method of thermodynamics, which can be regarded as a purely deductive science based upon certain postulates (notably the First and Second Laws of Thermodynamics). That such abstract reasoning should in the hands of Gibbs and others lead to fruitful theorems testifies to the validity of the original hypotheses.

Moreover, it is possible to derive operationally meaningful restrictive hypotheses on consumers' demand functions from the assumption that consumers behave so as to maximize an ordinal preference scale of quantities of consumption goods and services. (Of course, this does not imply that they behave rationally in any normative sense.)

It is not to be thought that in principle all economic results emerge from these maximizing assumptions.[3] For, as we have seen, it was also possible to deduce conclusive qualitative results from certain stability assumptions. Nevertheless, many of these stability conditions rest implicitly upon maximizing behavior.

Moreover, certain difficulties arise here. While, of course, it is always possible to lay down arbitrary definitions of stability, it is impossible to *deduce* them without the implicit introduction of dynamical considerations concerning the behavior of a system *out* of stationary equilibrium. Depending upon the dynamical set-up envisaged, different stability conditions are implied. Thus, given supply adjustments of the type assumed in the cobweb cycle phenomenon, it is well known that the ordinary Marshallian condition of a positively rising supply curve may not result in "stable" equilibrium.[4]

It is true that the identification of equilibrium with a stable maximum position in a sense begs the question of stability. However, where these extremum conditions are realized, it can be shown that many dynamic set-ups will give rise to dampened oscillations as a result of small displacements. The relations between dynamic theory and the stability of equilibrium are discussed in the last chapters.

There remains still another possibility by which conclusive theorems may be deduced. We may know in advance certain qualitative properties of our equilibrium equations. Thus, reference may be made to alleged technological and psychological laws,

[3] Thus, the definition of economic theory as the study of scarce means with alternative uses I would regard as too broad from one point of view, and much too narrow from another.

[4] A stationary equilibrium is stable, providing the specification of initial conditions differing only slightly from the stationary equilibrium values results in an evolution which tends (at least in the limit) to approach the equilibrium values. See Part II below.

held to be plausible upon a priori grounds.[5] Even here, as many economists have pointed out, the reasoning may rest in the last analysis upon certain maximum considerations. Thus, in demonstrating the validity of the law of diminishing marginal physical productivity we ordinarily point to the fact that firms in pure competition are in equilibrium under a given set of factor prices. This would not be possible if the law of diminishing marginal productivity did not hold. Again we point to the fact that farmers do not devote all their attention to raising grain on one square inch of land; they use much land of the same kind, and even inferior grades of land. Thus, we really argue backwards from maximizing economic behavior to the underlying physical data consistent with it.

There is still another type of problem for which the study of maximizing behavior is illuminating. In some cases, as we shall see later, it is possible to formulate our conditions of equilibrium as those of an extremum problem, even though it is admittedly not a case of any individual's behaving in a maximizing manner, just as it is often possible in classical dynamics to express the path of a particle as one which maximizes (minimizes) some quantity despite the fact that the particle is obviously not acting consciously or purposively.

For all of these reasons the study of maximizing behavior affords a unified approach to wide areas of current and historical economic thought. There is, moreover, considerable advantage in discussing the problem at first in its full generality. The high degree of abstractness will be more than compensated for in the ease with which numerous applications can be deduced as special cases.

A Calculus of Qualitative Relations

Before I enter upon the theory of maximizing behavior, it may be illuminating to show why intuition and a general feeling for the direction of things does not carry one far in the analysis of a complex many-variable system, such as is characterized by equation

---

[5] In a problem of any complexity involving a number of variables, intuition is a poor guide for the reasons discussed in the next section. All presumptions become dubious. In such cases the economist often falls prey to the perils of assuming the equiprobability of the unknown. As a result, every reformulation of the problem results in changed presumptions. This is no doubt one reason why every terminological revolution in economic thought brings with it a recasting of belief.

(1) of the previous chapter. To make matters even simpler than they usually are in reality, let us suppose that we know the qualitative direction of movement of each of our equilibrium equations with respect to a change in all of the variables and parameters. Thus, we know at least the algebraic sign of each of the first partial derivatives of the form $f_{x_j}{}^i$ or $f_\alpha{}^i$. It does not matter how we came about such knowledge; for example, we might confidently believe that individuals will divide an additional dollar of income fractionally between consumption and saving, not in consequence of some economic theory of maximization, but simply as a result of everyday observation.

What then can we say concerning the direction of change of any particular variable in response to a change in some parameter? According to equation (7) of chapter ii, this is given by a complicated expression which can be written as the quotient of two n by n determinants, whose elements are made up of these first partial derivatives. Now in order for our question to have an immediate definite answer, we must be able to determine unambiguously the signs of each of these determinants. From the original fundamental definition of a determinant, each consists of $n!$ terms, each term involving the product of n elements. From our hypothesized knowledge, we can be sure of the sign but not the magnitude of each term. Only if all of the $n!$ terms happen to be of the same sign will the sign of the determinant be unambiguous. If our system involves ten variables, the determinants will have more than three million terms. Regarded simply as a problem in probability, the chance that a run of this length should always have one sign is about one out of one with a million zeros after it. Therefore, unless some special feature is present, we are almost sure to find it necessary to weigh the magnitude of some terms against others, which is to enter upon quantitative problems admitting no answer by qualitative methods.

Nevertheless, let us see how far qualitative methods will take us in the slightly simpler case where only one parameter is changed in such a manner as to alter only one of the equilibrium relations. As before, the signs of all first partial derivatives are known. Consideration of all possible cases that may arise will show that there is no loss in generality in assuming that it is the first equation which is shifted, that the partial derivative of each implicit equation with respect to its own variable $f_{x_i}{}^i$ is always positive, and that the change in the first equation with respect to the given parameter is positive. If these conditions are not realized, they can be brought about by changes in sign of one or more of the equations or variables and the parameter.

By our qualitative knowledge we are able to specify a matrix of the form

$$
\text{sign } f_j{}^i =
\begin{pmatrix}
+ & \pm & \pm & \cdots & \pm \\
\pm & + & \pm & \cdots & \pm \\
\pm & \pm & + & \cdots & \pm \\
\cdot & \cdot & \cdot & & \cdot \\
\cdot & \cdot & \cdot & & \cdot \\
\cdot & \cdot & \cdot & & \cdot \\
\pm & \pm & \pm & \cdots & +
\end{pmatrix}
\tag{1}
$$

where the n columns represent $(x_1, \cdots, x_n)$, and the n rows represent $(f^1, \cdots, f^n)$. The sign in each element will represent the assumed known sign of the partial derivative of the variable corresponding to that row taken with respect to changes in the variable corresponding to that column. By our previous convention, we have made all diagonal elements plus. All the remaining elements can be of either sign, but in any one case they are assumed to be of definite known signs. All in all, there are a vast number of possible matrices of this kind which could arise in any problem, in fact all together 2 raised to the $n(n-1)$ power.

We are interested in the direction of change of our unknowns, or in the signs of $(dx_1/d\alpha, \cdots, dx_n/d\alpha)$. If nothing is known a priori, these may take on any one of all the possible 2^n arrangements of signs.

$$
\begin{matrix}
& & n & & \\
\begin{pmatrix}
+ & + & + & \cdots & + \\
- & + & + & \cdots & + \\
+ & - & + & \cdots & + \\
- & - & + & \cdots & + \\
\cdot & \cdot & \cdot & & \cdot \\
\cdot & \cdot & \cdot & & \cdot \\
\cdot & \cdot & \cdot & & \cdot \\
+ & - & - & \cdots & - \\
- & - & - & \cdots & -
\end{pmatrix} & 2^n
\end{matrix}
\tag{2}
$$

How many of these can now be eliminated as inadmissible on the basis of our qualitative knowledge as embodied in the specification of the matrix (1)?   Ideally, we should hope to be able to rule out all but one of the possible combinations so as to get a unique answer.   However, it would be at least desirable to be able to determine the sign of at least one of our unknowns, or, what comes to the same thing, to be able to rule out a particular half of all the possible combinations.

So much for our aspirations; turning to the exact procedure by which we rule out a combination, we find ourselves in for disappointment.   If we substitute into equation (6) of chapter ii the signs of the indicated elements, we shall be able to rule out a combination if, and only if, it leads to a contradiction, i.e., if it does not add up to zero, or to a negative number as it should.

Concretely, this can be seen to mean that we can rule out any one of the above combinations of sign in (2) which exactly duplicates any of the last $(n - 1)$ rows of (1), or which is the exact antithesis of any of these same rows.   Otherwise, one of the last $(n - 1)$ equations of (6), chapter ii, could not add up to zero as required by the present hypothesis.   In addition, we may rule out any combination of (2) which exactly duplicates the first row; but we are not able to rule out its antithesis.

All told then, we are at most able to rule out by qualitative considerations only $(2n - 1)$ combinations out of a grand total of 2^n possible combinations.   Even for moderate sizes of n this leaves us with all but a minute fraction of possibilities.   And this is the largest number that we can rule out on such a hypothesis.   In many cases we are not able to rule out even this many.   Thus, if any two rows in our original matrix have exactly the same signs, they will both rule out the same combinations, which cannot therefore be added together for fear of double counting.

It can be seen then that purely qualitative considerations cannot take us very far as soon as the simple cases are left behind. Of course, if we are willing to make more rigid assumptions, either of a qualitative or quantitative kind, we may be able to improve matters somewhat.   Ordinarily, the economist is not in possession of exact quantitative knowledge of the partial derivatives of his equilibrium conditions.   None the less, if he is a good applied economist, he may have definite notions concerning the relative importance of different effects; the better his judgment in these matters, the better an economist he will be.   These notions, which are anything but a priori in their original derivation, may suggest to him the advisability of neglecting completely certain effects as being of a second order of magnitude. In other words, zeros are inserted into the matrix of (1). In fact, the so-called method of *partial equilibrium* consists of nothing more than a liberal sprinkling of zeros into the equations of general equilibrium. In the hands of a master practitioner, the method will yield useful results; if not handled with caution and delicacy, it can easily yield nonsensical conclusions.

By simple extensions of the above argument we can show how the presence of a zero in any row permits that row to rule out four instead of only two combinations. Similarly, r zeros in a row permits that row to eliminate 2^{r+1} combinations. As before, there may be duplications in the eliminating influence of different rows. It is also apparent that definite knowledge concerning the sign of any one of the variables will enable us to rule out one-half of the original number of combinations, or 2^{n-1} combinations. Because of duplicating effects, definite knowledge of the signs of the changes in two of the unknowns will enable us to eliminate *less* than twice as many as one unknown; actually, by two known signs we can eliminate $3(2^{n-2})$ combinations in all. Definite knowledge of the signs of k unknowns will permit the elimination of all but 2^{n-k} combinations.

It would be possible to illustrate the above calculus of qualitative relations by reference to a number of well-known economic problems. Space will permit brief mention of a few. In the market illustration of the previous chapter [6] there was considered the case of a simple Marshallian partial equilibrium market involving two unknowns, price and quantity, whose equilibrium values are determined by the intersection of supply and demand schedules. We may apply our analysis to the determination of the changes in our variables resulting in an assumed shift of a negatively inclined demand curve. If the supply curve is known to be positively inclined, the sign matrix can be written in the form

$$\begin{bmatrix} + & + \\ - & + \end{bmatrix} \tag{3}$$

[6] Page 17.

In this case, we are able to rule out the maximum number of combinations, $(2n - 1)$, or three in all. Since there are only four combinations, we are left with a unique answer, as is apparent from the algebraic analysis of the previous chapter. If the supply curve is assumed to be negatively inclined, the signs in the second row both become plus, and we are able to rule out only the minimum number possible, or two. We are left then with a final ambiguity which cannot be settled except by quantitative knowledge or by means of various stability hypotheses.

A more illuminating and more difficult example is that of the simplified Keynesian system, described in greater detail in chapter ix. Without going into details here, it can be stated that this gives rise to a system of three variables, interest rate, x_1, income, x_2, and investment, x_3, whose equilibrium values are determined by three equations, liquidity preference, f^1, marginal efficiency schedule, f^2, and propensity to consume, f^3. Making the usual assumptions concerning the signs of the various first order effects, e.g., that investment varies inversely with the rate of interest and that the effect of interest on consumption is of an order of magnitude which can be neglected, we end up with a sign-matrix of the form

$$(\text{sign } f_j{}^i) = \begin{bmatrix} + & - & 0 \\ - & + & - \\ 0 & - & + \end{bmatrix} \tag{4}$$

We may now consider a shift in any one of the schedules, e.g., a change in the liquidity preference schedule brought about by some policy measure. If we apply the above calculus, we are still left with three possible combinations for (sign change in x_i), namely, $(+ + +)$, $(- + +)$, or $(- - -)$. In the case of a shift of the marginal efficiency schedule, we narrow the choice down to two, $(+ + +)$ or $(- - -)$. For a shift in the propensity to consume schedule we end up with three choices, $(+ + +)$, $(+ + -)$, or $(- - -)$.

It will be noted that in none of the cases are we able to make a definite statement about even one of the variables. In the second case, which is the most favorable, we can only say that an increase in the marginal efficiency schedule will either raise interest, income, and investment, or else lower all three of them. This is a highly unsatisfactory state of affairs, particularly since it seems on the face of it doubtful that an increase in the marginal efficiency of capital should lower interest, income, and investment. But it is only by bringing in the stability considerations of later chapters that a more definite, and more reasonable deduction can be made. In the discussion in chapter ix it is shown that stability hypotheses will leave us with only one combination for the first case, $(- + +)$; for the second case, $(+ + +)$; and for the third case the two possibilities, $(+ + +)$ or $(+ + -)$. This last ambiguity is irremovable unless still stronger quantitative assumptions are made.

Numerous other economic examples could be mentioned, but these may be left to the reader.[7] Before returning to the problem of maximizing behavior, I should like to call attention to the fact that the qualitative calculus is not invariant under transformation of the variables.

Maximum Conditions of Equilibrium

Let us consider a new variable, z, defined by a single-valued function of our previous variables,

$$z = f(x_1, \cdots, x_n, \alpha_1, \cdots, \alpha_m), \tag{5}$$

where f and its partial derivatives of at least second-order exist and are continuous in a wide region. If for any preassigned values of the α's, there exists a set of values for the x's, $(x_1{}^0, \cdots, x_n{}^0)$, corresponding to which z is at a maximum, then we must have

$$f(x_1, \cdots, x_n, \alpha_1{}^0, \cdots, \alpha_m{}^0) \leqq f(x_1{}^0, \cdots, x_n{}^0, \alpha_1{}^0, \cdots, \alpha_m{}^0). \tag{6}$$

As a matter of notational convenience this may be written

$$f(X, \alpha^0) \leqq f(X^0, \alpha^0), \tag{7}$$

[7] One last illustration taken from the field of international trade may be dealt with briefly. Professor Leontief has produced a numerical example illustrating the possibility that a unilateral payment from one country to another may so shift the terms of trade in favor of the *paying* country as to cause it to be better rather than worse off as a result of the transfer. "Note on the Pure Theory of Transfer," in *Explorations in Economics* (New York, 1936), pp. 84–92. The example is carefully framed so as to guarantee indifference curves of the proper curvature for both countries. However, if one sets up an analytical system, along the lines of the numerical example, one will find that the *Leontief Effect* can only happen for a system in which an increase in demand for a commodity lowers rather than raises its price. If the latter phenomenon is ruled out as being anomalous, or incompatible with stability (defined arbitrarily or in terms of a dynamic set up), then we can by the same action rule out the possibility of the *Leontief Effect*.

where X stands for the arguments $(x_1, \cdots, x_n)$, and α stands for the arguments $(\alpha_1, \cdots, \alpha_m)$.

If z^0 represents an absolute maximum with respect to all admissible values of our independent variables, then

$$f(X, \alpha^0) < f(X^0, \alpha^0). \qquad (8)$$

On the other hand, z^0 may merely represent a maximum relative to all x's lying in some restricted neighborhood of the point (X^0, α^0).

We know from Mathematical Appendix A, Section II, that in order for z^0 to enjoy a relative maximum it is necessary that

$$\frac{\partial z}{\partial x_i} = 0 = f_{x_i}(x_1{}^0, \cdots, x_n{}^0, \alpha_1{}^0, \cdots, \alpha_m{}^0), \qquad (i = 1, \cdots, n) \quad (9)$$

and

$$\sum_1^n \sum_1^n f_{x_i x_j}{}^0 h_i h_j \leqq 0, \qquad (10)$$

where the h's are arbitrary numbers. For a *regular* relative maximum the last condition can be written

$$\sum_1^n \sum_1^n f_{x_i x_j}{}^0 h_i h_j < 0, \qquad (11)$$

not all h's equal to zero. In other words, this symmetrical homogeneous quadratic form must be negative definite. (See Mathematical Appendix A, Section II.)

DISPLACEMENT OF EQUILIBRIUM

The set of equations in (9) can be regarded as our conditions of equilibrium corresponding to the set (1) of the second chapter, and may be assumed to yield an explicit solution for our unknown equilibrium values in terms of the preassigned parameters.[8]

$$x_i{}^0 = g^i(\alpha_1{}^0, \cdots, \alpha_m{}^0). \qquad (i = 1, \cdots, n) \quad (12)$$

Using the method of the previous chapter we may easily solve for the rates of change of our solution values with respect to the

[8] From the implicit function theorem it is known that assuming the definiteness of the quadratic form throughout the whole region under discussion will insure us of the uniqueness of our relative maximum position. Also our maximum conditions are essentially invariant under any non-singular transformation of variables. Furthermore, any properly monotonic function of z enjoys an extremum position for the same values of the arguments as does z.

kth parameter by means of the following:

$$\sum_{1}^{n} f_{x_i x_j}{}^{0} \frac{\partial x_j}{\partial \alpha_k} = -f_{x_i \alpha_k}{}^{0}, \qquad (i = 1, \cdots, n) \tag{13}$$

where of course,

$$\frac{\partial x_j}{\partial \alpha_k} = g_{\alpha_k}{}^{j}(\alpha_1{}^{0}, \cdots, \alpha_m{}^{0}). \qquad \begin{array}{l}(j = 1, \cdots, n) \\ (k = 1, \cdots, m)\end{array} \tag{14}$$

As in (8) of chapter ii, our solution may be written in the determinantal form

$$\frac{\partial x_j}{\partial \alpha_k} = -\frac{\sum_{1}^{n} f_{x_i \alpha_k}{}^{0} H_{ij}}{H}, \tag{15}$$

where

$$H = \begin{vmatrix} f_{x_1 x_1}{}^{0} & \cdots & f_{x_1 x_n}{}^{0} \\ \cdot & & \cdot \\ \cdot & & \cdot \\ f_{x_n x_1}{}^{0} & \cdots & f_{x_n x_n}{}^{0} \end{vmatrix} = |f_{x_i x_j}{}^{0}|, \tag{16}$$

and H_{ij} is the cofactor corresponding to the element of the ith row and the jth column of the Hessian H. As will appear later, we are able in a large class of cases to evaluate the algebraic sign of this expression. In what follows where there is no risk of ambiguity, I shall omit the superscript zero.

First let us derive a relationship of complete generality. Multiply the ith equation in (13) by $\partial x_i/\partial \alpha_k$ respectively to get

$$\frac{\partial x_i}{\partial \alpha_k} \sum_{1}^{n} f_{x_i x_j} \frac{\partial x_j}{\partial \alpha_k} = -f_{x_i \alpha_k} \frac{\partial x_i}{\partial \alpha_k}. \qquad (i = 1, \cdots, n) \tag{17}$$

Summing with respect to i over all equations we have

$$\sum_{1}^{n} \sum_{1}^{n} f_{x_i x_j} \frac{\partial x_i}{\partial \alpha_k} \frac{\partial x_j}{\partial \alpha_k} = -\sum_{1}^{n} f_{x_i \alpha_k} \frac{\partial x_i}{\partial \alpha_k}. \tag{18}$$

But from (11)

$$\sum_{1}^{n} \sum_{1}^{n} f_{x_i x_j} h_i h_j < 0,$$

holding for any h's. In particular, for

$$h_i = \frac{\partial x_i}{\partial \alpha_k} \tag{19}$$

we get

$$\sum_1^n \sum_1^n f_{x_i x_j} \frac{\partial x_i}{\partial \alpha_k} \frac{\partial x_j}{\partial \alpha_k} < 0, \tag{20}$$

or from (18)

$$\sum_1^n f_{x_i \alpha_k} \frac{\partial x_i}{\partial \alpha_k} > 0, \tag{21}$$

for not all $\partial x_i / \partial \alpha_k$ equal to zero. In words this compound term consisting of the weighted sum of our unknown rates of change must definitely be positive in sign. However, this does not add very much to our knowledge since we do not know which terms will be positive.

As mentioned earlier, however, we are not always interested in parameters which shift each and every one of our equilibrium conditions. For this would necessitate a knowledge of the relative quantitative importance of each shift before we could hope to evaluate the composite result. For this reason we often narrow our problem by considering parameters which cause only one of our equilibrium equations to shift. Let us restrict our attention, therefore, to a set of such parameters $(\alpha_1, \cdots, \alpha_n)$ equal in number to our unknowns. We may number each in the order corresponding to the respective equilibrium equation which it shifts. Then since a change in the kth parameter must leave all other equations unchanged, we have

$$f_{x_j \alpha_k} = 0, \qquad \text{for} \qquad j \neq k. \tag{22}$$

Now our inequality of (21) reduces to the more simple and more readily applicable condition

$$f_{x_k \alpha_k} \frac{\partial x_k}{\partial \alpha_k} > 0 \tag{23}$$

In words, for the class of parameters now under consideration the rate of change of the kth variable with respect to its corresponding parameter must be of the same sign as $f_{x_k \alpha_k}$, which in turn is positive if the shift of the equilibrium equation is in the direction of an increase in x_k.

This can be verified by the computation indicated in (15). According to our present hypothesis

$$\frac{\partial x_k}{\partial \alpha_k} = -\frac{f_{x_k \alpha_k} H_{kk}}{H}. \tag{24}$$

In Mathematical Appendix A, Section **IV**, it is shown that

$$\frac{H_{kk}}{H} < 0, \qquad (k = 1, \cdots, n) \tag{25}$$

as a condition for a true maximum. Hence,

$$f_{x_k \alpha_k} \frac{\partial x_k}{\partial \alpha_k} = (f_{x_k \alpha_k})^2 \left(\frac{-H_{kk}}{H} \right), \tag{26}$$

or

$$f_{x_k \alpha_k} \frac{\partial x_k}{\partial \alpha_k} > 0. \tag{27}$$

Let us examine more closely the nature of our hypothesis embodied in (22) that each parameter shifts but one condition of equilibrium, leaving all others unchanged. In the first place this does not mean that a change in the ith parameter results in a change in the ith variable alone. On the contrary, a change in any parameter will typically result in a change in all variables. Our hypothesis merely says that this must come about through a shift in but one schedule with movements along the remaining schedules.

As I shall later argue, the assumption of this hypothesis does not involve any serious loss of generality and still includes the vast majority (in fact, it is hard to find exceptions) of relationships contained in current economic theory.

The most general function for which the partial differential equations of (22) hold may be written

$$z = \theta(x_1, \cdots, x_n) + B^1(x_1, \alpha_1) + B^2(x_2, \alpha_2) + \cdots + B^n(x_n, \alpha_n). \tag{28}$$

This may be verified by successive differentiation to obtain

$$\frac{\partial^2 z}{\partial x_j \partial \alpha_k} = f_{x_j \alpha_k} = \frac{\partial^2 B^j}{\partial x_j \partial \alpha_k} = 0, \qquad \text{for} \qquad j \neq k. \tag{29}$$

For the rest of this chapter unless otherwise indicated I shall consider functions of this restricted type. The inequality of (21) still holds in any case, but is less immediately applicable. After all, generality is not an end in itself. A theory may be so general as to be useless. It is for simple theories which have wide applicability that we must look.

DISPLACEMENT OF QUANTITY MAXIMIZED

We have seen how the equilibrium quantities $(x_1, \cdots, x_n)$ change when parameters vary. Any function of them also varies in a determinable way. In particular, the quantity to be maximized, z, will change; and its laws of change take on a very simple form. Let

$$z = f(x_1, \cdots, x_n, \alpha), \tag{30}$$

where α is any parameter. Let the x's be functions of α determined by a maximum position, i.e., by

$$\frac{\partial z}{\partial x_i} = f_i(x_1, \cdots, x_n, \alpha) = 0. \qquad (i = 1, \cdots, n) \tag{31}$$

Then

$$\frac{dz}{d\alpha} = \sum_1^n f_i \frac{dx_i}{d\alpha} + f_\alpha = 0 + f_\alpha = \frac{\partial z}{\partial \alpha}. \tag{32}$$

That is, the first-order change in z is exactly equal to the change in z when the x's are not varying optimally so as to keep z at a maximum; only to terms of a higher order is there a difference in the way z is changing. A similar relation can be shown to hold in the case of a constrained maximum.

This is the familiar relation of tangency between the envelope of a family of curves and the curves which it touches. It has many economic applications of which only a few need be mentioned. In the famous dispute between Professor Viner and his draftsman, Dr. Wong, the question arose as to the correct relationship between long and short-run curves.[9] The short-run curve is drawn up by minimizing total (and average) costs for each and every output, *as of given amounts of some fixed factor.* The long-run curve requires lowest total (and unit) costs for every output, as plant is optimally adjusted. But according to our theorem a change in the parameter output will to the first-order result in the same change in total (and unit) costs when plant is fixed as when plant is optimally adjusted. Dr. Wong was right then in insisting upon tangency.

Another example is provided by Professor Viner.[10] Let labor-marginal cost be the rate of increase of total costs when only labor

[9] J. Viner, "Cost Curves and Supply Curves," *Zeitschfift fur Nationalökonomie,* III (1932), 23–46.

[10] J. Viner, *Studies in the Theory of International Trade* (New York: Harper, 1937), 515–516.

is varying so as to produce the extra output. It is to be distinguished from marginal cost of labor which appears in monopsony theory, and the marginal labor cost which means the increase in one component of costs as all factors are optimally varying. Let marginal cost be the rate of increase of total costs with respect to output as all factors vary optimally. Then our theorem states that labor-marginal cost equals marginal cost equals any other factor-marginal cost. As Professor Viner has pointed out with great insight, at the margin (i.e., neglecting differential coefficients of higher-orders) all factors are perfectly indifferent substitutes. The classical economists, lacking the precise notion of an infinitesimal, were forced to employ the concept of a *broad* extensive margin. (Viz., Ricardo's no-rent land, and J. B. Clark's famous zone of indifference.) [11]

For finite movements, however small, higher-order terms will make the change in the quantity maximized (minimized) different when the unknowns are optimally adjusted from the change when they are held constant. Actually,

$$\frac{d^2z}{d\alpha^2} = \sum_1^n f_i \frac{d^2x_i}{d\alpha^2} + \sum_1^n \frac{dx_i}{d\alpha} \frac{d(f_i)}{d\alpha} + \sum_1^n f_{i\alpha} \frac{dx_i}{d\alpha} + f_{\alpha\alpha} \qquad (33)$$

$$= 0 + 0 + \sum_1^n f_{i\alpha} \frac{dx_i}{d\alpha} + f_{\alpha\alpha},$$

since $f_i = 0$.

The higher-order change in z when all x's are held constant is given by

$$\frac{\partial^2z}{\partial\alpha^2} = f_{\alpha\alpha}. \qquad (34)$$

The difference between the former change and the latter is as follows:

$$\frac{d^2z}{d\alpha^2} - \frac{\partial^2z}{\partial\alpha^2} = \sum_1^n f_{i\alpha} \frac{dx_i}{d\alpha} > 0 \qquad (35)$$

because of equation (21) above.

If the changing parameter affects profits or ordinal utility adversely, it does so less when output and consumption are optimally adjusted to the new circumstances. If the parameter improves

---

[11] For still other examples see Marshall's *Principles*, Mathematical Appendix, Note XIV, pp. 846–852.

profits (etc.), it does so most when the unknowns are optimally adjusted.

One could go on to still higher terms. These would be seen to depend upon the various partial derivatives of f and upon $dx_i/d\alpha$, $d^2x_i/d\alpha^2$, etc. The changes in z are of higher order than the changes in the x's. In fact, the nth derivative of z depends at most upon the $(n - 1)$th derivative of the x's. This is brought out in the above equations.

Auxiliary Constraints and the Generalized Le Chatelier Principle

If the equilibrium of a system is determined by extremum conditions where all unknowns are independently variable, the addition of auxiliary constraints (satisfied by the equilibrium position) will leave the equilibrium unchanged. If a true relative maximum is attained, a movement in *any* direction leads downhill; a fortiori movements along certain subsets of directions will be downhill. The usefulness of what may at first seem a strange process lies in the fact that it enables us to deduce *necessary* conditions which the equilibrium must satisfy.

Thus, with plant fixed a variable factor will be hired until its wage (marginal cost) equals its marginal value productivity. In the long-run, plant cannot be taken as fixed. Nevertheless, the short-run condition holds in the long-run as well (but not vice versa) since long-run total costs cannot be at a minimum unless short-run total costs are as low as possible. Again, in discriminating monopoly the condition that any given output be divided optimally between two markets (equal marginal revenues) holds even when total output is not given but is determined by cost considerations.

How is the equilibrium displaced when there are no auxiliary constraints as compared to the case when constraints are imposed? How does the demand for a factor vary with its price when other factors cannot be optimally adjusted because of time lags, etc.? This type of question is important in thermodynamics as well as in economic systems. It admits of a simple answer.

Let z be of the following special form

$$z = \theta(x_1, \cdots, x_n) - \alpha_1 x_1 - \alpha_2 x_2 - \cdots - \alpha_n x_n. \qquad (36)$$

If all unknowns are independently variable, a maximum is determined by the equilibrium conditions

$$\frac{\partial z}{\partial x_i} = \theta_i(x_1^0, \cdots, x_n^0) - \alpha_i = 0, \qquad (i = 1, \cdots, n) \quad (37)$$

and

$$[H] = [\theta_{ij}]$$

is the matrix of a negative definite form. How does x_i change when its "conjugate" parameter α_i varies?

$$\frac{dx_i}{d\alpha_i} = \frac{H_{ii}}{H} < 0. \quad (38)$$

Let r independent additional linear constraints be imposed such that

$$\sum_1^n g_j^\beta(x_j - x_j^0) = 0, \qquad (\beta = 1, \cdots, r) \quad (39)$$

where

$$[g_j^\beta]$$

is of rank r.

The introduction of constraints requires that our equilibrium system be modified to assume the following form

$$\theta_i + \sum_1^r \lambda_\beta g_i^\beta - \alpha_i = 0, \qquad (i = 1, \cdots, n)$$

$$\sum_1^n g_j^\beta(x_j - x_j^0) = 0, \qquad (\beta = 1, \cdots, r) \quad (40)$$

where the λ's are Lagrangean undetermined multipliers.

Let ^rH represent the determinant formed by bordering H with r rows and columns consisting of the coefficients g_j^β; i.e.,

$$^rH = \begin{vmatrix} \theta_{ij} & g_i^\gamma \\ g_j^\beta & 0 \end{vmatrix}. \qquad (\beta, \gamma = 1, \cdots, r) \quad (41)$$

Then the change in x_i with respect to α_i when r auxiliary constraints are imposed, is given by

$$\left(\frac{dx_i}{d\alpha_i}\right)_r = \frac{^rH_{ii}}{^rH} < 0 \quad (42)$$

if $[H]$ is the matrix of a negative definite form, and the matrix

$\frac{dx_i}{d\alpha_j}$ is negative semi-definite. (Cf. Mathematical Appendix A, Section IV.) Adopting the convention that

$$H = {}^0H,$$

equation (38) fits in as a special case of (42).

What is the effect upon the rate of change of x_i with respect to α_i of adding an additional constraint? Clearly

$$
\begin{aligned}
\left(\frac{dx_i}{d\alpha_i}\right)_r - \left(\frac{dx_i}{d\alpha_i}\right)_{r-1} &= \frac{{}^rH_{ii}}{{}^rH} - \frac{{}^{r-1}H_{ii}}{{}^{r-1}H} \\
&= \frac{{}^rH_{ii}}{{}^rH} - \frac{{}^rH_{n+r,\,n+r.ii}}{{}^rH_{n+r,\,n+r}} \\
&= \frac{{}^rH_{ii}{}^rH_{n+r,\,n+r} - {}^rH{}^rH_{n+r,\,n+r.ii}}{{}^rH{}^rH_{n+r,\,n+r}} \\
&= \frac{({}^rH_{i,\,n+r})^2}{{}^rH{}^rH_{n+r,\,n+r}}
\end{aligned}
\tag{43}
$$

by a well-known theorem on determinants (Jacobi).

The denominator is positive because such bordered principal minors regardless of the number of bordering rows must be of the same sign.[12] Hence, the difference is positive.

We have the following general theorem:

$$\left(\frac{dx_i}{d\alpha_i}\right)_0 \leqq \left(\frac{dx_i}{d\alpha_i}\right)_1 \leqq \cdots \leqq \left(\frac{dx_i}{d\alpha_i}\right)_{n-1} \leqq 0. \tag{44}$$

While the change in an x with respect to its own parameter is always negative regardless of the number of constraints, it is most negative when there are no constraints, only less so when there is a single constraint, and so forth, until the number of auxiliary constraints reaches the maximum possible, namely $(n - 1)$.[13]

This explains why economically long-run demands are more elastic than those in the short-run. A lengthening of the time

[12] See Mathematical Appendix A, equation (48). It should be noted that our r corresponds to m there, and r there corresponds to n here.

[13] This is a purely mathematical theorem. It corresponds to some of the phenomena which fall under the heading of the celebrated principle of Le Chatelier. Because of the almost metaphysical vagueness of its formulation, the latter's meaning is often in doubt, and it is used at one and the same time to cover diverse phenomena. The above formulation explains why the change in volume with respect to a given change in pressure is greater when temperature is constant than when entropy is held constant and temperature is permitted to vary in accordance with the conditions of equilibrium.

period so as to permit new factors to be varied will result in *greater* changes in the factor whose price has changed, *regardless* of whether the factors permitted to vary are complementary or competitive with the one whose price has changed.

Economic Illustrations

It is not hard to point out the relevance of the above for a large number of economic problems. First, let us repeat the result of our previous analysis.

$$f_{z_i \alpha_i} \frac{\partial x_i}{\partial \alpha_i} > 0. \tag{45}$$

This states that the direction of the change of the ith variable with respect to its corresponding parameter is of the same sign as $f_{z_i \alpha_i} (= B_{z_i \alpha_i}{}^i)$. This quantity may be taken as a criterion. If its algebraic sign is definite, i.e., unambiguously determinable, then the sign of $\partial x_i / \partial \alpha_i$ is also definite.

We have merely to show, therefore, that a wide variety of economic problems can be so formulated as to yield a conclusive determination of the sign of our criterion.

It may be noted that for maximum problems involving a single variable no restrictions need be placed upon z in order that our criterion be applicable. Let

$$z = f(x, \alpha). \tag{46}$$

Then our criterion becomes

$$f_{z\alpha} \frac{\partial x}{\partial \alpha} > 0. \tag{47}$$

I list below some random examples chosen to illustrate the applicability of the criterion.

(a) Let us go back to the example of the second chapter of the effect of a unit tax on output. It will be remembered that the relationship between the equilibrium output and the tax was determined to be unambiguously negative. This conclusion can be quickly obtained by our present method. Profit is defined as follows:

$$\pi = \varphi(x, t) = [xp(x) - C(x)] - tx. \tag{48}$$

Our criterion may be easily computed.

$$\pi_{xt} = \varphi_{xt} = -1. \tag{49}$$

Therefore,

$$(-1)\frac{\partial x}{\partial t} > 0. \tag{50}$$

or

$$\frac{\partial x}{\partial t} < 0. \tag{51}$$

Also, as shown in the previous section,

$$\frac{d\pi}{dt} = \frac{\partial \pi}{\partial t} = -x.$$

To a first approximation, the change in profits is unaffected by the adjustment of output. To a more accurate approximation, profits are reduced less if output is optimally altered.

(b) The effects of three other kinds of taxes are also simply derivable. Consider respectively a percentage tax on gross sales, a lump-sum tax, and a percentage tax on profits. The corresponding profit functions may be written:

$$\begin{aligned}
\pi &= [xp(x) - C(x)] - t'xp(x), \\
\pi &= [xp(x) - C(x)] - t'' \\
\pi &= [xp(x) - C(x)] - t'''[xp(x) - C(x)].
\end{aligned} \tag{52}$$

Our criteria are respectively

$$\begin{aligned}
\pi_{xt'} &= -\frac{\partial}{\partial x}[xp(x)] < 0, \\
\pi_{xt''} &= 0, \\
\pi_{xt'''} &= -\frac{\partial \pi(x, t''')}{\partial x} = 0.
\end{aligned} \tag{53}$$

Obviously, therefore, for the first case of a tax on gross sales, the effect of an increase in the tax rate is to reduce output. The last two cases, however, present a new feature. Our criterion is neither positive nor negative, but equal to zero. A little reflection reveals that our equilibrium maximum conditions are essentially independent of the parameters changed. Hence, our equilibrium values remain unchanged, i.e.,

$$\begin{aligned}
\frac{\partial x}{\partial t''} &\equiv 0, \\
\frac{\partial x}{\partial t'''} &\equiv 0.
\end{aligned} \tag{54}$$

These conclusions are, of course, familiar from the Marshallian analysis.

(c) Let us now consider a problem which has nothing to do with taxation, but which figured prominently in the famous cost controversy of a few years back. Let us suppose a firm in pure competition, i.e., one which can sell as much of its output as it wishes without affecting the price. Given total cost in function of output, there will be a determinable output reaction to each given price. What is the nature of this dependence? From the fact that the firm is assumed to be in stable equilibrium when it enjoys a proper relative maximum, we can easily apply our criterion to deduce the properties of the supply curve. Here

$$\pi = \varphi(x, p) = px - C(x), \tag{55}$$

$$\frac{\partial \pi}{\partial x} = p - C'(x) = 0. \tag{56}$$

Equation (56) can be solved to determine output in function of price.

$$x = g(p). \tag{57}$$

It is easily verified that

$$\pi_{xp} \equiv \varphi_{xp} \equiv 1. \tag{58}$$

Therefore,

$$\frac{dx}{dp} = g'(p) > 0. \tag{59}$$

Even if we relax the requirement that a regular relative maximum be realized, it still remains true that the supply curve cannot be negatively inclined. Of course, this does not mean that the marginal cost curve cannot be negatively inclined, but merely that in such ranges it cannot serve as a supply curve.

(d) It must not be thought, however, that the assumption of our equilibrium as the solution of a maximum problem is the "open sesame" to the successful unambiguous determination of all possible questions which we may ask. For it is extremely easy to specify simple and important problems which cannot be answered even qualitatively without further knowledge.

Consider the problem of the effect of the introduction of advertising expense upon the output of a monopolist. Will an increased advertising expense result in a larger or smaller output? Here

$$\pi = \varphi(x, \alpha) = R(x, \alpha) - C(x) - \alpha, \tag{60}$$

where

$R(x, \alpha)$ = the maximum amount of total revenue which can be secured for a given output as of a given advertising expense optimally directed.

$C(x)$ = minimum total production cost in function of output.

α = total advertising expense in dollars.

For any given α, there is an optimal output which maximizes profit. What is the sign of $dx/d\alpha$?

Applying our criterion we have

$$f_{x\alpha} = R_{x\alpha}, \tag{61}$$

or

$$R_{x\alpha} \frac{dx}{d\alpha} > 0. \tag{62}$$

Thus, the direction of change of output depends upon the direction of shift of the marginal revenue schedule (upwards or downwards) as advertising changes. Now there is nothing in the formulation of the problem which requires that this shift be of any particular direction. Hence, short of quantitative empirical investigation of sales responses to advertising no presumption is possible. Moreover, since there is ambiguity as to the instantaneous rate of direction of quantity response to a change in advertising expense, there is *a fortiori* ambiguity as to the effect of a finite change in advertising expense. It is not possible, therefore, to state whether output will be larger or smaller under positive advertising expenditures as compared to no advertising expenditure. It may be pointed out that the effect of advertising upon price is also incapable of unambiguous inference, as one should intuitively expect from the arguments which have been presented on both sides of the case.

(e) Another problem which has attracted much interest is that of whether output will be larger under discriminating monopoly or under simple monopoly. Suppose a firm with two markets with independent demand curves.

$$x_i = D^i(p_i), \qquad (i = 1, 2) \tag{63}$$

and a schedule of costs in function of total output,

$$C = C(x_1 + x_2). \tag{64}$$

Under discriminating monopoly all prices are regarded as independently variable and are adjusted so as to maximize profit. Profit may be written as

$$\pi = p_1 D^1(p_1) + p_2 D^2(p_2) - C[D^1(p_1) + D^2(p_2)]. \quad (65)$$

For simplicity we rule out the possibility that all of the demand at a given price in a given market may not be satisfied by the entrepreneur. The removal of this restriction can be easily made. Here the conditions of equilibrium are

$$\frac{\partial \pi}{\partial p_1} = 0 = D^1(p_1) + (p_1 - C') \frac{dD^1}{dp_1},$$

$$\frac{\partial \pi}{\partial p_2} = 0 = D^2(p_2) + (p_2 - C') \frac{dD^2}{dp_2}. \quad (66)$$

This results in an optimal set of prices (p_1^0, p_2^0) and quantities (x_1^0, x_2^0), and total quantity (X^0), or $(x_1^0 + x_2^0)$.

In the case of simple monopoly we impose the condition upon our problem that the price be equal in both markets. Thus,

$$p_1 = p_2 = p, \quad (67)$$

$$\pi = p D^1(p) + p D^2(p) - C[D^1(p) + D^2(p)]. \quad (68)$$

$$\frac{d\pi}{dp} = 0 = D^1(p) + D^2(p) + (p - C')\left(\frac{dD^1}{dp} + \frac{dD^2}{dp}\right). \quad (69)$$

This yields as a solution (p', p'), (x_1', x_2'), and (X'). Is it possible to determine whether

$$X' \gtreqless X^0? \quad (70)$$

At first glance there is little resemblance between this and the examples hitherto discussed. No data have been introduced as parameters; furthermore, we are not comparing two situations indefinitely close to one another. On the contrary, we seem to be dealing with two entirely different kinds of behavior. The two solutions seem to result from qualitatively different types of maximum problems. Nevertheless, we may avail ourselves of an artifice by means of which we can bring to bear the methods used above. Let us introduce a parameter k, defined as follows:

$$\frac{p_2}{p_1} = k. \quad (71)$$

We may now treat as independent variables (p_1, k) instead of (p_1, p_2) since there is a one to one relationship between the two sets. Therefore,

$$\pi = F(p_1, p_2) = F(p_1, kp_1) = G(p_1, k). \tag{72}$$

In the case of discriminating monopoly both prices are varied independently so as to maximize profit. This is equivalent to the condition that both p_1 and k must be allowed to vary so as to maximize profit. Our conditions of equilibrium are

$$\frac{\partial \pi}{\partial p_1} = \frac{\partial G}{\partial p_1} = 0,$$
$$\frac{\partial \pi}{\partial k} = \frac{\partial G}{\partial k} = 0. \tag{73}$$

This must, of course, determine the same solution as given in (66) since we have only transformed our variables.

For simple monopoly it is a preassigned condition of the problem that both prices be the same, or that k be equal to unity. Thus, by continuous movement of k from unity to $p_2{}^0/p_1{}^0$, we may pass from simple to discriminating monopoly. If then we could unambiguously state the direction of the rate of change of output with respect to k at each point, it would be possible to determine whether output would be larger or smaller.

In order to ascertain the rate of change of total output with respect to k, let us still further transform our variables as follows:

$$k = \frac{p_2}{p_1},$$
$$X = D^1(p_1) + D^2(p_2). \tag{74}$$

Solving inversely, we get

$$p_1 = f^1(k, X),$$
$$p_2 = f^2(k, X). \tag{75}$$

Thus,

$$\pi = F(p_1, p_2) = F[f^1(k, X), f^2(k, X)] = \varphi(k, X). \tag{76}$$

Our equilibrium condition for a given k is

$$\frac{\partial \pi}{\partial X} = \frac{\partial \varphi(k, X)}{\partial X} = 0. \tag{77}$$

According to our criterion

$$\varphi_{Xk} \frac{dX}{dk} > 0. \tag{78}$$

Now the computation of φ_{Xk}, while laborious, is nevertheless possible. It will be found to depend in a complicated way upon the curvatures of our demand curves. Its algebraic sign will be ambiguous, as must therefore be the effect upon total output. However, anyone who cares to go through the computation can by so doing determine what additional restrictions must be placed upon the demand functions in order to insure that output be larger or smaller.

(f) In later chapters the methods outlined here will be systematically applied to different branches of theory. In order to illustrate that it is possible to derive unambiguous conclusions even with a large number of variables a small part of our later analysis will be anticipated here.

Let us consider the demand of a firm for a factor of production. We assume as given a production function embodying the technological relationships between inputs and output, the demand curve for the finished product, and the prices at which all factors of production can be bought in unlimited quantities. The condition that profit be at a maximum is sufficient to determine the value of all unknowns in terms of these data. Thus,

$$\pi = \text{total revenue} - \text{total factor cost}$$
$$= R(x) - (w_1 a_1 + w_2 a_2 + \cdots + w_n a_n), \tag{79}$$

where w_i and a_i are the respective prices and quantities of the ith factor of production. But we are also given a production function (assumed continuous),

$$x = x(a_1, \cdots, a_n). \tag{80}$$

Hence,

$$\pi = f(a_1, \cdots, a_n, w_1, \cdots, w_n)$$
$$= R[x(a_1, \cdots, a_n)] - (w_1 a_1 + \cdots + w_n a_n). \tag{81}$$

Recall from (21) our generalized criterion.

$$\sum_1^n f_{a_j w_i} \frac{\partial a_j}{\partial w_i} > 0. \tag{82}$$

Obviously here

$$f_{a_j w_i} \equiv 0. \qquad (i \neq j) \tag{83}$$

Hence,

$$f_{a_i w_i} \frac{\partial a_i}{\partial w_i} > 0. \qquad (i = 1, \cdots, n) \tag{84}$$

But

$$f_{a_i w_i} \equiv -1. \qquad (i = 1, \cdots, n) \tag{85}$$

So

$$\frac{\partial a_i}{\partial w_i} < 0. \qquad (i = 1, \cdots, n) \tag{86}$$

This conclusion holds for any number of factors.

The above examples are but a small sample of economic problems which can be regarded as determined by the solution of maxima problems. For these, the criteria outlined above may be employed to deduce meaningful unambiguous qualitative theorems.

ANALYSIS OF FINITE CHANGES

Up until now the analysis has been confined almost exclusively to the determination of the algebraic signs of instantaneous rates of change. One cannot leave the matter here, for in the world of real phenomena all changes are necessarily finite, and instantaneous rates of change remain only limiting abstractions. It is imperative, therefore, that we develop the implications of our analysis for finite changes. Fortunately, despite the impression current among many economists that the calculus can only be applied to infinitesimal movements, this is easily done.

Let us consider for simplicity a functional relationship between one variable, x, and one parameter, α, continuous and twice differentiable everywhere on a given interval.

$$x = g(\alpha). \qquad a \leqq \alpha \leqq b \tag{87}$$

Suppose that we have already ascertained the fact that the algebraic sign of the instantaneous rate of change of this function is everywhere negative on the defined interval; i.e.,

$$\frac{dx}{d\alpha} = g'(\alpha) < 0. \qquad a \leqq \alpha \leqq b \tag{88}$$

It follows then that any finite change in α within this interval will be accompanied by a finite change in x in the opposite sense.

For let

$$\Delta\alpha = \alpha^1 - \alpha^0, \qquad\qquad a \leqq \alpha^1 \leqq b \qquad (89)$$
$$\Delta x = x^1 - x^0 = g(\alpha^1) - g(\alpha^0). \qquad a \leqq \alpha^0 \leqq b$$

We wish to prove that

$$\Delta x \Delta\alpha < 0. \qquad \Delta\alpha \neq 0. \qquad (90)$$

By the theorem of the mean

$$\Delta x = g(\alpha^1) - g(\alpha^0) = \int_{\alpha^0}^{\alpha^1} g'(\alpha)d\alpha = g'(\epsilon)\Delta\alpha, \qquad (91)$$

where

$$\epsilon = \alpha^0 + \theta(\alpha^1 - \alpha^0). \qquad 0 < \theta < 1$$

But since the derivative g' is negative everywhere on the defined interval, it must be negative for $\alpha = \epsilon$. Therefore, Δx and $\Delta\alpha$ are of opposite sign, for

$$\Delta x \Delta\alpha = g'(\epsilon)(\Delta\alpha)^2 < 0. \qquad (92)$$

This result is intuitively obvious. If, starting from a given point, a curve is always falling, then one should not expect it to be higher after a finite distance, continuity being assumed.

The above proof rested on the assumption that the derivative be unambiguously negative everywhere. This is often an admissible hypothesis as we have seen. But what about the cases in which the derivative is known to be unambiguously negative only at a point? Thus,

$$g'(\alpha^0) < 0. \qquad a < \alpha^0 < b \qquad (93)$$

Can anything be said then about finite changes? Our answer is in the affirmative. *It can be shown that for all finite changes in α smaller than some assignable quantity, there exist corresponding finite changes in x of the opposite sense.*

For by hypothesis $g'(\alpha)$ is continuous on the given interval, and of course at α^0. Hence, from the elementary definition of continuity there exists a neighborhood around α^0 in which $g'(\alpha)$ is always negative, i.e.,

$$g'(\alpha) < 0. \qquad |\alpha - \alpha^0| < h \qquad (94)$$

Thus, from our previous theorem

$$\Delta x \Delta\alpha = (x - x^0)(\alpha - \alpha^0) < 0. \qquad |\alpha - \alpha^0| < h \qquad (95)$$

The implication of the last theorem is important. In order that the results of all finite movements be unambiguous, it is necessary that the sign of the instantaneous derivative be definite everywhere. For let the derivative change sign, and it will be possible to find contradictory finite movements.

Thus far we have assumed that our equilibrium equations are such as to enable us to solve for our unknowns uniquely in terms of our parameters. Under what conditions will this be possible? It will be readily seen that even where our equilibrium conditions are defined as the result of a maximum problem there remains the possibility of multiple relative maximum positions. Under what conditions are we able to get a unique explicit solution of our implicit equations? What shall be done if multiple solutions are possible?

Assume the implicit equations

$$f^i = f_{x_i}(x_1, \cdots, x_n, \alpha_1, \cdots, \alpha_m) = 0, \qquad (i = 1, \cdots, n) \quad (96)$$

and a set of values $(x_1{}^0, \cdots, x_n{}^0, \alpha_1{}^0, \cdots, \alpha_m{}^0)$ satisfying these equations. It is known from the Implicit Function Theorem [14] that there exists one and only one explicit solution of the form

$$x_i = g^i(\alpha_1, \cdots, \alpha_m), \qquad (i = 1, \cdots, n) \quad (97)$$

in a region around $(x_1{}^0, \cdots, x_n{}^0, \alpha_1{}^0, \cdots, \alpha_m{}^0)$ where the following functional determinant does not vanish,

$$H = |f_{x_i x_j}| = \begin{vmatrix} f_{x_1 x_1} & f_{x_1 x_2} & \cdots & f_{x_1 x_n} \\ f_{x_2 x_1} & f_{x_2 x_2} & \cdots & f_{x_2 x_n} \\ \cdot & \cdot & & \cdot \\ \cdot & \cdot & & \cdot \\ \cdot & \cdot & & \cdot \\ f_{x_n x_1} & f_{x_n x_2} & \cdots & f_{x_n x_n} \end{vmatrix} \neq 0 \quad (98)$$

Since we shall be considering chiefly the selection of regular maximum positions, we may assume

$$(-1)^n H^0 = (-1)^n |f_{x_i x_j}{}^0| > 0 \quad (99)$$

at the point of equilibrium. Providing this expression remains positive everywhere, we may be sure of a unique equilibrium. Of course, this is sufficient, but not necessary.

[14] See any Advanced Calculus.

Suppose, however, that the Hessian does change sign a finite number of times within the region of economically admissible values. Then the functions in (97) will be multiple-valued with a finite number of branches. Some of these may be ruled out immediately as not constituting maximum positions, namely those for which

$$(-1)^n H < 0. \tag{100}$$

It is possible to choose from the remaining branches only by referring back to our original maximum problem. Let $(x_1{}^1, \cdots, x_n{}^1)$, $(x_1{}^2, \cdots, x_n{}^2), \cdots$ correspond to a preassigned set $(\alpha_1, \cdots, \alpha_m)$ as multiple solutions of (96). That set (or sets) is retained for which f is greatest. This will ordinarily serve to define our x's as single-valued functions of the α's except at a finite number of points. At these points it is a matter of indifference which of the possible alternative solutions is embraced.

Broadly speaking this possibility of multiple equilibrium offers no serious difficulty. For all qualitative results remain. To illustrate this let us consider the problem in full generality. Let

$$z = f(x_1, \cdots, x_n, \alpha_1, \cdots, \alpha_n) = \theta(x_1, \cdots, x_n) + B^1(x_1, \alpha_1) \\ + B^2(x_2, \alpha_2) + \cdots + B^n(x_n, \alpha_n). \tag{101}$$

Consider a preassigned set of values of our parameters $(\alpha_1{}^0, \cdots, \alpha_n{}^0)$, and a corresponding optimal set of values for our unknowns $(x_1{}^0, \cdots, x_n{}^0)$, not assumed to be necessarily unique. Then by definition of a maximum

$$f(x_1, \cdots, x_n, \alpha_1{}^0, \cdots, \alpha_n{}^0) \leqq f(x_1{}^0, \cdots, x_n{}^0, \alpha_1{}^0, \cdots, \alpha_n{}^0) \tag{102}$$

where $(x_1, \cdots, x_n)$ take on any values. For brevity this may be written

$$f(X, \alpha^0) - f(X^0, \alpha^0) \leqq 0. \tag{103}$$

Consider any other preassigned values of our parameters $(\alpha_1{}^1, \cdots, \alpha_n{}^1)$, and a corresponding optimal set $(x_1{}^1, \cdots, x_n{}^1)$. Then

$$f(X^1, \alpha^1) - f(X^0, \alpha^1) \geqq 0, \tag{104}$$
$$f(X^0, \alpha^0) - f(X^1, \alpha^0) \geqq 0.$$

Adding both sides, we get

$$[f(X^1, \alpha^1) - f(X^0, \alpha^1)] - [f(X^1, \alpha^0) - f(X^0, \alpha^0)] \geqq 0. \tag{105}$$

From the definition of a definite integral this can be written

$$\sum_1^n \int_{x_i^0}^{x_i^1} [f_{x_i}(x_1, \cdots, x_n, \alpha_1^1, \cdots, \alpha_n^1)$$
$$- f_{x_i}(x_1, \cdots, x_n, \alpha_1^0, \cdots, \alpha_n^0)]dx_i \geqq 0. \quad (106)$$

From the same definition this can be further transformed

$$\sum_1^n \sum_1^n \int_{x_i^0}^{x_i^1} \int_{\alpha_j^0}^{\alpha_j^1} f_{x_i\alpha_j}(x_1, \cdots, x_n, \alpha_1, \cdots, \alpha_n)dx_id\alpha_j \geqq 0. \quad (107)$$

But from (101)

$$f_{x_i\alpha_j} = B_{x_i\alpha_j}^{\ i} \equiv 0, \qquad (i \neq j)$$
$$f_{x_i\alpha_i} = B_{x_i\alpha_i}^{\ i}, \quad (108)$$

so

$$\sum_1^n \int_{x_i^0}^{x_i^1} \int_{\alpha_i^0}^{\alpha_i^1} f_{x_i\alpha_i}(x_1, \cdots, x_n, \alpha_1, \cdots, \alpha_n)dx_id\alpha_i \geqq 0. \quad (109)$$

By the theorem of the mean this may be written

$$\sum_1^n \overline{f_{x_i\alpha_i}}\Delta x_i\Delta \alpha_i \geqq 0, \quad (110)$$

where $\overline{f_{x_i\alpha_i}}$ is evaluated at an intermediate point. If we consider movements of the kth parameter alone, others being held constant, this becomes

$$\overline{f_{x_k\alpha_k}}\Delta x_k\Delta \alpha_k \geqq 0. \qquad (k = 1, \cdots, n) \quad (111)$$

Hence, if our criterion is definite in sign everywhere, e.g.,

$$f_{x_k\alpha_k} = B_{x_k\alpha_k}^{\ k} < 0, \qquad (k = 1, \cdots, n) \quad (112)$$

then,

$$\Delta x_k\Delta \alpha_k \leqq 0. \qquad (k = 1, \cdots, n) \quad (113)$$

This is proof that multiplicity of equilibrium values does not alter the definiteness of our conclusions with respect to finite changes. It also shows that the criterion which we applied in earlier sections to determine the definiteness of instantaneous rates of change can be generalized to determine the definiteness of finite changes. In fact, by a proper limiting process our previous theorems relating to instantaneous rates of change can be deduced as special cases from this more general analysis.

The equality sign can be dropped if $\Delta\alpha \neq 0$, and if the maximum is proper. It will be noted that in this proof we did not require that θ be continuous, but merely that the B^i be continuous with the derivatives of the required order. This will turn out to be of considerable importance in the later consideration of discontinuities in the production function of a firm.

A very important case is that in which z takes the form

$$z = \theta(x_1, \cdots, x_n) - \sum_1^n \alpha_i x_i. \tag{114}$$

Then

$$\theta(x^1) - \sum_1^n \alpha_i{}^1 x_i{}^1 \geqq \theta(x^0) - \sum_1^n \alpha_i{}^1 x_i{}^0, \tag{115}$$

$$\theta(x^0) - \sum_1^n \alpha_i{}^0 x_i{}^0 \geqq \theta(x^1) - \sum_1^n \alpha_i{}^0 x_i{}^1. \tag{116}$$

Adding and collecting terms, we get

$$\sum_1^n (\alpha_i{}^1 - \alpha_i{}^0)(x_i{}^1 - x_i{}^0) \leqq 0, \tag{117}$$

or

$$\sum_1^n \Delta\alpha_i \Delta x_i \leqq 0. \tag{118}$$

As illustration of the direct application of our methods to finite changes, let us revert back to the firm with a given total cost function producing in a purely competitive market. For a preassigned price, p^0, the firm will supply a given output, x^0 (not necessarily uniquely defined, since the firm may be indifferent in its selection among two or more outputs). Since profit is at a maximum for this output

$$[p^0 x^1 - C(x^1)] - [p^0 x^0 - C(x^0)] \leqq 0, \tag{119}$$

where x^1 may be any output, in particular that output appropriate to a second price, p^1, such that

$$[p^1 x^0 - C(x^0)] - [p^1 x^1 - C(x^1)] \leqq 0. \tag{120}$$

Adding we get

$$\Delta p \Delta x = (p^1 - p^0)(x^1 - x^0) \geqq 0, \tag{121}$$

and

$$\Delta p \Delta x > 0 \quad \text{for} \quad \Delta x \neq 0, \quad \Delta p \neq 0. \tag{122}$$

For this analysis it is not necessary that the cost curve be continuous, or be such as to yield a unique optimum output. The marginal cost curve may be undefined at points, have kinks, and turn up and down many times.

ANALYTIC FUNCTIONS

In cases where z is an analytic function of the x's and the α's, finite changes can be evaluated by an infinite power series in the $\Delta\alpha$'s, whose coefficients depend upon partial derivatives of all orders of z at the original position of equilibrium. That is,

$$\Delta x_i = \sum_1^n \left(\frac{dx_i}{d\alpha_j}\right)^0 \Delta\alpha_j + \tfrac{1}{2}\sum_1^n \sum_1^n \left(\frac{d^2 x_i}{d\alpha_j d\alpha_k}\right)^0 \Delta\alpha_j \Delta\alpha_k + \cdots.$$

$$(i = 1, \cdots, n) \quad (123)$$

The general coefficient is of the form

$$\left(\frac{d^n x_i}{d\alpha_1{}^{m_1} \cdots d\alpha_n{}^{m_n}}\right)^0,$$

where

$$\sum_1^n m_s = n. \quad (124)$$

These coefficients can be computed from the equilibrium equations by differentiating as many times as is necessary with respect to the α's. If the Hessian is not zero, this will yield recursion relations sufficient to get the desired higher derivatives in terms of the already computed lower derivatives and the higher partial derivatives with respect to the x's.

CONVERTIBILITY INTO A MAXIMUM PROBLEM

Earlier in this chapter it was indicated that some problems which do not appear to involve extremum positions can at times be converted into an equivalent maximum or minimum problem. The advantage to be derived from so doing is merely notational, since it will require fully as much knowledge to ascertain whether the conditions of a maximum position are met as would be necessary to answer any questions which might be asked. Furthermore, there is the danger that unwarranted teleological and normative welfare significance will be attributed to a position of equilibrium so defined. To avoid misunderstanding it is well to emphasize that the conversion of a problem whose economic context does not suggest any human, purposive, maximizing behavior into a maximum problem is to be regarded as merely a technical device for the purpose of quickly developing the properties of that equilibrium position.

Our problem may be stated in the following way. Given initial conditions of equilibrium

$$f^i(x_1, \cdots, x_n, \alpha_1, \cdots, \alpha_m) = 0, \qquad (i = 1, \cdots, n) \quad (125)$$

such that our unknowns are determined in function of the given parameters, namely,

$$x_i = g^i(\alpha_1, \cdots, \alpha_m), \qquad (i = 1, \cdots, n) \quad (126)$$

under what conditions can the set (125) be regarded as the solution of an extremum problem so that the n indicated equilibrium loci correspond to the vanishing of the partial derivatives of some function? That is, does there exist a function

$$z = f(x_1, \cdots, x_n, \alpha_1, \cdots, \alpha_m) \quad (127)$$

such that

$$f_{x_i}(x_1, \cdots, x_n, \alpha_1, \cdots, \alpha_n) = 0, \qquad (i = 1, \cdots, n) \quad (128)$$

represents the same locus for each value of i as

$$f^i(x_1, \cdots, x_n, \alpha_1, \cdots, \alpha_m) = 0? \qquad (i = 1, \cdots, n) \quad (129)$$

Now the same implicit function may be represented in an infinity of ways without changing the locus it denotes.[15] It is desirable, therefore, that we represent the loci which are our conditions of equilibrium in a definite unambiguous form. One such way is provided by solving explicitly for each variable in turn,

$$x_i = M^i(x_1, \cdots, x_{i-1}, x_{i+1}, \cdots, x_n). \qquad (i = 1, \cdots, n) \quad (130)$$

What conditions are necessary on these functions or on the functions f^i so that there exists a z as defined by equations (127) and (128)?

Define

$$\lambda_{ij} = - \left(\frac{dx_i}{dx_j} \right)^0_i = - \left(\frac{\partial M^i}{\partial x_j} \right)^0 = \left(\frac{f^i_j}{f^i_i} \right)^0. \quad (131)$$

---

[15] For example, $(f^i)^2 = 0$, $(i = 1, \cdots, n)$ or $F(f^i) = 0$, where $F(0) = 0$; $F(a) \neq 0$, $a \neq 0$.

The λ's are unambiguously determinable independently of the representation of the f's. In general,

$$\lambda_{ij} \neq \lambda_{ji}.$$

If there exists a function z, the vanishing of whose partial derivatives is equivalent to the equations (125), then

$$\lambda_{ij} = \frac{f_{ij}}{f_{ii}}. \qquad (132)$$

Also for every possible triplet

$$\lambda_{ij}\lambda_{jk}\lambda_{ki} = \frac{f_{ij}{}^0 f_{jk}{}^0 f_{ki}{}^0}{f_{ii}{}^0 f_{jj}{}^0 f_{kk}{}^0} = \frac{f_{ji}{}^0 f_{kj}{}^0 f_{ik}{}^0}{f_{jj}{}^0 f_{kk}{}^0 f_{ii}{}^0} = \lambda_{ji}\lambda_{kj}\lambda_{ik} \qquad (133)$$

because $f_{ij} = f_{ji}$ for all possible pairs.

These conditions are necessary. They are not identities for all values of $(x_1, \cdots, x_n)$, but only for those satisfying

$$f^i(x_1, \cdots, x_n) = 0; \qquad (i = 1, \cdots, n)$$

i.e., they hold only at the point $(x_1{}^0, \cdots, x_n{}^0)$.[16] They are not to be confused with the integrability conditions of chapter v. Though necessary, they are probably not sufficient. Quite possibly similar point reciprocity relations can be found between various derivatives of higher order. If all of these should hold, perhaps a complete set of sufficient conditions would be attained.

The relationships given in equation (133) are vacuous if the number of variables is less than three. All together $n(n - 1)(n - 2)/6$ independent conditions are involved.[17]

[16] In addition, for all values of (x) satisfying a subset of $r(< n)$ equations $f^i = 0$, there will be defined similar relations which are *identities* in the remaining $(n - r)$ variables.

[17] Any completely non-specialized set of n equations in n variables, $f^i(x_1, \cdots, x_n) = 0$, can be regarded as equivalent to a stationary position of a function of $2n$ variables. Let

$$F(x_1, \cdots, x_n; x_{n+1}, \cdots, x_{n+n}) = \sum_1^n f^i(x_1, \cdots, x_n)x_{n+i}.$$

$dF = 0$ implies among other things that $f^i(x_1, \cdots, x_n) = 0$. This is definitely not an extremum position as shown by reference to the secondary conditions. The fact that in a larger set of variables a stationary value corresponds to a non-specialized system seems devoid of economic significance. See G. D. Birkhoff, *Dynamical Systems* (New York: 1927), pp. 33–34.

As we have seen, it is not enough that our equilibrium equations be expressible as the partial derivatives of some function.   In order to be able to derive definite theorems it is desirable that this function be at a regular maximum or minimum.   This requires as is shown in Mathematical Appendix A, Section II, that certain quadratic forms be either negative or positive definite.   Thus, for a maximum

$$\sum_1^n \sum_1^n f_{ij} h_i h_j < 0, \qquad \text{not all } h_i = 0. \tag{134}$$

As shown in Appendix A, Section III, this requires that the following inequalities hold.

$$|f_{11}| < 0; \qquad \begin{vmatrix} f_{11} & f_{12} \\ f_{21} & f_{22} \end{vmatrix} > 0; \qquad \begin{vmatrix} f_{11} & f_{12} & f_{13} \\ f_{21} & f_{22} & f_{23} \\ f_{31} & f_{32} & f_{33} \end{vmatrix} < 0; \quad \text{etc.} \tag{135}$$

For a regular minimum these determinants are all positive.   It can be easily shown that either of these is equivalent to the following conditions.

$$\begin{vmatrix} 1 & \lambda_{ij} \\ \lambda_{ji} & 1 \end{vmatrix} > 0; \qquad \begin{vmatrix} 1 & \lambda_{ij} & \lambda_{ik} \\ \lambda_{ji} & 1 & \lambda_{jk} \\ \lambda_{ki} & \lambda_{kj} & 1 \end{vmatrix} > 0; \qquad \text{etc.} \tag{136}$$

for i, j, and k all unequal.   This proves that it is not important that our problem be either a maximum or minimum one, but only that it be one or the other.

As an example of a problem which can artificially be converted into an equivalent maximum problem, consider a number of independent firms buying the same kinds of productive services in purely competitive markets.[18]   The demand of any firm for the factors of production can be written

$$v_i = r^i(p_1, \cdots, p_n), \qquad (i = 1, \cdots, n) \tag{137}$$

where $(v_1, \cdots, v_n)$ represent respective amounts of n factors of production, and $(p_1, \cdots, p_n)$ their respective prices.   It can be shown

[18] H. Hotelling, "Edgeworth's Taxation Paradox and the Nature of Demand and Supply Functions," *Journal of Political Economy*, XL (1932), 577–616.   L. Court, "Invariable Classical Stability of Entrepreneurial Demand and Supply Functions," *Quarterly Journal of Economics*, LVI (1941), 134–144.   R. Roy, *De l'Utilité, Contribution à la Théorie des Choix* (Paris: 1942).

that

$$\frac{\partial v_i}{\partial p_j} \equiv \frac{\partial v_j}{\partial p_i}. \tag{138}$$

Where we sum over the individuals and use capital letters for the total amounts demanded.

$$V_i = \sum v_i = R^i(p_1, \cdots, p_n), \qquad (i = 1, \cdots, n) \qquad . \tag{139}$$

From (138)

$$\frac{\partial R^i}{\partial p_j} \equiv \frac{\partial R^j}{\partial p_i}. \tag{140}$$

There exists, therefore, a function

$$Z = R(p_1, \cdots, p_n) - (V_1 p_1 + V_2 p_2 + \cdots + V_n p_n), \tag{141}$$

where

$$\frac{\partial R}{\partial p_i} = R^i(p_1, \cdots, p_n). \qquad (i = 1, \cdots, n) \tag{142}$$

The conditions of equilibrium represented by the general demand functions of (139) are, therefore, equivalent to those derived from the condition that Z be at a maximum with respect to the p's, i.e.,

$$\frac{\partial Z}{\partial p_i} = R^i - V_i \equiv 0. \qquad (i = 1, \cdots, n) \tag{143}$$

CHAPTER IV

A COMPREHENSIVE RESTATEMENT OF THE THEORY OF COST AND PRODUCTION

ECONOMIC THEORY as taught in the textbooks has often tended to become segmentalized into loosely integrated compartments, such as production, value, and distribution. There are, no doubt, pedagogical advantages in such a treatment, and yet something of the essential unity and interdependence of economic forces is lost in so doing. A case in point is the conventional assuming of a cost curve for each firm and the working out of its optimum output with respect to its demand conditions. Only later is the problem of the purchase of factors of production by the firm investigated, and often its connection with the previous process is not clearly brought out.

I should like here to investigate from the point of view of the previous chapters the cost curves of the firm as usually presented and the production function embodying technical relations between inputs and output which lie behind it, and also to show clearly its relevance to the problem of the determination of the optimum output. In particular, I shall attempt to derive all possible operationally meaningful theorems. Much of what is said will be found to apply regardless of the elasticity of the demand curve for the firm; i.e., under "impure" as well as "pure" competition. By employing a suitable notation it is possible from a purely technical point of view to consider the case of any number of productive factors as easily as one or two.

STATEMENT OF PROBLEMS

In the beginning the revenue side of the firm is completely ignored. We assume as given by technical considerations the maximum amount of output, x, which can be produced from any given set of inputs $(v_1, \cdots, v_n)$. This catalogue of possibilities is the production function and may be written

$$x = \varphi(v_1, \cdots, v_n). \tag{1}$$

In general, there will be a maximum output for each set of inputs, and so this function is single-valued, and will be assumed initially to have continuous partial derivatives of desired order. Furthermore, no marginal physical productivities can be negative, else output would not be maximal since it could be improved for the same set of factors by leaving some idle. Regardless of this consideration, in the relevant region under consideration we will have

$$\varphi_i \geqq 0, \qquad (i = 1, \cdots, n) \qquad (2)$$

where as a convention of notation

$$\varphi_i = \frac{\partial x}{\partial v_i} = \text{marginal physical (degree of) productivity. Simi-}$$

larly, we define

$$\varphi_{ij} = \frac{\partial^2 x}{\partial v_i \partial v_j}.$$

It is also assumed that each firm is small relative to the market for each input so that unlimited amounts of each can be bought at the respective prices $(w_1, \cdots, w_n)$.

As a matter of definition the total cost of the firm may be written as the sum of the costs for each input item and any other costs which are independent of the purchase of the designated inputs and output; i.e.,

$$C = A + \sum_1^n w_i v_i, \qquad (3)$$

where A represents costs which do not vary with the designated inputs and output (taxes, etc.). Of course, these fixed charges may be zero.

A brief survey of our field by economic intuition will aid in phrasing the problems to be investigated, after which mathematical analysis may be employed in stating the conditions imposed on our various functions. Our aim is to derive the total cost for each output. More precisely, with given prices of productive factors and given production function, we are interested in deriving the *minimum total cost for each output*. This will be a function as follows:

$$C = A + V(x, w_1, \cdots, w_n). \qquad (4)$$

If we regard the prices of the productive factors as constant, the resulting relationship between C and x is the usual total cost curve, from which average and marginal curves can be derived.

The question arises as to the relationship between (3) and (4). It is clear that the same output can be produced by an infinity of combinations of productive factors so that in the absence of other considerations it is impossible to determine the total cost uniquely for each output. In view of the consideration that total cost for each output be a minimum, our indeterminacy disappears. Out of the set of all possible input combinations which will produce a given output, that combination is selected which minimizes the total cost defined in (3). In other words, with given prices of productive factors and for a preassigned output, there is an optimum value for each productive factor; i.e.,

$$v_i = f^i(x, w_1, \cdots, w_n). \qquad (i = 1, \cdots, n) \tag{5}$$

By substitution into (3), we have

$$C = A + \sum_{1}^{n} w_i f^i(x, w_1, \cdots, w_n) = A + V(x, w_1, \cdots, w_n). \tag{6}$$

Thus, the relationship between (3) and (4) is revealed.

It is part of the purpose of this book to investigate the properties of the functions (4) and (5). It is true that theoretical economics does not deal with particular forms of functions (e.g., polynomials, etc.). However, it does concern itself with the general character of various functions; that is, their slopes, curvature, etc. In this case we are interested in the following properties of these functions:

$$\frac{\partial C}{\partial x}, \frac{\partial^2 C}{\partial x^2}, \frac{\partial C}{\partial w_j}, \frac{\partial^2 C}{\partial x \partial w_j}; \tag{7}$$

i.e., how are total and marginal costs affected by changes in output or prices of productive services? On what properties of the production function does this depend?

We are also interested in

$$\frac{\partial v_i}{\partial w_i}, \frac{\partial v_i}{\partial w_j}, \frac{\partial v_i}{\partial x}; \tag{8}$$

i.e., what is the reaction of demand for a productive service with a change in its own price? With a change in another price? With a change in output?

These are obviously important theoretical questions, and yet, curiously enough, the answers to some of them do not appear to be in the literature. In the next section these will be mathematically evaluated, and the results summarized. It will be found that under very general assumptions the knowledge of the signs of these differential quotients will give us the direction of change with respect not only to sufficiently small finite movements, but also to finite movements of any size.

Conditions of Equilibrium

Thus far we have employed only the notation of mathematics. By so doing, the problem has been clearly framed, which in many economic problems is more than half the battle. It remains now to state the derivations of (4) and (5) from (1) and (3).

Our problem is to minimize

$$C = A + \sum_1^n w_i v_i \tag{9}$$

subject to

$$\varphi(v_1, \cdots, v_n) = \bar{x} = \text{constant.} \tag{10}$$

Mathematically, this is a constrained minimum problem, and we may avail ourselves of the method of the Lagrangean (undetermined) multiplier. We define a new function

$$G = A + \sum_1^n w_i v_i - \lambda[\varphi(v_1, \cdots, v_n) - \bar{x}], \tag{11}$$

where $(-\lambda)$ is a Lagrangean multiplier, whose economic interpretation will be brought out later. G may be regarded as a function of all the inputs as independent variables. It is necessary for a proper relative minimum that

$$\frac{\partial G}{\partial v_i} = 0 = w_i - \lambda\varphi_i. \qquad (i = 1, \cdots, n) \tag{12}$$

These may be rewritten as

$$\frac{1}{\lambda} = \frac{\varphi_1}{w_1} = \frac{\varphi_2}{w_2} = \cdots = \frac{\varphi_n}{w_n}. \tag{13}$$

This is the well-known economic theorem that in order for total costs to be a minimum for any given output, the marginal productivity of the last dollar $(1/\lambda)$ must be equal in every use. Alternatively, it may be stated that the marginal physical productivity of any factor must be proportional to the price at which it can be hired, the factor of proportionality being the term λ.[1] *It will be noted that this condition is independent of the revenue curve of the firm and must hold at every point on the cost curve, not only at the final point of optimal output.*

Provided that certain secondary conditions to be discussed presently hold, the n equations in (12) and the one equation in (10) are sufficient to determine each of our $(n + 1)$ unknowns $(v_1, \cdots, v_n, \lambda)$ in terms of x and the factor prices $(w_1, \cdots, w_n)$ regarded as parameters. Thus, our equations (5) are defined implicitly by these minimum conditions.

One may well question the advantage of this formulation. Apparently we have substituted an indirect statement of our final conditions for a direct one. But, and this is typical of all sound economic theory, we are trying to deduce the consequences of our hypothesized data, and we do know (by hypothesis) much about the functions in (12). Merely to state the relations in (4) and (5) is formal and empty. By means of (12) we can place positive restrictions upon them and know their general properties.

Now there remains the purely mathematical problem of translating our assumptions into terms of the functions (4) and (5), and computing their respective partial derivatives designated in (7) and (8).

SECONDARY EXTREMUM CONDITIONS

To do so we must first state all that we know about the conditions defined in (12), in particular the secondary necessary and sufficient conditions for a proper relative constrained minimum. It is clear that in order for total cost to be a minimum for a preassigned x, the locus of all possible inputs yielding that preassigned quantity (isoquant surface) must be tangential to a locus of all possible inputs yielding the same total cost (isocost plane). But of course this is not enough. The isoquants must also be convex to the origin in all directions in order that its contact with the isocost plane represent a true proper minimum. The analogy with the theory of consumer's preference suggests itself. This is brought out more clearly if we phrase the problem not as that of minimizing

---

[1] Later λ will be shown to be equal to marginal cost, i.e., $\partial C/\partial x$.

total cost for a preassigned output, but rather in the equivalent form of maximizing output for any preassigned total expenditure. Mathematically, our secondary conditions are

$$\sum_1^n \sum_1^n \varphi_{ij}\xi_i\xi_j < 0, \tag{14}$$

for

$$\sum_1^n \varphi_i\xi_i = 0,$$

and not all

$$\xi_i = 0.$$

Consider the bordered determinant

$$D = \begin{vmatrix} \varphi_{ij} & \varphi_i \\ \varphi_j & 0 \end{vmatrix} = \begin{vmatrix} \varphi_{11} & \varphi_{12} & \cdots & \varphi_{1n} & \varphi_1 \\ \varphi_{21} & \varphi_{22} & \cdots & \varphi_{2n} & \varphi_2 \\ \cdot & \cdot & & \cdot & \cdot \\ \cdot & \cdot & & \cdot & \cdot \\ \cdot & \cdot & & \cdot & \cdot \\ \varphi_{n1} & \varphi_{n2} & \cdots & \varphi_{nn} & \varphi_n \\ \varphi_1 & \varphi_2 & \cdots & \varphi_n & 0 \end{vmatrix} \tag{15}$$

and respective principal minors

$$D^{12} = \begin{vmatrix} \varphi_{11} & \varphi_{12} & \varphi_1 \\ \varphi_{21} & \varphi_{22} & \varphi_2 \\ \varphi_1 & \varphi_2 & 0 \end{vmatrix}; \quad D^{123} = \begin{vmatrix} \varphi_{11} & \varphi_{12} & \varphi_{13} & \varphi_1 \\ \varphi_{21} & \varphi_{22} & \varphi_{23} & \varphi_2 \\ \varphi_{31} & \varphi_{32} & \varphi_{33} & \varphi_3 \\ \varphi_1 & \varphi_2 & \varphi_3 & 0 \end{vmatrix}; \quad \text{etc.} \tag{16}$$

It is well known [2] that (14) implies that any such minor of the order m must have the sign of $(-1)^{m-1}$, and conversely: i.e.,

$$(-1)^{m-1}D^{12\ldots(m-1)} > 0. \qquad (m \leqq n + 1) \tag{17}$$

Specifically,

$$\varphi_{ii}\varphi_j{}^2 - 2\varphi_{ij}\varphi_i\varphi_j + \varphi_{jj}\varphi_i{}^2 < 0; \text{ etc.} \qquad (i \neq j)$$

It will be noted that this condition does *not* necessarily imply or require the law of diminishing marginal physical productivity to hold.[3]

[2] Compare H. Hotelling, "Demand Functions with Limited Budgets," *Econometrica*, January, 1935, pp. 66–78.

[3] I am assuming that these secondary conditions hold not only at the minimum point, but everywhere. Mathematically, this assures us of the *uniqueness* of our equilibrium, since this stronger assumption definitely rules out multiple relative minima.

The secondary conditions are not always mentioned in the literature. It is not for elegance or completeness that they are included here, but rather because they are wholly relevant to the problem under discussion, since it is upon them that all our results depend.

DISPLACEMENT OF EQUILIBRIUM

It is now possible to derive in compact form the rates of change of our dependent variables $(v_1, \cdots, v_n)$ with respect to changes in the variables $(x, w_1, \cdots, w_n)$. The reader not interested in the mathematical derivation of these conditions is referred to a summary of results at the end of this section. First we write the total differential of our equilibrium equations (12) and (10).

$$\sum_1^n \varphi_{ij} dv_j + \frac{\varphi_i}{\lambda} d\lambda = \frac{dw_i}{\lambda}, \qquad (i = 1, \cdots, n) \qquad (18)$$

$$\sum_1^n \varphi_j dv_j = dx.$$

These are $(n + 1)$ linear equations in $(n + 1)$ unknowns $(dv_1, \cdots, dv_n, d\lambda)$, and may be solved in determinantal notation as follows:

$$dv_k = \frac{\sum_1^n \frac{dw_i}{\lambda} \Delta_{ik} + dx \Delta_{n+1,k}}{\Delta}, \qquad (19)$$

where

$$\Delta = \begin{vmatrix} \varphi_{ij} & \varphi_i \\ \varphi_j & \frac{\varphi_i}{\lambda} \\ & 0 \end{vmatrix} = \begin{vmatrix} \varphi_{11} & \varphi_{12} & \cdots & \varphi_{1n} & \frac{\varphi_1}{\lambda} \\ \varphi_{21} & \varphi_{22} & \cdots & \varphi_{2n} & \frac{\varphi_2}{\lambda} \\ \cdot & \cdot & & \cdot & \cdot \\ \cdot & \cdot & & \cdot & \cdot \\ \cdot & \cdot & & \cdot & \cdot \\ \varphi_{n1} & \varphi_{n2} & \cdots & \varphi_{nn} & \frac{\varphi_n}{\lambda} \\ \varphi_1 & \varphi_2 & \cdots & \varphi_n & 0 \end{vmatrix} \qquad (20)$$

and Δ_{qr} is the cofactor of the element in the rth column and the qth row.

Also,

$$d\lambda = \frac{\sum_{1}^{n} \frac{dw_i}{\lambda} \Delta_{i,n+1} + dx\Delta_{n+1,n+1}}{\Delta}. \tag{21}$$

Hence,

$$\frac{\partial v_k}{\partial w_j} = \frac{\Delta_{jk}}{\lambda\Delta}. \tag{22}$$

As a special case

$$\frac{\partial v_k}{\partial w_k} = \frac{\Delta_{kk}}{\lambda\Delta}. \tag{23}$$

Also,

$$\frac{\partial v_k}{\partial x} = \frac{\Delta_{n+1,k}}{\Delta} \tag{24}$$

and

$$\frac{\partial \lambda}{\partial w_k} = \frac{\Delta_{k,n+1}}{\lambda\Delta}, \tag{25}$$

$$\frac{\partial \lambda}{\partial x} = \frac{\Delta_{n+1,n+1}}{\Delta}. \tag{26}$$

It is clear on inspection of the determinant Δ, that

$$\Delta = \frac{1}{\lambda} D. \tag{27}$$

Also

$$\Delta_{jk} = \frac{1}{\lambda} D_{jk} = \Delta_{kj}, \qquad (j, k = 1, \cdots, n) \tag{28}$$

$$\Delta_{j,n+1} = D_{j,n+1} = \lambda\Delta_{n+1,j}, \qquad (j = 1, \cdots, n) \tag{29}$$

and

$$\Delta_{n+1,n+1} = D_{n+1,n+1}. \tag{30}$$

Therefore, from (28)

$$\frac{\partial v_k}{\partial w_j} = \frac{\partial v_j}{\partial w_k}. \tag{31}$$

That is to say, *the change in the kth factor with respect to a change in the jth price, output being constant, must be equal to the change in the jth factor with respect to the kth price, output being constant;* a result which is not intuitively obvious.

From (27) and (28)

$$\frac{\Delta_{jk}}{\Delta} = \frac{D_{jk}}{D}. \tag{32}$$

But from our stability conditions in (17)

$$\frac{D_{jj}}{D} < 0. \qquad (j = 1, \cdots, n) \tag{33}$$

Therefore,

$$\frac{\partial v_j}{\partial w_j} < 0. \qquad (j = 1, \cdots, n) \tag{34}$$

That is, *any fixed output will always be produced with less of any given factor as its respective price rises, other prices not changing. By the law of the mean this can be shown to hold for finite changes.*

Let us now determine the economic meaning of λ. Rewriting (11)

$$G = A + \sum_{1}^{n} w_i v_i - \lambda[\varphi(v_1, \cdots, v_n) - \bar{x}],$$

and differentiating G, which is total cost with a term added on, we get

$$\frac{\partial G}{\partial x} = \lambda.$$

This suggests that λ may be marginal cost. This can be proved rigorously in two ways. Of course,

$$dC = \sum_{1}^{n} w_i dv_i, \tag{35}$$

and

$$dx = \sum_{1}^{n} \varphi_i dv_i. \tag{36}$$

Dividing (35) by (36), we get

$$\frac{\partial C}{\partial x} = \frac{\sum\limits_{1}^{n} w_i dv_i}{\sum\limits_{1}^{n} \varphi_i dv_i}. \tag{37}$$

Substituting from (12),

$$\frac{\partial C}{\partial x} = \frac{\sum\limits_{1}^{n} \lambda \varphi_i dv_i}{\sum\limits_{1}^{n} \varphi_i dv_i} = \lambda(x, w_1, \cdots, w_n). \tag{38}$$

More rigorously the proof is as follows:

$$\frac{\partial C}{\partial x} = \sum_1^n w_i \frac{\partial v_i}{\partial x}. \tag{39}$$

Substituting from (24),

$$\frac{\partial C}{\partial x} = \sum_1^n w_i \frac{\Delta_{n+1,i}}{\Delta} = \lambda \sum_1^n \varphi_i \frac{\Delta_{n+1,i}}{\Delta}. \tag{40}$$

But expanding Δ in terms of the elements of the last row,

$$\Delta = \sum_1^n \varphi_i \Delta_{n+1,i}. \tag{41}$$

Hence,

$$\frac{\partial C}{\partial x} = \lambda \frac{\Delta}{\Delta} = \lambda. \tag{42}$$

Therefore, we may rewrite (12) as follows:

$$w_i = \frac{\partial C}{\partial x} \varphi_i. \tag{43}$$

Thus, it may be stated as a theorem that *in order for total costs to be a minimum for any given output, the price of each factor must be equal to marginal physical productivity times marginal cost.*[4] *This holds regardless of revenue considerations.*
Of course,

$$\frac{\partial \lambda}{\partial x} = \frac{\partial^2 C}{\partial x^2}, \tag{44}$$

and

$$\frac{\partial \lambda}{\partial w_k} = \frac{\partial^2 C}{\partial x \partial w_k}. \tag{45}$$

From (24), (25), and (29),

$$\frac{\partial \lambda}{\partial w_k} = \frac{\partial v_k}{\partial x}, \tag{46}$$

or

$$\frac{\partial^2 C}{\partial x \partial w_k} = \frac{\partial v_k}{\partial x}. \tag{47}$$

[4] This has been pointed out in another connection in lectures by Professor Viner with illuminating insight into the relationship of the external to the internal margin, and the broad zone of indifference as a substitute for the infinitesimal. Paradoxically, it is this condition which is basic to Mr. Wong's famous envelope theorem!

That is, *the change in any input item with respect to an increase in output must be equal to the change in marginal cost with respect to a change in the price of that input item.*

Recall from (26)

$$\frac{\partial \lambda}{\partial x} = \frac{\partial^2 C}{\partial x^2} = \frac{\Delta_{n+1,n+1}}{\Delta}. \tag{48}$$

Now it is known from (17) and (27) that Δ has the sign of $(-1)^n$. Also

$$\Delta_{n+1,n+1} = \begin{vmatrix} \varphi_{11} & \cdots & \varphi_{1n} \\ \cdot & & \cdot \\ \cdot & & \cdot \\ \cdot & & \cdot \\ \varphi_{n1} & \cdots & \varphi_{nn} \end{vmatrix} = H, \tag{49}$$

where H is called the Hessian determinant of the production function. *Obviously, therefore, the slope of the marginal cost curve must have the same or opposite sign as compared to this Hessian, depending upon whether the number of inputs is even or odd;* i.e.,

$$(-1)^n H \frac{\partial^2 C}{\partial x^2} > 0. \tag{50}$$

Thus the stability of pure competition is intimately tied up with the Hessian of the production function, a result not intuitively obvious.

I should also like to indicate certain other results, leaving their rigorous derivation to the interested reader. Consider equation (5),

$$v_i = f^i(x, w_1, \cdots, w_n). \qquad (i = 1, \cdots, n)$$

These functions are defined by (10) and (12),

$$x = \varphi(v_1, \cdots, v_n)$$

and

$$w_i - \lambda \varphi_i = 0. \qquad (i = 1, \cdots, n)$$

(12) may be rewritten as follows:

$$\frac{\varphi_i}{\varphi_1} = \frac{w_i}{w_1}. \qquad (i = 2, \cdots, n) \tag{51}$$

Obviously, the changing of all prices in the same proportion will leave the solution of (51) unchanged; hence, the functions in (5) must be homogeneous of order zero in the variables $(w_1, \cdots, w_n)$, x being constant; i.e.,

$$v_i = f^i(x, w_1, \cdots, w_n) = f^i(x, \gamma w_1, \cdots, \gamma w_n), \quad (i = 1, \cdots, n) \quad (52)$$

where γ is arbitrary.   Hence, from Euler's theorem on homogeneous functions,

$$0 = \sum_1^n w_j \frac{\partial v_i}{\partial w_j}. \quad (i = 1, \cdots, n) \quad (53)$$

This can be verified by substitution from (22).

By analogous reasoning,

$$C = A + \sum_1^n w_i \frac{\partial C}{\partial w_i}, \quad (54)$$

where

$$\frac{\partial C}{\partial w_i} = v_i. \quad (55)$$

Actually, from the considerations of the previous chapter it is possible to deduce a more general condition which includes (34) as one minor part.   The minimization of total expenditure for a given output, price being fixed, implies (10) and (12).   In addition, at a regular minimum we must have [5]

$$\sum_1^n \sum_1^n \frac{\partial v_i}{\partial w_j} \xi_i \xi_j < 0, \quad (56)$$

for not all ξ_i proportional to w_i.   Consider the determinant

$$G = \frac{\partial(v_1, \cdots, v_n)}{\partial(w_1, \cdots, w_n)} = 0 = \left| \frac{\partial v_i}{\partial w_j} \right|, \quad (57)$$

and

$$G_{12} = \frac{\partial(v_1, v_2)}{\partial(w_1, w_2)} = \begin{vmatrix} \dfrac{\partial v_1}{\partial w_1} & \dfrac{\partial v_1}{\partial w_2} \\ \dfrac{\partial v_2}{\partial w_1} & \dfrac{\partial v_2}{\partial w_2} \end{vmatrix}; \quad G_{123} = \frac{\partial(v_1, v_2, v_3)}{\partial(w_1, w_2, w_3)}; \text{ etc.} \quad (58)$$

Then each such principal minor of order m (less than n) must be negative or positive depending upon whether m is odd or even; i.e.,

$$(-1)^m G_{12\cdots m} > 0. \quad G_{12\cdots n} = G = 0. \quad (59)$$

[5] Compare chap. iii, p. 30, Mathematical Appendix A, Sections IV and V, and chap. v, pp. 113–116.

Specifically,

$$\frac{\partial v_j}{\partial w_j} < 0; \qquad \frac{\partial v_j}{\partial w_j}\frac{\partial v_k}{\partial w_k} - \left(\frac{\partial v_j}{\partial w_k}\right)^2 > 0; \quad \text{etc.} \qquad (60)$$

It may be well to summarize our results of this section:

$$\frac{\partial v_j}{\partial w_j} < 0; \qquad \frac{\partial(v_j, v_k)}{\partial(w_j, w_k)} > 0; \quad \text{etc.} \qquad \text{(34) and (59)}$$

$$\frac{\partial v_k}{\partial w_j} = \frac{\partial v_j}{\partial w_k}, \qquad (31)$$

$$\frac{\partial^2 C}{\partial x \partial w_j} = \frac{\partial v_j}{\partial x}, \qquad (47)$$

$$w_i = \lambda \varphi_i = \frac{\partial C}{\partial x}\varphi_i, \qquad (i = 1, \cdots, n) \quad \text{(12) and (42)}$$

$$(-1)^n H \frac{\partial^2 C}{\partial x^2} < 0, \qquad (50)$$

$$\sum_1^n \frac{\partial v_i}{\partial w_j} w_j = 0, \qquad (i = 1, \cdots, n) \qquad (53)$$

$$\frac{\partial C}{\partial w_i} = v_i, \qquad (55)$$

$$C = A + \sum_1^n w_i \frac{\partial C}{\partial w_i}. \qquad (54)$$

Boundary or Corner Minima

Even in the case where the production function and its derivatives are continuous with the proper convexity to insure a uniquely determined optimal position, the interesting case may arise where some factor may not be used at all. That is to say, the more that others are used and the less of it, the lower will costs be for any given output. In this case the conditions for equilibrium do not require the equalization of the marginal productivity of the last dollar spent on it to that of other factors. Rather do we have a boundary minimum due to the fact that no negative values are economically admissible. Hence, the conditions of equilibrium are given by the statement that for any input, potentially usable but not actually used, the marginal productivity of the last dollar

spent on it must *not* be greater than the marginal productivity of the last dollar spent on factors which are used.[6]
Mathematically,

$$\frac{\varphi_u}{w_u} \lesseqgtr \frac{1}{\lambda},\qquad(61)$$

where the uth factor is one not actually used.

As the price w_u changes, it may still remain unused until some critical level at which it will begin to be used, and hence will fall into the analysis of the previous section. Of course, the critical level may very well depend on the scale of operations; i.e., output, so that with the same price it may still be brought into use by an increase in output.[7]

The demand function for such a factor of production will have the following properties:

$$v_u = f^u(x, w_u, w_1, \cdots, w_n),\qquad(62)$$

$$\frac{\partial v_u}{\partial w_u} \equiv 0 \text{ in some domain defined by } \psi(x, w_u, w_1, \cdots, w_n) < 0,\quad(63)$$

$$\frac{\partial v_u}{\partial w_u} < 0 \text{ in some domain defined by } \psi(x, w_u, w_1, \cdots, w_n) > 0,\quad(64)$$

where ψ is so constructed as to form the locus of all critical points described above.

DISCONTINUITIES IN THE PRODUCTION FUNCTION

I should now like to drop the assumption that the production function is necessarily continuous with continuous partial derivatives at every point. This assumption has been challenged by many economists, who have alleged that production coefficients

---

[6] There is an interesting discussion of an exactly analogous equilibrium system in the famous paper of J. Willard Gibbs, "The Equilibrium of Heterogeneous Substances," *Collected Papers*, I, 55–349.

[7] An analogy is suggested to the case of items which do not enter into a consumer's budget until income increases or their relative prices decrease to some critical levels. Be it noted that this phenomenon here described can occur even though there be increasing marginal physical productivity, just as the budget case does *not* restrict the behavior of marginal utility. It can be mathematically proved that this result is independent of the cardinal measure of product (utility). Another analogy is provided by the classical comparative cost doctrine—according to which a country specializes completely in one good; the equilibrium is defined by a certain inequality between prices and marginal costs.

are technically fixed, that some factors are "limitational," some factors of production "must" be used in certain joint proportions, etc. These discontinuities, if true of the real world, have been thought by many economists to offer serious problems to the analysis of distribution and the pricing of the factors of production.

It will be argued here that the fact of discontinuity offers no problems to the firm—on the contrary, its task is made much easier. As an *obiter dictum* I hold that it also offers no particular difficulty to the analysis of the wider problem of determining the prices of the factors of production with which each firm is to be confronted. As before, these are to be determined by general equilibrium analysis of supply and demand.[8]

As before, we have a production function relating maximum output to any given set of inputs:

$$x = \varphi(v_1, \cdots, v_n). \tag{65}$$

Precisely as argued in the first section this must be single-valued. However, it need not be continuous nor have partial derivatives at every point. In order that there be no contradiction to our definition of output as maximal, we must have

$$\Delta\varphi \geqq 0, \quad \text{for} \quad \Delta v_i \geqq 0. \quad (i = 1, \cdots, n) \tag{66}$$

That is, as we increase all factors together, output cannot decrease, since otherwise product would not in the next position be maximal.

For definiteness I assume that along an isoquant the production function contains only a finite number of points which do not possess continuous partial derivatives. At a point of discontinuity it is assumed that left-handed and right-handed partial derivatives exist. Of course, at a point of discontinuity there does not exist a uniquely defined plane tangent to the isoquant, but limiting direction cosines can be found for all planes which touch but do not cut the isoquant surface. It is also assumed that the isoquants are of a "single concavity," to be defined later. The production function so defined is general enough to include the case of fixed coefficients of production, "perfectly complementary" factors, limitational factors, etc.

---

[8] It is possible that within a narrow range the price may be indeterminate due in special cases to coincidental inelasticity of supply and demand.

Note that all the inputs are to be regarded as independent variables. It is never true that they must be used in fixed proportions. It is true that it may be unprofitable not to do so, but this is a result of economic calculation. Even in the continuous case, given certain economic data, the factors must (on consideration of profitability) be used finally in given proportions, and in determined amounts for each output. The only difference between these cases is that in the discontinuous case the required optimum point may be more obvious and less sensitive to changes in the prices of all factors of production. Be it understood that I do not minimize discontinuity. On the contrary, I should like to indicate the outline of a method which will handle both cases.

Along an isoquant it is assumed that we have convexity as defined below. Consider any point on an isoquant, $(v_1^1, \cdots, v_n^1)$. There must exist constants, $(\alpha_1^1, \cdots, \alpha_n^1)$, (not necessarily unique) such that

$$\sum_1^n \alpha_i^1(v_i^2 - v_i^1) \geqq 0, \tag{67}$$

where $(v_1^2, \cdots, v_n^2)$ is any other point along the same isoquant. This merely says that there exist one or more tangent planes at each point which touch but never cross the isoquant. Similarly, at the second point there exist constants, $(\alpha_1^2, \cdots, \alpha_n^2)$, such that

$$\sum_1^n \alpha_i^2(v_i^1 - v_i^2) \geqq 0, \tag{68}$$

or

$$- \sum_1^n \alpha_i^2(v_i^2 - v_i^1) \geqq 0. \tag{69}$$

Adding (69) and (67) and changing sign, we get

$$\sum_1^n (\alpha_i^2 - \alpha_i^1)(v_i^2 - v_i^1) \leqq 0. \tag{70}$$

Since these are two arbitrary points, taking one as fixed, say $(v_1^0, \cdots, v_n^0)$, we must have along an isoquant

$$\sum_1^n \alpha_i^0 \Delta v_i \geqq 0 \tag{71}$$

for

$$\varphi(v_1^0, \cdots, v_n^0) = \varphi(v_1^0 + \Delta v_1, \cdots, v_n^0 + \Delta v_n),$$

and

$$\sum_1^n \Delta\alpha_i\Delta v_i \leqq 0. \tag{72}$$

Actually, it can be verified that the necessary and sufficient conditions imposed on $(\alpha_1^0, \cdots, \alpha_n^0)$ in order that (71) holds are the following inequalities:

$$\frac{\varphi_i^S}{\varphi_1^L} \leqq \frac{\alpha_i^0}{\alpha_1^0} \leqq \frac{\varphi_i^L}{\varphi_1^S}, \tag{73}$$

where φ_i^L and φ_i^S are respectively the largest and smallest of the left- or right-hand derivatives at the given point. At any point where there is no discontinuity, the right-hand and the left-hand derivatives are identical; hence, the inequality converges to the equality,

$$\frac{\alpha_i^0}{\alpha_1^0} = \frac{\varphi_i(v_1^0, \cdots, v_n^0)}{\varphi_1(v_1^0, \cdots, v_n^0)}. \tag{74}$$

All of the above are merely elaborations of the definition of concavity. It remains to show its relevance to the problem at hand.

CONDITIONS OF EQUILIBRIUM

Suppose we are given a set of prices $(w_1^0, \cdots, w_n^0)$ corresponding to which there is one combination of factors $(v_1^0, \cdots, v_n^0)$ which minimizes total cost for given output. As a definition of our minimum

$$\Delta C \geqq 0 \tag{75}$$

for

$$\Delta x = 0, \qquad \Delta v_i \gtreqless 0.$$

In other words, for any point $(v_1, \cdots, v_n)$ along the same isoquant we must have

$$\sum_1^n w_i^0 v_i \geqq \sum_1^n w_i^0 v_i^0 \tag{76}$$

for

$$\varphi(v_1, \cdots, v_n) = \varphi(v_1^0, \cdots, v_n^0),$$

or

$$\sum_1^n w_i^0 \Delta v_i \geqq 0 \tag{77}$$

for

$$\varphi(v_1{}^0 + \Delta v_1, \cdots, v_n{}^0 + \Delta v_n) = \varphi(v_1{}^0, \cdots, v_n{}^0).$$

Obviously from (73) this implies

$$\frac{\varphi_i{}^S}{\varphi_1{}^L} \leqq \frac{w_i{}^0}{w_1{}^0} \leqq \frac{\varphi_i{}^L}{\varphi_1{}^S}. \tag{78}$$

In the case that the maximum point is one at which continuous derivatives exist, we have the conditions of the previous section,

$$\frac{\varphi_i}{\varphi_1} = \frac{w_i{}^0}{w_1{}^0}. \tag{79}$$

Thus, condition (78) is the general condition which includes (79) as a special case.

Furthermore, it is still possible to place definite restrictions on the demand functions for the factors of production, output being constant. As before,

$$v_i{}^0 = f^i(x, w_1{}^0, \cdots, w_n{}^0), \tag{80}$$

or

$$\Delta v_i = f^i(x, w_1{}^0 + \Delta w_1, \cdots, w_n{}^0 + \Delta w_n) - v_i{}^0. \tag{81}$$

From (72) we have

$$\sum_1^n \Delta w_i \Delta v_i \leqq 0 \tag{82}$$

for

$$\Delta x = 0.$$

Suppose that only the price of the kth factor varies. Then (82) becomes

$$\Delta w_k \Delta v_k \leqq 0. \tag{83}$$

That is, an increase in the price of a factor cannot result in an increase in its use. Likewise, a decrease in its price cannot result in a decrease in its use. Still more generally, it can be stated that a change in the price of any number of factors cannot result in a change in amounts of all the factors in the same direction: i.e.,

$$\sum_1^r \Delta w_j \Delta v_j \leqq 0, \qquad (r \leqq n) \tag{84}$$

for all $\Delta w_j \geqq 0$, not all $\Delta v_j > 0$; likewise, all $\Delta w_j \leqq 0$ implies not all $\Delta v_j < 0$.

Determinateness of Equilibrium

Clearly our minimum cost is unambiguously determined even in the case of discontinuity. The task of the firm is easier because the penalty for not being at the minimum point is greater and more obvious. To be at the top of a smooth hill requires fine balancing and judgment. To find a maximum which is a cusp or spire is much easier. Moreover, such an equilibrium is extremely stable. It is sometimes called "too stable" equilibrium. In order to move it a very large change in prices may be necessary. In the limiting case where the increase of each factor in more than the optimum proportion results in no increase in product, the wage may fluctuate from zero to infinity without changing the proportions of factors employed for each output. And yet the problem is completely determined.

It is curious to see the logical confusion into which many economists have fallen. The primary end of economic analysis is to explain a position of minimum (or maximum) where it does not pay to make a *finite* movement in any direction. Now in the case that all functions are continuous, it is possible as a means towards this end to state certain *equalities* on differential coefficients which will (together with appropriate secondary conditions) insure that certain *inequalities* will hold for finite movements. It is no exaggeration to say that infinitesimal analysis was developed with just such finite applications in view. Unfortunately, the means have become confused with the ends, and so conventions and artifices are continually sought in order to be able to make statements concerning marginal equivalences. A case in point is the Marshallian marginal net productivity. It is only in the singular case that the production function is differentiable (i.e., possesses certain properties of continuity) in a certain direction (i.e., for certain composite movements) that it is possible to employ this device; whereas the inequalities of condition (78) always give necessary and sufficient conditions, and include the marginal net productivity relations whenever these happen to be applicable.[9]

[9] An example of another improper use of marginal net productivity curves is provided by the treatment in Mrs. Robinson's *The Economics of Imperfect Competition* (London: Macmillan, 1933), chap. xx. The reasoning is mathematically circular; the so-called demand curves *shift* with changes in the wage of one factor! This follows from the fact that they are drawn up *as of appropriate amounts of the other factors*. These appropriate amounts are necessarily a function of the prices of all factors of production.

Although equilibrium is determinate for the single firm confronted with prices of the factors of production, discontinuities of the production function may introduce some difficulties into the general equilibrium problem whereby all firms and individuals together through the interplay of their demands and supplies determine the prices with which each is confronted. For discontinuities may introduce perfect inelasticities of demand in certain domains; there emerges the possibility, however remote, of coincidental inelasticities leading to indeterminacy of price within certain limited ranges. But this is outside the scope of the present discussion.

MAXIMIZATION OF PROFIT

By now we have attained to the point where most discussions begin. We have seen how to derive the locus of factor combinations which give lowest total costs for each output. But as yet the scale of operations, level of output, actually to be undertaken has not yet been determined. This can only be done in the face of a new set of considerations, those relating to the terms at which different amounts of the commodity can be sold. I take as a datum the maximum amount of gross total revenue which can be secured for each level of output. This may be written

$$R = R(x). \tag{85}$$

Let us define profit, net revenue, as the difference between gross revenue and total expenditure,

$$\pi = \pi(x, w_1, \cdots, w_n) = R(x) - A - V(x, w_1, \cdots, w_n). \tag{86}$$

Output will be optimum when profit is at a maximum. Necessary conditions that this be so when all functions are differentiable are

$$\frac{\partial \pi}{\partial x} = \frac{\partial R}{\partial x} - \frac{\partial V}{\partial x} = 0, \tag{87}$$

$$\frac{\partial^2 \pi}{\partial x^2} = \frac{\partial^2 R}{\partial x^2} - \frac{\partial^2 V}{\partial x^2} \leqq 0. \tag{88}$$

Assuming that we have a regular relative maximum, this becomes

$$\frac{\partial R}{\partial x} = \frac{\partial V}{\partial x}, \tag{89}$$

$$\frac{\partial^2 R}{\partial x^2} < \frac{\partial^2 V}{\partial x^2}. \tag{90}$$

This is the familiar theorem that at the optimal output the marginal revenue curve must intersect the marginal cost curve from above.[10]

Regardless of whether or not the profit function has derivatives at each point our proper maximum conditions are

$$\Delta\pi < 0, \qquad \text{for} \qquad \Delta x \gtrless 0. \qquad (91)$$

or

$$\frac{\Delta R}{\Delta x} < \frac{\Delta C}{\Delta x}, \qquad \text{for} \qquad \Delta x > 0, \qquad (92)$$

$$\frac{\Delta R}{\Delta x} > \frac{\Delta C}{\Delta x}, \qquad \text{for} \qquad \Delta x < 0. \qquad (93)$$

The economic common sense of this is obvious.[11]

Equation (89) gives us a relation to determine optimum output x^0. By substituting the value of x^0, so obtained, in (5) we get a new set of demand curves for factors of production, drawn up as of a given total revenue curve.

$$v_i = f^i(x^0, w_1, \cdots, w_n) = g^i(w_1, \cdots, w_n). \qquad (i = 1, \cdots, n) \quad (94)$$

It is possible to derive the positions of output, input, etc., in a more direct fashion by treating all the inputs as independent variables.

Let

$$\pi(v_1, \cdots, v_n, w_1, \cdots, w_n) = R[\varphi(v_1, \cdots, v_n)] - A - \sum_1^n w_i v_i. \quad (95)$$

At a proper maximum

$$\frac{\partial R}{\partial x} \varphi_i - w_i = 0, \qquad (i = 1, \cdots, n) \qquad (96)$$

and

$$T = [R_x \varphi_{ij} + R_{xx} \varphi_i \varphi_j]$$

must form the coefficients of a negative definite quadratic form.

---

[10] The famous cost controversy may be interpreted as an argument over the implications of these conditions.

[11] In the case of pure competition, when price is independent of sales, these conditions become

$$p < \frac{\Delta C}{\Delta x} \qquad \text{and} \qquad p > \frac{\Delta C}{\Delta x}, \qquad \text{respectively.}$$

It can also be shown that $\Delta p \Delta x \gtreqless 0$; i.e., that an increase in prices cannot, *ceteris paribus*, result in a decrease in quantity supplied. Hence, the firm's supply curve cannot be negatively inclined.

The results in (96) follow from (43) and (89), since for any output factor price must equal marginal cost times marginal physical productivity, while for optimum output marginal cost equals marginal revenue. These are n equations from which we can solve for the n factors of production in terms of the n prices to get the demand functions of (94).

$$v_i = g^i(w_1, \cdots, w_n). \qquad (i = 1, \cdots, n)$$

Actually, it is known that [12]

$$\frac{\partial v_i}{\partial w_j} = g_j{}^i = \frac{T_{ij}}{T}, \qquad (97)$$

where T_{ij} is the cofactor of the element of the ith row and the jth column of the above matrix. From the definiteness of the above quadratic form it follows that these last must form the coefficients of a negative definite form; i.e.,

$$\frac{\partial v_j}{\partial w_j} < 0; \qquad \frac{\partial(g^j, g^k)}{\partial(w_j, w_k)} > 0; \quad \text{etc.} \qquad (98)$$

INDETERMINACY IN PUREST COMPETITION?

If competition is "pure" in the commodity and factor markets, and the production function is homogeneous of the first order, then it is a classical fact that the matrix T, which except for factors of proportionality is by the first assumption identical with the Hessian of the production function, is singular. Therefore, a regular maximum for the firm is impossible. Unit costs being constant, and demand being horizontal, there are only three possibilities: price being everywhere greater than marginal cost, it will pay the firm to expand indefinitely, i.e., until competition ceases to be pure; or if price is less than marginal cost, no output will be produced; or, finally, if price is identically equal to marginal cost, the exact output of the firm will be a matter of indifference. Thus, what was usually regarded as the most favorable case for pure competition turns out to yield indeterminate output for each firm.

However, too much should not be made of this paradox. Even though the output of every firm may be indeterminate, their sum

[12] Compare H. Hotelling, "Edgeworth's Taxation Paradox and the Nature of Demand and Supply Functions," *Journal of Political Economy*, XL, 577–616.

may be determinate, in the same way that the sum of two discontinuous functions may be continuous.   For if many firms expand output, others will contract; for price will fall along the industry's demand curve causing contraction.   It has been argued, however, that competition will disappear since any one firm, with no obstacles to its expansion, will grow until it is a "significant part of the market," at which time it will be able to affect the price of its product.

This is similar to the familiar argument by which it is shown that decreasing marginal cost within a firm will lead to monopoly. Nevertheless, the analogy is faulty.   For the demand curve of any firm is equal to the demand curve of the industry minus the supply curve of the remaining firms, already in the industry or potentially therein.   This being the case, it is easy to show that under uniform constant costs the demand curve for a firm is horizontal even though it produces 99.9 per cent of all that is sold,   Geometrically, the long-run supply curve of potential rivals is horizontal, and a horizontal curve subtracted laterally from any curve must always yield a horizontal curve.   Economically if the firm were to begin to restrict output so as to gain monopoly profit, it would cease to sell 99.9 per cent of the output or even anything at all.   Consequently, it would not attempt to do so, but would find its maximum advantage in behaving like a pure competitor.

Thus, it remains true that the classical assumptions underlying pure competition are actually consistent.   It is no accident that Walras and Marshall paid so little attention to the firm and so much to the industry.   For under the purest conditions of competition the boundaries of the former become vague and ill-defined, and also unimportant, since through reactions to prices the factors of production adjust themselves in the right proportions and in the right total amounts for the industry.

Perhaps to a greater extent than in the case of increasing cost will the industry be subject to oscillation around its equilibrium. However, once displaced, output will tend to return to the correct value, so that the equilibrium may be said to be stable even though it would appear that a limitingly small individual would have no incentive to keep his output unchanged.   However, the same is true of the situation where the price of the same good in two markets just balances the transportation costs necessary to transfer a unit of the good from one market to the other. Any one arbitrager has no special inducement to ship more or less than he is actually doing, nor even to ship just the amount that he is doing. Yet the equilibrium is stable; for if the right amount were not to flow, the spatial price differential would change so as to return the system to its previous position. To an infinitely near-sighted olive the bottom of the cocktail glass appears level, and it no doubt regards itself as being in neutral equilibrium. Actually, the equilibrium is stable as any finite movement will show.

Discontinuous Case

In the general case where the production function is not necessarily differentiable we have still for a maximum

$$\Delta \pi \leqq 0, \qquad \text{for} \qquad \Delta v_i \gtreqless 0. \qquad (99)$$

As a special case of this, for a movement of one factor, all others constant, we must have

$$\frac{\Delta R}{\Delta x} \frac{\Delta x}{\Delta v_i} < w_i, \qquad \text{for} \qquad \Delta v_i > 0, \ \Delta v_j = 0, \qquad (100)$$

$$\frac{\Delta R}{\Delta x} \frac{\Delta x}{\Delta v_i} > w_i, \qquad \text{for} \qquad \Delta v_i < 0, \ \Delta v_j = 0. \qquad (101)$$

That is, it must pay to move neither backward nor forward.

Moreover, consider a given set of factor prices $(w_1^0, \cdots, w_n^0)$. Corresponding to this there is a set of factors $(v_1^0, \cdots, v_n^0)$ which give a maximum profit. In order that this be a real maximum

$$R[\varphi(v_1^1, \cdots, v_n^1)] - A - \sum_1^n w_i^0 v_i^1 \leqq R[\varphi(v_1^0, \cdots, v_n^0)]$$

$$- A - \sum_1^n w_i^0 v_i^0. \quad (102)$$

Consider a set of prices $(w_1^1, \cdots, w_n^1)$ for which the (arbitrary) point $(v_1^1, \cdots, v_n^1)$ is the point of maximum profits. Then

$$R[\varphi(v_1^0, \cdots, v_n^0)] - A - \sum_1^n w_i^1 v_i^0 \leqq R[\varphi(v_1^1, \cdots, v_n^1)]$$

$$- A - \sum_1^n w_i^1 v_i^1. \quad (103)$$

Now adding (102) and (103) and canceling terms we get

$$\sum_1^n (w_i{}^1 - w_i{}^0)(v_i{}^1 - v_i{}^0) \leqq 0, \qquad (104)$$

or

$$\sum_1^n \Delta w_i \Delta v_i \leqq 0. \qquad (105)$$

For only the jth price varying, this becomes

$$\Delta w_j \Delta v_j \leqq 0. \qquad (106)$$

In other words, a decrease in a price cannot result in a decrease in the factor used. Further possible interpretations are of course possible.

As before, the general case is simpler than that of the special continuous case. Moreover, the method of finite increments appears to be mathematically simpler in the sense that it is possible to state the qualitative direction of changes without solving inversely for the actual demand functions.

The method employed here is that which underlies Le Chatelier's principle in physics. By making use of Professor E. B. Wilson's suggestion that this is essentially a mathematical theorem applicable to economics, it has been possible to gain increased generality without increased complexity and emptiness.

It is important to realize just how much content there is to a particular economic theory. As far as the single firm is concerned, everything fundamental which can be said is implied in the statement that in equilibrium there must exist no movement by which the firm can improve its profits; i.e., $\Delta \pi \leqq 0$ for all movements of variables possible to the firm. In the case of continuity certain necessary relations of differential coefficients (marginal equivalences) are implied. Moreover, assuming certain specific forms to our functions (independence of prices, etc.), it is possible to deduce formally the implications of an equilibrium position (e.g., negative demand curves, positive supply curves, etc.). It appears that no more than this can be validly stated.

EXTERNAL CONDITIONS OF EQUILIBRIUM

Thus far we have been discussing the conditions of equilibrium imposed from within the enterprise by its desire to maximize profits. This has resulted in certain marginal inequalities. Economists have not stopped here, but have also tried to analyze certain conditions of equilibrium resulting from inter-competition among firms. That is to say, they have tried to state conditions upon the market situation (obstacles) with which each firm will be confronted. In particular, they have been interested in the determination of the rate of profit which any firm can earn.

It has often been argued that not only must price (average revenue) under "perfect" competition equal marginal cost, but also it must be equal to average cost so that net revenue will be zero. This second condition has not always been recognized as being of an entirely different nature from the first. In this section an attempt will be made to distinguish between them. It is hoped that in so doing it will be possible to put the famous "adding up" problem and homogeneity of the production function in its proper place.

In the beginning, to avoid confusion, no use is made of the term "perfect" competition. The term "pure" competition will be understood to mean that the demand curve for any producer is infinitely elastic, that his sales cannot affect prices. The problem of discontinuity is ignored. Under these conditions the internal conditions of equilibrium are that marginal cost be equal to marginal revenue (price), and hence, that the marginal physical productivity of each factor times the sales price of the good be equal to the price of the respective factor.

$$\frac{\partial R}{\partial x} = p = \frac{\partial C}{\partial x}, \tag{107}$$

$$w_i = \frac{\partial C}{\partial x} \varphi_i = p\varphi_i. \tag{108}$$

These are marginal conditions and say nothing about the totals involved. It is also true by definition of the "long-run" as that period in which all costs can be avoided by going out of business, that the firm must never have a negative net revenue. As a condition internally imposed we know that

$$\pi \geqq 0, \tag{109}$$

or

$$R(x) \geqq \sum_1^n w_i v_i. \tag{110}$$

Some writers, by a curious play on words, have been able to arrive at the condition that average cost equals price. A typical form of the argument is as follows: (1) a firm will equate marginal cost to price; (2) it will also try to minimize its unit cost; (3) at the point of minimum unit cost average cost equals marginal cost; (4) hence, average cost must equal price (average revenue) and profits will be zero.

Stated explicitly, it is obvious that the second statement is false. The play on words arises from the confusion of the condition that for each and every output total and unit costs must be a minimum with the statement that of all outputs possible that one is chosen at which unit cost is the lowest. The first implies the valid condition that the marginal productivity of the last dollar in every use must be equal. The second implies the invalid (from internal considerations) condition that output be determined irrespective of the sales price.

On the other hand, some have tried to argue as follows: (1) the production function from the nature of things must be homogeneous of the first order; (2) by Euler's theorem it follows that if factors are paid "according to the marginal productivity principle," product will be exhausted.

As an example of the lack of integration between the theory of production and that of cost, we find many writers asking whether product will be exhausted at the same time that they have already agreed that price equals average cost, and total revenue equals total cost. Of course, the latter condition is merely another way of stating the former.

Once the problem is properly stated as that of determining the relation between gross revenue per unit and expenditure per unit, it should be reasonably clear that this cannot be determined by the properties of the production function alone, but must depend upon the marketing situation of the firm, which in turn depends upon the competition of other firms. It is quite clear that as far as the single firm is concerned it is possible that it be making huge profits regardless of the homogeneity of the production function. This condition is neither necessary nor sufficient to the exhaustion of the product. If the production function were homogeneous, but demand were sufficiently favorable, of course product would not be exhausted—even under pure competition. .

The problem of homogeneity of the production function is one about which much controversy has raged. It has long been held on philosophical grounds that product must be a homogeneous function of the first order of all the variables, and that if this is not so, it must be either because of "indivisibility" or because not all "factors" have been taken into account. With regard to the first point, it is clear that labeling the absence of homogeneity as due to indivisibility changes nothing and merely affirms by the implication that "indivisibility" does exist, the absence of homogeneity.

With respect to the second point, we may reverse the Aristotelian dictum and affirm that anything which must be true self-evidently ("philosophically"), intuitively—i.e., by conventional definition of the terms involved—that such a principle can have no empirical content. It is a scientifically meaningless assertion that doubling all factors must double product. This is so not because we do not have the power to perform such an experiment; such an objection is of course irrelevant. Rather the statement is meaningless because it could never be refuted, in the sense that no hypothetically conceivable experiment could ever controvert the principle enunciated. This is so because if product did not double, one could always conclude that some factor was "scarce." [13]

It is useful, I believe, to avoid the expression "factor of production" entirely. This has been used in at least two senses, neither of which is quite satisfactory. First, it has been used to denote broad composite quantities such as "labor, land, and capital." On the other hand, it has been used to denote any aspect of the environment which has any influence on production. I suggest that only "inputs" be explicitly included in the production function, and that this term be confined to denote measurable quantitative economic goods or services. The production function must be associated with a particular institution (accounting, decision-making unit, etc.), and must be drawn up as of any unique circumstances pertaining to this unit. Other definitions are of

---

[13] Any function whatsoever in n variables may be regarded as a subset of a larger function in more than n variables which is homogeneous of the first order. It is because this is true of *any* arbitrary function that this generalization is useless. For example, the volume of a sphere not being a homogeneous function of the radius, a new factor can be defined whose "scarcity" will explain this fact. Like a false proposition in logic from which every proposition can be derived, this overgenerality renders such a convention useless.

course possible, but it is clear that our previous conditions cannot be expressed in terms of them.

So defined, the production function need not be homogeneous of the first order. If really homogeneous, marginal costs would always be constant.[14] It is indicative of the lack of integration mentioned above that many writers assume U-shaped cost curves in the same breath with homogeneity of the production function.

In reality, it is not on philosophical grounds that economists have wished to assume homogeneity, but rather because they were afraid that, if they did not do so, contradictions would emerge to vitiate the marginal productivity theory. This is simply a misconception as will be indicated below.

Our discussion can be confined to the relation of total cost and total revenue. The implications for marginal productivities can then be indicated.

It is clear that the firm does not of its own volition act so as to equate average gross revenue to average expenditure, although it may in the long-run prevent average revenue from being less than average cost by going out of business.

It is only through the competition of new firms that the demand curve of the firm may so shift downward as to make the position of maximum profit one at which total gross revenue equals total expenditure.

Reserving for later investigation the conditions under which the demand curve will so shift, let us investigate the implications of the assumption of zero net revenue. Given

$$\frac{\partial R}{\partial x} = \frac{\partial C}{\partial x}, \tag{111}$$

and

$$\pi = R - C = 0, \tag{112}$$

it follows that the demand curve must be tangential to the total unit cost curve.

In the case of pure competition the demand curve is a horizontal line, and under the conventional assumptions as to the shape of the cost curve, the tangency will be at a unique point, that of

---

[14] It follows from Euler's generalized theorem on homogeneous functions that the Hessian of a homogeneous function of the first order is identically zero. Obviously, stable equilibrium for a firm under pure competition is impossible in these circumstances.

minimum average cost. This follows from the fact that average cost must be equal to marginal cost, and that the latter is rising.

$$\frac{\partial R}{\partial x} = p = \frac{\partial C}{\partial x} = \frac{C}{x} = \text{minimum average cost.[15]} \qquad (113)$$

Of course,

$$px = \sum_1^n w_i v_i \text{ by assumption,} \qquad (114)$$

and

$$w_i = \frac{\partial C}{\partial x} \varphi_i = p\varphi_i. \qquad (115)$$

Hence,

$$x = \sum_1^n \varphi_i v_i. \qquad (116)$$

This looks superficially like Euler's theorem, but it is not. For Euler's theorem is an identity and should be written

$$x \equiv \sum_1^n \varphi_i v_i, \qquad (117)$$

whereas this is merely a condition of equilibrium holding at a single output.

Moreover, in the case that the demand curve may be negatively inclined, we get the more general formulation

$$x = \frac{\frac{\partial R}{\partial x}}{p} \sum_1^n \varphi_i v_i. \qquad (118)$$

This formulation differs from that of Walras, Wicksell, and Hicks in that the condition of minimum unit cost is derived as a theorem from the condition that total revenue equal total expendi-

---

[15] At a minimum of average cost

$$\frac{\partial \left(\frac{C}{x}\right)}{\partial x} = 0 = \frac{x \frac{\partial C}{\partial x} - C}{x^2} \quad \text{and} \quad \frac{\partial^2 \left(\frac{C}{x}\right)}{\partial x^2} = \frac{\frac{\partial^2 C}{\partial x^2}}{x} - 2 \frac{x \frac{\partial C}{\partial x} - C}{x^3} > 0;$$

i.e.,

$$\frac{\partial C}{\partial x} = \frac{C}{x} \quad \text{and} \quad \frac{\partial^2 C}{\partial x^2} > 0.$$

ture. It is this last condition and the forces which lead to it that are of importance, and not the question of homogeneity at all.

It is quite clear that in the real world net revenue is not zero for all firms, nor is it tending towards zero. This is true under pure competition as well as impure competition. It is clear that this residuum must be "due" to something, and it may be labeled by any name we please (rent to institutional advantage, etc.).

The existence of this residuum does not imply any indeterminacy whatsoever. Optimal output, revenue, expenditure, and the difference between these two terms are all fully determined. Of course, under ideal conditions this residuum will be capitalized by going concern valuations. Economists, remembering the classical solution of the problem of distribution in which the shares of two or more factors were simultaneously residually determined, have swung too far in the opposite direction. The attempt to "explain" all residua in terms of marginal productivity analysis applied to a wider production function can always be done by convention, but is devoid of empirical content.

It is convenient to have an analytic definition for the case in which "competitive" conditions between firms are such that the demand curve of any firm will always shift until net revenue is equal to zero. The term "free entry" may be defined as the condition under which this holds. Of course, this classification cuts across that of pure or impure competition. Thus defined, free entry is a condition to be looked for empirically, rather than one imposed upon the data a priori.

I suspect that part of the economists' intuitive desire to define a category of "profits" as distinct from "rent to institutional advantage" stems from a subconscious remembrance of the old-fashioned distinction between "natural" and "contrived" scarcity. Perhaps too little is heard today of this distinction, which has important connotations for social policy and welfare economics.

SUMMARY

In conclusion, a summary formulation of the analysis is presented to replace the famous three Theorems of Walras. These, aside from being redundant and ambiguous, are not each of the same order of meaning. The formulation here is for the continuous case and in terms of marginal equivalences, but the more general formulation in terms of marginal inequalities readily suggests itself. Throughout a firm with given production function, factor prices, and demand conditions is posited. The general case of pure or impure competition is considered.

I. The first fundamental assumption is that the firm tries to maximize its profits, and from this the following internal conditions of equilibrium can be deduced.

A. Any output which is produced must be produced with factor combinations such that total cost is a minimum. As a result of this we have two corollaries.

1. The marginal productivity of the last dollar must be equal in every use.

2. The price of each factor of production must be proportional to marginal physical productivity, the factor of proportionality being marginal cost.

B. That output will be selected which maximizes net revenue, total cost being optimally determined by the previous conditions. This implies

1. The equality of marginal cost and marginal revenue, the slope of the latter being the smaller.

2. In combination with the previous conditions under A we also have the marginal value productivity of each factor equal to its price, the first term being defined as marginal revenue times marginal physical productivity.

3. Total cost must not exceed total revenue, since otherwise the firm would go out of business.[16]

II. If we impose by arbitrary assumption or hypothesis the external conditions that entry be free, i.e., that total revenue be equal to total cost, then

A. Product will be exhausted by definition.

B. The demand curve must be tangent to the unit cost curve. In the case of pure competition this implies minimum average cost.

---

[16] If the enterprise under consideration owns productive resources which have a sale value on the market, it is necessary that net revenue be at least as large as the sale (liquidation) value of these resources. As an internal condition of equilibrium $\pi \geqq$ sale value of owned resources. Alternative uses elsewhere introduce "opportunity costs."

Aside from the above general conditions of equilibrium, it has been shown how the definition of an extremum position may be utilized (a) to evaluate the direction of change of variables with respect to parameters (prices) taken as data, regardless of conditions of continuity, and (b) to develop reciprocal relations imposed upon demand derivatives, where these exist.

CHAPTER V

THE PURE THEORY OF CONSUMER'S BEHAVIOR

IF ONE were looking for a single criterion by which to distinguish modern economic theory from its classical precursors, he would probably decide that this is to be found in the introduction of the so-called subjective theory of value into economic theory. This revolution in thought broke out almost simultaneously along three fronts, and with it we associate the names of Jevons, Menger, and Walras.

Moreover, it is this part of economic doctrine which has proved to be the center of so much controversy. Indeed, many critics of the orthodox tradition have identified the whole body of economic theory with the belief in that abstraction, *homo economicus*. In fact, many economists, well within the academic fold, would separate economics from sociology upon the basis of rational or irrational behavior, where these terms are defined in the penumbra of utility theory. It would seem extremely important, therefore, to know clearly what is contained in the conventional utility analysis, if only to understand the consequences of denying its validity.

EVOLUTION OF UTILITY CONCEPT

The concept of utility may be said to have been undergoing throughout its entire history a purging out of objectionable, and sometimes unnecessary, connotations. The result has been a much less objectionable doctrine, but also a less interesting one. Without doing justice to the subject, these developments may be summarized in a brief way. It must be clearly understood, however, that these are the movements of the pioneers of thought. Their work appears chiefly in academic journals, and has little influenced the general class of economists.

(a) One clearly delineated drift in the literature has been a steady tendency towards the rejection of utilitarian, ethical, and welfare connotations of the Bentham, Sidgwick, Edgeworth variety. These matters still receive consideration in questions of normative policy, but they are clearly separated from the problem of consumer's behavior. Although especially marked in regard to inter-individual welfare comparisons, there is the same tendency in connection with the analysis of the behavior of a single individual. Only as *obiter dicta* do we find in the modern literature discussions of particular pleasures as being pure or impure, etc.[1]

(b) Concomitantly, there has been a shift in emphasis away from the physiological and psychological hedonistic, introspective aspects of utility. Originally great importance was attached to the ability of goods to fill basic biological needs; but in almost every case this view has undergone extreme modification. At the same time, there has been a similar movement away from the concept of utility as a sensation, as an introspective magnitude. It is not merely that the modern economist replaces experienced sensation or satisfaction with anticipated sensation, desire, according to the now familiar distinction between *ex post* and *ex ante* analysis. But much more than this, many writers have ceased to believe in the existence of any introspective magnitude or quantity of a cardinal, numerical kind. With this skepticism has come the recognition that a cardinal measure of utility is in any case unnecessary; that only an *ordinal* preference, involving "more" or "less" but not "how much," is required for the analysis of consumer's behavior.

Indeed, so far has the reaction gone that it is the belief of many that nothing remains but an empty convention. Others, who do not admit the hollowness of utility, have in some cases embraced a formulation of the analysis which is meaningless in any operational, empirical sense.[2] The result is a curious jargon of dogmatic precepts.

Thus, the consumer's market behavior is explained in terms of preferences, which are in turn defined only by behavior. The result can very easily be circular, and in many formulations undoubtedly is. Often nothing more is stated than the conclusion that people behave as they behave, a theorem which has no em-

---

[1] The Cambridge tradition is perhaps an exception in this respect, although even here the change in emphasis is notable.

[2] Cf. Alan R. Sweezy, "The Interpretation of Subjective Value Theory in the Writings of the Austrian Economists," *Review of Economic Studies*, vol. I, no. 3 (1934), pp. 176–185.

pirical implications, since it contains no hypothesis and is consistent with all conceivable behavior, while refutable by none.[3]

Nevertheless, as we shall see, the modern utility theory with all its qualifications is not in a technical sense *meaningless*. It *is* a hypothesis which places definite restrictions upon demand functions and price-quantity data; these could be refuted or verified under ideal observational conditions. One should have thought that these empirical implications would have been the sole end of the theorists who have concerned themselves with these matters. Strangely enough, means and ends have been so confused that only a small fraction of the literature has been concerned with this problem even indirectly; moreover, in this there are scarcely half a dozen papers in which valid demand restrictions have been developed.

I do not propose to defend the fruitfulness of these empirical restrictions. The extent to which they satisfy and unify the factual behavior of consumers cannot be settled by argumentation. However, for better or worse the theory of utility has occupied an important position in economic thought for the last half century. This alone makes it desirable that its meaning be clearly understood.

PROGRESSION IN MATHEMATICAL THOUGHT

From the beginning mathematical methods have figured prominently in the analysis of utility. Despite the unfavorable reaction produced among some writers who felt that a spurious precision was implied by the use of these supposedly "exact" tools, it is demonstrable from the literature that symbolic methods have been an aid to clear thinking and the advancement of the analysis.[4] For those who used this abstract language were forced to formulate their concepts unambiguously, and so the way was opened for modification and qualification.

It is interesting, therefore, to review very briefly the history of some mathematical aspects of the theory to bring out clearly the progression in thought through time.

[3] Still another "meaningless" theory is held by those writers who speak of behavior in terms of the *economic principle*, regardless of whether any empirical behavior related to it exists.

[4] Thus, Edgeworth's *Mathematical Psychics* offers penetrating insight into the views commonly held in his day.

As early as 1854, Gossen is credited with presenting what is essentially marginal utility. He assumed this to be a decreasing linear function of the quantity of any particular good. The utility function would therefore be as follows:

$$U = K + (a_1 x_1 - b_1 x_1^2) + (a_2 x_2 - b_2 x_2^2) + \cdots. \qquad (1)$$

Jevons, writing fifteen years later, proposed that the utility function be written as the sum of utilities pertaining to each good separately.

$$U = V_1(x_1) + V_2(x_2) + \cdots + V_n(x_n), \qquad (2)$$

where the functions V_i obey the law of diminishing marginal utility.[5] Specifically,

$$V_i'(x_i) > 0, \qquad (3)$$
$$V_i''(x_i) < 0.$$

In his *Mathematical Psychics* (1881), Edgeworth, going further than Jevons, suggested that the requirement that utility be a sum of functions pertaining to each good was an unnecessary and indeed unjustifiable assumption. He proposed, therefore, that the utility function be written in the form [6]

$$U = \varphi(x_1, \cdots, x_n), \qquad (4)$$

where φ is any joint function of the quantities of all goods, and where

$$\varphi_{ij} = \frac{\partial^2 \varphi}{\partial x_i \partial x_j} \gtreqless 0. \qquad (i \neq j) \qquad (5)$$

By the end of the nineteenth century many writers, notably Pareto, had come to the realization that it was an unnecessary and unwarranted assumption that there even exist utility as a *cardinal* magnitude. Since only more or less comparisons are needed for consumer's behavior and not comparisons of how much more or less, it is only necessary that there exist an *ordinal* preference field.

---

[5] Walras and Marshall also made the assumption that utility may be written as in (2). In the case of Marshall, as will be discussed later, it is not clear whether he really intended to be taken literally when making the assumption that utilities are independent, or whether he regarded this as an approximation for small movements under certain conditions.

[6] Professor Irving Fisher is also credited with the independent discovery of this possibility at a later date.

For any two combinations of goods, respectively $(x_1^0, \cdots, x_n^0)$ and $(x_1^1, \cdots, x_n^1)$, or for brevity, (X^0) and (X^1), it is only necessary that the consumer be able to place them in one of the following mutually exclusive categories.

    a. (X^0) preferred to (X^1)
    b. (X^1) preferred to (X^0) (6)
    c. (X^0) and (X^1) equally preferred or indifferent.

For convenience, we may attach a number to each combination; this is assumed to be a continuous differentiable function. This function (or rule of numbering) may be written

$$\varphi = \varphi(X) = \varphi(x_1, \cdots, x_n). \tag{7}$$

It is so constructed that the following three conditions correspond to the above three respectively:

    a'. $\varphi(X^1) < \varphi(X^0)$
    b'. $\varphi(X^0) < \varphi(X^1)$ (8)
    c'. $\varphi(X^0) = \varphi(X^1)$.

φ may be designated as a utility index. The one parameter family of loci defined by

$$\varphi(x_1, \cdots, x_n) = C,$$

where C is regarded as a parameter, are designated as indifference loci.

It is clear that any function

$$U = F(\varphi), \qquad F'(\varphi) > 0 \tag{9}$$

defined by any monotonic transformation of φ, is also a utility index. For

$$\varphi(X^1) \gtreqless \varphi(X^0) \text{ implies } U(X^1) \gtreqless U(X^0), \text{ respectively.}$$

The converse also holds. Thus, from any one utility index all others can be derived by a suitable functional transformation.

To summarize, our ordinal preference field may be written

$$U = F[\varphi(x_1, \cdots, x_n)], \qquad F'(\varphi) > 0, \tag{10}$$

where φ is any one cardinal index of utility.

It is clear that the choice of any one numbering system or utility index is arbitrary. The indifference loci are left unchanged by any alteration of the tags attached to each, provided ordinal relationships are maintained. In order, therefore, to avoid the asymmetry of employing any one favored utility index, many writers (Pareto, W. E. Johnson, Hicks and Allen, *et al.*) have suggested that a notation be employed which is dependent only upon the invariant elements of the ordinal preference field, namely, the indifference loci.

The direction cosines of the tangent plane to an indifference locus at any point must be in determined ratios. Given any one utility index, we have

$$1 : \left(\frac{\partial x_1}{\partial x_2}\right)_{U=c} : \left(\frac{\partial x_1}{\partial x_3}\right)_{U=c} : \cdots : \left(\frac{\partial x_1}{\partial x_n}\right)_{U=c}, \tag{11}$$

as

$$F' \varphi_1 : F' \varphi_2 : \cdots : F' \varphi_n.$$

We may take as given the invariant slope functions

$$-\left(\frac{\partial x_1}{\partial x_i}\right)_{U=c} = {}^1R^i(x_1, \cdots, x_n). \qquad (i = 2, \cdots, n) \tag{12}$$

These are invariant under any change of utility index, for

$$^1R^i = \frac{U_i(x_1, \cdots, x_n)}{U_1(x_1, \cdots, x_n)} = \frac{F' \varphi_i(x_1, \cdots, x_n)}{F' \varphi_1(x_1, \cdots, x_n)}$$

$$= \frac{\varphi_i(x_1, \cdots, x_n)}{\varphi_1(x_1, \cdots, x_n)}. \qquad (i = 2, \cdots, n) \tag{13}$$

However, if we consider more than two commodities, the functions $^1R^i$ cannot be all arbitrarily chosen. In order that there exist an ordinal preference field of the type described above they must, as Professor Fisher has pointed out, satisfy the following integrability conditions:

$$^1R_j{}^i - {}^1R^j \, {}^1R_1{}^i \equiv {}^1R_i{}^j - {}^1R^i \, {}^1R_1{}^j, \tag{14}$$

so that the following so-called Pfaffian

$$dx_1 + {}^1R^2 dx_2 + \cdots + {}^1R^n dx_n \tag{15}$$

admits of an integrating factor $\gamma(x_1, \cdots, x_n)$, and may be converted into the exact differential

$$d\varphi = \gamma dx_1 + (\gamma \, {}^1R^2) dx_2 + \cdots + (\gamma \, {}^1R^n) dx_n$$
$$= \varphi_1 dx_1 + \varphi_2 dx_2 + \cdots + \varphi_n dx_n, \tag{16}$$

where

$$\varphi_1 = \gamma,$$

and

$$\varphi_i = (\gamma^1 R^i).[7] \tag{17}$$

From this stage it was but one small step to the rejection of the integrability conditions. Thus, Pareto, Hicks and Allen, and others have been content to start out with the assumption of a planar element embodying indifference directions at each point. The latter two writers call these the respective marginal rates of substitution between the ith and first goods. These are written as in (12), but the functions are not required to satisfy the partial differential equations of integrability presented in (14).

$$^1R^i = {}^1R^i(x_1, \cdots, x_n). \qquad (i = 2, \cdots, n) \tag{18}$$

The Demand Functions as a Goal

We have seen an account of the transformations which the preference field has undergone through time. However, nothing has been said as yet as to the use to which these concepts are put in the explanation of consumer's behavior. This we must now do in order to investigate the meaning—in the technical operational sense—of the various hypotheses.

Following traditional assumptions of the pure theory of consumer's behavior, we consider a single idealized consumer buying goods and services per unit time in a market whose prices he cannot appreciably affect. The selling of personal goods and services may be at times regarded as negative purchases. For present purposes each good and service is taken as clearly defined, homogeneous, divisible, etc. Let us designate all goods and services $(x_1, \cdots, x_n)$ with respective given prices $(p_1, \cdots, p_n)$. Total expenditure or income is defined as

$$I = x_1 p_1 + x_2 p_2 + \cdots + x_n p_n = \sum_1^n p_i x_i. \tag{19}$$

As of any given total expenditure and a given set of prices, it is assumed that our idealized individual will select some determined amounts of each and every good. (Of course, the amount of some goods may be zero.) That is to say, the quantity of each good is

[7] Of course, $F'(\varphi)\varphi_1$ is also an integrating factor.

a function of all prices and income.

$$x_1 = h^1(p_1, \cdots, p_n, I)$$
$$x_2 = h^2(p_1, \cdots, p_n, I)$$
$$\vdots \qquad \vdots \qquad\qquad (20)$$
$$x_n = h^n(p_1, \cdots, p_n, I).$$

These are the general demand functions. Their derivation is the whole end and purpose of our analysis of consumer's behavior. As has been reiterated again and again, the utility analysis is meaningful only to the extent that it places hypothetical restrictions upon these demand functions. This is the point of view from which we shall proceed.

The Marshallian partial equilibrium demand functions for the first good would be, of course,

$$x_1 = h^1(p_1, \bar{p}_2, \cdots, \bar{p}_n, \bar{I}) = D^1(p_1), \qquad (21)$$

where all other prices and income are held constant by *ceteris paribus* assumptions. A meaningful restriction upon our price-quantity data would be the hypothesis that an increase in one good's price will, *ceteris paribus*, result in a decrease in its quantity; i.e.,

$$\frac{\partial x_i}{\partial p_i} = h_i{}^i < 0. \qquad (22)$$

Is this derivable from the utility analysis? Can anything be said about $\partial x_i/\partial p_j$, the change in the quantity of one good when some other price varies? What about $\partial x_i/\partial I$, the rate of change in the quantity of the ith good with respect to a change in income? These are the questions whose answers we must seek.

CONDITIONS OF EQUILIBRIUM

It is not necessary that the demand curves be derived for each of the preference fields defined by (1), (2), (4), and (10), respectively. Fortunately, the last includes all previous formulations as special cases. I start out from the general case of an ordinal preference field, later considering the meanings of the special cases.

The utility analysis rests on the fundamental assumption that the individual confronted with given prices and confined to a given total expenditure selects that combination of goods which is highest on his preference scale. This does not require (a) that the individual behave rationally in any other sense; (b) that he be deliberate and self-conscious in his purchasing; (c) that there exist any *intensive* magnitude which he feels or consults.

Our problem, therefore, is the comparatively simple one of finding a maximum for

$$U = F[\varphi(x_1, \cdots, x_n)], \tag{10}$$

subject to

$$\sum_1^n p_i x_i = I, \tag{19}$$

where $(p_1, \cdots, p_n, I)$ are each preassigned parameters.

This is a constrained maximum problem, since equation (19), familiarly termed the budget equation, must be satisfied. This restricts the choice of quantities. Without such a restriction the individual could presumably purchase an unlimited amount of goods up to the point of satiation. But in point of fact, goods are not all free; with a fixed income the more of one good which is bought, the less must be consumed of another.

In the Appendix it is shown that we must have as a necessary condition for such a constrained relative maximum:

$$U_i + \lambda p_i = 0, \qquad (i = 1, \cdots, n) \tag{23}$$

where λ is a so-called Lagrangean undetermined multiplier. This may also be rewritten in either of the two following equivalent forms:

$$\frac{U_i}{U_1} = \frac{p_i}{p_1}, \qquad (i = 2, \cdots, n) \tag{24}$$

or

$$\frac{U_1}{p_1} = \frac{U_2}{p_2} = \cdots = \frac{U_n}{p_n} = -\lambda. \tag{25}$$

This means that in equilibrium the ratio of the marginal utilities of two goods is equal to the ratio of their prices, i.e., marginal utilities are proportional to prices.

It is clear from the formulation of (24) that it does not matter which utility index we use, for

$$U_i = F'\varphi_i. \qquad (i = 1, \cdots, n) \tag{26}$$

Therefore,

$$\frac{U_i}{U_1} \equiv \frac{F'\varphi_i}{F'\varphi_1} = \frac{\varphi_i}{\varphi_1}. \tag{27}$$

Our conditions of equilibrium yield the same solution, therefore, regardless of our choice of a particular utility index. It is as meaningless to argue that one particular utility index is really the true measure of utility as it is to argue that the earth really revolves about the sun and not vice versa. Only in terms of observations other than those envisaged in our market place can a cardinal utility magnitude be defined.

The formulation of (25) gives rise to the familiar interpretation that in a maximum position the marginal utilities of the last dollars spent for each and all commodities must be identical. This magnitude $(= -\lambda)$ has been termed the marginal utility of money, or better still, the marginal utility of income. It will be noted that it is *not* invariant under a change of the utility index, and so for an ordinal field no significance attaches to its magnitude, nor to the rates of changes of its magnitude with respect to any variables.

Employing the notation of indifference loci, the same conditions may be derived. For from (13)

$$^1R^i = \frac{U_i(x_1, \cdots, x_n)}{U_1(x_1, \cdots, x_n)}. \qquad (i = 2, \cdots, n)$$

Therefore, the conditions of equilibrium of (24) may be written

$$^1R^i(x_1, \cdots, x_n) - \frac{p_i}{p_1} = 0. \qquad (i = 2, \cdots, n) \tag{28}$$

This is the familiar tangency of the budget plane with the indifference locus passing through the point of equilibrium. Figuratively, the consumer moves along the budget plane until he attains the position lying highest on his preference scale, which must in the continuous case be a position of tangency; for if the budget plane crossed the indifference locus, he could advance to a still higher position.

We have stated our equations of equilibrium in several different, but mathematically equivalent ways. The formulation of (23) is one in which the symmetry of all variables is maintained, and so for definiteness we may concentrate upon it. Our budget equation of (19) must also be satisfied, and so our full conditions of equilibrium can be written

$$U_i(x_1, \cdots, x_n) + \lambda p_i = 0, \qquad (i = 1, \cdots, n)$$
$$p_1 x_1 + p_2 x_2 + \cdots + p_n x_n - I = 0. \tag{29}$$

These conditions of equilibrium correspond to the set (1) of the second chapter. We wish to derive from them our demand functions,

$$x_i = h^i(p_1, \cdots, p_n, I), \tag{30}$$

which correspond to the equations (2) of the second chapter. Prices and income are regarded as data for this analysis, and we should like to know how our equilibrium quantities vary with changes in these parameters.

Our conditions of equilibrium are $(n + 1)$ in number, and involve $2(n + 1)$ unknowns, namely $(- \lambda, x_1, \cdots, x_n, p_1, \cdots, p_n, I)$. Avoiding now all problems of multiplicities of solution, we may assume that $(n + 1)$ of our variables may be solved for in terms of the remaining $(n + 1)$. In particular $(- \lambda, x_1, \cdots, x_n)$ may be each solved for in terms of $(p_1, \cdots, p_n, I)$. Hence, we get the following functions:

$$x_i = h^i(p_1, \cdots, p_n, I), \qquad (i = 1, \cdots, n) \tag{30}$$

and

$$(- \lambda) = f(p_1, \cdots, p_n, I). \tag{31}$$

Thus, our demand functions can be derived from our conditions of equilibrium. We have also introduced a new variable $(- \lambda)$, the marginal utility of income, which could, of course, have been eliminated, but only with a loss of symmetry. Had we employed one of the other equivalent sets, such as (28), we should have had n equations between $(2n + 1)$ variables, and so our n quantities could have been expressed as before in terms of the $(n + 1)$ prices and income parameters.

DISPLACEMENT OF EQUILIBRIUM

We have counted our equations and unknowns, and found them to be equal in number. Subject to certain restrictions, this assures us that all our equilibrium variables are determined. There is a temptation to stop at this point and rest content with these achievements.

In view of all that has been said in earlier chapters, it requires no further argument to show that our task has hardly begun. There remains the sizable problem of deducing the qualitative properties of our demand functions from our knowledge of the properties of our equilibrium maximizing equations.

To do so, we employ the same methods outlined in the second and third chapters. Let us write the total differential of the equilibrium equations (29)

$$U_{i1}dx_1 + U_{i2}dx_2 + \cdots + U_{in}dx_n + p_i d\lambda$$
$$= (-\lambda)dp_i, \qquad (i = 1, \cdots, n)$$
$$p_1dx_1 + p_2dx_2 + \cdots + p_ndx_n$$
$$= dI - (x_1dp_1 + x_2dp_2 + \cdots + x_ndp_n),$$

or

$$\sum_1^n U_{ij}dx_j + p_i d\lambda = (-\lambda)dp_i, \qquad (i = 1, \cdots, n)$$

$$\sum_1^n p_j dx_j = dI - \sum_1^n x_k dp_k. \tag{32}$$

These are $(n + 1)$ linear equations in the $(n + 1)$ unknowns $[dx_1, \cdots, dx_n, d(-\lambda)]$. Their solution may be indicated as follows:

$$dx_j = \frac{\sum_1^n (-\lambda)D_{ij}dp_i + (dI - \sum_1^n x_k dp_k)D_{n+1,j}}{D},$$

$$d(-\lambda) = \frac{-[\sum_1^n (-\lambda)D_{i,n+1}dp_i + (dI - \sum_1^n x_k dp_k)D_{n+1,n+1}]}{D}, \tag{33}$$

where

$$D = \begin{vmatrix} U_{ij} & p_i \\ p_j & 0 \end{vmatrix} = \begin{vmatrix} U_{11} & U_{12} & \cdots & U_{1n} & p_1 \\ U_{21} & U_{22} & \cdots & U_{2n} & p_2 \\ \cdot & \cdot & & \cdot & \cdot \\ \cdot & & & \cdot & \cdot \\ \cdot & \cdot & & \cdot & \cdot \\ U_{n1} & U_{n2} & \cdots & U_{nn} & p_n \\ p_1 & p_2 & \cdots & p_n & 0 \end{vmatrix} \tag{34}$$

and D_{ij} indicates the cofactor of the element of the ith row and the jth column.

The formulae in (33) give the changes in our unknowns for any changes in the parameters, prices, and income. As special cases, the following partial derivatives may be evaluated:

$$\frac{\partial x_j}{\partial p_i} = \frac{(-\lambda)D_{ij} - x_iD_{n+1,j}}{D}, \qquad (i, j = 1, \cdots, n)$$

$$\frac{\partial x_j}{\partial I} = \frac{D_{n+1,j}}{D},$$

(35)

where, of course,

$$\frac{\partial x_j}{\partial p_i} = h_i{}^j, \qquad \frac{\partial x_j}{\partial I} = h_I{}^j.$$

Also,

$$\frac{\partial(-\lambda)}{\partial p_i} = \frac{-\left[(-\lambda)D_{i,n+1} - x_iD_{n+1,n+1}\right]}{D},$$

$$\frac{\partial(-\lambda)}{\partial I} = \frac{-D_{n+1,n+1}}{D}.$$

(36)

It is convenient to consider a compound term introduced first by Slutsky, defined as follows:

$$K_{ji} = \frac{\partial x_j}{\partial p_i} + x_i\frac{\partial x_j}{\partial I}. \qquad (i, j = 1, \cdots, n)$$

(37)

From (35) by substitution

$$K_{ji} = (-\lambda)\frac{D_{ij}}{D}. \qquad (i, j = 1, \cdots, n)$$

(38)

Also define

$$r_i = \left[\frac{\partial(-\lambda)}{\partial p_i} + x_i\frac{\partial(-\lambda)}{\partial I}\right]\frac{1}{(-\lambda)}, \qquad (i = 1, \cdots, n)$$

(39)

or

$$r_i = \frac{-D_{i,n+1}}{D}. \qquad (i = 1, \cdots, n)$$

(40)

The expressions $\partial x_j/\partial p_i$, $\partial x_j/\partial I$, K_{ji} are all properties of the demand functions and are empirically determinable under ideal conditions. We seek restrictions on them.

Inspection of the determinant D reveals that it is symmetrical with respect to i and j, since

$$U_{ij} = U_{ji}.$$

Hence,

$$K_{ji} = \frac{(-\lambda)D_{ij}}{D} = \frac{(-\lambda)D_{ji}}{D} = K_{ij}; \qquad (41)$$

i.e.,

$$\frac{\partial x_j}{\partial p_i} + x_i \frac{\partial x_j}{\partial I} = \frac{\partial x_i}{\partial p_j} + x_j \frac{\partial x_i}{\partial I}. \qquad (i, j = 1, \cdots, n) \qquad (42)$$

What is the economic interpretation of the compound term

$$K_{ji} = \frac{\partial x_j}{\partial p_i} + x_i \frac{\partial x_j}{\partial I} ?$$

It has been called by Slutsky the *residual variability of the jth good for a compensated change in the ith price*.[8]

This can be made more clear by the following considerations. Thus far, we have imagined the individual to be maximizing his utility as of given prices and total expenditure. A little thought will reveal that utility will be maximized as of a given expenditure only if the level of utility which is being realized is being achieved in the cheapest possible way; i.e., expenditure must be minimized as of any level of utility. If this were not so, the same level could be achieved with some money left over; this remnant could be spent to buy more goods, and hence a still higher level of utility could be attained.

Along any indifference locus there exists for any set of prices an optimum set of purchases which minimizes total expenditure. That is,

$$x_j = \psi^j[p_1, \cdots, p_n, F(\varphi)]. \qquad (j = 1, \cdots, n) \qquad (43)$$

For

$$U = F(\varphi) = \text{constant},$$

we are confined to the same level of utility. It could be easily shown [9] that

$$K_{ji} \equiv \left(\frac{\partial x_j}{\partial p_i}\right)_{U = \text{constant}} \equiv \psi_i{}^j. \qquad (i, j = 1, \cdots, n) \qquad (44)$$

In words, K_{ji} is equal to the change in the quantity of the jth good with respect to the ith price, where the individual moves

[8] E. Slutsky, "Sulla teoria del bilancio del consumatore," *Giornale degli economisti*, LI (1915), 19–23.

[9] See chap. iv, pp. 62–65.

along the same indifference locus and keeps his expenditure down to a minimum before and after the change in price.[10]

From the formulation of our equilibrium equations in (29) we have seen that the properties of the demand functions are *not* affected by our choice of utility index. This may be shown explicitly from the identities

$$U = F(\varphi), \tag{45}$$

$$U_i = F'\varphi_i, \tag{46}$$

$$U_{ij} = F'\varphi_{ij} + F''\varphi_i\varphi_j, \tag{47}$$

$$(-\lambda) = F'(-\lambda'), \tag{48}$$

where $(-\lambda')$ is the marginal utility of income for the utility index φ. Let

$$D' = \begin{vmatrix} \varphi_{ij} & p_i \\ p_j & 0 \end{vmatrix}. \tag{49}$$

From (47)

$$D = \begin{vmatrix} U_{ij} & p_i \\ p_j & 0 \end{vmatrix} = \begin{vmatrix} F'\varphi_{ij} + F''\varphi_i\varphi_j & p_i \\ p_j & 0 \end{vmatrix} = \begin{vmatrix} F'\varphi_{ij} & p_i \\ p_j & 0 \end{vmatrix}$$
$$\equiv (F')^{n-1} D'. \tag{50}$$

Similarly, the following relationship holds for all cofactors.

$$D_{ij} = (F')^{n-2} D'_{ij}. \qquad (i, j = 1, \cdots, n) \tag{51}$$

Hence,

$$\frac{(-\lambda)D_{ij}}{D} \equiv \frac{(-\lambda')D'_{ij}}{D'}, \tag{52}$$

so that K_{ji} is an invariant under any transformation of utility index. *Literally nothing is implied for empirical price behavior by the choice of any particular utility index.*

Inspection of our equilibrium conditions in the form of (24) and (19) reveals that they are unaffected by a proportional change in all prices and income; our equilibrium values remain intact for such a change; i.e.,

$$x_i = h^i(p_1, \cdots, p_n, I) = h^i(mp_1, \cdots, mp_n, mI), \qquad (i = 1, \cdots, n) \tag{53}$$

where m is any positive number. Mathematically, our demand

---

[10] For another interpretation, see H. Schultz, *The Theory and Measurement of Demand* (Chicago: University of Chicago Press, 1938), pp. 43–45.

functions must be *homogeneous of order zero*. Employing Euler's theorem for homogeneous functions, we have [11]

$$\frac{\partial x_i}{\partial p_1} p_1 + \frac{\partial x_i}{\partial p_2} p_2 + \cdots + \frac{\partial x_i}{\partial p_n} p_n + \frac{\partial x_i}{\partial I} I = 0. \quad (i = 1, \cdots, n) \quad (54)$$

Dividing through by x_i yields the following relationships in terms of elasticity coefficients:

$$\eta_{i1} + \eta_{i2} + \cdots + \eta_{in} + \eta_{iI} = 0, \quad (i = 1, \cdots, n) \quad (55)$$

where

$$\eta_{ij} = \frac{\partial x_i}{\partial p_j} \frac{p_j}{x_i}$$

is the elasticity of the ith good with respect to the price of the jth good, and

$$\eta_{iI} = \frac{\partial x_i}{\partial I} \frac{I}{x_i}$$

is the income elasticity of demand of the ith good. Intuitively, we should expect this equality, since an upward movement in all prices is equivalent to a decrease in money income.

Thus far our analysis has not been completely devoid of meaning. The following empirical restrictions have been found to hold for the demand functions.

I. They are homogeneous of order zero; i.e., a simultaneous doubling of all prices and income leaves all quantities demanded invariant. This implies as we have seen

$$\frac{\partial x_i}{\partial p_1} p_1 + \frac{\partial x_i}{\partial p_2} p_2 + \cdots + \frac{\partial x_i}{\partial p_n} p_n = - \frac{\partial x_i}{\partial I} I, \quad (i = 1, \cdots, n) \quad (56)$$

or in elasticity terms

$$\eta_{i1} + \eta_{i2} + \cdots + \eta_{in} = - \eta_{iI}; \quad (i = 1, \cdots, n) \quad (57)$$

i.e., the sum of the elasticities of a good with respect to each and every price is equal in absolute value, but opposite in sign, to the

[11] This may also be proved by substitution from (35).

$$\sum_1^n \frac{\partial x_i}{\partial p_i} p_i + \frac{\partial x_i}{\partial I} I \equiv \sum_1^n \left(\frac{\partial x_i}{\partial p_i} + x_i \frac{\partial x_i}{\partial I} \right) p_i \equiv (- \lambda) \sum_1^n \frac{D_{ii} p_i}{D} \equiv 0$$

by a well-known theorem on determinants that the expansion of the elements of one column with respect to the cofactors of a different column must vanish.

income elasticity of demand for that good. These are n restrictions which are not compatible with any and all price-quantity behavior, and so are meaningful.[12]

Because of this homogeneity condition, it is not necessary to take as independent variables the n prices and income. These $(n + 1)$ variables may be reduced to n variables by considering the ratios between any n and the remaining variable.

Thus, we may divide through by any price, say the price of the first good, to get

$$x_i = h^i(p_1, \cdots, p_n, I) = h^i\left(1, \frac{p_2}{p_1}, \cdots, \frac{p_n}{p_1}, \frac{I}{p_1}\right)$$
$$= g^i\left(\frac{p_2}{p_1}, \frac{p_3}{p_1}, \cdots, \frac{p_n}{p_1}, \frac{I}{p_1}\right). \qquad (i = 1, \cdots, n) \quad (58)$$

This is equivalent to setting the price of the first good equal to unity, and using it as our *numeraire*.

However, a more symmetrical measure suggests itself. Dividing through by I, we get

$$x_i = h^i(p_1, \cdots, p_n, I) = h^i\left(\frac{p_1}{I}, \frac{p_2}{I}, \cdots, \frac{p_n}{I}, 1\right)$$
$$= H^i\left(\frac{p_1}{I}, \frac{p_2}{I}, \cdots, \frac{p_n}{I}\right). \qquad (i = 1, \cdots, n) \quad (59)$$

---

[12] From our definition of income or total expenditure as

$$I = \sum_1^n p_i x_i$$

we have the following $(n + 1)$ restrictions on elasticities of demand

$$\sum_1^n k_i \eta_{iI} \equiv 1$$

and

$$\sum_1^n k_i \eta_{ij} = -k_j,$$

where

$$k_i = \frac{p_i x_i}{I}$$

is the proportion of income spent on the ith good. However, these are not meaningful restrictions, since they are consequences of our definition. At best, they could but reveal that we have not applied our defined operations with numerical accuracy.

Let

$$\alpha_j = \frac{p_j}{I}. \qquad (j = 1, \cdots, n)$$

Hence,

$$x_i = H^i(\alpha_1, \cdots, \alpha_n). \tag{60}$$

The α's here are very natural units to employ, since they involve only the dimensions of the respective quantities. In words, α_j may be defined as the proportion of total income required to purchase a single unit of the jth good.

II. We have also the following reciprocal "integrability" conditions.

$$K_{ji} = \frac{\partial x_j}{\partial p_i} + x_i \frac{\partial x_j}{\partial I} = \frac{\partial x_i}{\partial p_j} + x_j \frac{\partial x_i}{\partial I} = K_{ij}; \qquad (i, j - 1, \cdots, n) \tag{61}$$

i.e., the residual variability of the jth good for a compensated change in the ith price is identically equal to the corresponding term for the ith good with respect to the jth price. These are $n(n - 1)/2$ independent meaningful conditions.[13]

Meaningful Theorems

Thus far almost nothing has been said about the *directions* of change in our equilibrium quantities of goods demanded with respect to changes in prices and income. Does the utility analysis have nothing to say upon this question? The answer can be sought along lines indicated in previous chapters.

Before clouding the air with determinants, let us make a common sense appraisal of the situation to see whether we cannot suggest a simple answer.

First, suppose the individual to be constrained to move along the same indifference locus. Let him be confronted with a set of prices, and attempt to attain this level of "utility" in the cheapest

---

[13] They hold, of course, only for the individual demand functions. Moreover, they reflect differential properties of our demand functions which are hard to visualize and hard to refute. For our empirical data consists of isolated points. These must be smoothed in some sense before our relations can be tested; the smoothing, even by the best known statistical methods, is to a degree arbitrary, and so refutation and verification are difficult.

I have tried, but thus far with no success, to deduce implications of our integrability conditions which can be expressed in finite form, i.e., be conceivably refutable merely by a finite number of point observations.

possible way. Consider the set of prices $(p_1^0, \cdots, p_n^0)$. There will correspond to this an optimal set of quantities $(x_1^0, \cdots, x_n^0)$, such that total expenditure is as low as possible, i.e.,

$$\sum_1^n p_i^0 x_i \geqq \sum_1^n p_i^0 x_i^0, \tag{62}$$

where (X) is any other point on the locus

$$F[\varphi(X)] = F[\varphi(X^0)]. \tag{63}$$

Consider now a second set of prices, $(p_1^1, \cdots, p_n^1)$, and the corresponding optimal set of goods, $(x_1^1, \cdots, x_n^1)$, lying on the same indifference locus as the first. Then

$$\sum_1^n p_i^1 x_i \geqq \sum_1^n p_i^1 x_i^1. \tag{64}$$

In equations (62) and (64) any values of x (along the same locus) may be inserted in the respective left-hand sides. In particular, we may write them respectively

$$\sum_1^n p_i^0 x_i^1 \geqq \sum_1^n p_i^0 x_i^0, \tag{65}$$

and

$$\sum_1^n p_i^1 x_i^0 \geqq \sum_1^n p_i^1 x_i^1. \tag{66}$$

This means that the optimal set of goods for each respective set of prices cannot cost more than the other set of goods (optimal for a different set of prices).

Rewriting the equations, we get

$$\sum_1^n p_i^0 (x_i^0 - x_i^1) \leqq 0, \tag{67}$$

$$\sum_1^n p_i^1 (x_i^1 - x_i^0) \leqq 0. \tag{68}$$

Add these two equations to get

$$\sum_1^n (p_i^1 - p_i^0)(x_i^1 - x_i^0) \leqq 0. \tag{69}$$

If the two equilibrium points are assumed to be always distinct, and if a proper *absolute* minimum is assumed to be always realized, then the equality sign may be dropped, and this may be rewritten

$$\sum_1^n (p_i{}^1 - p_i{}^0)(x_i{}^1 - x_i{}^0) < 0, \tag{70}$$

This may also be written

$$\sum_1^n \Delta p_i \Delta x_i < 0, \qquad \text{not all } \Delta p_i = 0. \tag{71}$$

Suppose we allow but one price to change, say the kth; then all but one term of (71) vanishes and we have

$$\Delta x_k \Delta p_k < 0; \qquad (k = 1, \cdots, n) \tag{72}$$

i.e., *as the kth price increases, all other prices being held constant, less will be bought of the kth good.* It must be emphasized that this holds only for a movement along the same indifference locus, i.e., for a compensated change in price, and does not mean that with a *given money income* a change in one price will necessarily result in a decreased amount taken of the corresponding commodity. It will be noted that the above proof does not involve the calculus at all; using only the operations of addition and subtraction, the definition of a maximum position may be utilized to derive meaningful finite demand restrictions.

Employing only the most elementary logical and arithmetical operations, we can advance matters still further. Consider any initial set of prices and income $(p_1{}^0, \cdots, p_n{}^0, I^0)$. Corresponding to this there will exist one or more optimal sets of goods. Select one of these and designate it by $(x_1{}^0, \cdots, x_n{}^0)$. Consider now a second set of prices and income $(p_1{}^1, \cdots, p_n{}^1, I^1)$, and a corresponding optimal set of goods $(x_1{}^1, \cdots, x_n{}^1)$.

Let us consider what would have been the cost of the second batch of goods at the prices of the first. This will be

$$p_1{}^0 x_1{}^1 + p_2{}^0 x_2{}^1 + \cdots + p_n{}^0 x_n{}^1 = \sum_1^n p_i{}^0 x_i{}^1. \tag{73}$$

If this cost is equal to or less than the amount of money that the first batch actually cost, we have conclusive evidence that the second batch is not higher on the individual's preference scale than the first batch; for if it were, the individual could not have been in equilibrium in the first place, since he would not be minimizing total expenditure for the attained level of satisfaction. In other words, if he could have bought the second batch, and he bought the first, we rule out the possibility that he prefers the second to the first.

Our theorem is

$$\sum_1^n p_i{}^0 x_i{}^1 \le \sum_1^n p_i{}^0 x_i{}^0 \text{ implies } F[\varphi(X^1)] \le F[\varphi(X^0)]. \quad (74)$$

More specifically,

$$\sum_1^n p_i{}^0 x_i{}^1 < \sum_1^n p_i{}^0 x_i{}^0 \text{ implies } F[\varphi(X^1)] < F[\varphi(X^0)]. \quad (75)$$

Similarly,

$$\sum_1^n p_i{}^1 x_i{}^0 \le \sum_1^n p_i{}^1 x_i{}^1 \text{ would imply } F[\varphi(X^0)] \le F[\varphi(X^1)]. \quad (76)$$

It is obvious that

$$\sum_1^n p_i{}^0 x_i{}^1 < \sum_1^n p_i{}^0 x_i{}^0, \quad (77)$$

and

$$\sum_1^n p_i{}^1 x_i{}^0 \le \sum_1^n p_i{}^1 x_i{}^1 \quad (78)$$

cannot both hold simultaneously, for this would imply

$$F[\varphi(X^1)] < F[\varphi(X^0)], \quad (79)$$

and

$$F[\varphi(X^1)] \ge F[\varphi(X^0)], \quad (80)$$

which is a contradiction.

This gives us a condition which holds for any movements, not merely for compensated ones.

Equations (77) and (78) may be written

$$\sum_1^n p_i{}^0 (x_i{}^1 - x_i{}^0) < 0 \text{ implies } \sum_1^n p_i{}^1 (x_i{}^1 - x_i{}^0) < 0, \quad (81)$$

òr

$$\sum_1^n p_i \Delta x_i < 0 \text{ implies } \sum_1^n (p_i + \Delta p_i) \Delta x_i < 0. \quad (82)$$

If we assume that our demand functions are single-valued, and agree to consider only distinct points, this may be broadened to the following form:

$$\sum_1^n p_i \Delta x_i \leqq 0 \text{ implies } \sum_1^n (p_i + \Delta p_i)\Delta x_i < 0. \qquad (83)$$

The importance of this result can hardly be overemphasized. In this simple formula are contained almost all the meaningful empirical implications of the whole pure theory of consumer's choice. Moreover, these are expressed in the form which is most suitable for empirical verification. So fundamental is this condition that (as I have shown elsewhere) it provides a foundation for the theory of economic index numbers and the utility analysis, and affords the most convenient path for the derivation of all known restrictions upon the individual and general demand functions.[14]

From this condition alone can be derived the following restrictions upon the demand functions:

(a) They must be single-valued; i.e., to each set of prices and income there corresponds a unique set of goods.

(b) They must be homogeneous of order zero; i.e., a change in all prices and income in the same proportion must leave all quantities unchanged. All the properties of condition I of the previous section must therefore hold.

(c) All known valid qualitative restrictions upon the slopes of the demand functions. These will be indicated below.

Elsewhere [15] I have suggested as new foundations for the pure theory of consumer's behavior the conditions (a) and (b) and equations (83). At that time I did not realize that (a) and (b) were redundant in the sense that they themselves could be deduced as theorems from the assumption of (83) alone. In other words, this single condition provides us with complete foundations for the theory (with the reservation concerning integrability).

The proof of (a) and (b) as theorems can be indicated simultaneously. Consider an initial price and income situation $(p_1^0, \cdots, p_n^0, I^0)$. Corresponding there is a set of goods $(x_1^0, \cdots, x_n^0)$. Suppose now all prices and income to be multiplied by the same

---

[14] The only point upon which this formulation does not throw light is that of integrability. Even here, a proof may still be forthcoming by which this condition may be slightly generalized to include the question of integrability.

[15] "A Note on the Pure Theory of Consumer's Behavior," *Economica*, February, 1938, pp. 61–71.

positive quantity, m, $(mp_1{}^0, \cdots, mp_n{}^0, mI^0)$. Corresponding there is a second set of quantities $(x_1{}^1, \cdots, x_n{}^1)$. We wish to prove that the second batch of goods is identical, commodity for commodity, with the first.

By hypothesis,

$$I^1 = mI^0. \tag{84}$$

Hence,

$$\sum_1^n p_i{}^1 x_i{}^1 = m \sum_1^n p_i{}^0 x_i{}^0. \tag{85}$$

Also,

$$p_i{}^1 = mp_i{}^0. \qquad (i = 1, \cdots, n) \tag{86}$$

Therefore,

$$\sum_1^n p_i{}^0 x_i{}^1 = \sum_1^n p_i{}^0 x_i{}^0. \tag{87}$$

But also

$$\sum_1^n p_i{}^1 x_i{}^0 = \sum_1^n p_i{}^1 x_i{}^1. \tag{88}$$

But this is a contradiction, for condition (83) says that

$$\sum_1^n p_i{}^0 x_i{}^1 = \sum_1^n p_i{}^0 x_i{}^0 \text{ implies } \sum_1^n p_i{}^1 x_i{}^0 > \sum_1^n p_i{}^1 x_i{}^1. \tag{89}$$

Therefore, these cannot be two *distinct* points. Hence,

$$x_i{}^1 = x_i{}^0. \qquad (i = 1, \cdots, n) \tag{90}$$

For $m = 1$, condition (a) is deduced as a special case of (b).

Thus far, we have made no use of the calculus. We may now proceed to derive conditions upon the various partial derivatives of our demand functions.

Let us go through a limiting process and write (83) in the following differential form:

$$\sum_1^n dp_i dx_i < 0, \tag{91}$$

for

$$\sum_1^n p_i dx_i = 0,$$

not all dx_i or $dp_i = 0$.

In this expression the dx's and the dp's are differentials, not infinitesimal increments.

Regarding prices and income as independent variables, from our demand functions of (20) we have

$$dx_i = \sum_1^n h_j{}^i dp_j + h_I{}^i dI. \qquad (i = 1, \cdots, n) \qquad (92)$$

But for $\sum_1^n p_j dx_j = 0$,

$$dI = \sum_1^n p_j dx_j + \sum_1^n x_j dp_j = \sum_1^n x_j dp_j. \qquad (93)$$

Therefore,

$$dx_i = \sum_1^n (h_j{}^i + x_j h_I{}^i) dp_j = \sum_1^n K_{ij} dp_j. \qquad (94)$$

Equation (91) becomes

$$\sum_1^n \sum_1^n (h_j{}^i + x_j h_I{}^i) dp_i dp_j \leqq 0, \qquad (95)$$

or

$$\sum_1^n \sum_1^n (K_{ij}) dp_i dp_j \leqq 0. \qquad (96)$$

This is a negative semi-definite form; semi-definite because for all prices changing in the same proportion, it vanishes due to the homogeneity condition.

This is also derivable in at least two other ways. From equation (71)

$$\sum_1^n \Delta p_i \Delta x_i \leqq 0 \text{ along an indifference locus} \qquad (97)$$

This may be written

$$\sum_1^n dp_i dx_i < 0 \text{ along an indifference locus.}$$

$$\text{(not all differentials vanishing).} \qquad (98)$$

But along an indifference locus, from (43)

$$x_i = \psi^i[p_1, \cdots, p_n, F(\varphi)], \qquad (i = 1, \cdots, n) \qquad (99)$$

where ψ^i is homogeneous of order zero in the p's.   Also

$$dx_i = \sum_1^n \psi_j{}^i dp_j. \qquad (i = 1, \cdots, n) \qquad (100)$$

Therefore,

$$\sum_1^n \sum_1^n \psi_j{}^i dp_i dp_j \leqq 0. \qquad (101)$$

But, of course, for a movement along an indifference locus, i.e., for a compensated price change,

$$\frac{\partial x_i}{\partial p_j} \equiv \psi_j{}^i \equiv K_{ij}. \qquad (102)$$

Therefore, (101) may be written

$$\sum_1^n \sum_1^n K_{ij} dp_i dp_j \leqq 0. \qquad (103)$$

Finally, in the Mathematical Appendix the following algebraic theorem is stated: Let

$$[A_{ij}] = \left[\frac{D_{ij}}{D} \right] = [A_{ji}], \qquad (i, j = 1, \cdots, n) \qquad (104)$$

be the first n by n matrix of the inverse matrix of $[D]$.   Then

$$\sum_1^n \sum_1^n A_{ij} h_i h_j \leqq 0 \qquad (105)$$

because $[D]$ is the matrix of a negative definite form under constraint.   Now from (38)

$$K_{ij} = (-\lambda) A_{ji}. \qquad (106)$$

Since $(-\lambda) > 0$, our theorem again follows.   This is a direct algebraic proof of our theorem.

The meaning of the requirement that the form in (96) be negative semi-definite may be briefly indicated.[16] Let

$$K = |K_{ij}| = \begin{vmatrix} K_{11} & K_{12} & \cdots & K_{1n} \\ K_{21} & K_{22} & \cdots & K_{2n} \\ \cdot & \cdot & & \cdot \\ \cdot & \cdot & & \cdot \\ \cdot & \cdot & & \cdot \\ K_{n1} & K_{n2} & \cdots & K_{nn} \end{vmatrix}. \tag{107}$$

Then because of the semi-definiteness

$$|K| \equiv 0 \text{ and } \sum_1^n \sum_1^n K_{ij} p_i p_j = 0. \tag{108}$$

However, the principal minors beginning with the first alternate in sign from negative to positive, i.e.,

$$|K_{11}| < 0; \quad \begin{vmatrix} K_{11} & K_{12} \\ K_{21} & K_{22} \end{vmatrix} > 0; \quad \begin{vmatrix} K_{11} & K_{12} & K_{13} \\ K_{21} & K_{22} & K_{23} \\ K_{31} & K_{32} & K_{33} \end{vmatrix} < 0, \text{ etc.} \tag{109}$$

Thus, the following demand restrictions are implied.

$$\frac{\partial x_i}{\partial p_i} + x_i \frac{\partial x_i}{\partial I} < 0, \qquad (i = 1, \cdots, n) \tag{110}$$

$$\left(\frac{\partial x_i}{\partial p_i} + x_i \frac{\partial x_i}{\partial I} \right) \left(\frac{\partial x_j}{\partial p_j} + x_j \frac{\partial x_j}{\partial I} \right) - \left(\frac{\partial x_i}{\partial p_j} + x_j \frac{\partial x_i}{\partial I} \right)^2 > 0,$$

$$(i, j = 1, \cdots, n), (i \neq j), \text{ etc.} \tag{111}$$

Condition (110) was first developed by W. E. Johnson and Eugen Slutsky, presumably independently. We see that it is not possible to deduce that

$$\frac{\partial x_i}{\partial p_i} < 0, \tag{112}$$

the ordinary expression for the "law of demand." For if $\partial x_i/\partial I$ be sufficiently negative, $\partial x_i/\partial p_i$ can be algebraically positive. This is the phenomenon alluded to in the well-known Giffen's Paradox.[17]

---

[16] If integrability is not assumed and $K_{ij} \neq K_{ji}$, the exposition may be easily modified by the substitution throughout of the term $(K_{ij} + K_{ji})/2$.

[17] It is only by making additional, and demonstrably arbitrary, assumptions that various writers have been able to derive the so-called law of diminishing demand.

The assumption that the form in (96) be symmetrical and negative semi-definite completely exhausts the empirical implications of the utility analysis. All other demand restrictions can be derived as theorems from this single assumption. These are bold statements, but they are substantiated by the fact that it is possible to work backwards from the assumption of (96) to an integrable preference field displaying the properties necessary for a maximum.[18]

Conclusion

We have come a long way in this chapter. Despite its lofty beginnings, the pure theory of consumer's behavior, when its empirical meaning is finally distilled from it, turns out to be one simple hypothesis on price and quantity behavior. This may be written

$$\sum_1^n (p_i + \Delta p_i)\Delta x_i < 0,$$

for

$$\sum_1^n p_i \Delta x_i \leqq 0, \qquad \text{not all } \Delta x_i = 0,$$

subject to the qualifications indicated above. Alternatively, we may write this as

$$\sum_1^n \sum_1^n \left(\frac{\partial x_i}{\partial p_j} + x_j \frac{\partial x_i}{\partial I} \right) dp_i dp_j \leqq 0,$$

[18] Only a sketch of the proof of this statement need be given. Write

$$x_i = H^i(\alpha_1, \cdots, \alpha_n), \qquad (i = 1, \cdots, n)$$

$$K_{ij} = \frac{\partial x_i}{\partial p_j} + x_j \frac{\partial x_i}{\partial I} = \frac{1}{I}\left(\frac{\partial x_i}{\partial \alpha_j} - x_j \sum_1^n \frac{\partial x_i}{\partial \alpha_k} \alpha_k \right).$$

Define a new set of variables

$$\beta_i = f^i(\alpha_1, \cdots, \alpha_n), \qquad \text{or} \qquad \alpha_k = F^k(\beta_1, \cdots, \beta_n)$$

such that

$$x_i = H^i[F^1(\beta_1, \cdots, \beta_n), \cdots, F^n(\beta_1, \cdots, \beta_n)] = G^i(\beta_1, \cdots, \beta_n),$$

and

$$\frac{\partial x_i}{\partial \beta_j} \equiv G_j{}^i \equiv K_j{}^i \equiv K_i{}^j \equiv G_i{}^j \equiv \frac{\partial x_j}{\partial \beta_i}.$$

Then there exists a function

$$\varphi = \psi(\beta_1, \cdots, \beta_n),$$

or

$$\varphi = \varphi(x_1, \cdots, x_n),$$

which satisfies the properties of our preference field.

where the equality sign holds only for all prices changing in the same proportion.

Many writers have held the utility analysis to be an integral and important part of economic theory. Some have even sought to employ its applicability as a test criterion by which economics might be separated from the other social sciences. Nevertheless, I wonder how much economic theory would be changed if either of the two conditions above were found to be empirically untrue. I suspect, very little.

A Note on the Demand for Money

One special problem in the theory of value has been touched upon at various places in the previous discussions, namely, the value of *money* itself. Probably more has been written upon this subject than upon any other in economics, and most of the issues raised are not germane to the present investigation. However, it is a fair question as to the relationship between the demand for money and the ordinal preference fields met in utility theory. In this connection, I have reference to none of the tenuous concepts of money, as a numeraire commodity, or as a composite commodity, but to money proper, the distinguishing features of which are its indirect usefulness, not for its own sake but for what it can buy, its conventional acceptability, its not being "used up" by use, etc., etc.

The most interesting problems arising in connection with money are linked up with the fact of "uncertainty" in the most general sense, leading into liquidity considerations which cannot be discussed here. However, it should be possible to indicate in a few pages the way out of certain false dilemmas connected with the demand for money for so-called transactions purposes.[19]

On the one hand, there are writers like Mises who would explain the value of money in marginal utility terms such as might be applicable to any commodity; on the other hand, to economists like Schumpeter the peculiarity of money lies in its essential lack of direct usefulness and in the fact that its value is not capable of explanation in the usual utility terms. On the whole the latter

---

[19] For a summary of the extensive Continental speculations on these matters see Howard S. Ellis, *German Monetary Theory, 1905–1933* (Cambridge, Mass., 1934), Part I.

view is the least misleading, but, as Walras showed many years ago, it is possible to modify utility analysis so as to take account of the peculiar properties of money. The latter, who above all others developed the notion of *general equilibrium* in which all magnitudes are simultaneously determined by efficacious interdependent relations, was able to remain undisturbed by the fears of literary writers that there was something viciously circular in assuming the existence of prices and of a "value for money" in the midst of the process by which that value was to be determined. Today after the recent contributions of Keynes, it is particularly rewarding to go back to reëxamine the elaborate discussion of liquidity preference, *encaisse desirée*, etc., in Walras. The latter was so sophisticated as to have outgrown the quantity equation in later editions of his work, although he continued to believe in what is today called the "quantity theory"; very rightly, in my opinion, he in effect reversed the commonly met dictum that "the quantity theory should be scrapped, but the quantity equation is useful."

Here I shall only consider the demand for the holding of money by the consumer. As before, ordinal utility or preference depends upon all commodities, but the $(n + 1)$th good, M, will be taken to be money, which yields benefit only in its ultimately being given up. Possession of an average amount of it yields convenience in permitting the consumer to take advantage of offers of sale, in facilitating exchanges, in bridging the gap between receipt of income and expenditure, etc. The average balance is both used and at the same time not used; it revolves but is not depleted; its just being there to meet contingencies is valuable even if the contingencies do not materialize, *ex post*. Possession of this balance then yields a real service, which can be compared with the direct utilities from the consumption of sugar, tobacco, etc., in the sense that there is some margin at which the individual would be indifferent between having more tobacco and less of a cash balance, with all of the inconvenience which the latter condition implies.

But there is this difference. Given physical amounts of tobacco, food, ballet, etc. have significance in terms of the want pattern of the consumer, but it is not possible to attach similar significance to a given number of physical units of money, say to a number of ounces of gold. It would be otherwise in the case of gold which was to be used to fill teeth, but such uses of money in the industrial arts we purposely neglect. The amount of money which is needed depends upon the work that is to be done, which in turn depends upon the prices of all goods in terms of gold.

The above remarks are by now so well known as to appear trite and trivial. But let us translate them into mathematics. Our ordinal utility is now a function, not alone of the physical quantities of goods, but it has within it prices as well. This is a serious, significant alteration, for, as we shall see, the empirical properties of the demand functions are changed by this innovation. This is not the only case in which economists have found it necessary to introduce prices into the indifference loci; there is also the example of goods which have snob appeal, or scarcity appeal, which are valued for their exclusiveness so that preference for them is altered by changes in their relative prices. This Veblenesque effect need not detain us here.

Our utility function will be of the form

$$U(x_1, \cdots, x_n, Mp_m, p_1, \cdots, p_n)$$
$$\equiv U(x_1, \cdots, x_n, M\lambda p_m, \lambda p_1, \cdots, \lambda p_n)$$
$$= F\left(x_1, \cdots, x_n, \frac{Mp_m}{p_1}, \cdots, \frac{Mp_m}{p_n} \right), \qquad (113)$$

where the function is homogeneous of order zero in *all* of the prices, so that a doubling of all prices (including the price of gold) at the same time that quantities are unchanged will leave ordinal utility unchanged. This stems from the hypothesis, which need not be true in the short run or under particular expectations, that money is evaluated only in terms of the work which it has to do. It will be noted that I have not set the price of money equal to one. Actually, we shall avoid confusion in thought if we refrain from doing so. Any other commodity may be used as numeraire, or we may express prices in any units we like. Of course, it will still be possible to speak of the gold price of things, and after we have learned to do without the use of the money commodity gold as numeraire, we can then fall back upon the simple convention of expressing prices in terms of it. Of course no reader will think that I attach any particular importance to gold or any other metal; any conventional unit which serves as money will do.

Walras was careful to point out another important distinction: consumption of goods is a flow per unit time, so much tobacco per year, etc., but the gold balance is an inventory or stock. We may speak of its price in two senses, the price of gold compared to the prices of other things, as one ounce of gold is worth two beaver skins, while a pound of tobacco is worth three beaver skins, or an ounce of gold is worth two "anythings," while a pound of tobacco is worth three "anythings." In our notation this is p_m. But we may also speak of the price of the *use* of gold per unit time. In a capital market where people can both borrow and lend at a given rate of interest, this price is necessarily related to the rate of interest. This is true even if the individual in question does not have to stay in debt for the amount of his cash balance; in any case there is the opportunity cost of holding money in the sense of the interest he might have earned by lending this sum.

If we wish to exclude dynamical considerations from our discussion as much as possible, the simplest assumption would seem to be that the individual maximizes the above expression subject to the following budget equation,

$$\sum_1^n p_j x_j + r p_m M = I. \tag{114}$$

where prices, income, and interest, r, are given to the individual. Thus, the amounts paid out (or foregone) in every period for the use of money are treated as subtractions from income available for expenditure upon consumer's goods. The conditions of equilibrium are exactly as in chapter v, equation (29), except that the marginal utilities of the goods are affected by the level of prices directly, and we now have an additional unknown, M, to be determined. But we also have an additional equation,

$$\frac{\partial U}{\partial M} + \lambda p_m r = 0. \tag{115}$$

Thus, the use of money is bought up to the point where its marginal utility (convenience) is proportional to its cost, or the interest charges which must be paid for its use. The secondary inequalities are exactly as in the usual case, i.e., the principal minors of the

bordered Hessian must oscillate in sign, with money treated as an
$(n + 1)$th good.

From the conditions of equilibrium our demand curves are as
follows,

$$x_i = h^i(p_1, \cdots, p_n, p_m, I, r), \qquad (i = 1, \cdots, n)$$
$$M = M(p_1, \cdots, p_n, p_m, I, r). \tag{116}$$

These equations are homogeneous of order zero in all prices and
income just as in the usual case of demand. With the interest
rate unchanged, doubling all prices (including the price of gold)
and income will leave all quantities unchanged. However, if we
double all prices and income in terms of the price of gold, then
with r unchanged, the demand for physical quantities of money
will be exactly doubled. Mathematically M is a homogeneous
function of order one in terms of all *other* prices and income. This
is the peculiar feature of money. Another way of saying the same
thing is the assertion that the demand for money in terms of its
own price, all other prices held constant, is necessarily of unitary
elasticity. This is a familiar proposition in the history of the
quantity theory. The reader will note that this is a meaningful,
refutable hypothesis which is capable of being tested under ideal
observational conditions.[20]

The further qualitative properties of the demand schedules can
be determined by differentiation of our equilibrium equations.
However, they will not be so simple as those in the usual demand
case, because in varying any one price, we shift every equilibrium
equation through the direct influence of each price on marginal
utilities. Still, income elasticities behave more or less the same as
before; also the demand for money in terms of the interest rate
behaves just like the demand for any good in terms of its own price
under the usual utility assumptions. Thus, if interest is raised,
and at the same time income is increased so as to leave the individual equally well off, then the amount of money demanded must
fall. If money is not an inferior good, and we should expect it not
to be, then an increase in interest will lower the amount of money
demanded even for an uncompensated change.

[20] Jacob Marschak, "Money Illusion and Demand Analysis," *Review of Economic
Statistics*, February, 1943, pp. 40–48.

The complete results of such differentiations are given below in partitioned matrix form.[21]

$$
\begin{bmatrix}
h_j{}^i & \cdot & h_{p_m}{}^i & \cdot & h_I{}^i & \cdot & h_r{}^i \\
& \cdots & & & & & \\
M_j & \cdot & M_{p_m} & \cdot & M_I & \cdot & M_r
\end{bmatrix}
$$

$$
= -
\begin{bmatrix}
U_{ik} & \cdot & \dfrac{\partial U_i}{\partial M} & \cdot & p_i \\
& \cdots & & & \\
\dfrac{\partial U_k}{\partial M} & \cdot & \dfrac{\partial^2 U}{\partial M^2} & \cdot & rp_m \\
& \cdots & & & \\
p_k & \cdot & rp_m & \cdot & 0
\end{bmatrix}^{-1}
\begin{bmatrix}
\dfrac{\partial U_i}{\partial p_j}+\lambda\delta_{ij} & \cdot & \dfrac{\partial U_i}{\partial p_m} & \cdot & 0 & \cdot & 0 \\
& \cdots & & & & & \\
\dfrac{\partial^2 U}{\partial M\partial p_j} & \cdot & \dfrac{\partial^2 U}{\partial M\partial p_m}+\lambda r & \cdot & 0 & \cdot & \lambda p_m \\
& \cdots & & & & & \\
x_j & \cdot & rM & \cdot & -1 & \cdot & p_m M
\end{bmatrix} \quad (117)
$$

We may leave as an exercise to the interested reader to verify this and to work out the interesting and special case where the ordinal preference field takes the simple form $U(x_1, \cdots, x_n, p_m M / I)$.

Qualifications Introduced by Uncertainty

The above analysis of the demand for money confines itself to the so-called transaction aspects. The really interesting problems arise when uncertainty as well as transaction friction is admitted into the picture. Some of the best lines ever written in this connection are those to be found in Keynes's *General Theory* and in Hicks's *Value and Capital*. Space can be devoted to only one comment here. In the past the structure of interest rates and assets has been subject to only perfunctory notice so that the recent analysis in terms of liquidity preference is of the greatest importance. But it would be a mistake, which would be as damaging to further analysis of liquidity preference as it would be to classical doctrines, if it were thought that uncertainty and liquidity differentials are the *sine qua non* for the existence of a rate of interest.

[21] Reference may be made here to the valuable contribution of C. E. V. Leser, "The Consumer's Demand for Money," *Econometrica*, vol. XI, no. 2 (April, 1943), pp. 123–140.

Such a view can be compared with a theory of land rent based upon differences in the quality of different kinds of land. I believe that the analogy is not a superficial one.

Specifically I think it would be misleading to say that interest is simply the price of money; it would be quite possible to have an economy in which money did not exist, and in which there still was a substantial rate of interest.[22] Nor can I agree with all of the formulations of Hicks's brilliant chapter xiii on Interest and Money, such as ". . . it must be the trouble of making transactions which explains the short rate of interest" (p. 165);" . . . if bills are are perfectly safe, [there would be] no reason for the bills to fall to a discount" (p. 165); "Securities which are not generally acceptable in payment of debts bear some interest because they are imperfectly 'money' "(p. 167).

It is true that in a world involving no transaction friction and no uncertainty, there would be no reason for a spread between the yield on any two assets, and hence there would be no difference in the yield on money and on securities. Hicks concludes, therefore, that securities will not bear interest but will accommodate themselves to the yield on money. It is equally possible and more illuminating to suppose that under these conditions money adjusts itself to the yield of securities. In fact, in such a world securities themselves would circulate as money and be acceptable in transactions; demand bank deposits would bear interest, just as they often did in this country in the period of the twenties.[23] And if money could not make the adjustment, as in the case of metal counters which Aristotle tells us are barren, it would pass out of use, wither away and die, become a free good.

In the preface to the reissue of *Risk, Uncertainty and Profit* [24] Frank Knight makes the penetrating observation that under the conditions envisaged above the velocity of circulation would become infinite and so would the price level. This is perhaps an

---

[22] Elsewhere I have developed this notion briefly under the title "The Rate of Interest under Ideal Conditions," *Quarterly Journal of Economics*, LIII (February, 1939), 286–297.

[23] In a world without uncertainty where money has the same yield as other assets, its velocity becomes indeterminate. Note that this is the case when the interest rate is zero.

[24] *Risk, Uncertainty and Profit* (London School of Economics and Political Science: Series of Reprints of Scarce Tracts, no. 16, 1933), p. xxii.

over-dramatic way of saying that nobody would hold money, and it would become a free good to go into the category of shells and other things which once served as money. We should expect too that it would not only pass out of circulation, but it would cease to be used as a conventional numeraire in terms of which prices are expressed. Interest bearing money would emerge.

Of course, the above does not happen in real life, precisely because uncertainty, contingency needs, non-synchronization of revenues and outlay, transaction frictions, etc., etc., all are with us. But the abstract special case analyzed above should warn us against the facile assumption that the average levels of the structure of interest rates are determined solely or primarily by these differential factors. At times they are primary, and at other times, such as the twenties in this country, they may not be. As a generalization I should hazard the hypothesis that they are likely to be of great importance in an economy in which there is a "quasi-zero" rate of interest. I think by this hypothesis one can explain many of the anomalies of the United States money market in the thirties.

A further defect of the reasoning that I have been criticizing lies in the tendency to regard as universal the hypothesis that interest yield is inversely correlated with an asset's nearness to money so that normally long rates are above short rates. This is not in accord with much of economic history for reasons which I do not think are difficult to elucidate.[25]

[25] See D. Durand, "Basic Yields of Corporate Bonds, 1900–1942," Technical Paper 3 (New York: National Bureau of Economic Research, 1942). Also F. A. Lutz, "The Structure of Interest Rates," *Quarterly Journal of Economics*, LV (1940), 36–63.

CHAPTER VI

TRANSFORMATIONS, COMPOSITE COMMODITIES, AND RATIONING

Logarithmic Transformations and Elasticities

Through the influence of Alfred Marshall economists have developed a fondness for certain dimensionless expressions called elasticity coefficients. On the whole, it appears that their importance is not very great except possibly as mental exercises for beginning students.[1] As we have seen, most of the "laws of economics" are qualitative and ordinal rather than quantitative, and where such are concerned the problem of dimensions is of no consequence.

Furthermore, while elasticity expressions are invariant under changes of scale, they are not invariant under changes of origin. Since there are no natural zeros from which we measure economic magnitudes, the elasticity expressions can be seen to be essentially arbitrary. Thus we meet in economic analysis such concepts as exports, net purchases, amount of factors supplied, etc., all of which are differences measured from arbitrary bases.[2]

Mathematically an elasticity expression between two magnitudes, such as price and quantity, consists simply of the logarithm of one of these quantities differentiated with respect to the logarithm of the other. Thus,

$$\eta_{xp} = (dx/dp)(p/x) = d \log x/d \log p = Ex/Ep.[3]$$

[1] There is perhaps some usefulness of the concept of elasticity of demand as giving an indication of the qualitative behavior of total revenue, but even this is only the consequence of neglecting to deal with total revenue directly.

[2] This was realized, somewhat inadequately, by Wicksteed who denied the validity of the concept of supply, preferring to use the notion of "reserve demand"; only he went to the opposite extreme in attaching sacredness to his reformulation.

[3] A calculus of operations with elasticity terms can be devised on the basis of the properties of logarithmic derivatives. See R. G. D. Allen, *Mathematical Analysis for Economists* (London, 1937), chap. x, particularly the reference there to the work of D. G. Champernowne.

Not only are elasticity expressions more or less useless, but in more complicated systems they become an actual nuisance,[4] converting symmetrical expressions into asymmetrical ones, and hiding the definiteness of quadratic forms. This could be illustrated by utility analysis, but can be amply demonstrated by the slightly simpler case of profit maximization, where constraints do not enter the picture. Let us consider a firm buying inputs $(v_1, \cdots, v_n)$ in perfectly competitive markets at given prices $(w_1, \cdots, w_n)$. With the demand curve for its product and its production function being known, total revenue becomes a determinate function of the inputs bought. Total expenditure being defined as the sum of the amounts paid to all the factors of production, it is clear that the firm's profit can be written in the form

$$\pi = R(v_1, \cdots, v_n) - \sum_1^n w_j v_j. \tag{1}$$

For profits to be at a regular maximum, we must have

$$R_i(v_1, \cdots, v_n) - w_i = 0, \qquad (i = 1, \cdots, n)$$
$$[R_{ij}] \text{ negative definite.} \tag{2}$$

Suppose we are interested in the inverse demand functions giving the amount of each factor of production which will be bought at each set of prices. By explicit differentiation of our equilibrium conditions above, we find

$$\left[\frac{\partial v_i}{\partial w_j} \right] = [R_{ij}]^{-1}. \tag{3}$$

Since the inverse of a symmetrical negative definite matrix is itself

---

[4] Actually it is a little misleading to say that an elasticity expression is necessarily "without dimension." For take any absolute *derivative*, such as dx/dp, which is certainly *not* dimensionless, involving as it does the dimensions [output times output divided by value]. Even though it has dimensions, it is still the elasticity of *some* expression. Thus if

$$x = f(p),$$

and

$$y = s(q),$$

where

$$y = e^x, \qquad q = e^p,$$

then

$$\frac{Ey}{Eq} = \frac{dx}{dp}.$$

symmetrical and negative definite, the complete conditions on the demand functions are summarized in the above expression.

If one were interested in the corresponding elasticity coefficients $[Ev_i/Ew_j]$, one could as an afterthought introduce suitable factors into the matrix of equation (3). This usual procedure has been termed by Professor Lange the *"indirect" method.*[5] He suggests an alternative "direct" method. I should like to point out a third method, which carries out the Lange procedure to its logical conclusion. Before doing so, however, I should like to express the opinion that in this matter "indirectness" is a virtue rather than a drawback.

It will simplify the discussion if we adopt a mnemonic notation whereby the Jacobian of one set of variables with respect to another is written in a form reminiscent of that for a single derivative; i.e.,

$$J(y_1, \cdots, y_n; x_1, \cdots, x_n) = \left[\frac{\partial y_i}{\partial x_j}\right] = \frac{dy}{dx}. \tag{4}$$

The reader may then verify the identities

$$\frac{dz}{dy}\frac{dy}{dx} = \frac{dz}{dx},$$

$$\frac{dx}{dy} = \left[\frac{dy}{dx}\right]^{-1} \tag{5}$$

which parallel exactly those for single derivatives.

In terms of this notation the Jacobians of the transformations

$$\begin{aligned} V_i &= \log v_i, & v_i &= e^{V_i} \\ W_i &= \log w_i, & w_i &= e^{W_i} \end{aligned} \qquad (i = 1, \cdots, n) \tag{6}$$

can be written as

$$\begin{aligned} \frac{dV}{dv} &= \left[\frac{\delta_{ij}}{v_i}\right], & \frac{dv}{dV} &= [v_i\delta_{ij}] \\ \frac{dW}{dw} &= \left[\frac{\delta_{ij}}{w_i}\right], & \frac{dw}{dW} &= [w_i\delta_{ij}], \end{aligned} \tag{7}$$

where δ_{ij} is the Kronecker delta, equal to one for like subscripts and vanishing for all others.

[5] Oscar Lange, "Theoretical Derivation of Elasticities of Demand and Supply: The Direct Method," *Econometrica*, X (1942), 193–214.

Then it follows that

$$\frac{dV}{dW} = \frac{dV}{dv}\frac{dv}{dw}\frac{dw}{dW} = \left[\frac{\delta_{ij}}{v_j}\right][R_{ij}]^{-1}[w_i\delta_{ij}]. \tag{8}$$

This is the so-called indirect method.   The Lange direct method involves computing the same matrix by the following equality

$$\frac{dV}{dW} = \left[\frac{dW}{dV}\right]^{-1} = \left[\frac{v_j R_{ij}}{w_i}\right]^{-1} \tag{9}$$

There seems to be no special advantage in this procedure; on the other hand, there is the great disadvantage of loss of symmetry *prior to inversion*, and a cloaking of the definiteness properties of R and its inverse.   Of course, what is covered up can later be unscrambled, but a good deal of waste motion would seem to be involved.

However, if we wish to carry the direct method to its final conclusion, it would seem logical to replace the v's and w's in the original profit expression by their equivalences in terms of the variables V and W.   With the latter being given, the firm would vary the V's so as to maximize profits.   The conditions of equilibrium would be

$$S_i(V_1, \cdots, V_n) - e^{V_i}e^{W_i} = 0, \qquad (i = 1, \cdots, n) \tag{10}$$

and

$$[S_{ij} - v_i w_i \delta_{ij}] = H$$

negative definite.   In the above expressions it is to be understood that

$$S(V_1, \cdots, V_n) = R(e^{V_1}, \cdots, e^{V_n}), \tag{11}$$

and that subscripts stand as usual for differentiation.

If we differentiate our equilibrium conditions, we easily derive the identity

$$\frac{dV}{dW} = H^{-1}[v_j w_j \delta_{ij}], \tag{12}$$

where H^{-1} is symmetrical and negative definite.   Thus, except for column factors the elasticity matrix is symmetrical.   By dividing through with these factors, and defining $K_i = v_i w_i / \sum v_j w_j$, we easily arrive at the familiar identity [6]

$$K_i \eta_{ij} = K_j \eta_{ji}. \tag{13}$$

---

[6] H. Schultz, *Theory and Measurement of Demand* (Chicago, 1938), chap. xix.

Also we may verify the relations

$$\eta_{ii} < 0, \qquad \begin{vmatrix} \eta_{ii} & \eta_{ij} \\ \eta_{ji} & \eta_{jj} \end{vmatrix} > 0, \quad \text{etc.} \tag{14}$$

Relations (13) and (14) are also immediately derivable from the indirect method, but not easily from the Lange method.

If one must use "dimensionless" expressions, it would seem desirable to replace the usual elasticity expression by the more symmetrical coefficient

$$M_{ij} = \frac{\partial v_i}{\partial w_j} \frac{\sqrt{w_i w_j}}{\sqrt{v_i v_j}}. \tag{15}$$

The reader can easily verify that symmetry and definiteness are preserved in all matrices, that these coefficients are pure numbers, which in the case of diagonal elements reduce to the old definition of elasticity.

I should like to conclude this discussion of elasticity expressions with a warning that the transformations break down when any of the variables are zero or change sign. In earlier sections it has been shown that productive services or inputs can be regarded simply as negative outputs. These can be converted into logarithms only after a reversal of sign. This would offer no problems were it not for the fact that many of the magnitudes are neither always positive nor always negative. As an illustration of the difficulties which may arise, consider the classical case where the total of all expenditure is taken as zero. Here the partial derivatives of the various goods with respect to hypothetical income changes have a definite meaning, whereas their elasticities cannot be defined.

General Transformation of Independent Variables

The logarithmic transformation discussed in the previous section is but one special case of the transformation of our independent variables. It is desirable to examine the behavior of our equilibrium conditions under general transformation of our independent variables because in economics as in other disciplines we wish to free ourselves from any particular scheme of reference, or coördinate space, in favor of *generalized coördinates*. This desire is not only aesthetic but is necessitated by the fact that in real life we do not always meet *naturally* defined commodities. In business cycle theory we often use the concept of "the cost of living," taken to be the price of some composite market basket of commodities. But even if we confine our attention to what is ordinarily called a commodity, such as "wheat," we find ourselves dealing with a composite commodity made up of winter wheat, spring wheat, of varying grades. Each of these in turn is a composite of heterogeneous components, and so forth in infinite regression.

There is a related reason for analyzing the effects of a general transformation. Among the many recent advances contained in Professor J. R. Hicks's *Value and Capital* perhaps the most important from an analytical point of view was the enunciation of the principle that a group of commodities has the property of a single commodity if their prices all change in the same proportion. This theorem had been partially anticipated by Professor Leontief,[7] but it was Professor Hicks who made it the cornerstone of his exposition. Every mathematical economist, working in many variables, finds difficulty in explaining his theories in words or diagrams. By means of the Hicks-Leontief theorem all but one of the variables can be lumped together as a single variable, and a tolerably simple literary explanation can be phrased. We shall see how this theorem emerges as a special case of general theorems concerning transformations.

The most general conditions of equilibrium are of the type first encountered in chapter ii, equation (1), which we may rewrite in matrix form with suppressed subscripts as

$$f(x; \alpha) = 0. \tag{16}$$

If we subject the independent variables to the non-singular transformation

$$x = T(\bar{x}), \tag{17}$$

whose Jacobian

$$\frac{dx}{d\bar{x}} = [T_j{}^i]$$

never vanishes, then our equilibrium conditions become

$$f[T(\bar{x}); \alpha] = \bar{f}(\bar{x}; \alpha) = 0. \tag{18}$$

---

[7] W. Leontief, "Composite Commodities and the Problem of Index Numbers," *Econometrica*, vol. IV (1936).

If the relationship between the equilibrium values of our unknowns and the parameters was given by

$$x = g(\alpha),\tag{19}$$

the new relationship will be

$$\bar{x} = \mathfrak{g}(\alpha),\tag{20}$$

which will be equivalent to

$$T(\bar{x}) = g(\alpha).\tag{21}$$

Most importantly, it can be easily verified that

$$\frac{dx}{d\alpha} = \frac{dx}{d\bar{x}}\frac{d\bar{x}}{d\alpha}.\tag{22}$$

We may turn directly to the general extremum problem where some quantity is to be at a relative maximum or minimum with respect to n independent variables, which are themselves under m constraints.[8] In matrix notation we have

$$z = f(x)\tag{23}$$
$$G(x) = 0.$$

At a regular maximum it is necessary that the matrix

$$[f_x, G_x]\tag{24}$$

be of rank m, and that

$$h'H_{xx}h\tag{25}$$

be negative definite subject to

$$h'G_x = 0.$$

where

$$H_{xx} = [f_{x_i x_j} + \sum_1^m \lambda_k G_{x_i x_j}{}^k].\tag{26}$$

where the λ's are Lagrangean multipliers.

After transformation we have

$$[\overline{f}_{\bar{x}}, \overline{G}_{\bar{x}}] \equiv \left[\frac{dx}{d\bar{x}}\right]' [f_x, G_x].\tag{27}$$

[8] See Mathematical Appendix A, Section III.

where prime on a matrix $[a_{ij}]$ indicates its "transpose" $[a_{ji}]$. Since the first matrix on the right-hand side is non-singular, the first order rank conditions are invariant under transformation. It is also easy to show that

$$\bar{h}'\bar{H}_{\bar{x}\bar{x}}\bar{h} \equiv h'H_{xx}h, \tag{28}$$

where

$$\bar{h}'\bar{G}_{\bar{x}} \equiv h'G_x \equiv 0,$$

$$h = \left[\frac{dx}{d\bar{x}}\right]\bar{h}$$

so that the second order conditions are invariant under transformation.

Alternatively this might have been proved by showing the invariance of the relevant bordered determinants in consequence of the relation:

$$\begin{bmatrix} \bar{H}_{\bar{x}\bar{x}} & \bar{G}_{\bar{x}} \\ \bar{G}_{\bar{x}}' & 0 \end{bmatrix} = \begin{bmatrix} \dfrac{dx'}{d\bar{x}} & 0 \\ 0 & I \end{bmatrix} \begin{bmatrix} H_{xx} & G_x \\ G_x' & 0 \end{bmatrix} \begin{bmatrix} \dfrac{dx}{d\bar{x}} & 0 \\ 0 & I \end{bmatrix} \tag{29}$$

It will be noted that the Lagrangean multipliers $(\lambda_1, \cdots, \lambda_m)$ are invariant under transformations of independent variables. There are economic as well as mathematical explanations of this. If we insert parameters $(\alpha_1, \cdots, \alpha_m)$ in our equations above, so that our constraints become

$$G^k(x) - \alpha_k = 0, \tag{30}$$

then one can easily verify by direct differentiation that

$$\left[\frac{dz}{d\alpha_k}\right]_{\text{other } \alpha\text{'s constant}} = [-\lambda_k]. \tag{31}$$

Earlier we have derived special cases of this in connection with the marginal utility of income (chapter v, p. 100) and marginal cost (chapter iv, p. 65).

The above relationship can be derived heuristically by differentiating H with respect to α_k, holding all other variables constant. As with other operations involving Lagrangean multipliers, this is an analytic "trick" whose justification lies in its equivalence with expressions which can be rigorously derived by more roundabout methods.

Explicit attention is called to the fact that transformation of the independent variables of an extremum problem subjects the matrix of the relevant quadratic forms to a cogredient congruent transformation which leaves the definiteness of the quadratic form unchanged, and also leaves the signs of principal minors of a given order intact. This is in consequence of the equivalence of our equilibrium equations to an extremum condition, and need not be true for other types of equilibrium.

Thus, when Hicks [9] sets down as a condition of perfect stability under general market exchange the requirement that all the principal minors of a matrix

$$- \left[\frac{\partial x_i}{\partial p_j} \right]$$

be positive, we have as yet no way of knowing whether or not this is independent of the particular coördinate system chosen. The same may be said of his concept of "imperfect stability." The reason for the ambiguity lies in the inapplicability of the proofs given above to asymmetrical matrices.[10]

This section has dealt with the invariance of an extremum position under transformation of independent variables. We turn now to the problem of transformation of the dependent variable.

TRANSFORMATION OF DEPENDENT VARIABLE

It is by now well known that the equations of demand are independent of the particular choice of utility index; [11] i.e., all of their properties are invariant under a general transformation

$$U = F(\varphi), \tag{32}$$

where the latter is a one to one, always increasing function. For simplicity we may assume that it is twice differentiable.

In the most general case where $f(x)$ is to be made a maximum subject to one or more constraints on the x's given by

$$G(x) = 0, \tag{33}$$

[9] J. R. Hicks, *Value and Capital* (London, 1939), chap. v and Mathematical Appendix, pp. 315–317.

[10] This problem is discussed again later in this chapter.

[11] See chap. v, pp. 94, 99, and 104.

the equilibrium conditions are completely expressed by the condition that $[f_x G_x]$ be of certain rank, and that the quadratic form $h' H_{xx} h$ be of certain definiteness for values of h satisfying

$$h' G_x = 0.^{12} \tag{34}$$

Now if we subject z and the G's to the transformation

$$F = F(z) \quad \text{and} \quad E = E(G), \tag{35}$$

and ask that the new variable F be maximized subject to the new constraints, our conditions involve the rank of $[F_x E_x]$ and the definiteness of $h' R_{xx} h$, subject to

$$h' E_x = 0, \tag{36}$$

where

$$R_{xx} = \left[F_{ij} + \sum_1^r m_k E_{ij}{}^k \right]. \tag{37}$$

By actual differentiation we easily find the relationships between the new and old matrices, namely

$$[F_x E_x] = [f_x G_x] \begin{bmatrix} F'(\varphi) & 0 \\ 0 & E'(G) \end{bmatrix}. \tag{38}$$

Since the last of these matrices is a diagonal matrix which is to be non-singular, the first order rank properties are clearly invariant under this transformation, as is the actual solution in x itself.

We may similarly verify by differentiation that

$$h' R_{xx} h = h' \left[F' f_{ij} + \sum_1^n m_k E_k'(G^k) G_{ij}{}^k \right] h$$

$$+ h' \left[F'' f_i f_j + \sum_1^n m_k E_k'' G_i{}^k G_j{}^k \right] h. \tag{39}$$

From the first order rank conditions, there must be linear dependence between the f_x and G_x columns of precisely the sort to make the second part of the right-hand side of the above equation vanish for admissible h's. From the monotonic property of the functions F and E it follows that $[F' E_k']$ are non-vanishing; hence the transformed quadratic form retains its definiteness.

[12] See Mathematical Appendix A, Section V.

This completes a sketchy proof of the invariance of our equilibrium conditions. This whole problem is of interest primarily in connection with utility and consumer's choice theory, but our theorem applies just as well to the maximization of profit. If we maximize the square of profit, or the log of profit, or 90 per cent of profit, or that monotonic function of profit which the Treasury tells us we can retain as net income, there will be no change in our optimum price and output policy. In connection with the production function the combining of the factors of production so as to produce a given output most cheaply could be done as well if we worked with some indicator of output rather than with output itself; alternatively, we might work with the iso-product contours alone, taken without regard to their numbering. However, it is important to realize that the variables, profit and output, are measurable under ideal conditions; consequently it is artificial and unnecessary to replace them by a transformed variable.[13]

Explicit evaluation of the new Lagrangian multipliers shows that they have been changed by the transformation as follows:

$$m_k = \frac{F'(f)\lambda_k}{E_k'(G^k)}. \tag{40}$$

The significance of this for the marginal utility of income appears in the discussion in chapter vii.

TRANSFORMATION OF PRICES

Thus far I have considered transformations of the unknown variables, leaving the parameters, α, unchanged. We are able to evaluate changes of the new variables with respect to α by equation

---

[13] Can those who have a fondness for cardinal utility find support for their position by analogy to other disciplines, such as physics? In my opinion, no. Certain physical concepts, such as temperature, were for a long time treated by the physicists as ordinal magnitudes. Their behavior could be described by any one of many different indicators, whose relationship to each other was not linear. Finally it was deemed convenient to give conventional, privileged position to one such index, namely that based upon the properties of a "perfect gas." Nor is the use of the word "force" in physics books a good precedent for utility analysis; much of physics can dispense with the term, and in any case the things for which it stands, such as rate of change of momentum, or derivative of a potential function, can be given strict observational values, which are not invariant under monotonic transformation. Perhaps a better precedent for economics is that of statistics, where likelihood or its logarithm is used indifferently depending upon numerical convenience, and without metaphysical connotations.

(22). However, in the new coördinate system we are no longer able to state definite theorems regarding the signs of these changes.

In the old system we could definitely state that

$$\frac{\partial v_1}{\partial w_1} < 0, \tag{41}$$

but our new coefficient $(\partial \bar{v}_1 / \partial w_1)$ is a linear combination of terms of the form $(\partial v_i / \partial w_1)$, the sign of which can be anything.

And yet, since there was nothing privileged about the first coördinate system, it is manifest that there must be somewhere in the new coördinate system theorems no less definite than in the old. As we shall see, this "hunch" is correct. There are such theorems, and they are to be derived by considering the changes of our new variables with respect to specified *composite* changes in our parameters. That is, at the same time that we subject our equilibrium unknowns to a transformation, we subject our parameters to a transformation. The latter transformation is *not* the same as the former, but, as will be shown presently, the transformation of parameters is related in a definite manner to the transformation of quantities.

For the present purpose, it is not necessary to examine the problem in full generality. We may consider the important case of a firm maximizing profit as in the first section of this chapter. The case of an extremum under constraint, such as appears in production and utility theory, can be developed in a straightforward manner by the reader.

Let profits be written in the form

$$\pi(v\,;w) \;=\; R(v_1, \,\cdots, v_n) \;-\; \sum_{1}^{n} w_j v_j, \tag{42}$$

where the w's are parameters taken as given by the firm, and the v's are productive inputs. The v's and w's are just special cases of x's and p's, having specific reference to inputs.

If now we define new commodities $(\bar{v}_1, \,\cdots, \bar{v}_n)$, we ought to be able to find definite relations between their changes and changes in *their* prices, just as we have been able to do in the old coördinate system. But what are we to mean by the *prices of the new commodities*, $(\bar{w}_1, \,\cdots, \bar{w}_n)$. Only one answer is possible, as must be obvious to anyone who has worked with the price of a market basket of goods.

The price of the latter is reckoned as a weighted sum of the individual prices, where the weights are chosen so that the total *value* of the new commodity, equal to $\bar{w}\bar{v}$, is the same as the value of the component parts. This suggests a general rule to be followed. Throughout all transformations, value magnitudes are to be conserved; i.e.,

$$\sum_{1}^{n} w_k v_k = \sum_{1}^{n} \bar{w}_k \bar{v}_k \tag{43}$$

regardless of the transformation. For this is a value magnitude (dollars, pounds, etc.), which is not arbitrary once prices and quantities in any coördinate system are given. On the other hand, prices and quantities involve the particular reference system being used, and are thus arbitrary.

It is a familiar mathematical problem to subject two sets of variables to transformations, now assumed to be linear, so as to conserve their inner products as in equation (43).[14] Variables related in this way are called *contragredient variables*.[15]

If we subject the quantities v to the non-singular linear transformation

$$v = c\bar{v}, \qquad \bar{v} = c^{-1}v, \tag{44}$$

then

$$w'v = w'c\bar{v}. \tag{45}$$

If, and only if,

$$w' = \bar{w}'c^{-1}, \qquad \text{or} \qquad \bar{w} = c'w, \tag{46}$$

will (43) be realized. Thus, the related transformations of prices and quantities are

$$\begin{aligned} v &= c\bar{v}, & \bar{v} &= c^{-1}v, \\ w &= c^{-1'}\bar{w}, & \bar{w} &= c'w, \end{aligned} \tag{47}$$

where the transposition and inversion of the matrices is to be noted, along with the fact that the relationship between the two transformations is reflexive.

---

[14] This problem arises in higher geometry, in many branches of mathematics, and in multiple regression analysis where predicted dependent variables are to be independent of transformations of the predicting variables. As the latter undergo a linear transformation, the regression coefficients must be adjusted accordingly so as to leave the predictions unchanged.

[15] M. Bocher, *Introduction to Higher Algebra*, p. 108.

After transformation profits become

$$\pi(v \, ; w) \equiv \bar{\pi}(\bar{v} \, ; w) \equiv \bar{R}(\bar{v}) - \sum_1^n w_j \bar{v}_j. \tag{48}$$

In form this is the same as the original; consequently, it follows from the maximization conditions that everything that could be said about (dv/dw) can be said about $(d\bar{v}/d\bar{w})$. Thus,

$$\frac{d\bar{v}}{d\bar{w}} = (\bar{\pi}_{vv})^{-1} \tag{49}$$

is symmetrical and negative definite.

This might also have been deduced from the fact that

$$\frac{d\bar{v}}{d\bar{w}} \equiv \frac{d\bar{v}}{dv} \frac{dv}{dw} \frac{dw}{d\bar{w}}. \tag{50}$$

Substituting into this the equations of (47), we find

$$\frac{d\bar{v}}{d\bar{w}} = c^{-1} \frac{dv}{dw} c^{-1\prime}. \tag{51}$$

It is a classical mathematical fact that a matrix's properties of negative definiteness and symmetry are preserved after a congruent transformation of the above type.[16]

There are many equilibrium systems encountered in economics which do not arise from an extremum problem and which cannot be converted into this form. The various simplified versions of the Keynesian system provide but a first example of what is after all the general case. A second example is that of the *general equilibrium* equations of Walras. An intermediate case is a third example in which we assume consistent preference behavior, infinitesimal indifference loci at every point subject to certain generalized convexities, but without the assumption that "integrability" conditions are satisfied so that the "local" indifference planar elements can be "joined" together to form a family of indifference loci. Thus, our preference field may be characterized by a differential

---

[16] Mathematical Appendix A, p. 368. The first proof above can be used to derive a proof for this classical theorem. Also, if we set $c = [a]$, it is easy to show that the inverse of a definite matrix, a, is itself definite. This is related to the "inverse" profit function or "price potential" discussed in chapter iii, p. 56. The latter in turn seems related to the so-called Legendre transformation. See A. Wintner, *Analytical Foundations of Celestial Mechanics* (Oxford: 1941), chap. i.

expression, or Pfaffian, for which no integrating factor can be found. Only in the case of two goods can we always find an integrating factor which will lead to an "exact differential" which can be integrated.[17] The first of the above three examples is of no interest in this connection since we cannot pair a set of "price" variables as "conjugate" variables to "quantities."

Turning to the second example of *general* equilibrium, I should like to point out a grave difficulty with the Hicksian concept of stability of general exchange and production. In later chapters it is argued that stability is an essentially dynamic concept, and that the formal statical treatment of Hicks leads to conditions which are neither necessary nor sufficient from a dynamical point of view. Here it will be argued that the Hicks stability conditions are unsatisfactory from a purely statical point of view.

This may be illustrated by the somewhat simplified system of chapter v of *Value and Capital*, whose equilibrium is given by a set of equations of the form

$$x^k(p_1, \cdots, p_n) = 0. \quad (k = 1, \cdots, n) \tag{52}$$

To be *perfectly* stable the Jacobian, $[dx/dp]$, must have all its principal minors oscillate in sign. A matrix with this property I shall call *Hicksian*. To be imperfectly stable, we only impose the weaker condition that the $(n - 2)$ and $(n - 1)$ order minors be of the opposite sign.[18]

Since no particular definition of commodities or frame of reference is fundamental, if the Hicks conditions are fundamental, they must be invariant under transformations of price and quantity. A single example suffices to show that a matrix a which is Hicksian becomes under transformation $c^{-1}[dx/dp]c^{-1\prime}$, and this need not be Hicksian, nor even *imperfectly stable.*

[17] The problem of integrability goes back to the "classical" discussions of Irving Fisher and Pareto. In their "A Reconsideration of the Theory of Value," Parts I and II, *Economica*, XIV (1934), 52–76, 196–219, Hicks and Allen touch upon it, but not in an altogether satisfactory fashion. The most illuminating treatment is that of Georgescu-Roegen, "The Pure Theory of Consumer's Behavior," *Quarterly Journal of Economics*, L (1935–36), 545–593. See also the discussion of chap. v, p. 95 above, and P. Samuelson, "A Note on the Pure Theory of Consumer's Behavior," *Economica*, V (1938), 61–71, 353–354, for some unsolved problems in this connection.

[18] *Value and Capital*, pp. 67, 315.

Thus for

$$\frac{dx}{dp} = \begin{bmatrix} -1 & 10 \\ 0 & -1 \end{bmatrix}$$

$$c^{-1} = \begin{bmatrix} 1 & .2 \\ .2 & 1 \end{bmatrix} \tag{53}$$

we get

$$\frac{d\bar{x}}{d\bar{p}} = \begin{bmatrix} .96 & 9.6 \\ 0 & .96 \end{bmatrix} \tag{54}$$

which is neither perfectly stable nor imperfectly stable.

Of course, if $[dx/dp]$ had been symmetrical and definite (as when income effects can be neglected), this could not have happened; but then our system would have been convertible into a maximum problem.

I have shown elsewhere that convexity in non-integrable cases implies that the "symmetrical part" [19] of certain matrices be definite. This follows in consequence of the relation

$$\sum_{1}^{n} \Delta x_i \Delta p_i \leqq 0, \tag{55}$$

where the p's and the x's may or may not be under constraints. By going to the limit, we find that $[dx/dp + dx/dp']/2$ and $[dp/dx + dp/dx']/2$ must be non-positive.

It is not hard to show that this property, which we shall call *quasi-definiteness*, is invariant under redefinition of commodities, or under a general non-singular congruent transformation. Thus, let $[a + a']/2$ be negative definite. Then the quadratic form

$$h'ah \equiv h' \frac{[a + a']}{2} h + 0 \tag{56}$$

is negative definite. Conversely, if $h'ah$ is negative definite, then a is negative quasi-definite.

With the aid of a non-singular matrix b we subject a to a congruent transformation so that

$$\bar{a} = b'ab. \tag{57}$$

---

[19] Every matrix a can be decomposed into a symmetrical and an asymmetrical part. Thus,

$$a \equiv \frac{a + a'}{2} + \frac{a - a'}{2}.$$

Then

$$\bar{h}'\bar{a}\bar{h} = [\bar{h}'b']a[b\bar{h}] = h'ah, \tag{58}$$

and the extreme right-hand member is always negative, as must be the left-hand side. Thus, $[\bar{a} + \bar{a}']/2$ is negative definite, and $\bar{a}$ is negative *quasi-definite*.

The above analysis may be of interest even where there is integrability. If income effects cannot be neglected, the Jacobians of general exchange equilibrium need not be symmetrical. However, if the income effects are symmetrical and definite, or if their symmetrical parts are definite, or if their symmetrical parts are not so lacking in definiteness as to outweigh the definiteness of the substitution effect, then the Jacobians will be quasi-definite. Not only is this property preserved under transformation, but it is possible to establish the Theorem: *If a is quasi-definite, it is necessarily Hicksian, but not conversely.*

This important theorem can be proved in a variety of ways. One is to write each principal minor of a in a Taylor's expansion around $[a + a']/2$ so that the skew elements $(a_{ij} - a_{ji})/2$ appear in a power series. Then it can be shown that all of these elements enter in even powers so that the complete a matrix is "more Hicksian" than its symmetrical part. This confirms my previous remark that asymmetry, *per se*, makes for greater rather than less stability. The real significance of quasi-definiteness can only become apparent from the dynamical discussions of stability in later chapters.

Demand for a Group of Commodities

Value and Capital will take its place in history along with the classic works of Cournot, Walras, Pareto, and Marshall. Like the latter, Hicks has succeeded in keeping formidable mathematical analysis below the surface of things and locked up in appendices, thereby securing for his work a much wider audience than would otherwise be possible. This *tour de force* was made possible in considerable degree by the repeated use of the already mentioned theorem relating to the demand for a group of commodities when their prices all change in the same proportion. We are now in a position to derive this theorem rigorously in a more general form.

When a group of prices, say $(p_1, \cdots, p_r)$, all move together, it is natural to define a new commodity, $\bar{x}_1$, by the relation

$$\bar{x}_1 = p_1x_1 + p_2x_2 + \cdots + p_rx_r. \tag{59}$$

Strictly speaking, we are *not* thereby enabled to replace n commodities by $(n - r + 1)$ commodities. We are merely changing our frame of reference, and so we must lose no dimensions or degrees of freedom in the process. Our complete transformation of quantities can be given by

$$\bar{x} = \left[\begin{array}{c|cccccc} p_1 & p_2 & \cdots & p_r & 0 & \cdots & 0 \\ \hline 0 & & & I & & & \end{array} \right] x \tag{60}$$

Here we have simply defined all commodities but one to be identically the same as before; [20] the first commodity has been replaced by the new composite commodity. The contravariant price variable must then satisfy the equation

$$\bar{p} = \left[\begin{array}{c|ccc} \dfrac{1}{p_1} & 0 & \cdots & 0 \\ -\dfrac{p_2}{p_1} & & & \\ \cdot & & & \\ \cdot & & & \\ -\dfrac{p_r}{p_1} & & I & \\ 0 & & & \\ \cdot & & & \\ \cdot & & & \\ \cdot & & & \\ 0 & & & \end{array} \right] p \tag{61}$$

so as to leave $\sum px = \sum \bar{p}\bar{x}$. Even though $(n - 1)$ commodities are the same as before, their prices must have changed. This will not seem strange if it is remembered that a price is *not* a property of a good itself independently of the frame of reference involved. In fact, it is quite possible for either prices or quantities to become negative, although $\sum px$ will conserve its original sign.

Now if we change prices $(p_1, \cdots, p_r)$ in the same proportion, λ, holding constant $(p_{r+1}, \cdots, p_n)$, it can be shown by explicit differ-

[20] This is only one of an infinite number of possible transformations which will serve the present purpose.

entiation, $d\bar{p}/d\lambda$, that in the new price-quantity coördinates only the $\bar{p}_1$ is changed with all other $\bar{p}$'s remaining constant. Consequently, if this price changes, and if income is changed in such a way as to keep utility constant, then

$$\frac{d\bar{x}_1}{d\bar{p}_1} = \bar{K}_{11} < 0. \tag{62}$$

Also

$$\bar{K}_{11}\bar{K}_{22} - \bar{K}_{12}^2 > 0, \quad \text{etc.}, \tag{63}$$

so that all of the properties of the demand functions given in the previous chapter are satisfied.

Thus, the demand for a group whose relative prices are unchanged satisfies the same inequalities as in the case of a single good.

This is the fundamental Hicksian theorem.[21] It can easily be broadened so that we may work with $s(\leqq n)$ composite goods. Their substitution terms form a negative definite quadratic form.

This is a very useful theorem. It states that any group of commodities whose relative prices remain unchanged can be lumped together into a single commodity, and that indifference curves in fewer dimensions can be constructed which will have all the usual properties of indifference curves. Thus, all goods but one can be lumped into one commodity which Hicks calls "money," and then concave indifference curves can be drawn between the good in question and "money." [22]

It would seem that this involves rather a strained use of the term "money," and one almost certain to lead to confusion.[23] Very properly when Hicks later comes to discuss monetary matters, he rejects this earlier notion.

[21] Proved in his Mathematical Appendix, pp. 311–312, as a consequence of his sixth rule relating to substitution terms. All six of these rules are contained in the statement $h'[X_{ij}]h$ is non-positive definite quadratic form of rank $(n-1)$, which vanishes for values of h proportional to prices, this being an immediate consequence of the primary conditions of equilibrium and the secondary conditions guaranteeing an extremum under constraint.

[22] *Value and Capital*, p. 33, *passim*, diagram on p. 39. Also see A. G. Hart, "Peculiarities of Indifference Maps Involving Money," *Review of Economic Studies*, VIII (1941), 126–128.

[23] Such an instance is provided by a writer who interprets Hicks literally and confusedly attempts to throw light on the "inflationary gap" by means of an indifference diagram in which money is taken as a catchall for all but one commodity. M. W. Reder, "Welfare Economics and Rationing," *Quarterly Journal of Economics*, vol. LVII (1942).

The General Problem of Composite or Aggregate Commodities

Any economic system when viewed carefully will be found to consist of an almost uncountably large number of variables. It is almost a necessity if advances in analysis are to be made to simplify matters artificially so as to reduce the number of variables which are to be handled. This is done in a number of different ways. Some authors retreat to a one or two commodity world in order to derive more precise results; the penalty for this lies in the difficulty in establishing the relation between the simplified construct and complex reality. This, however, is at least an honest procedure. Other writers wish to have their cake and eat it too: to work with only a few variables and at the same time retain an air of realism and versimilitude.

Here too a variety of artful dodges are open to the investigator. (1) He may hold other things equal. (2) He may concentrate on a representative firm or family, each of whom is doing about what all are doing. (3) Or he may work with certain aggregate, composite magnitudes, such as bales of output, "socially necessary" labor, "wage units," cost of living, real national output, etc.

It is the third device which is of interest here. There is nothing intrinsically reprehensible in working with such aggregate concepts. On the contrary, abstraction from complexity is a necessary thought process. And in any case the most general equilibrium set up must necessarily stop short of the full total of all possible economic variables. But it is important to realize the limitations of these aggregates and to analyze the nature of their construction.

Broadly speaking, we replace a number of variables by a single variable under two diametrically opposite conditions. In the first, the variables have each the same effect (except possibly for scale differences which disappear upon redefinition) upon all of the economic functions under discussion. In this case, they can be summed and treated as one. Thus, we might define as the same commodities all goods which have exactly the same influence on consumption preference fields and production functions, which are so to speak infinitely substitutable. In practice rigid adherence to perfect substitutability might lead to the unmanageable result that no two things are quite the same. Consequently, goods which do not significantly (for the purpose at hand) differ are treated as identical.

Actually the above case of substitutability is but one example of the more general mathematical theorem whereby the identical vanishing of a Jacobian, or of all of its minors of a given order, implies that there exists functional relationships between sets of the variables, so that many may be dropped out of the picture completely. It is clear from the implicit function theory that such simplifications are possible only in the case where the original system was indeterminate.[24] This may or may not be a matter of concern. What if the variables which are extraneous cannot be given determinate values by the system of equations which define equilibrium? The *indeterminate* variables may be a matter of *indifference* to the economist. Thus, take any determinate system of economic goods. Let each unit of one type of good be marked with an invisible serial number, and now let us ask how many odd numbered units will be bought by a given consumer. Clearly the answer is indeterminate, but also of no possible interest. If consumers did have preferences as between different serial numbers, then the indifference schedules would be affected by this fact, and additional equations would be available to determine the final allocation. And notice that even in the case of complete indifference the final allocation is not really indeterminate on any particular occasion. It is just that the determining factors, which are taken as due to "chance" by the economist, would be of a different character.

Unlike the first condition under which variables are lumped together because they are infinitely substitutable, at the other extreme we combine variables which bear an invariant, "perfectly joint" relationship to each other. A notable example is provided by the classical "dose" of labor and capital applied to land. Here, too, the economist customarily relaxes the rigid requirement of perfect collinearity in favor of an approximate condition. Thus, the most primitive justification for a price level construct is provided by the indisputable fact that prices do generally rise and fall in about the same proportions.

---

[24] This must be qualified. Our original equilibrium equations may be imbedded in a still wider set of equations so that the total is determinate, but the original subset taken by itself is not.

Geometrically this differs from the first case in which indifference curves or iso-quants are straight lines. Here the contours are broken lines meeting at right angles in such a way that the goods or factors will by obvious choice be combined together in the given proportions almost regardless of price ratios. Unlike the Hicksian bundle of goods the physical composition is the same regardless of relative prices.

Of all composite magnitudes perhaps the most interesting to the theorist is that of an index of the cost of living, or of an index of consumption output. Such an index is designed to meet certain special requirements and need not be satisfactory for other purposes. In particular, it need not represent the *desideratum* from the standpoint of the questions which Jevons and other pioneers in the use of index numbers sought to answer. Yet the theory of these indices is of some interest for its own sake and because in the course of investigation of these index numbers economists inadvertently stumbled upon certain ordinal relationships which are basic to welfare economics and to consistent consumer's behavior.

THE ECONOMIC THEORY OF INDEX NUMBERS

Economists such as Jevons, Edgeworth, Marshall, Allyn Young, Warren Persons, Irving Fisher, Edwin Frickey, and others have made contributions to what may be called the statistical theory of index numbers. But what has come to be called the economic theory of index numbers is concerned with quite distinct matters. To this theory many economists have made contributions. A partial list would include the names of Wicksell, Konus, Bortkiewicz, Bowley, Haberler, Pigou, Keynes, Staehle, Leontief, Allen, Lerner, Frisch, and Wald.[25]

With the exception of Leontief all of these writers are unduly preoccupied with the problem of the *price* index number, instead of being occupied with the more fundamental question to which it is only a partial, and somewhat arbitrary, answer. *The fundamental problem upon which all the analysis rests is that of determining merely from price and quantity data which of two situations is higher up on*

---

[25] Reference may be made to the survey article by R. Frisch, "Annual Survey of General Economic Theory; The Problems of Index Numbers," *Econometrica*, IV (1936), 1–38; also to the article by W. Leontief in the same issue. The early volumes of the *Review of Economic Studies* may be consulted for other discussions.

an individual's preference scale. This problem admits of a partial answer if certain rigid assumptions are fulfilled.

It is assumed that there is only one individual, whose tastes do not change in the period under consideration; or if there are more than one, that their tastes are identical. It is not necessary to assume that the regime of commodities is the same in the two situations provided we follow the convention of setting at infinity the price of any good which is unavailable. At whatever the prices named, the individual is presumed to buy as many or as few of the goods as he wishes. This rules out such phenomena as rationing or monopsony. Ordinarily, a comparison is made between two situations which differ in time, but we might just as well compare two situations different in any respect, as in the case of comparisons in the cost of living between two regions.

Our fundamental data consist of prices and commodities, including productive services which can be treated as negative commodities, in the two situations, represented respectively by (P^a, X^a) and (P^b, X^b), where these are shorthand notations for the prices and quantities of n goods. Of course, if we know completely the individual's whole preference field, we may simply insert into it the two amounts of commodities and read off which is the better, or whether they are indifferent. Since we do not know the field, our problem is to go as far as we can on what we do know.

If for the moment we restrict ourselves to the quantity data, we ordinarily cannot say which of the two situations is the better. However, in the exceptional circumstance in which one of the situations contains more of some of the goods than the other, and not less of any of the other goods, then it is clear which is the better. Taking situation A as our reference point, and thinking of the simpler two-dimensional case, we can definitely divide up the whole of the commodity space into four regions with respect to X^a by letting two perpendicular horizontal and vertical lines (not shown in the figure) intersect at this point. Treating this as the origin, we can definitely classify all points in the northeast quadrant as better than X^a, and all points in the southwest quadrant as definitely worse. We are left then with ignorance concerning the interior points of the other two quadrants. In these more of one commodity has been acquired at the expense of less of another, and until we have further information concerning the preference field this is as far as we can go.

But it should be possible to utilize our price information. If the individual is supposed .to be maximizing his ordinal preference field subject to the given budget relation, we may be sure that the point X^a is better (or not worse) than any point between the budget

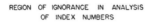

REGION OF IGNORANCE IN ANALYSIS
OF INDEX NUMBERS

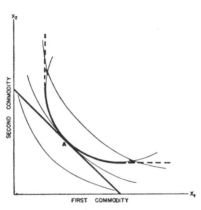

FIGURE 1

locus and the axes. For all such points were available to the individual in the initial situation, and he nevertheless preferred to select X^a. It follows that for all such points

$$U(X) \leqq U(X^a). \tag{67}$$

Thus, we have narrowed down the region of our ignorance, but not completely.

It will be noted that the two situations have not been treated symmetrically, A always being the reference point. It might well happen that X^a lay inside the budget line of the point X^b. Assuming for the moment that knowledge of the complete preference field were available, for what values of X^b would this be possible? Applying the requirement that X^a must cost less than X^b at the prices, P^b, the boundary of this region will be given by the equality

$$\sum P^b X^a = \sum P^b X^b. \tag{68}$$

Geometrically, this locus is the result of swinging the budget line through the point X^a, and determining for each position the point where it reaches the highest indifference curve, to which it is clearly tangent. If we connect all such points, we have a familiar offer curve. All points above this offer curve, are definitely better than X^a, in the same sense that all points under the budget line of X^a are definitely inferior to X^a. (It is to be emphasized that a knowledge of two points does not give us this locus in the way that it gives all the previous boundaries. Nevertheless, given two such points, it would always be possible to decide just where X^b was with respect to X^a.)

We have now narrowed our ignorance down still further. Actually this is as far as we can go on the basis of the given data. Note that the old boundaries of our ignorance derived from the utilization of quantity data alone have been made obsolete by the additional light furnished by the auxiliary price information.

We have gone a long way, but there is still left a definite area of darkness—the space between the two heavy lines. I should like to state as strongly as possible that this final indeterminacy is intrinsic and inherent. No amount of ingenuity can remove it, grounded as it is in the fundamental convexity properties of the indifference field, or more accurately in the consistency behavior of the individual. It is important to prove this rigorously, for peculiarly in the literature of index numbers is an attempt made to search for limits within which the truth must lie without at the same time investigating whether or not these are the *best possible* limits. Moreover, the limits themselves are sometimes derived under special approximations, such as the neglect of "squares of small quantities," etc.

To see that these are indeed the best possible limits under the circumstances, let us suppose that someone proposes narrower limits. Since our preference field is arbitrary except possibly for certain curvature properties, we can draw the true indifference curve through X^a so as to contradict any more definite result. If the proposer claims that a given point in the area of darkness is worse than X^a, we can pass the indifference curve below that point but above the correct lower boundary in such a way as to make this statement wrong. Similarly, the opposite statement can be shown not to hold universally. (It is of course understood that "we" do not actually change the indifference field of the economic unit under observation; but "we" can find a consistent field for which the given result holds.)   Where the offer curves bend back, we are able from quantity considerations alone to extend our boundaries along the dotted lines indicated in the figure.

For well-behaved indifference fields with the proper continuous derivatives, the offer curve which gives the upper boundary of the area of darkness will be tangential to the indifference curve going through X^a and to the lower budget boundary through X^a.   Even if there is a corner in the indifference curve at X^a, there must be generalized tangency in the sense of touching from above without crossing.   One might be tempted to say that the area of indeterminacy narrows down to a point in the vicinity of X^a, but nothing is gained thereby.   Nevertheless, the mathematician is tempted to consider Taylor's expansions in the neighborhood of the X^a point and to neglect terms of higher order.   Perhaps there is even some empirical statistical usefulness in the handling of budgetary data to be found in this practice, which has been associated with the names of Bowley and Wald.

But from a fundamental viewpoint there is no getting around the fact that for any finite move, *however small*, there remains a region of ignorance; this region may narrow down as the size of the movement decreases, but it never vanishes, except for the trivial case of a vanishing movement.[26]   Thus, there is nothing to be gained for the present purpose from following the practice of Divisia [27] in working with differentials or infinitesimals.   The fact that these avoid difficulties connected with the time reversal and factoral reversal is not an indication of their superiority, but of the fact that they sidestep the intrinsic difficulties of the subject matter.

By the examination of value sums we can sometimes, but not always, state definitely whether one situation is worse than another. But we can *never* by these means state that two situations are equally desirable.   In fact, as will become evident from later dis-

[26] It may be worth mentioning that even a knowledge of the curvature of the indifference curve at X^a will not enable us to narrow down our region of ignorance.   It will enable us to assert with confidence that the indifference curve will approach arbitrarily near to the osculating circle, but the departures for any finite small movement may be of either sign and of any magnitude.

[27] F. Divisia, *Economique Rationnelle* (Paris: 1928).

cussion, knowledge of prices and quantities on a finite number of points will not permit us to determine the equality of two points; but in the limit as the number of points becomes infinite we can in fortunate circumstances determine points of indifference.

This result may be approached by a consideration of the additional information which a third point will yield. We now have three pairs of points, and it may turn out that any two of them when put to the test of our computed value sums gives a definite answer. In that case each pair can be considered by itself without regard to the third point. Of course, from the discussion of chapter v it will be clear that a consistent ordinal preference field can never give contradictory testimony whereby point A is better than B, which is better than C, and at the same time the latter is better than A. For the relations of ordinal utility are transitive.

But the relations of better or worse as revealed by the value sums are not transitive; that is why I have elsewhere proposed a new notation to represent "revealed" preference in this special sense. Thus, if our value sums give a definite result so that

$$\sum P^a X^b \leqq \sum P^a X^a, \tag{69}$$

this fact may be represented by the symbol

$$X^b \otimes X^a. \tag{70}$$

Since

$$X^b \otimes X^a \quad \text{implies} \quad U(X^b) < U(X^a), \tag{71}$$

and this in turn implies

$$U(X^a) \nless U(X^b), \tag{72}$$

then to avoid a contradiction in logic, we must be able to state the theorem

$$X^b \otimes X^a \quad \text{implies} \quad X^a \oslash X^b.$$

But this is not the same thing as the meaningless assertion that

$$X^b \otimes X^a \quad \text{implies} \quad X^a \oslash X^b, \tag{73}$$

or the incorrect assertion that

$$X^b \otimes X^a \quad \text{and} \quad X^c \otimes X^b \quad \text{implies} \quad X^c \otimes X^a. \tag{74}$$

The most that can be stated under the above hypothesis is that

$$X^a \oslash X^c. \tag{75}$$

This is much weaker than transitivity. An additional indication that the algebra of revealed preference is quite distinct from that of cardinal or ordinal numbers is the fact that equality is not defined; consequently, two points cannot be placed in one of the three categories: A worse than B, or B worse than A, or the two equally good. All we can say is: either A is revealed to be worse than B, or B is revealed to be worse than A, or there is no indication one way or another. These are mutually exclusive categories only if a consistent preference field is postulated.

It is precisely because of this lack of transitivity that knowledge of a third point may add knowledge to a comparison between two given points. Our value sums may give no indication with respect to points X^a and X^c taken by themselves, but an intermediate point X^b may serve to indicate their true ordinal relationship to each other. We are in a position now to indicate just how much points X^b and X^c may narrow down our ignorance in relationship to X^a.

If the two additional points both lie in our old area of darkness, we are no better off than before. But if X^b lies in the upper region of certainty with respect to X^a, and X^c lies in the upper region of certainty with respect to X^b, then even though X^c lies in the X^a's region of uncertainty, it can still be definitely said to be better than X^a. Therefore, we have narrowed down our area of darkness. How much can this area be reduced in the most favorable case?

From the geometry of the problem it can be shown that X^b must lie on X^a's offer curve for the best results. We then proceed to draw the offer curve through X^b. This will cross the old one and thereby narrow our region of ignorance, since every point above the new offer curve is definitely better than X^a. If now we let X^b take each and every position on the old offer curve, the process can be duplicated as many times as we wish, giving us a one parameter family of new offer curves. The lower envelope to this family of curves gives us our new upper boundary of uncertainty.

In the same way, we can secure a best lower boundary by letting X^b travel along the original budget line, generating through each such point a new budget line, or a one parameter family of such lines in all. The upper envelope of this family of lines is our new lower boundary. Our new boundaries must of necessity lie within the old ones, but there is still left an area of darkness.

If a fourth point is added, we may narrow our ignorance still further; similarly with a fifth point. It is intuitively clear that the boundaries will never meet for any finite number of points; but in the limit as the number of points becomes infinite, the upper and lower boundaries approach a common limit, which is of course the indifference curve through X^a. Points along this curve, and only such points, can never find their place in a finite chain of points which serve to relate them unambiguously to the initial situation. Thus, with a single dimensional infinity of points any indifference curve may be traced out. With a two-dimensional infinity of points, the whole indifference field can be determined. In fact, with this much knowledge we may dispense completely with revealed preference, and instead "integrate" completely our elements of slope at each point into a one parameter family of indifference curves.

The above discussion is concerned with the narrowing of our field of ignorance under the best circumstances. In actual practice we shall not necessarily do nearly so well. An instance is provided by the frequently met case in which we know a complete budget line (expenditure path, income consumption curve, etc.) giving the behavior of changes in all of the commodities with changes in money income but with unchanged prices. Such a situation is provided by observations of the behavior of more or less similar people, all confronted with the same prices but differing with respect to total expenditure.

Not only is this of considerable statistical importance, but it is of special relevance in connection with the usual economic theory of index numbers, where a comparison is made between two price situations, rather than between two particular price-commodity situations. By applying our previous analysis it will be seen that the knowledge of an infinite number of points along two budget lines will not be sufficient to determine the whole preference field, or even a single indifference curve, or even be sufficient to enable us to match points of equivalent satisfaction on the two budget lines. If we select a given point on one line and through it draw a budget line and an offer curve, then these last two loci will split the other budget line into three parts. The lower part will consist of points all worse than the initial point, the upper part will consist of points all better than that point, while the intermediate part will constitute our area of indeterminacy.

Of course, the closer together are the two price situations, the smaller will be the indeterminacy. Therefore, we can narrow down our ignorance by a knowledge of many intermediate budget lines. In the limit, as the number of budget lines becomes infinite in such a way as to decrease indefinitely the distance between each, we shall approach the complete indifference field.

The value sums considered up until now have all had the disadvantage of being capable of yielding indeterminate results. We shall put up with this if need be, but first we must determine whether it is not possible to devise an index of quantity, computable only from the prices and amounts of all the commodities, which will be an unfailing indicator of ordinal utility. Can we not find a magic formula which will have these properties when applied to any preference field whatsoever, or at least to those of the proper convexity?

The answer is no. As yet no one has devised such a formula, and the following mathematical reasoning shows why no one ever can, even if we permit more general functions than simple value sums. Any such general formula will from the nature of the problem be a function of quantities and prices in one or more (usually two) situations. Without loss of generality we may consider the prices and quantities of all but one of the situations as fixed, while the one situation represents an arbitrary variable point. In terms of its prices and quantities, (P, X), we must be able to construct a single-valued function Q, which is constant so long as the X points remain on the same indifference curve of the (unknown) preference field. Because this is to be a quantity index, it is clear that relative prices only can be important, and so we may express all prices in terms of the first good as numeraire. Then Q may be written as

$$Q = \theta \left(x_1, \cdots, x_n, \frac{p_2}{p_1}, \cdots, \frac{p_n}{p_1} \right). \tag{76}$$

For observable equilibrium quantities the ratios of prices are equal to marginal rates of substitution $({}^1R^2, \cdots, {}^1R^n)$, or to ratios of marginal utilities $(U_2/U_1, \cdots, U_n/U_1)$. Although the form of the relationship will change from preference field to preference field, and is in any case unknown to us, there will still nevertheless in each specific instance be a functional relationship between these ratios and quantities of goods. Therefore Q will be a uniquely determined function of the x's alone. In fact, since Q is constant along an indifference curve, it must itself be one cardinal index of utility; its partial derivatives with respect to each commodity (computed by adding to the direct effect of each x on Q all indirect effects via influence on price changes) can be interpreted as marginal utilities, whose ratios are equal to observable price ratios, etc.

In consequence of this last fact, equation (76) can be written in the form

$$\theta\left(x_1, \cdots, x_n, \frac{\partial Q}{\partial x_1}\bigg/\frac{\partial Q}{\partial x_2}, \cdots, \frac{\partial Q}{\partial x_1}\bigg/\frac{\partial Q}{\partial x_n}\right) - Q \equiv 0. \qquad (77)$$

This identity is a first order partial differential equation which the preference field must satisfy, and only a limited small subset of all preference fields will do so. Consequently we have proved the impossibility of finding a magic formula to serve as a quantity indicator in the general case of a consistent ordinal preference field.

In actual fact it is customary to restrict the form of a quantity index still further, to require that it be a homogeneous function of the first order in the component quantities, etc. This restricts the range of applicability still further, to preference fields possessing expenditure proportionality, etc.

For any particular θ it may be a problem of some mathematical difficulty to determine the exact restriction on the preference field. But where θ represents the Laspeyre quantity index, thought of as a function of the quantity components of the second point, with base point fixed, it will be immediately seen that the only possible preference field for which it is exact is that of a family of parallel straight line indifference curves. Of course, this is almost a *reducto ad absurdum*, since convexity is denied, and since all relative prices (of goods which are bought) cannot vary.

The "ideal index number" is one of the most popular index numbers. It is the geometric mean between Laspeyre's and Paasche's index numbers. A. Konus and S. Buscheguennce,[28] as well as S. Alexander (in an unpublished Harvard paper), have shown that it is exact only for certain hyperbolic indifference curves. This theorem may be derived by solving explicitly the

[28] See the reference in H. Schultz, "A Misunderstanding in Index-Number Theory," *Econometrica*, VII (1939), 8.

implied differential equation. Similar results can be derived for other "approximate" formulae which have been suggested.

As a result of the analysis of this section, the conclusion may be ventured that the important economic content of index number theory resides in the fact that it attempts to utilize limited price and quantity data to infer ordinal preference comparisons. The above formulation seems best designed to reveal this essential content, and to show the intrinsic limitations necessarily involved. In the next section the same analysis is shown to be useful in connection with the more commonly met formulation of the index number problem.

PRESENT FORMULATIONS OF INDEX NUMBERS

We are now in a position to apply our tools of analysis to the more familiar branch of index numbers. First, we consider price of living comparisons between two different price situations. The price of living index number in going from the situation (X^a) to (X^b) is familiarly defined as the ratio of the cost of the cheapest bundle of goods at the prices of the second situation which will yield satisfaction equivalent to that of the initial situation, to the cost of the initial bundle at the initial prices.

We assume as known (say from empirical studies on "identical" individuals with varying incomes) the price expansion paths in two price situations, (P^a) and (P^b). These are defined by the following sets of parametric equations:

$$x_i = h_i(p_1{}^a, \cdots, p_n{}^a, I), \qquad (i = 1, \cdots, n) \qquad (78)$$

$$x_i = h_i(p_1{}^b, \cdots, p_n{}^b, I). \qquad (i = 1, \cdots, n) \qquad (79)$$

Consider an initial situation (X^a) on the initial expansion path. The indifference locus corresponding to this point will intersect the second expansion path in a point called (X^{ab}) such that

$$U(X^{ab}) = U(X^a). \qquad (80)$$

An index number of the price of living is defined as follows:

$$I^{ab} = \frac{\sum P^b X^{ab}}{\sum P^a X^a}. \qquad (81)$$

Similarly,

$$I^{ba} = \frac{\sum P^a X^{ba}}{\sum P^b X^b}, \qquad (82)$$

where
$$U(X^{ba}) = U(X^b), \tag{83}$$

and (X^{ba}) lies on the "initial" expansion path.

These respective index numbers are not rigidly related; in general they are *not* reciprocals. Since we do not know the hypothetical preference field, (X^{ab}) is not known, and so our index number cannot be computed.

However, from the considerations indicated above we know that all of the points on the expansion path (b) fall into three classes with respect to (X^a):

$$1. \quad (X) \otimes (X^a) \qquad \sum P^a X \leqq \sum P^a X^a \tag{84}$$

$$2. \quad (X^a) \otimes (X) \qquad \sum P^b X^a \leqq \sum P^b X \tag{85}$$

$$3. \quad (X) \oplus (X^a) \qquad \sum P^a X > \sum P^a X^a \tag{86}$$
$$\quad\quad (X^a) \oplus (X) \qquad \sum P^b X^a > \sum P^b X.$$

In particular, consider the equality signs in (84) and (85) and we get the boundary points defined by the intersection of

$$\sum P^b X = \sum P^b X^a \tag{87}$$
and
$$x_i = h_i(p_1{}^b, \cdots, p_n{}^b, I). \qquad (i = 1, \cdots, n) \tag{88}$$

Call this point $({}^u X^{ab})$.

Consider the intersection of

$$\sum P^a X = \sum P^a X^a \tag{89}$$
and
$$x_i = h_i(p_1{}^b, \cdots, p_n{}^b, I). \qquad (i = 1, \cdots, n) \tag{90}$$

Call it $({}^l X^{ab})$. By definition

$$({}^l X^{ab}) \otimes (X^a) \otimes ({}^u X^{ab}). \tag{91}$$
Hence,
$$U({}^l X^{ab}) < U(X^a) < U({}^u X^{ab}), \tag{92}$$
or
$$U({}^l X^{ab}) < U(X^{ab}) < U({}^u X^{ab}). \tag{93}$$

Since along an expansion path the cost of a batch of goods and its "utility" are monotonically related, we have

$$\sum P^b \, {}^l X^{ab} < \sum P^b X^{ab} < \sum P^b \, {}^u X^{ab}. \tag{94}$$

Hence, dividing by the appropriate factor (if it does not vanish), we have

$$\frac{\sum P^b \, {}^l X^{ab}}{\sum P^a X^a} < \frac{\sum P^b X^{ab}}{\sum P^a X^a} < \frac{\sum P^b \, {}^u X^{ab}}{\sum P^a X^a}, \tag{95}$$

or

$$\frac{\sum P^b \, {}^l X^{ab}}{\sum P^a X^a} < I^{ab} < \frac{\sum P^b \, {}^u X^{ab}}{\sum P^a X^a}. \tag{96}$$

These are valid double limits for our index number computable under our specified assumptions. More directly from the definition of $({}^u X^{ab})$, we have

$$\sum P^b \, {}^u X^{ab} = \sum P^b X^a. \tag{97}$$

Hence, our double limits are

$$\frac{\sum P^b \, {}^l X^{ab}}{\sum P^a X^a} < I^{ab} < \frac{\sum P^b X^a}{\sum P^a X^a}. \tag{98}$$

By symmetry we have

$$\frac{\sum P^a \, {}^l X^{ba}}{\sum P^b X^b} < I^{ba} < \frac{\sum P^a X^b}{\sum P^b X^b}, \tag{99}$$

where $({}^l X^{ba})$ is symmetrically defined with respect to $({}^l X^{ab})$. Again, these four limits are not rigidly related, no pair being necessarily reciprocals. Furthermore, it follows from the analysis of the earlier sections that these are the best possible double limits under our hypothesis, and will never converge to equality for convex indifference curves.

It is clear that the two upper limits are determinable from price and quantity figures alone. The points $({}^l X^{ab})$ and $({}^l X^{ba})$, however, can be computed only if certain subsections of the respective expansion paths are empirically known. Dropping this assumption, we may ask the question as to what lower limits can be computed from price and quantity figures alone. This being a more difficult problem, the answer will in general be less satisfactory.

Recall that $({}^l X^{ab})$ was the intersection of the budget plane of (X^a) with the expansion path of the second price situation. Since we do not know the expansion path, we cannot compute $({}^l X^{ab})$. But if we restrict ourselves to positive quantities, it is always possible to find a point on the budget plane whose cost is less than $({}^l X^{ab})$, and which must *a fortiori* be a lower limit. Such a point is that point on the budget plane whose cost at the prices (P^b) furnishes a minimum with respect to *all* points on the budget plane.

Let us designate this point $(^\lambda X^{ab})$. It may be derived by minimizing

$$F = \sum_1^n p_i^b x_i \tag{100}$$

subject to

$$\sum_1^n p_i^a x_i = \sum_1^n p_i^a x_i^a. \tag{101}$$

This is a constrained minimum problem, and, since the equations are linear, the minimum is a restricted or boundary one, derived from the fact that no negative quantities are admissible. Actually, it is easily verified that the minimum quantity $(^\lambda X^{ab})$ is $(0, 0, \cdots, {}^\lambda x_m^{ab}, \cdots, 0, 0)$ where x_m is the good whose price ratio between the two situations is lowest, i.e., ,

$$\frac{p_m^b}{p_m^a} \leqq \frac{p_i^b}{p_i^a}. \tag{102}$$

$(^\lambda X^{ab})$ is easily computed since

$$^\lambda x_m^{ab} = \frac{\sum P^a X^a}{p_m^a}. \tag{103}$$

Hence this lower limit developed by Mr. Lerner is as follows:

$$\frac{\sum P^b {}^\lambda X^{ab}}{\sum P^a X^a} = \frac{p_m^b}{p_m^a} \frac{\sum P^a X^a}{\sum P^a X^a} = \frac{p_m^b}{p_m^a}. \tag{104}$$

By symmetry, p_l^a/p_l^b is a lower limit for I^{ba}, where

$$\frac{p_l^a}{p_l^b} \leqq \frac{p_i^a}{p_i^b}. \tag{105}$$

In particular cases other lower limits are possible. It is possible that our actually observed situation (X^b) is such that

$$(X^b) \ominus (X^a), \tag{106}$$

i.e.,

$$\sum P^a X^b \leqq \sum P^a X^a. \tag{107}$$

Recalling the definition of $(^l X^{ab})$, obviously

$$\sum P^a X^b \leqq \sum P^a \, {}^l X^{ab}$$

and (108)

$$\sum P^b X^b < \sum P^{b\ l} X^{ab},$$

and so in this case we have a lower limit as follows:

$$\frac{\sum P^b X^b}{\sum P^a X^a} < I^{ab}. \tag{109}$$

Note that this holds only if (106) is realized. On the other hand given

$$(X^a) \ominus (X^b), \tag{110}$$

we have

$$\frac{\sum P^a X^a}{\sum P^b X^b} < I^{ba}. \tag{111}$$

Except in the coincidental case where the equality sign holds, these limits will be worse than those deducible from the whole expansion path. They may be better or worse than the Lerner limits given in (104) depending upon the case selected. Note that it is impossible for

$$(X^a) \ominus (X^b)$$

simultaneously with

$$(X^b) \ominus (X^a).$$

Hence it is not possible to derive lower limits to both indexes simultaneously. In fact, given

$$(X^b) \oslash (X^a)$$

and

$$(X^a) \oslash (X^b),$$

it is impossible to compute either lower limit in this manner.

If we widen our assumptions as to initial information, still other limits are possible. Knowledge of a third point may be utilized by the methods of the previous section; as may also knowledge of any intermediate expansion paths. In fact, in the limit as all intermediate expansion paths are known, i.e., as we know the functions

$$x_i = h^i(p_1, \cdots, p_n, I), \qquad (i = 1, \cdots, n)$$

the indifference map itself may be solved for implicitly.[29]

It is possible to develop similar relationships between usual quantity indexes. Let us define our quantity index from the *a*th

---

[29] I do not discuss the effect of imposing the assumption of monotonic expansion paths, since there is no reason to rule out "inferior" goods.

situation to the bth as follows:

$$Q^{ab} = \frac{\sum P^b X^b}{\sum P^b X^{ab}} = \frac{\sum P^b X^b}{\sum P^a X^a} \frac{\sum P^a X^a}{\sum P^b X^{ab}} = \frac{I^b}{I^a I^{ab}} , \qquad (112)$$

i.e., this index is the ratio between the actual cost of the batch (X^b) to the cost of the cheapest bundle at (P^b) prices which would yield an equivalent satisfaction to that of (X^a).

Similarly,

$$Q^{ba} = \frac{\sum P^a X^a}{\sum P^a X^{ba}} = \frac{I^a}{I^b I^{ba}} , \qquad (113)$$

Obviously, if one situation is preferred to the other, the index number between them will be less than one, i.e.,

$$U(X^a) < U(X^b) \text{ implies } Q^{ba} < 1, \qquad (114)$$

and conversely. Likewise

$$U(X^a) < U(X^b) \text{ implies } Q^{ab} > 1. \qquad (115)$$

Hence,

$$Q^{ba} > 1 \text{ implies } Q^{ab} < 1, \qquad (116)$$

and

$$Q^{ab} > 1 \text{ implies } Q^{ba} < 1. \qquad (117)$$

More generally,

$$Q^{ab} \gtreqless 1 \text{ implies } Q^{ba} \lesseqgtr 1, \qquad (118)$$

where the inequalities are to be taken in the indicated order.

However,

$$Q^{ab} \neq \frac{1}{Q^{ba}} , \qquad (119)$$

except under special circumstances. The above relations are consequences of the concavity of the indifference loci.

Of course in the absence of knowledge of the preference field, it is impossible to compute these index numbers, since we do not know (X^{ab}) and (X^{ba}). From the last section we know that

$$\sum P^{b \, \lambda} X^{ab} \leqq \sum P^{b \, l} X^{ab} < \sum P^b X^{ab} < \sum P^{b \, u} X^{ab}. \qquad (120)$$

Hence,

$$\frac{\sum P^b X^b}{\sum P^{b \, \lambda} X^{ab}} \geqq \frac{\sum P^b X^b}{\sum P^{b \, l} X^{ab}} > Q^{ab} > \frac{\sum P^b X^b}{\sum P^{b \, u} X^{ab}} , \qquad (121)$$

or

$$\frac{\sum P^b X^b}{\sum P^b {}^\lambda X^{ab}} \geqq \frac{\sum P^b X^b}{\sum P^b {}^l X^{ab}} > Q^{ab} > \frac{\sum P^b X^b}{\sum P^b X^a}. \tag{122}$$

As before, $({}^l X^{ab})$ can be computed only if we know the expansion paths. From (103) we find

$$\frac{\sum P^b X^b}{\sum P^b {}^\lambda X^{ab}} = \frac{p_m{}^a}{p_m{}^b} \frac{\sum P^b X^b}{\sum P^a X^a}. \tag{123}$$

Therefore,

$$\frac{p_m{}^a}{p_m{}^b} \frac{\sum P^b X^b}{\sum P^a X^a} \geqq \frac{\sum P^b X^b}{\sum P^b {}^l X^{ab}} > Q^{ab} > \frac{\sum P^b X^b}{\sum P^b X^a} = \text{``Paasche''}. \tag{124}$$

Similarly,

$$\frac{p_l{}^b}{p_l{}^a} \frac{\sum P^a X^a}{\sum P^b X^b} \geqq \frac{\sum P^a X^a}{\sum P^a {}^l X^{ba}} > Q^{ba} > \frac{\sum P^a X^a}{\sum P^a X^b} = \frac{1}{\text{``Laspeyres''}};$$

As before, if we have

$$(X^b) \lessgtr (X^a),$$

or

$$(X^a) \lessgtr (X^b),$$

still other limits are possible.

Now it is only in the case where the "Paasche" index is greater than one or the "Laspeyres" index is less than one that it is possible to say which of the situations is better. But, and this is what makes this whole branch of theory a sterile exercise, it is always possible to determine this fact without any limits or without even introducing such index numbers. For our question is always answered, when it can be answered, by the previous analysis of "revealed" preference, and the introduction of quantity and price indexes is indirect, unnecessary, and misleading. It is indirect and unnecessary because it is a deduction from the previous simpler analysis. It is misleading because of the tendency to attach significance to the numerical value of the index computed.[30] There is not a single valid *general* theorem in the present field of index numbers which is not deducible from the analysis of the previous section.

Of course, in the case of *expenditure proportionality*, certain new invariances do emerge. (1) It is always possible to derive double

[30] See the penetrating remarks of W. Leontief, "Composite Commodities and the Problem of Index Numbers," *Econometrica*, vol. IV (1936).

limits; (2) The respective index numbers are reciprocals, i.e.,

$$Q^{ba}Q^{ab} = 1 = I^{ab}I^{ba}. \tag{125}$$

One last serious drawback to the present formulations of index number theory rests in the fact that these are expressed as ratios. If we admit productive factors as negative commodities, and for many purposes this greatly enlarges the generality of our analysis, denominators may vanish or change sign. Since all we wish is an algebraic comparison between value sums, it is unnecessary and undesirable to work with ratios. Instead the methods of the previous section are preferable.

Pure Theory of Choice under Rationing

Thus far in this chapter we have discussed the effects of general transformations of our dependent and independent variables. This led naturally into a study of composite commodities and of index numbers. At this point there is also suggested the interesting and important related problem of placing constraints upon the consumer in addition to that imposed by fixed total income. Of course, rationing involves such constraints.

The simplest kind of rationing is that in which the government specifies the maximum amount of a particular commodity that each individual can consume. Sugar provides a common example, being relatively homogeneous and universally in demand. Ordinarily in rationing the individual is subjected to an inequality. He must not consume more than a given amount, but he need not consume as much as that amount. Of course, if the rationing is to be of any use, it will be applied to situations in which for many individuals the allotted amount will actually be bought. Otherwise the law has no teeth, and individual behavior is left unchanged.

The single individual maximizes ordinal utility as before except that he is now subjected to additional constraints of the form

$$x_i \leqq b_i, \qquad x_j \leqq b_j, \qquad \cdots, \tag{126}$$

where the commodities i, j, $\cdots$ are given maximum individual quotas of respective amounts per unit time, b_i, b_j, $\cdots$. To present the conditions of equilibrium in these circumstances we must distinguish carefully between various possible cases. The simplest is that in which the rationing quotas are so small that each is effective.

In this case, the equality signs will hold in the above equation. Here we lose as many degrees of freedom as there are commodities effectively rationed. In terms of the *remaining* commodities our conditions of equilibrium are just as before since each partial differentiation assumed other commodities constant. However, overall consistency is maintained by the fact that we write down partial derivative conditions only for those commodities which are not frozen at given levels. Thus, for each equation added in (126) we drop one equation of the form

$$\varphi_i + \lambda p_i = 0, \qquad (127)$$

replacing the equality sign by the inequality "greater than." For only with respect to goods whose amounts can be voluntarily augmented will the marginal utility of their last dollar of expenditure be equated to the marginal utility of expenditure in all other lines. Goods which are arbitrarily limited at some quota have a marginal utility of expenditure which may and ordinarily will exceed that of the non-rationed goods.

So far, we have been discussing the case where all quotas are effective. If any particular one is not effective, then the inequality rather than the equality sign is relevant, and we may disregard completely the fact that it is rationed and treat it exactly as we would an unrationed commodity.

So much for the theory of single commodity rationing, a theory which is elementary and intuitively obvious. Before leaving it, however, one final point should be noted. The above analysis would suggest that the authorities could independently ration $(n - 1)$ commodities but not all n. For if all commodities but one are rationed, the amount of the last would seem to be effectively frozen by the budget equation, and therefore would not be subject to the control of the government. Actually, this is not the case. The budget equation itself is not, strictly speaking, an equality. It gives the maximum that total expenditure can attain, not the amount it must attain. The authorities *can* ration all n commodities even if this means that the individual cannot spend all his income.

However, this raises a problem of terminology. Cannot money itself be counted as a commodity? Secondly, when we speak of total expenditure, do we include as one of its components "saving" in the sense of expenditure on future goods? Upon reflection I think the reader will conclude that this is primarily a verbal problem, much aggravated by the customary loose and ambiguous usage of the concepts of "money" and numeraire.

Various conventions are open to us, any of which is satisfactory provided that it is adhered to consistently. We may include among our commodities goods of different periods of time, and we may assume certain expectations with respect to future prices. For the present purpose it is simpler to assume that total expenditure upon present commodities can differ from present income by the algebraic amount of saving without going into the problem of the form (cash, securities, etc.) that these savings take. If saving is determined by the usual preference calculus, certain implicit assumptions are made with respect to future incomes, prices, ordinal rates of time preference, etc.

If it wishes to, a powerful government can arbitrarily limit the consumption of all present goods, and at the same time permit only an arbitrarily small amount of the surplus of income to be carried over for future uses. Ordinarily, in connection with a rationing program the State does not so limit saving, relying instead upon a personal tax program to bring about this desired result. Further discussion of this point may therefore be deferred.

Single commodity rationing has certain shortcomings which give rise to a demand for some form of "point-rationing." Instead of limiting the amount of a single commodity, the individual is limited to a weighted sum of a number of commodities, the point-prices providing the relative weights. But such a weighted sum represents nothing more than a single commodity in a new transformed set of variables. It is for this reason that the general theory of rationing belongs in the present chapter on transformations and composite commodities.

It would lead us into the field of welfare economics if we were to discuss the criteria used in classifying commodities into groups and the determination of their point values. Suffice it to say that administrative considerations, criteria of substitutability on the consumption and production sides, all contribute to the decision as to which commodities shall fall in the same group, what the relative values of each shall be, how many groups there shall be, etc. Moreover, although this is not strictly necessary, each commodity is usually restricted to but one group so as to obviate the necessity of handling many kinds of tokens or stamps in making a given purchase.

In addition then to the dollar prices, $(p_1, \cdots, p_n)$, and money income, I, each consumer is confronted with r classes of point prices, $(p_1', \cdots, p_n'), (p_1'', \cdots, p_n''), \cdots, (p_1^r, \cdots, p_n^r)$, and fixed totals of expendable points per unit time, $(I', I'', \cdots, I^r)$. Each of the sets of point prices will have zeros for most commodities, and for a given commodity all but one point price will usually be zero.

This being the case, the consumer will maximize $U(x_1, \cdots, x_n)$ subject to the generalized budgetary constraints

$$\sum_1^n p_j x_j \leqq I, \qquad \sum_1^n p_j' x_j \leqq I', \qquad \cdots, \qquad \sum_1^n p_j^r x_j \leqq I^r. \quad (128)$$

For the moment the matrix $[p_j{}^k]$ will be assumed to be of rank $(r+1)$. There will result optimal amounts of each good for each specified complete set of point-prices and expenditure allotment. We may summarize this result by writing down the generalized demand schedule for each good, written as a function of all prices and points and all total incomes or expenditures. Thus,

$$x_i = h^i(p_1, \cdots, p_n; p_1', \cdots, p_n'; \cdots; p_1^r, \cdots, p_n^r; I, I', \cdots, I^r).$$
$$(i = 1, \cdots, n) \quad (129)$$

It is the purpose of the regulating authorities so to determine point prices and allotments as to result in "equitable" inter-individual amounts of consumption, appropriate total output, at appropriate dollar prices. In addition to such policy matters, the economist is interested in the purely positive problem of determining the properties of these demand functions implied by the ordinal maximization process.

For this purpose we must examine the maximum conditions of equilibrium. By the usual Lagrangean multiplier technique the first order conditions are easily seen to be

$$U_i + \lambda p_i + \lambda' p_i' + \cdots + \lambda^r p_i^r = 0, \qquad (i = 1, \cdots, n) \quad (130)$$

provided that all of the group allotments are "effective" as indicated by the presence of the equality signs in (128). If any particular group allotment is ineffective for the individual in question, its Lagrangean multiplier may be set equal to zero in the above equations.

In words: the consumer will purchase each good up to the point where its marginal utility is equal to a weighted average of its various dollar and point prices, the weights being the marginal utilities of the last dollar or group ration coupons.[31]

For a regular maximum our necessary and sufficient secondary conditions are contained in the statement that the Hessian of the utility function must represent the matrix of a quadratic form which is negative definite under the $(r + 1)$ linear constraints. This is equivalent to certain conditions on the matrix formed by bordering the Hessian with the matrix of the constraints, the transpose of the latter, and zeros. If we strike out rows and columns corresponding to each of $(n - r + 1)$ commodities in turn, the resulting $(n - r + 1)$ principal minors must oscillate in sign, the smallest one being negative, the next positive, etc. Thus let

$$\Delta_m = \begin{bmatrix} U_{ij} & p_i^{\ k} \\ p_j^{\ s} & 0 \end{bmatrix} \quad \begin{array}{l} (i, j = 1, \cdots, m) \\ (k, s = 0, \cdots, r) \\ [m = (n - r + 1), \cdots, n] \end{array} \tag{131}$$

Then

$$(-1)^m \Delta_m > 0. \tag{132}$$

As throughout this book, the fundamental observationally meaningful restrictions on observable prices and quantities emerge as consequences of these secondary extremum conditions. In this case such implications can most simply be stated after the concept of a compensated price change has been suitably generalized. At least since the time of Slutsky it has been customary to deal with a compound change in price and income, where the latter is varied along with the former so as to leave the individual on the same indifference curve.

When rationing enters the picture so that we have auxiliary constraints, the problem is made more complex. An increase in a

---

[31] This seems to have been pointed out in print for the first time by T. Scitovsky, "The Political Economy of Consumers' Rationing," *Review of Economic Statistics*, XXIV (1942), 114–124. Other theoretical aspects of rationing are discussed in H. P. Neisser, "Theoretical Aspects of Rationing," *Quarterly Journal of Economics*, LVII (1943), 378–397. Also see N. Kalecki, "General Rationing," *Oxford Bulletin of Statistics*, vol. III (1941).

given price, or in a given point price, will make the individual worse off. But he can be compensated for this in many different ways—by a change in money income, by a change in his point allotments of the same or of a different group, or by any combination of these. It is most useful for the present purpose to consider that special compensated change in the dollar or point price of a commodity in which the individual is kept just as well off as before by means of a simultaneous change in the same total expenditure allotment (dollar or particular group point allotment). Let the change in the ith good resulting from a change in the kth group point price of the jth good when compensated as above be written in the form $(\partial x_i/\partial p_j{}^k)_{\text{comp.}}$. Then regarded as an n by n matrix, with k a fixed number, this must be negative semi-definite of rank $(n - r + 1)$. Thus, the compensated change in a good with respect to one of its *own* point prices must always be negative; in addition, we have inequalities on certain cross product and inter-action terms. These are expressed completely by the statement that the smallest naturally ordered principal minor of the above matrix must be negative, the next positive, etc., and finally the $(n - r + 2)$th and all higher principal minors must vanish. The last part of this statement is equivalent to the obvious proposition that the demand functions are homogeneous of order zero in each set of point prices and expenditure.

If one wishes, off diagonal terms may be interpreted as generalized complementarity coefficients, and it may be left as an exercise to the reader to show that these obey the usual symmetry rules. In fact, the reader may easily show that the matrix of compensation terms is nothing more than the northwest partition of the inverse of the Δ_n matrix, after this submatrix has been premultiplied by the scalar $(-\lambda^k)$[32]

The interested reader may also develop for himself the generalized Le Chatelier-Braun principle introduced in chapter iii. In words, its economic significance may be summarized as follows: if in a given position of equilibrium a (compensated) change in price is made, the resulting change in amount demanded of that good will be greater if the individual is not subjected to the extra constraints of rationing than if he is subjected to such constraints;

[32] See chap. v, p. 103. Also see p. 378.

furthermore, the introduction of each new constraint will make demand still more inelastic.

The tendency for demand to become inelastic under rationing has a number of important implications for policy. In particular, it helps to explain why in a system which has already been subjected to numerous direct controls, fiscal measures aimed at sopping up superfluous income have effects which are of only secondary importance. To explore this further would involve us in considerations of effective demand outside the scope of the present discussion.

Most economists will not be interested in the somewhat artificial compensated change in point-price, but rather in the ordinary *ceteris paribus* change, in which other point-prices and expenditure are kept constant. It is easy to show by explicit differentiation of the equilibrium conditions, as well as from general considerations, that this may be split up into two parts: the compensated change and the income effect. Thus,

$$(\partial x_i/\partial p_j{}^k)_{\text{cet. par.}} = (\partial x_i/\partial p_j{}^k)_{\text{comp.}} - x_j(\partial x_i/\partial I^k). \qquad (133)$$

Except for ("generalized") *inferior* consumption goods, the second term will be positive; consequently, a change in a good resulting from an increase in its point price must be negative in all normal cases. But if we have generalized inferiority, we may (but need not) have a generalized Giffen's paradox, in which raising the point-price of a commodity causes more of it to be bought.

Our discussion of rationing may be brought to a close with a few comments on the special mathematical features which distinguish it from the general analytic case of any linear constraints. First, it is almost universally the custom to make all point prices positive, even though one could in theory imagine a case in which there were negative prices. (For example, ration tickets might be given to a consumer who will take certain redundant staples, etc.)

Second, the authorities often set ration point-prices proportional to dollar prices. A special case of this is provided by dollar expenditure control on various commodities or groups of commodities. An even more special case is that of over-all expenditure control, in which the individual is given a quota of dollar expenditure, ordinarily less in amount than his disposable income. If savings are *not* treated as one of the n commodities, this is equivalent to introducing linear constraints whose rank is less than

$(r + 1)$; consequently the equations of (128) are inconsistent if equality signs are used.   We must then have recourse to inequalities; of course, in this case the dollar budget equation must be relaxed in favor of the new quota allotment.[33]   In rare cases where ration tickets or quotas are over-generous, the auxiliary constraint will become an inequality and the rationing will be ineffective.

A different mathematical problem arises if the consumer can pay for a commodity by giving up a certain number of ration stamps of one kind *or* by giving up some of another.   Depending upon the relative prices and scarcities of the different stamps, he will ordinarily choose to spend one rather than the other in a fashion reminiscent of Gresham's Law.   If he has similar options with respect to many commodities but at different relative ratios, he will spend a given kind of stamp on those commodities in which it is relatively advantageous in a manner formally identical with the classical theory of comparative advantage as applied to the determination of which of many commodities will be exported and which will be imported.

The above case merges into that in which the different kinds of stamps can be converted into each other at rates determined on a black or white market, or by the government.   Unless the government were explicitly to ban such transactions, there would inevitably arise trade in the different ration groups and money. Arbitrage would create ruling market ratios of exchange which any individual as a small consumer could not appreciably affect.   Once the individual is confronted with given rates at which he can buy or sell each type of ration points, the problem is no longer one of

[33] Since in practice a commodity is not given more than one ration point price, "degeneracy" cannot arise in any other way.   If the authorities should require multiple point prices for a given commodity, unless care is taken the consumer may be put into the position of not being able to spend all his points.   This difficulty may arise in two different ways: through true degeneracy and inconsistency in the auxiliary constraints, or from the fact that the admissible solutions of the linear equations do not yield positive amounts of all commodities.   When this is the case, the first order conditions of equilibrium given in (130) are modified, but not as before by setting certain of the Lagrangean multipliers equal to zero, but rather by replacing certain equality signs by greater than signs.   Any commodity which is *not* bought will have a marginal utility *less* than the above specified weighted average of point prices.   The problems raised in this footnote are similar to those discussed by Schlesinger, Wald, v. Neuman, Neisser, and v. Stackelberg in connection with the consistency and independence of the equations of the Walrasian theory of production in its simplest constant coefficient form.

many auxiliary constraints. Thus, if orange stamps can be bought or sold for five cents apiece, and if a commodity costs twenty-five cents and two orange stamps, it can simply be regarded as a commodity which costs thirty-five cents. The consumer simply reverts back to the standard type of budget equation, modified only by the fact that his money income may be increased or decreased by the need to buy or sell ration points; or, what is simply another way of saying the same thing, the individual has higher income and is confronted by a new higher set of prices. If the dollar values of the first, second, $\cdots$, and rth ration points are $(b', b'', \cdots, b^r)$, the new budget equation becomes

$$\sum_1^n (p_i + \sum_1^r b^k p_i{}^k)x_i = I + \sum_1^r b^k I^k. \tag{134}$$

Actually, from a welfare point of view it can be shown that the free interchange of different kinds of stamps, among themselves and against money, is in a certain sense optimal. In fact, it is an indirect way of permitting individuals to exchange goods so long as the exchange is mutually advantageous. These last two sentences must be qualified. They must not be taken to mean that every individual will be better off if coupons or goods can be interchanged. Thus, if the rich buy redundant ration coupons from the poor to the mutual advantage of both, their expenditure by the rich will cause an increase in the point price of the scarce rationed goods in question to the disadvantage of the middle classes.

Nevertheless, it can be shown that free interchange is optimal in the sense that its introduction accompanied by *appropriate* modifications in the point allocations to every individual could lead to an improvement for everybody. In the above example, the middle classes *could* be bribed into acquiescence, and there would still be a margin of advantage left for rich and poor. I do not imply by this that the middle classes *should* receive such a bribe since that would suggest a belief in the perfection of the previous *status quo*. Nor should it be thought that anything said here is an argument for making coupons interchangeable, since there might very well be in actual fact very grave difficulties in the way of devising a method of point allocation which would recognize the harm done to particular individuals.

CHAPTER VII

SOME SPECIAL ASPECTS OF THE THEORY OF CONSUMER'S BEHAVIOR

CHAPTER V exhausts the content of utility analysis in its most general form, involving only an ordinal preference field. There remains in the literature a great number of discussions of particular problems which involve special and extra assumptions. In order to present a fairly complete account of the present status of the theory I propose to examine some of these carefully to show their empirical meaning. This involves a break in the unity of exposition since each special assumption has often been made independently of all others. There is no choice but to go through the list with no regard for continuity. Among the topics to be discussed will be the cardinal measure of utility, independence of utilities and measures of complementarity, and constancy of the marginal utility of money.

It is clear that every assumption either places restrictions upon our empirical data or is *meaningless*. A price must be paid for any simplifications introduced into our basic hypotheses. This price is the limiting of the field of applicability and relevance of the theory because of the extra empirical restrictions to be imposed on the data. Many writers do not appear to be aware of this; in any case few have indicated the costliness of their assumptions or have adduced any evidence to support a presumption of their admissibility.

There is a further serious difficulty. Despite the fact that developments in this field are not recent, and that mathematical methods of exposition have been employed, ambiguity still permeates the contentions of many writers. This ambiguity can go unnoticed precisely because there has been so little interest in the operational significance of these assumptions. To put the matter somewhat harshly, ambiguously defined assumptions are used to give a semblance of deriving theorems which are themselves inconclusive.

A recurring source of difficulty in this connection which goes back as far as Marshall is the practice of introducing certain mathematical relations as alleged "approximations." These are presented as being valid in the neighborhood of a point of equilibrium. Even if such a relationship be admissible (as in the case of Taylor's expansion), precisely because it can be applied to any and all properly continuous functions it is devoid of meaningful significance. Moreover, in common usage the restrictions which are introduced as allegedly holding only for a restricted neighborhood of equilibrium are in fact used to deduce results which follow only from an entirely different interpretation of these assumptions. We shall have occasion to enter more deeply into these matters at later points in the discussion.

THE CARDINAL MEASURE OF UTILITY

We have seen from chapter v that all empirical market behavior is independent of the choice of a particular index of utility, or indeed of the choice of any measure of utility at all.[1] Nevertheless, many writers have wished to introduce the concept of a cardinal measure of utility, unique except for constants of scale and origin.

Lange,[2] Fisher,[3] and others have contended that measurable utility, while superfluous from the standpoint of positivistic behavioristic description, is necessary for the purpose of a normative science of welfare economics.

While I cannot consider this problem in detail, it is well to point out that this is not at all necessary. Assuming that Welfare Economics involves comparisons between individuals, it is sufficient that explicit welfare judgments be made such that we are able to relate *ordinally* all possible combinations of goods and services consumed by each and every individual. Nothing at all is gained by the selection of individual cardinal measures of utility.[4]

[1] Some writers have partially recognized this fact, but still maintain that the avoidance of the use of utility is a "stunt," an axiomatic experiment by means of which we make our way more difficult. From the present operational orientation this view is clearly superficial.

[2] Oscar Lange, "The Determinateness of the Utility Function," *Review of Economic Studies*, I (1934), 218–225.

[3] Irving Fisher, "A Statistical Method for Measuring 'Marginal Utility' and Testing the Justice of a Progressive Income Tax," in *Economic Essays in Honor of John Bates Clark* (New York, 1927).

[4] Of course, if one considers *general welfare* as the algebraic sum of individual cardinal

In any case it is clear that there are an infinity of ways of selecting a particular utility index and defining it as the true cardinal measure of utility. Thus, one might draw a straight line from the origin through a point representing an arbitrary bundle of goods and services. The numerical distance of any point on this line from the origin could serve as an index of utility, and might be dignified with a unique title.

THE ASSUMPTION OF INDEPENDENT UTILITIES

A method of selection such as that outlined above is obviously arbitrary. Others are more subtle, but equally arbitrary. Professors Fisher [5] and Frisch,[6] employing only price and quantity data, have measured what is alleged to be marginal and total utilities and how these magnitudes vary with changes in income, quantities, etc. Although the exact technique differs between these two writers, the fundamental principle remains the same. This can be illustrated with reference to a simplified case where only two consumption goods are involved.

Given a great number of observations on prices, quantities, and total income, one could in the limit more or less trace out the whole indifference map. We should still, however, have said nothing about the numbering of the one-parameter family of indifference loci so traced out. Both Professors Frisch and Fisher employ the following definition for selecting out a particular utility index to be designated the "true" measure of utility, subject to origin and scale constants. That utility index, if it exists, is to be selected which can be written in the form

$$\varphi = f(x) + g(y); \tag{1}$$

i.e., for which

$$\frac{\partial^2 \varphi}{\partial x \partial y} \equiv 0. \tag{2}$$

utilities, then one will require the cardinal measurability of utility. But such an assumption is arbitrary and gratuitous. Cf. A. Burk (Bergson), "A Reformulation of Certain Aspects of Welfare Economics," *Quarterly Journal of Economics*, vol. LII, no. 2, February, 1938, pp. 310–334.

[5] Fisher, *op. cit.*

[6] R. Frisch, "New Methods of Measuring Marginal Utility," *Beiträge zur ökonomischen Theorie*, no. 3 (Tübingen, 1932); H. Schultz, *The Theory and Measurement of Demand*, pp. 111–117.

If there exists one index of utility which can be written in the form of equation (1), then any other index which obeys the same law must differ from it only by a linear transformation. For, consider another index

$$F = F(\varphi), \tag{3}$$

for which

$$\frac{\partial^2 F}{\partial x \partial y} \equiv 0. \tag{4}$$

Successively differentiating (3) partially with respect to x and y, we get

$$\frac{\partial^2 F}{\partial x \partial y} = F' \varphi_{xy} + F'' \varphi_x \varphi_y. \tag{5}$$

This, together with (2), requires that

$$F'' \varphi_x \varphi_y \equiv 0, \tag{6}$$

or

$$F''(\varphi) \equiv 0. \tag{7}$$

Therefore,

$$F = a + b\varphi, \tag{8}$$

where a and b are origin and scale constants respectively.

It is clear, therefore, that the assumption that utilities shall be "independent" will help to select one utility index as the cardinal measure of utility. Nevertheless, even this convention is not in general applicable. It will guarantee us that we do not have two different utility scales, as has been shown in the above proof; it will *not*, in general, provide us with even one scale.

If we assume an indifference field obeying the ordinary concavity restrictions and nothing more, then there will not, in general, be even one utility index which can be written in the form

$$\begin{aligned} \varphi &= f(x) + g(y), \\ \varphi_{xy} &\equiv 0. \end{aligned} \tag{9}$$

Let us write out one legitimate utility index.

$$II = H(x, y). \tag{10}$$

Does there exist a transformation F such that

$$\varphi = F[H(x, y)] = f(x) + g(y)? \tag{11}$$

The answer in general must be in the negative. Further arbitrary restrictions must first be placed upon the indifference field.

Let the indifference field be defined in the following form, independent of any utility concept:

$$-\left(\frac{dy}{dx}\right)_{H=\text{constant}} = R(x, y), \tag{12}$$

where R is a function of x and y obeying the following curvature requirements

$$R_x - R_y R < 0. \tag{13}$$

The necessary and sufficient condition that there exist a utility index which can be written in the form

$$\varphi = f(x) + g(y),$$
$$\varphi_{xy} \equiv 0$$

is as follows:

$$RR_{xy} - R_x R_y \equiv 0, \tag{14}$$

or

$$\frac{\partial^2 \log R}{\partial x \partial y} \equiv 0. \tag{15}$$

The necessity is verified by the differentiation of

$$R(x, y) = \frac{f'(x)}{g'(y)}. \tag{16}$$

The sufficiency is also easily indicated.

If

$$\frac{\partial^2 \log R}{\partial x \partial y} \equiv 0,$$

$$\log R = \log h(x) - \log k(y) = \log \frac{h(x)}{k(y)}, \tag{17}$$

where h and k are arbitrary functions. Form the expression

$$Rdx + dy = \frac{h(x)}{k(y)} dx + dy. \tag{18}$$

This can easily be transformed into the exact differential

$$d\varphi = h(x)dx + k(y)dy, \tag{19}$$

or

$$\varphi = \int_a^x h(x)dx + \int_b^y k(y)dy + \text{constant}$$
$$= f(x) + g(y). \tag{20}$$

We must now investigate the meaning of the restriction in (14). The assumption of independence of utilities in order to define a cardinal measure of utility is seen to involve (1) a convention by means of which one out of an infinity of possible utility scales is designated as the true cardinal measure of utility; (2) an arbitrary *a priori* restriction upon the preference field, and hence upon empirical price-quantity behavior. The meaning of this restriction we must now investigate.

The functional restriction (14) is a partial differential equation of the second order of the general form

$$M(R, R_x, R_y, R_{xx}, R_{yy}, R_{xy}, x, y) = 0. \tag{21}$$

Subject to boundary conditions involving two arbitrary functions, it will serve to define a unique solution function

$$R = \bar{R}(x, y). \tag{22}$$

More specifically, if we are given as empirical observational data the two expenditure paths corresponding to the changes in quantities with income in each of two respective price situations, then from these observations, and these alone, the whole field of indifference curves can be determined by suitable extrapolation.

It is not easy to visualize intuitively why this should be so; indeed, few economists would be so bold as to claim that the behavior of an individual in all conceivable circumstances should be derivable from so few observations. And yet this is the conclusion to which we are forced by the apparently innocuous assumption of independence of utilities.

Moreover, (14) places definite restrictions on our demand functions, the validity of which are equally dubious and equally impossible to comprehend intuitively. For the simple two-commodity case our conditions of demand equilibrium can be written

$$\frac{P_x}{P_y} = R(x, y), \tag{23}$$

$$I = P_x x + P_y y.$$

These may be transformed into

$$x = m\left(\frac{P_x}{P_y}, \frac{I}{P_y}\right),$$

$$y = n\left(\frac{P_x}{P_y}, \frac{I}{P_y}\right).$$

(24)

These demand equations must be subject to the restriction

$$\frac{\partial^2 \log \dfrac{P_x}{P_y}}{\partial x \partial y} \equiv 0.$$

(25)

When there are more than two goods, the restrictions implied by the very possibility of an independent index of utility take on a different and more complicated form. If there exists an index F for which

$$F_{ij} \equiv 0, \qquad (i \neq j)$$

(26)

then

$$F_{ij} \equiv F'(\varphi)\varphi_{ij} + F''(\varphi)\varphi_i\varphi_j \equiv 0,$$

(27)

where φ is any other index. Thus,

$$\frac{\varphi_{ij}}{\varphi_i\varphi_j} = T(\varphi), \qquad (i \neq j)$$

(28)

where T is an arbitrary function, and φ is *any* index of utility. Taking into account the $(n-1)(n-2)/2$ conditions of integrability, this implies an additional $n(n-1)/2$ conditions. It is to be noted that these are identities, holding everywhere. Not only are they necessary, but the transformation

$$F = \int_a^\varphi e^{\int_c^v T(\theta)d\theta} dv$$

(29)

shows them to be sufficient as well.

In terms of the indifference varieties these take still another form. Let

$$\frac{p_j}{p_i} \equiv -\frac{dx_i}{dx_j} = {}^iR^j(x_1, \cdots, x_n).$$

(30)

These, of course, satisfy the identities

$$\frac{{}^iR^j}{{}^iR^k} \equiv {}^kR^j. \qquad (i, j, k = 1, \cdots, n)$$

(31)

If an independent index of utility is possible, then we must have

$$\frac{\partial \, ^iR^j}{\partial x_k} \equiv 0. \qquad (j \neq k \neq i) \qquad (32)$$

In view of the n^3 relations of (31), the above $n(n-1)^2$ relations are not all independent. At most $n(n-2)$ are independent, and these may be written in the form

$$\frac{\partial \, ^1R^i}{\partial x_j} \equiv 0, \qquad (i \neq j), \qquad (i, j = 2, \cdots, n)$$

$$\frac{\partial \left(\dfrac{^1R^i}{^1R^2} \right)}{\partial x_1} \equiv 0. \qquad (i = 3, \cdots, n) \qquad (33)$$

These conditions are both necessary and sufficient. They imply among other things the $(n-1)(n-2)/2$ integrability conditions of equation (14) of chapter v. On the other hand, if the latter are postulated at the beginning, then equations (33) cease to be all independent and can be reduced in number.

We have then $n(n-2)$ partial differential equations of the first order. Subject to an equal number of arbitrary functions, the *general* solution is uniquely determined. But empirically an observation of an expenditure path involves $(n-1)$ functions. Hence, observation of more than $n(n-2)/(n-1)$, or more than n expenditure paths, could be used to disprove the possibility of independence.

In words, the implications of independence are that the amount bought of any good x_i can be expressed in terms of its price p_i, the price of any other good p_j, and the amount of expenditure upon these two goods alone, i.e., upon the amount left over out of total expenditure after all other goods are bought. Thus, the general demand function

$$x_i = h^i(p_1, \cdots, p_n, I)$$

can be written in the special forms

$$h^i(p_1, \cdots, p_n, I) \equiv h^{ij}(p_i, p_j, I + p_i x_i + p_j x_j - \sum_1^n p_k x_k) \qquad (34)$$

for any i not equal to j. Subject to the conditions of (25) and certain consistency relationships, these conditions seem to be sufficient as well as necessary.

Except for R. G. D. Allen's derivation of equation (15) for the two-good case, I am not aware that these full price-quantity implications of independence have previously been derived.[7]   However, fragmentary sets of necessary but by no means sufficient conditions for independent goods have been derived by Slutsky and by Milton Friedman.[8]   They differ fundamentally from those above, and are of a species which I choose to call *local* implications of independence.   At a given point in the (X) space it *may* be possible to find a transformation $F(\varphi)$ such that

$$F_{ij} = F'\varphi_{ij} + F''\varphi_i\varphi_j \equiv 0. \qquad (i \neq j) \qquad (35)$$

Thus, if there are only two goods (x_1) and (x_2), this is always possible at every point so that the *local* conditions degenerate into trivial identities.   At any point $(X) = (x_1, x_2)$, let

$$-\frac{F''(\varphi)}{F'(\varphi)} = \frac{\varphi_{12}(X)}{\varphi_1(X)\varphi_2(X)}, \qquad (36)$$

and

$$F_{12}(X) = 0. \qquad (37)$$

This differs from the previous non-local conditions in that the above relation is *an equality at a point and not an identity.*

In the general case of n goods a local transformation of this type is possible only if the following relations hold,

$$\frac{\varphi_{12}(X)}{\varphi_1(X)\varphi_2(X)} = \frac{\varphi_{ij}(X)}{\varphi_i(X)\varphi_j(X)}. \qquad (i \neq j \neq 1) \qquad (38)$$

These are $[n(n-1)/2 - 1]$ independent conditions, and as before need *not* be identities.   Even if they hold *everywhere*, independence is *not* necessarily implied.   If the local conditions hold, the bordered determinant of the type given in equation (34) of chapter v takes on a special form, and consequently certain restrictions upon the demand functions can be derived.

Slutsky [9] shows that

$$\varphi_{ij} = (-\lambda)_\varphi \left(\frac{p_{ij}}{p} - \theta_\varphi \frac{p_{n+1,n+1.ij}}{p}\right), \qquad (39)$$

---

[7] R. G. D. Allen, "A Comparison between Different Definitions of Complementary and Competitive Goods," *Econometrica*, II (1934), 168–175.

[8] Milton Friedman, "Professor Pigou's Method for Measuring Elasticities of Demand from Budgetary Data," *Quarterly Journal of Economics*, November, 1935, pp. 151–163.

[9] E. Slutsky, "Sulla teoria del bilancio del consumatore," *Giornale degli Economisti*, LI (1915), 23–26.

where

$$
p = \begin{vmatrix}
K_{11} & K_{12} & \cdots & K_{1n} & \dfrac{\partial x_1}{\partial I} \\[1.2em]
K_{12} & K_{22} & \cdots & K_{2n} & \dfrac{\partial x_2}{\partial I} \\[0.8em]
\cdot & \cdot & & \cdot & \cdot \\
\cdot & \cdot & & \cdot & \cdot \\
\cdot & \cdot & & \cdot & \cdot \\[0.4em]
K_{1n} & K_{2n} & \cdots & K_{nn} & \dfrac{\partial x_n}{\partial I} \\[1.2em]
\dfrac{\partial x_1}{\partial I} & \dfrac{\partial x_2}{\partial I} & \cdots & \dfrac{\partial x_n}{\partial I} & 0
\end{vmatrix}, \tag{40}
$$

and the subscripts indicate appropriate cofactors. Also

$$
\theta_\varphi = - \frac{\partial \log (-\lambda)}{\partial I} \varphi \tag{41}
$$

in the notation of chapter v.

If an index exists such that

$$
F_{ij} \equiv 0, \qquad (i \neq j) \tag{42}
$$

at a point, then

$$
\theta_F = \frac{p_{12}}{p_{n+1,n+1.12}} = \frac{p_{ij}}{p_{n+1,n+1.ij}}. \quad (i \neq j \neq 1) \tag{43}
$$

These are $[n(n - 1)/2 - 1]$ independent and meaningful restrictions on the demand functions and completely exhaust the *local* implications of the independence assumption.

I should also like to point out that equations (43) might be used to determine the marginal utility of income if (1) independence is possible; (2) that utility index which can be written as an additive sum of independent utility is defined as the "true" cardinal index of utility. I commend it to the attention of the never lacking army of utility measurers.

Mr. Friedman has derived the following $n(n - 1)$ local independence conditions: [10]

$$
\frac{\eta_{ii}}{\eta_{jj}} = \left(\frac{\eta_{iI}}{\eta_{jI}} \frac{1 - k_i \eta_{iI}}{1 - k_j \eta_{jI}} \right) + \frac{\eta_{iI}}{\eta_{jj}} \left[\frac{(k_j - k_i) - k_i k_j (\eta_{iI} - \eta_{jI})}{1 - k_j \eta_{jI}} \right]. \tag{44}
$$

In the two-dimensional case the restriction is vacuous.

[10] Friedman, *op. cit.*, p. 162.

From the fact that their number is excessive, it is clear that they cannot all be independent. In fact, I am unable to prove that they are *complete*, i.e., equivalent to the above Slutsky conditions; indeed, I would venture the conjecture that they are not.[11]

It would be literally impossible for any individual to determine by introspection whether or not his demand functions satisfied the above relations. Indeed, the likelihood that such relations, selected arbitrarily from an infinity of possible functional relations, should hold is infinitely small. The minute amount of plausibility

[11] On page 162, footnote 2, Mr. Friedman argues against the admissibility of the Pigou theorem that

$$\frac{\eta_{ii}}{\eta_{ji}} = \frac{\eta_{iI}}{\eta_{jI}} \quad \text{when} \quad \frac{k_i}{\eta_{iI}} \doteq 0 \doteq \frac{k_j}{\eta_{jI}} \tag{*}$$

on the grounds that ". . . there is a presumption that η_{iI} and k_i [my notation] are *inversely* related." The whole problem is of course ambiguous until a particular set of indifference curves are specified. Nevertheless, within the realm of probability and presumption, Mr. Friedman's statement seems to be incorrect. In chapter v it is shown that

$$\frac{\sum_{1}^{n} k_i \eta_{iI}}{\sum_{1}^{n} k_i} = 1;$$

i.e., a weighted average of all income elasticities equals unity regardless of the number of goods. The average k is given by

$$\frac{\sum_{1}^{n} k_i}{n} = \frac{1}{n}.$$

This approaches zero as the number of goods increases.

A survey of empirical budget studies will convince the reader that the income elasticities are distributed around unity, while the proportions vary around $1/n$.

See also A. C. Pigou and N. Georgescu-Roegen, "Marginal Utility of Money and Elasticities of Demand," *Quarterly Journal of Economics*, vol. L, no. 3 (1936).

The above Pigou theorem rests, nevertheless, upon the restrictive assumption of independence. If it could be shown that it holds for small values of k_i/η_{iI} in every case, it would be much more useful.

That this cannot be true in general is shown by the following special case. Let consumption of n goods be completely "joint" in the sense that there are always fixed proportions. Then regardless of the number of goods, $\eta_{iI} \equiv 1$, and $\eta_{iI}/\eta_{jI} \equiv 1$. On the other hand, it is easily shown that $\eta_{ii} \equiv -x_i p_i/I$. Consequently, $\eta_{ii}/\eta_{jj} \equiv k_i/k_j$. Even though we make the k's become arbitrarily small as compared to the income elasticities, their ratio may take on any value other than unity. Thus, the Pigou theorem (*) is false.

Of course, this example rests upon discontinuities in the higher derivatives, but I should think that we could approximate this condition by appropriate choice of continuous derivatives.

to the proposition that independence is an admissible assumption comes from the fact that the question is usually posed in such a way that independence appears to be an intermediate class between the extreme classes of competitiveness and complementarity. Employing a rudimentary concept of the equal probability of the unknown, one is inclined at first blush to acquiesce to the independence assumption. The error involved in so doing is obvious from our previous discussion, completely aside from the crucial ambiguity attaching to the older notions of independence and complementarity.[12]

COMPLEMENTARITY

In my opinion the problem of complementarity has received more attention than is merited by its intrinsic importance. Nevertheless, as a result of the interest in this subject, crucial inconsistencies in the thought of Pareto were revealed by Hicks and Allen, and much light was thrown on the cardinal and ordinal conceptions of utility.

The older writers, Fisher, Pareto, and Edgeworth, suggested as a qualitative definition of complementarity between two goods, x_i and x_j, the sign of the cross derivative of the utility function; i.e., goods were complementary, independent, or competitive depending upon whether

$$\frac{\partial^2 \varphi}{\partial x_i \partial x_j} \gtreqless 0. \tag{45}$$

If one assumes only an ordinal preference field, all numerical utility indexes are equally admissible. This cross derivative is not invariant in sign under a change in the index of utility. Consider a monotonic transformation of φ.

$$U = F(\varphi), \qquad \frac{dF}{d\varphi} > 0$$

$$U_i = \frac{dF}{d\varphi} \varphi_i, \tag{46}$$

$$U_{ij} = \frac{dF}{d\varphi} \varphi_{ij} + \frac{d^2F}{d\varphi^2} \varphi_i \varphi_j.$$

---

[12] It may be argued that regarded purely as a working hypothesis the facts do not sharply contradict the independence assumption. A little investigation reveals that such a hypothesis has not been tested from this point of view. On the contrary, it is implicitly assumed from the beginning in the manipulation of the statistical data. Hence, one would have to go back to examine the original empirical data. It is interesting to note that observations on three expenditure paths would be sufficient to contradict the independence assumption in the case of two commodities.

By a proper selection of the arbitrary term, $d^2F/d\varphi^2$, the sign of the new cross derivative can be made to differ from that of the old. As a corollary of this lack of invariance, complementarity so defined will have nothing to do with the budgetary habits of individuals with respect to the two goods in question. Similarly, an individual's introspective, spontaneous, intuitive designation of two goods as complementary or competitive (sugar and coffee, beef or pork, etc.) corresponds not to such a measure as this, but rather to behavioristic properties of the preference field and demand functions.[13]

In the course of the last five years the world's best economists have spent considerable time and energy in the study of Professor Hicks's *Value and Capital*.[14] It is perhaps symptomatic of the essential unimportance of the concept of complementarity that in this period no one seems to have noticed that the author gives two or more distinct (and inconsistent?) definitions of complementarity. The verbal definition in the text (p. 44) seems to be different from that in the mathematical appendix (paragraph 8).[15]

---

[13] Hicks and Allen, Slutsky, and Schultz have suggested invariant measures of complementarity which are properties of the indifference curve system and demand function. Perhaps the simplest measure of complementarity between two goods, x_i and x_j, is the sign of

$$K_{ij} = \frac{\partial x_i}{\partial p_j} + x_j \frac{\partial x_i}{\partial I} = K_{ji}, \qquad \text{or} \qquad \epsilon_{ij} = \frac{K_{ij}p_j}{x_i}.$$

If there are but two commodities, this must always be positive in sign; in the many commodity case at least one must be of positive sign in order to satisfy the relationships

$$\sum_1^n p_i K_{ij} = 0, \qquad (i = 1, \cdots, n)$$

$$K_{ii} < 0.$$

Professor Leontief has suggested the following invariant measure of independence, corresponding most closely to the old notions:

$$\frac{\partial^2 {}^iR^j}{\partial x_i \partial x_j} = \frac{\partial^2 \log\left(\dfrac{U_i}{U_j}\right)}{\partial x_i \partial x_j} = 0.$$

Since the above lines were first written, Professor Hicks's two works, *Value and Capital* and *Theorie Mathematique de La Valeur*, have appeared. I still believe, however, that Hicks's own solid contributions to economic theory do not rest on his treatment of complementarity, and that the extended discussion of the concept is a tribute to an old love rather than the necessary consequence of the subject matter.

[14] J. R. Hicks, *Value and Capital* (Oxford, 1939).

[15] Actually, there is still a third definition in the footnote on page 44. Only in the case of three goods is it clearly equivalent to one of the other two; in the general case it

This may be seen in many ways. While the mathematical definition can be applied to the case where there are only two goods, the literary definition cannot. (It is irrelevant that in the case of two goods the mathematical definition of complementarity admits of only one possible algebraic sense.) There is no reason why two distinct definitions should give the same answer in any particular case, so it is not surprising that one can invent examples *ad inifinitum* for which two goods, such as wheat and linen, are on one of the definitions complements and on the other substitutes. But as we shall see in a moment, things are in even a worse state. According to the definition of the literary text, it is possible for wheat and linen to be complements and substitutes at the same time, depending on the selection of the third good which is to serve as numeraire. The definition is ambiguous; instead of reflecting the properties of two goods, it (or rather they) represents the properties of three goods.

The mathematical appendix definition gives as a coefficient of complementarity between the ith and jth good the element of the ith row and jth column of the matrix $(\psi_j{}^i)$ where

$$x = \psi(p, U) \tag{47}$$

represents in matrix notation the demand functions, for each indifference level.

Because of the homogeneity property discussed in chapter v it is clear that these n demand functions cannot be inverted to give each p in terms of the x's and U. Only relative prices can be determined. We can use any one price as numeraire, discard one of the above equations and invert the others so as to give $(n - 1)$ relative prices in terms of $(n - 1)$ goods and the ordinal level of U. It is most convenient to omit the quantity of the numeraire, x_k, and its demand equation. This gives us

$$\frac{p_i}{p_k} = {}^kN^i(x_1, \cdots, x_{k-1}, x_{k+1}, \cdots, x_n, U). \qquad (i \neq n) \tag{48}$$

is ambiguously worded, since the offer of the maximum amount of money by the consumer to attain given amounts of the two goods in question will change the amount bought of *all* other goods. It would appear that the author intends that all other (than the two goods in question and the numeraire good) goods are to be held constant, in which case it becomes identical with the verbal definition. The difficulty may reside in Hicks's unique use of the concept "money."

Let $(^kN_j{}^i) = N_k$ be the matrix of this transformation. Then the element corresponding to the ith price and jth quantity represents the literary definition of complementarity. It can easily be shown that this, like the first matrix, must be symmetrical. In fact, it is necessarily negative definite, like the ψ matrix.

These last two statements are consequences of the definition of the inverse demand functions according to which

$$N_k = \psi_k{}^{-1}(p_k{}^{-1}\delta_{ij}), \qquad (49)$$

where ψ_k is defined to be the matrix formed by omitting the kth row and kth column from the original ψ matrix. Since it is known from earlier chapters to be negative definite, so too will be its inverse.

While the diagonal elements of the N and ψ matrices must agree in sign, being negative, the off diagonal terms need not agree in sign except in the empirically unimportant case of three goods. Even more important, the element in a given row and column of the N matrix may be of different sign depending upon which good is called money or numeraire. A single instance will suffice to indicate this possibility. Suppose we have n goods in a preference field that can be typified by additive utilities. Let all but the last good have decreasing marginal utility. Then on the literary definition the first two goods will be substitutes if the third good is used as numeraire; unless the last good has decreasing marginal utility, when it is used as numeraire, the first two goods will be complements. There is no reason why one of the goods, which we may call the last, cannot be an inferior good. Indeed, in the interesting borderline case where one of the goods has constant marginal utility, every pair of goods is independent on the literary definition when the good with constant marginal utility is used as numeraire; if any other good is used as numeraire, all other pairs not involving the good with constant marginal utility are easily shown to be substitutes. But according to the definition of the mathematical appendix, all pairs of goods not involving the one with constant marginal utility must always be independent, whatever the numeraire.

A typical element of N_k can be written out in terms of the slopes of the indifference loci, and the reader may verify for himself the dependence upon the subscript k.

Walras was scrupulously careful in his use of the concept *numeraire*. He distinguished between it and money, in the sense of the portable, divisible, cognizable, durable, conventional commodity which served as a counter in performing exchanges. Marshall, when he spoke of money, ordinarily meant nothing more than income, as we shall see in the discussion of the constancy of the marginal utility of income. Hicks seems to alternate between the above uses, and a third sense in which money stands for a composite commodity made up of all but one or two of the total number of commodities. The result is a tendency toward ambiguity, of which the above example is only one instance.

If complementarity is not of interest for its own sake, can it not still be of importance as an indicator of conditions where certain "abnormal" phenomena are to be found? Thus, on page 71 in his discussion of the stability of a general equilibrium exchange system, Hicks says, "If income effects can be neglected, and if no complementarity is present, then the system of exchange equilibrium must be stable." It would seem, therefore, that the concept may be useful in indicating where a stable system will break down. Unfortunately, this is not correct. The author has made a momentary slip, as he has since indicated elsewhere. If income effects can be neglected, then his matrix (X_{rs}), being the sum of the negative definite symmetrical matrices of all individuals, must itself be negative definite and symmetrical. It must therefore be *perfectly stable* on the Hicksian definition, *regardless of complementarity*.[16] If income effects cannot be neglected, then the matrix may be asymmetrical; according to the author asymmetry tends to make for instability. This is not quite correct. Pure asymmetry, and nothing else tends to make for stability; the neglected income effects are the villains in the piece, and they do the most harm when their influence is *not* spent in creating asymmetry.

Again in Hicks' discussion of the effects upon the "period of production" of a change in the interest rate, the concept of complementarity is introduced.[17] But here, too, a correct rendition of the secondary maximum conditions shows that complementarity

---

[16] Since these lines were first written, I find that Hicks has detected his error. Cf. J. R. Hicks, "Consumers' Surplus and Index Numbers," *Review of Economic Studies*, vol. IX, no. 2, p. 133, n. 2.

[17] Hicks, *Value and Capital*, p. 222, n. 1 and p. 328.

cannot be such as to make the Hicksian period of production decrease with a reduced interest rate.

The Hicksian average period of production is defined as the elasticity [18] of discounted value, C, with respect to changes in the discount rate, $\beta = (1 + i)^{-1}$. Mathematically, it is given by $(\beta dC/d\beta)/C$. Its precise usefulness seems not to have been explicitly indicated. Among other things, the Hicksian "average period" has the anomalous property of not being an "internal mean," i.e., one whose value lies within the limits of the greatest and least of the time periods being averaged. Thus, it cannot be considered a generalization of the simple Bohm-Bawerkian average period of production. For example, consider the trivially simple "point-input-point-output" case where 99¢ worth of input is invested for one year to produce, say, $1.00 worth of output. The Bohm-Bawerkian average period, which unlike the Hicks concept requires a careful distinguishing between *plus* and *minus* items, is one year regardless of the interest rate. The Hicks period is 100 years if the interest rate is zero and infinite if the interest rate is one per cent. In fact, for the so-called "marginal investment" it is always infinite. By introducing discount factors into the average, the author hoped, perhaps, to meet the Knightian objection that the period is infinite; but in many cases he seems only to have succeeded in making the finite infinite.[19]

But this is not the place to go into the deeper Knightian objections to the Austrian theory. It will be sufficient, in passing, to state what seems to be the only essential theorem relating production planning to the interest rate. By the methods of earlier chapters, it can be easily shown that where the firm acts to maximize

$$C = x_0 + x_1\beta_1 + x_2\beta_2 + \cdots + x_n\beta_n, \qquad (50)$$

[18] As its author indicates, here is an example of an elasticity expression which is not dimensionless. For an analytic explanation of this the reader is referred to the first section of my chapter vi.

[19] Actually, it is not always necessary to introduce discount factors in order to make a process with infinite range yield a finite average. Many writers have shown how the distant elements receive smaller weights so as to create a convergent infinite series. Thus, imagine a perpetual stew, to which something is always being added and from which something is always being taken out, at random. Some part of what is now being added will never come out of the stew, just as some part of what is in the stew is of infinite age. But it is a simple exercise in infinite processes to show that the average age of the stew is finite, and the average expectancy of a particle's staying in the stew is also finite.

a change in the discount factors must see the following inequalities realized

$$\sum_{0}^{n} \Delta x_j \Delta \beta_j \geqq 0. \tag{51}$$

If the interest rates for all periods are equal, and if we go to the limit, we have the definite theorem

$$\sum_{1}^{n} (dx_j/d\beta)j\beta^{j-1} \geqq 0. \tag{52}$$

Constancy of the Marginal Utility of Income

I return after the above digression to an examination of another special restrictive assumption with which the analysis of consumer's behavior is often burdened. For its own sake the problem of constancy of the marginal utility of income is one of the least important in economic theory, but it has given rise to an endless amount of discussion, most of it not on a very high level, and it therefore deserves brief notice here. Inasmuch as I have given a rather complete analysis of this matter elsewhere,[20] I do not propose to do more than summarize matters here, and to comment upon some more recent contributions which became available after the writing of the cited essay.[21]

As will be seen in the next section, constancy of the marginal utility of income derives most of its importance from its relationships, real and alleged, to the subject of consumer's surplus. In the beginning, it is well to point out that one ambiguity runs through the whole literature; sometimes constancy is interpreted to mean constancy, and at other times it is intended to mean *almost* constancy. The last usage generally involves some sort of limiting process; either the change in question is supposed to be "small," whatever that might mean, or the percentage spent upon

[20] P. A. Samuelson, "Constancy of the Marginal Utility of Income," *Studies in Mathematical Economics and Econometrics: In Memory of Henry Schultz* (University of Chicago, 1942), pp. 75–91.

[21] A. Henderson, "Consumer's Surplus and the Compensating Variation," *Review of Economic Studies*, vol. VIII, no. 2 (February, 1941), pp. 117–121. J. R. Hicks, "The Rehabilitation of Consumers' Surplus," same issue as above, pp. 108–116. J. R. Hicks, "Consumers' Surplus and Index Numbers," *Review of Economic Studies*, vol. IX, no. 2, pp. 126–137. Robert L. Bishop, "Consumer's Surplus and Cardinal Utility," *Quarterly Journal of Economics*, vol. LVII, no. 3 (May, 1943), pp. 421–449.

some specified good is to be small, etc., etc.   The problem is still more complicated because the alleged result, itself rarely worded unambiguously, is more often than not held to be "likely" rather than necessary.[22]   I think, therefore, that we shall accomplish more if in the beginning we examine the literal implications of constancy of the marginal utility of income to show rigorously the empirical implications of this hypothesis.

We have already encountered the marginal utility of income in chapter v in the form of the $-\lambda$ of equation (31).   It is clear from the preceding equilibrium equations (29) that the marginal utility of expenditure upon each and every commodity must be the same, equal moreover to the marginal (rate of) utility derived from an extra dollar of expenditure distributed optimally over *all* of the goods.[23]

I have been meticulous in adhering to the usage of marginal utility of *income*, eschewing the more common terminology encountered in the literature of the marginal utility of *money*.   This brings up the second fatal ambiguity involved in the discussions of this subject.   Money has many different meanings in theoretical discussions, ranging from an abstract non-metallic, non-paper, conventional unit of account, to specific counters, to commodities commanding wide acceptance in exchange, to any commodity taken arbitrarily as *numeraire*, to income or expenditure.   It is reasonably clear from everything that Marshall has written and from the cast of his thought that he definitely intended to convey the meaning of money simply as a euphemism for income or expenditure, reckoned in pounds or dollars.   In his own words, it is "money or general purchasing power."[24]   In particular, it was foreign to his usage to think of money in the sense of *numeraire*, a concept which is not even listed in his index.

This is a matter of importance when we come to ask the question, with respect to what is the marginal utility of income or

---

[22] This is another one of the numerous places where Alfred Marshall left matters in a fog.   It was part of the flavor of the man not to bring things to a sharp focus.   But what is forgivable in a genius cannot be tolerated among lesser mortals.

[23] This is simply one example of the Wong-Viner theorem discussed in chapter iii, p. 34; chapter iv, p. 66.

[24] A. Marshall, *Principles of Economics*, 8th edition, p. 838.   For a more complete discussion and for detailed citations the reader is referred to my essay in the Schultz volume.

money to be held constant? That Pareto might have interpreted this to mean constant marginal utility of a particular commodity chosen as *numeraire*, taken with respect to changes in the amount of that commodity, is understandable in view of the Lausanne usage. But that Hicks and others in the Anglo-Saxon tradition should have thought this to be the Marshallian meaning is much more surprising. Now at this date it is not a very significant question as to what Marshall himself really meant, but it is of importance to show the implications of at least two distinct and inconsistent meanings. Furthermore, many writers have definitely fallen into misstatements concerning the necessity and sufficiency of parallel indifference curves (the geometrical embodiment of the first of the above formulations) if various identities are to be realized.[25]

A closer examination of equations (29) and (31) will show that the marginal utility of income *cannot* be constant with respect to *everything*. It is a function of all prices and income. If we were to *double* all prices and income, the marginal utility of income would have to become *halved*. For such a doubling of income and prices would by the homogeneity property described in chapter v leave all physical quantities unchanged, and hence all real marginal utilities unchanged. But the marginal utility of income is given by dividing each real marginal utility by the respective price. With the numerator unchanged, and with the denominator doubled, the whole expression must be halved. If the marginal utility of income were constant with respect to all prices and also with respect to income, it would have to be unaffected by a simultaneous change in them all; since it must be halved by such a change, we have a contradiction. Consequently, the marginal utility of income cannot be invariant under changes in income and each and every price.[26]

At most the marginal utility of income might be independent of *all but one* of these $(n + 1)$ magnitudes. We can set n first partial derivatives equal to zero, but not $(n + 1)$. Which n shall

[25] In addition there may be a misapprehension running through Hicks's treatment in his book and the two articles cited. As Bishop has pointed out, the problem is not primarily one of whether or not income effects can be neglected. Further, there is the question of keeping real income constant or "adjusting" for changes in real income as seems to be implied in certain of the Hicksian statements.

[26] See *Studies in Mathematical Economics and Econometrics*, p. 76.

we choose?   This can clearly be done in $(n + 1)$ alternative ways. One of these involves the constancy of the marginal utility of income with respect to n prices, but not with respect to income. Elsewhere I have argued that this is the pure Marshallian case. The other alternatives involve the constancy of marginal utility of income with respect to income and with respect to $(n - 1)$ prices, or with respect to all prices but one.[27]   This is the second hypothesis of constancy.

In the Schultz volume essay I worked out the implications of each of these distinct hypotheses.   In terms of everything that has ever been observed concerning price and budgetary data, the implications of each are highly unrealistic, although it is the second of these which leads to really fantastic conclusions.

Before summarizing these empirical implications I should first point out that the marginal utility of income, being from a formal point of view a Lagrangean multiplier, must by the results of chapter vi, p. 132, *not* be left unchanged if we go from one utility index to another, as is our privilege in an ordinal preference field. At each point, for each different utility indicator, we have a different marginal utility of income.   If the expression is constant for a given movement when we are using one indicator, it will not be constant if we use another indicator.   If, to get rid of the minus sign, we define a new expression to be equal to $-\lambda$, it is really necessary to indicate the cardinal index of utility to which it applies. We may represent the new expression by the letter m, and append a subscript to indicate the utility index in question.

Then,

$$m_\varphi = m_\varphi(p_1, p_2, \cdots, p_n, I) = -\lambda = f(p_1, p_2, \cdots, p_n, I). \quad (53)$$

As shown in the Schultz volume this function must be homogeneous of order minus one; by Euler's theorem on homogeneous functions the sum of its elasticities with respect to each of the independent variables must equal minus one, so that each cannot vanish.

---

[27] The good whose price changes have an effect upon the marginal utility of income need not be the commodity selected as numeraire, and it might prevent confusion if we made a point of selecting some other commodity as "money," especially since there is no special reason within the scope of static theory why this special good should be divisible, durable, and have all the other properties of money.   Nevertheless, in the literature the convention is followed of picking this good as numeraire.

If we subject our utility index, φ, to a monotonic transformation to give us a new index, $U = F(\varphi)$, in terms of our new utility index the marginal utility of income has the properties

$$m_U = F'(\varphi)m_\varphi,$$
$$\frac{dm_U}{d\alpha} = F' \frac{dm_\varphi}{d\alpha} + F''m_\varphi \frac{d\varphi}{d\alpha}. \tag{54}$$

Since we can make F'' of any sign, the marginal utility of income can be made to change in any direction and amount we like, except in the special case which I have discussed elsewhere.

Have we destroyed then all possibilities of speaking of constant marginal utility of income? Not quite, since we need only assume that there exists some one cardinal index (even if we ourselves prefer to use another cardinal index, or no one cardinal index) for which the strong, non-local restrictions of the two different hypotheses hold.

It is a mere exercise to show that the first, or pure Marshallian, hypothesis implies that the income elasticity of demand for each good must be unitary, and the price elasticity of demand for each good in terms of its own price must equal minus one. Moreover, the demand for each good is independent of changes in the prices of all other goods. There must exist one way of numbering the indifference curves so that utilities are additive and independent in the old sense; actually except for arbitrary origin and scale the utility function is a linear combination of terms like $k_i \log x_i$, where the k coefficients represent the unchanging proportions spent upon each commodity, x. These implications are both necessary and sufficient.

In view of the well-known Engel's laws and numerous budgetary studies it is hardly necessary to point out that this flies in the face of all observable reality, even as a first approximation in the sense of limitingly small changes.

Performing a scarcely more difficult exercise in connection with the second hypothesis, it can be shown that it implies that the demand for each good except the numeraire depends only upon its own price in relation to the numeraire's price, and is entirely independent of income, money or real. The demand for the numeraire depends in a corresponding way upon all prices and income. These conditions are both necessary and sufficient.

They imply among other things that the indifference varieties are parallel, their slopes being constant along the direction of change in the numeraire good alone.

Of course no one has observed, and presumably no one ever will, a preference pattern in which all of extra income is spent upon one commodity.[28] Note that this is not even approximately true for instantaneous rates of change even when we neglect "second order of smalls."

Before we go into the reasons why anyone should ever have wished the marginal utility of income to be constant, a word may be said concerning the quasi-constancy of this magnitude. Of course, for a very small change in the initial situation, the marginal utility of income will change very little, as with everything else in the system. But this is simply a consequence of continuity, and nothing else. It is quite another thing to say, and this is the only important thing, that the *rate* of change of marginal utility of income is small. Today the use of infinitesimals and of differentials is rather out of fashion with mathematicians, although a completely rigorous basis can be given for these processes. But in the Victorian era when Marshall was in his prime, these were old familiar standbys, and we may be sure that the man who was second wrangler to the great Lord Rayleigh was well at home with their use. It is strange, therefore, that he contented himself with gratuitous, and I believe incorrect, statements that changes in the marginal utility of income were of the "second order of smallness." [29] In the technical sense they are not; the fact that we are dealing with what can be regarded as a second derivative is not relevant here.

If it may be of comfort to anyone cherishing a fondness for constancy, the following formula may be given indicating how the relative amount of expenditure upon a good ties up with the elasticity of the marginal utility of income with respect to a change in

[28] Perhaps King Midas was an exception, although his case involves certain dynamic considerations outside the present scope. For a one commodity maniac of his type it might not be inappropriate to measure all values in terms of the commodity in question; thus, the food necessary to keep a book collector alive might be reckoned as simply some fraction of a first edition of Adam Smith.

[29] Marshall, *Principles*, p. 842. The small germ of truth in the argument concerning "second order of smallness" lies in the fact that if each of the half dozen different consumer's surplus concepts are plotted againts a variable price (later called $p_i{}^b$), then at the original point, $p_i{}^a$, they all have the common tangent, $-q_i$.

the price of this good.

$$\frac{Em_\varphi}{Ep_i} = -k_i \left(\frac{Em_\varphi}{EI} + \frac{Ex_i}{EI} \right). \tag{55}$$

Providing that the two expressions in brackets do not simultaneously become large, and the last of these must for all goods average out to unity, then our left-hand elasticity must go to zero in the limit as the per cent spent upon the good in question goes to zero. But then of course any "surpluses" connected with this good become small, and there is no reason to distinguish between the orders of smallness.

WHY CONSUMER'S SURPLUS IS SUPERFLUOUS

Of course, the problem of constancy derives its interest, I will not say importance, from the Marshallian concept of consumer's surplus, about which an earlier generation of economists were able to indulge in much argumentation. Since many of the points involved were essentially mathematical in character, and since most of the antagonists did not go beyond literary methods, the discussion was not able to advance beyond a certain point, although most of the essential difficulties with the concept had been brought out. Later when there came about a renascence of mathematical methods in economic theory, economists had lost interest in the problem, and the subject lived on primarily in the elementary textbook and in the classroom.

. In the present writer's opinion this is as it should be. The subject is of historical and doctrinal interest, with a limited amount of appeal as a purely mathematical puzzle. These statements are made in cognizance of the fact that Professor Hicks has recently attempted to rehabilitate the doctrine of consumer's surplus. It would carry us afield from the present task to analyze his contentions in detail, and so only a few *ex cathedra* remarks must suffice.

In the first place, any judgment as to the usefulness or lack of usefulness of consumer's surplus has nothing to do with the problem of the admissibility of welfare economics as a significant part of economic theory since nobody has ever argued that the latter subject presupposes the validity of consumer's surplus. Can it then be said that consumer's surplus if not necessary, is nevertheless a useful construct? Concerning this psychological question, no final answer can be given. Historically the important propositions concerning increasing and decreasing cost industries, which are attributed to Marshall's consumer's surplus notions, may be said at best to have been incomplete derivations, and at worst may be said to be absolutely incorrect statements which, by a pun or play on words, seem to resemble the Pigouvian doctrine concerning industries with external economies and diseconomies. In its earlier form the Pigouvian doctrine is close to that of Marshall, but from the writings of Knight and Pigou himself we know that earlier form to be quite wrong.[30] To Pigou the problem is not at all one of increasing or decreasing returns; it is only a question as to whether each unit is taking account of its full effect upon social magnitudes (other than prices), or whether it is not. If it is not, and that is all that we mean by external economies, then there is of course need to interfere with the "invisible hand." I have found nothing in the written work of Marshall which suggests that he ever saw matters in this way, and even if he had stumbled upon this result by means of consumer's surplus, it would not be the first time that a correct theorem had been reached by incorrect, heuristic reasoning.

Also it may be said that the merits or demerits of the concept in question have little to do with the applicability of partial equilibrium methods to any particular problem. As for its connection with the theory of index numbers, after the concept has been renovated and altered, it *is* simply the economic theory of index numbers in the Pigou, Könus, Haberler, Staehle, Leontief, Lerner, Allen, Frisch, Wald tradition.[31]

[30] F. H. Knight, "Fallacies in the Interpretation of Social Cost," *Quarterly Journal of Economics*, XXXVIII (1924), 582–606. A. C. Pigou, *The Economics of Welfare*, 4th edition (London: 1932), chap. xi and appendix iii.

[31] In the Hicks derivations (*Review of Economic Studies*, vol. IX, no. 2, pp. 126–137) certain well-known theorems which are *exact* are derived as approximations. Also his most interesting result, that the difference between the Laspeyre and compensating variation is equal to a generalized substitution term, is exactly true, not simply for small movements, being a transcription of the familiar notion that the two terms differ in consequence of the curvature of the preference field. The one application to welfare economics in section 8 would be of interest only in connection with a (misdirected) attempt to measure welfare in a cardinal sense: to say whether one movement is better than the sum of the benefits of two other movements. And even if one were interested in cardinalization of welfare, this would not be the way to do it, for it can be shown that the value sums which are used in index number theory are of importance only for the qualitative direction of change which they indicate; in general (except in the trivial case

If one were to begin afresh to give answers to the following problems, in no one of them would consumer's surplus be necessary or desirable: Should Robinson Crusoe, a Socialist state, or a capitalist economy build a particular bridge? Should indirect taxes be preferred to direct taxes? Should discriminatory prices be allowed if a uniform price will not keep an activity in business? Should the number of firms producing differentiated products be reduced, and in what way? Should a particular small industry be expanded or contracted by means of tax or subsidy? etc., etc. Aside from their extraneous inter-personal aspects, all of these questions can more conveniently (and more honestly!) be answered in terms of the consumer's ordinal preference field.

It is for these reasons that my ideal *Principles* would not include consumer's surplus in the chapter on welfare economics except possibly in a footnote, although in my perfect *Primer* the concept might have a limited place, provided its antidote and alternatives were included close at hand.

THE MANY FORMS OF CONSUMER'S SURPLUS

The Marshallian expression of consumer's surplus does not refer to any one thing but to at least half a dozen interrelated expressions. It is only too easy to accept tacitly one of these as primary and then to show that the others do not correctly measure this magnitude. Thus, Professor Viner [32] argues that Marshall is incorrect in using the area under the demand curve as an index of the gains from trade because this magnitude does not coincide with the amount which could be derived by an all or none offer, as if

of expenditure proportionality) they cannot constitute even an arbitrary cardinal index. Some of these implications will be seen from an application of the Hicks result to what I have called the pure Marshallian case. Let us suppose that utility "really" is measurable in a cardinal sense and is given by the additive logarithmic form mentioned above, so that demand for each good is unitary and *independent* of all other prices. Any two goods will nevertheless be substitutes in the Hicksian sense; if it seems strange that independence in the usual objective sense nevertheless implies substitutability in the latter sense, the reader is reminded of the formal definitions laid down by Hicks. Be cause each good is unaffected by a change in the other price, a change in both prices together leads to exactly the same cardinal change in utility as the sum of each change separately. Yet by the Hicks theorem of section 8 the combined reduction in price leads to a smaller "gain" than the sum of the two separate "gains," an eminently gratuitous conclusion.

[32] J. Viner, *Studies in the Theory of International Trade* (New York: 1937), chapter ix, section iv.

the latter were the primary and correct expression for consumer's surplus. As Bishop has shown,[33] the latter *may* be a worse approximation than the former to the cardinal utility gain, which Bishop takes as the primary measure of consumer's surplus. Hicks first took the all or none magnitude as being the primary one, but now adopts a fourth magnitude as primary, what he calls the compensating variation. Which is correct can only be a question of history of thought; which would Marshall have selected if confronted with a one or none offer? Unfortunately this is no longer an observably meaningful question. Although I think Marshall would have agreed with Bishop, looking upon the other measures as good or bad approximations, I prefer to treat no one as primary or privileged, but to give the relationships between each.

This was done in brief but fairly exhaustive fashion in the Schultz volume essay, from which I append the following few pages, copied verbatim except for minor changes.[34]

Before examining the Marshallian concept of consumer's surplus, let us consider the uses to which it is put. Among other things it is proposed as a measure of the gain (loss) of utility that results from a decrease (increase) in price of a single good. An attempt also has been made to apply it to the analysis of the burden involved in commodity taxation. It has been used to determine the maximum amount of revenue that a perfectly discriminating monopolist might exact from the consumer for a given amount of the good in question.

Since only an ordinal preference field is assumed in the theory of consumer's behavior, there is really little importance to be attached to any numerical measure of the gains from a price change. In particular, one cannot fruitfully compare the gain derived from a movement between two given price situations with the gain between two other price situations.[35] Moreover, all valid theorems relating to the burden of taxation can be stated independently of any numerical measure of utility change. We should not be greatly perturbed, therefore, if the concept of consumer's surplus should

[33] *Op. cit.*, p. 421, *passim.*

[34] Pages 87–90.

[35] One can, however, compare the gains derived from a change in the basic price situation with an alternative price change from the *same* basic situation, since this resolves itself into an *ordinal* comparison of the alternative new situations. The initial situation "cancels out" so to speak.

be found to be inadmissible. Its only advantage seems to lie in its deceptively easy two-dimensional representation.

Consider an initial price and income situation, $(p_1{}^a, \cdots, p_n{}^a, I^a)$, and the corresponding amount of goods purchased, $(x_1{}^a, \cdots, x_n{}^a)$. For any selected utility index, φ, there will also be a given amount of utility, $\varphi(X^a)$. Suppose that a change is made in but one price, p_i, and income is left unchanged. There will be new amounts of every commodity, $(x_1{}^b, \cdots, x_n{}^b)$, and of utility, $\varphi(X^b)$, corresponding to the new prices and income, $(p_1{}^b, \cdots, p_n{}^b, I^b)$, or $(p_1{}^a, \cdots, p_i{}^b, \cdots, p_n{}^a, I^a)$, where $p_i{}^b$ is less than $p_i{}^a$.

We are interested in the following magnitudes:

1. The gain (loss) in utility resulting from the price change, or $\varphi(X^b) - \varphi(X^a)$.

2. The area between the demand curve of the ith good and the p_i axis within the range of the price movement, or

$$-\int_{p_i{}^a}^{p_i{}^b} x_i dp_i.$$

3. The amount by which the expenditure on the ith good in the new situation is exceeded by the maximum amount of money which the consumer would be willing to pay for $x_i{}^b$ in preference to trading at the old set of prices. (This may be negative if we are dealing with a price increase rather than a decrease.) Call this $^bE_{ab}$.

4. The amount of extra income which the consumer would insist upon if he is to be as well off as in the new situation while consuming the old amount of x_i. Call this $^aE_{ab}$.

5. The change in income which will make trading at the new set of prices as attractive as trading at the old set of prices with the initial income. Call this $^b\Delta I_{ab}$.

6. The change in income which will make trading at the old set of prices as attractive as trading at the new set of prices with the initial income. Call this $^a\Delta I_{ab}$.[36]

According to the Marshallian doctrine of consumer's surplus, all six of these magnitudes are equal except for dimensional con-

[36] Interchanging subscripts changes algebraic signs. Thus, $^b\Delta I_{ab} = -\,^b\Delta I_{ba}$. $^a\Delta I_{ab}$, but not $^b\Delta I_{ab}$ nor $^bE_{ab}$, can exceed I.

stants.   We are explicitly warned, however, that his doctrine holds unqualifiedly only when the marginal utility of income is constant, and only if utilities are independent.   I shall now examine the value of each of these magnitudes in four cases: (a) in the general unrestricted case of stable demand; (b) under the first interpretation of constancy of the marginal utility of income; (c) under the second hypothesis when the ith good is not the *numeraire;* and (d) under the second hypothesis when the ith good itself has constant marginal utility of income.   Only the most sketchy proofs will be indicated.

In the general case we have the following relations:

$$\varphi(X^b) - \varphi(X^a) = \int_{p_i^a}^{p_i^b} \left(\frac{d\varphi}{dp_i} \right) dp_i = \int_{p_i^a}^{p_i^b} \sum_1^n \left(\frac{\partial \varphi}{\partial x_j} \frac{\partial x_j}{\partial p_i} \right) dp_i$$

$$= \int_{p_i^a}^{p_i^b} m_\varphi \sum_1^n \left(p_j \frac{\partial x_j}{\partial p_i} \right) dp_i = - \int_{p_i^a}^{p_i^b} m_\varphi x_i dp_i. \quad (56)$$

$$^b\Delta I_{ab} = \max \left(\sum_1^n p_j^b x_j^b - \sum_1^n p_j^b x_j \right), \quad \text{where} \quad \varphi(X) = \varphi(X^a), \quad (57)$$

$$\geqq \sum_1^n p_j^b (x_j^b - x_j^a), \quad (58)$$

$$\geqq \sum_1^n (p_j^a - p_j^b) x_j^a. \quad (59)$$

If only the ith price changes, this becomes

$$^b\Delta I_{ab} \geqq (p_i^a - p_i^b) x_i^a. \quad (60)$$

Similarly,

$$^a\Delta I_{ab} = \min \left(\sum_1^n p_j^a x_j - \sum_1^n p_j^a x_j^a \right), \quad \text{where} \quad \varphi(X) = \varphi(X^b) \quad (61)$$

$$^a\Delta I_{ab} \leqq \sum_1^n p_j^a (x_j^b - x_j^a), \quad (62)$$

and, the ith price alone changing,

$$^a\Delta I_{ab} \leqq \sum_1^n p_j^a (x_j^b - x_j^a) = (p_i^a - p_i^b) x_i^b. \quad (63)$$

It is impossible in the general case [37] to determine the relative magnitude of ${}^b\Delta I_{ab}$ and ${}^a\Delta I_{ab}$, or of ${}^bE_{ab}$ and ${}^aE_{ab}$.

$$
{}^b\Delta I_{ab} \gtreqless {}^a\Delta I_{ab}; \qquad {}^bE_{ab} \gtreqless {}^aE_{ab}. \tag{64}
$$

It can be shown in the two dimensional case that

$$
{}^bE_{ab} = - \int_{p_i a}^{p_i b} x_i dp_i + \int_{p_i a}^{p_i b} (\bar{p}_i - p_i) \frac{\partial x_i}{\partial p_i} dp_i, \tag{65}
$$

where $\bar{p}_i$ is the price which would have to prevail for the consumer *freely* to select the batch of goods which he actually does consume when presented with an "all or none" offer by the perfectly discriminating monopolist. The first term on the right-hand side of equation (65) is the area under the demand curve. The second "correction" term may be of either sign.[38] It also follows from the definition of ${}^a\Delta I_{ab}$ that

$$
{}^b\Delta I_{ab} \geqq {}^bE_{ab} \qquad \text{and} \qquad {}^a\Delta I_{ab} \leqq {}^aE_{ab}. \tag{66}
$$

In case (b) we find

$$
{}^bE_{ab} < {}^b\Delta I_{ab} < {}^a\Delta I_{ab} \leqq {}^aE_{ab}, \tag{67}
$$

and

$$
{}^a\Delta I_{ab} > \frac{\varphi(X^b) - \varphi(X^a)}{m_\varphi} = - \int_{p_i a}^{p_i b} x_i dp_i > {}^bE_{ab}.{}^{39} \tag{68}
$$

The following relations must be satisfied in case (c):

$$
\frac{\varphi(X^b) - \varphi(X^a)}{m_\varphi} = - \int_{p_i a}^{p_i b} x_i dp_i
$$
$$
= {}^bE_{ab} = {}^b\Delta I_{ab} = {}^a\Delta I_{ab} = {}^aE_{ab}. \qquad (i \neq 1) \tag{69}
$$

[37] If we rule out the inferior good phenomenon so that demand is "normal,"

$$
{}^b\Delta I_{ab} < {}^a\Delta I_{ab} \qquad \text{and} \qquad {}^bE_{ab} < {}^aE_{ab}.
$$

Actually,

$$
{}^b\Delta I_{ab} - {}^a\Delta I_{ab} = \int_{p_i a}^{p_i b} [x_i(p_1{}^a, \cdots, p_i, \cdots, p_n{}^a, \varphi^b) - x_i(p_1{}^a, \cdots, p_i, \cdots, p_n{}^a, \varphi^a)] dp_i
$$
$$
= \int_{p_i a}^{p_i b} \int_{\varphi^a}^{\varphi^b} \frac{\partial x_i}{\partial \varphi} d\varphi dp_i.
$$

For sufficiently small changes in price, concept 2 will always be halfway between any corresponding pair of Δ's, or E's, etc.

[38] In the "normal" two-dimensional case it will be of negative sign; i.e., a perfectly discriminating monopolist will be able to exact less than the area under the demand curve from the consumer.

[39] The last of these inequalities will certainly hold in the two-good case. I have not developed a satisfactory proof that it holds for the *n*-dimensional case.

Although this is not the Marshallian interpretation, consumer's surplus seems to be most justified in this case.   However, the above equalities cannot hold simultaneously for every good.[40]

For case (d) equation (67) must hold with the possible exception of the inequality referred to in a previous footnote, but (69) is definitely false.

Other results may be extended in at least two directions.   More than one price may be permitted to change, and also income, without changing many of the inequalities.[41]   This may be left to the interested reader as an exercise.   Also we may attempt to derive rigorous inequalities in the n commodity case.   This offers considerable complexities in connection with concepts (3) and (4).

[40] Case (c) is *sufficient* to insure the equalities of equation (69).   Some of them may hold in other cases.

[41] In general, line integrals will replace simple integrals with the path of integration of the former a matter of no consequence.

CHAPTER VIII

WELFARE ECONOMICS

BEGINNING as it did in the writings of philosophers, theologians, pamphleteers, special pleaders, and reformers, economics has always been concerned with problems of public policy and welfare. And at least from the time of the physiocrats and Adam Smith there has never been absent from the main body of economic literature the feeling that in some sense perfect competition represented an optimal situation. Of course, over time the exact form of this doctrine has undergone modification (not always in any one direction), and there is considerable diversity in the attempted proofs (in the amazingly few places where rigorous proof was attempted).

Although this doctrine is often thought to be conservative or reactionary in its implication and to reflect the "kept" status of the economist, it is important to emphasize that it was "radical" in the eighteenth century, and there is some evidence from events of the last decades (e.g., the T.N.E.C. and economists' role and views with respect to Anti-Trust) that it has become a thorn in the side of what are usually thought of as conservative interests. Furthermore, some Socialist writers, who in their youth became interested in analytical economics, find in this doctrine a possible device for expediting planning in a socialized state.

Early uncritical allegiance to this doctrine arose in part from the understandable eighteenth-century tendency to find teleological significance in the workings of what is after all an equilibrium system which is not devoid of aesthetic content regarded simply as a mechanism.[1] But it would be unfair to the older economists to believe that their case ended with a simple argument from design,

---

[1] It would be out of place here to discuss the relationship of this doctrine to that of "natural rights"; to that of competition as an immutable law with which man cannot interfere even if he should wish to; to the inverted doctrine of natural selection whereby the results of competition were judged to be best by means of a circular definition of the "fittest" as those who survive; the Malthusian view that hardship and competition are necessary to bring out the "best" in a man; to the view that competition was good enough for our predecessors and therefore good enough for us; and other arguments designed to preserve the *status quo*.

even if such a charge can be sustained with respect to certain Epigoni.

This can best be seen in the writings on International Trade where the issue of the tariff brings out most clearly the welfare and policy beliefs of economists, even down to the present day. For free trade is but one dramatic exemplification of pure competition, and in this field formal attempts at proof were made, or we can at least in many cases piece together the implicit beliefs of the author.

1. Perhaps the most common reason for believing competition to be optimal stemmed from the recognition that no party could be hurt by exchange as compared to his position before trade, since he could always refuse to trade. *Thus, trade is better than no trade; exchange is mutually beneficial; one party does not gain what the other loses.* If we examine the argument carefully, we find that it does not really imply that pure competition is optimal, even though properly interpreted it can provide a case against *prohibitive tariffs.*

2. A second more sophisticated argument, which includes the first and more, rests upon the fact that the equilibrium position reached in pure competition represents an optimum for each individual, consistent with his original endowment of commodities and the market situation with which he is confronted. But every individual may be making the best of a situation without implying that that best is very good or is optimal; although each individual in pure competition takes price as given, for the market it is a variable, and it is quite possible that conditions other than pure competition might lead to better results in terms of any of the usual ethical notions. But, leaving aside all ethical notions, is it not equally clear that under (say) monopoly, both buyer and seller are doing the best that they can for themselves under existing market situations? The only distinguishing feature of pure competition, as compared to any other mode of behavior, is that the market conditions facing each individual are taken (by him) to be "straight lines" involving trade at unchanging price ratios. And it is precisely the question of the sense in which this is optimal which is left unanswered.

It does not appear that Walras ever reached beyond this second stage of the argument.[2] His cardinal failing consists not so much

---

[2] Compare the very penetrating remarks of Wicksell on this point. K. Wicksell, *Lectures on Political Economy* (English translation, New York: Macmillan, 1934), I, 72–83.

in the fact that he jumps from incomplete premises to sweeping conclusions, but in the fact that he is satisfied with this very limited kind of an optimum, which by a play on words he seems to confuse with the more usual and important senses in which perfect competition is conceived to be optimal.[3]

3. Still a third stage of reasoning attempts to show, *not* that *each* individual is made best off by competition since this is impossible unless each can take all, but that in some sense the sum total of satisfactions is maximized, that perfect competition effects an ideal compromise of mutual benefit, or in its most nebulous form that free trade (perfect competition) maximizes world (all individuals') *income*. Of course, this involves the notion of adding the utilities of different individuals, of somehow being able to compare and weight the utilities of different individuals. Although the marginal utility economists, with the exception of Jevons who made an interesting slip in connection with the concept of the utility of the "trading body," knew that it was not necessary to make interpersonal comparisons of utility in describing exchange under pure competition, they nevertheless did not have the modern reticence about making such assumptions.

Launhardt seems to have been the only economist who attempted to give rigorous proof of this theorem. As Wicksell has pointed out in the section just cited, his argument is mathematically and logically false. Yet he must be given credit for having made an attempt at rigor, and we can learn more from his unambiguous failure than from many pages of fuzzy literary effusion.

To many modern economists the difficulty with this third line of reasoning lies in the fact that it assumes that the utilities of different individuals can be compared, in fact added together.

---

[3] If interpreted literally, he would seem to imply that each and every person is made better off by perfect competition, a conclusion which, as Wicksell observes, goes farther than the free traders themselves, "for the latter have not denied that a restriction of free competition might be most advantageous to a small privileged minority." *Ibid.*, p. 76.

Actually there is one qualification in Walras' argument which makes it not so much wrong as trivial. He maintains that perfect competition creates a maximum of satisfaction, *consistent with trading at uniform prices*. Waiving the trivial objection that under nondiscriminating monopoly trading is also done at uniform prices, I find this confusing. Except for positions of multiple equilibria which we may provisionally ignore, the equilibrium position under competition is uniquely determined. Instead of being the *optimum* condition under these conditions, it is the only one possible. Thus, it is the worst position as well as the best.

This they would regard as "unscientific." But to the preceding generation of economists, interindividual comparisons of utility were made almost without question; to a man like Edgeworth, steeped as he was in the Utilitarian tradition, individual utility— nay social utility—was as real as his morning jam. And with Marshall the apostrophe in consumers' surplus was always after the *s*.

Both Marshall and Wicksell objected to what they considered to be a prevalent notion that perfect competition leads to the maximum of satisfaction. Both enter as a minor objection the fact that there may be multiple positions of equilibrium; actually this is largely irrelevant since each stable equilibrium might be a relative maximum as compared to points in its immediate neighborhood (*im kleinen*) even if it were not the *maximum maximorum*. But their major objection consists in the fact that with existing distributions of wealth and ability, the processes of imputation under competition will give rise to great inequalities in the personal distribution of income so that unless individuals are very different in their natures the marginal utilities of income will not be equal for each individual. Both recognize that in these circumstances any interference (à la Robin Hood) with perfect competition which transfers income from rich to poor would be beneficial.

4. It might be thought that at this stage Marshall and Wicksell would enunciate a fourth proposition, that exchange under perfect competition is optimal provided the distribution of income is optimal. In the case of Wicksell the proof which he gives (*Lectures*, p. 80) to show why perfect competition is *not* optimal when the distribution of income is inappropriate paves the way for a proof as to why perfect competition is optimal when the distribution of income is appropriate.[4] Wicksell also realizes that when the distribution of income is not optimal, the creation of a condition of

[4] Actually his proof seems to suffer from one minor drawback. In effect, his evaluation of the change in utility resulting from a change in price from the competitive level assumes that in the noncompetitive situation all individuals are still on their offer curves. Strictly speaking, this is not possible. It would perhaps be correct to say that his proof (with slight modifications) shows that transfer of goods or income from one individual to another could not improve the competitive conditions. There is also an unfortunate minor slip in expression, perhaps in translation, in the statement that "free competition would secure a maximum satisfaction *to all* parties to the exchange." (*Ibid.*, p. 81, my italics.) Actually, it is the sum of all and not the utility *of each* that is maximized.

imperfect competition may improve the situation, but that this is not the best way of improving the situation, since perfect competition is a necessary condition to "maximize production." I return to this point a little later in this historical review.

Although inappropriateness in distribution is thought by Marshall to render the competitive position suspect, he was of the belief that many decisions involve alternatives which affect all classes more or less equally. He has been criticized for this too facile assumption, but it is nevertheless true that many modern economists, and this includes some purists, by use of the principle of sufficient reason (or is it insufficient reason?) argue in such terms for or against a price change of a commodity which is not presumed to relate more to the poor than to the rich.

However, aside from problems raised by the inappropriateness of the distribution of income, Marshall had important objections to the equilibrium position realized under perfect competition. These objections resulted from his analysis of consumers' surplus, an analysis which was regarded as almost the most significant contribution of his *Principles*. By a comparison of geometrical areas he arrived at the conclusion that increasing cost industries would be pushed to too great a margin under competition, and that the output of decreasing cost industries would be too small under competition. From the modern standpoint it is clear that these conclusions are true in only a very limited sense. And if Marshall did arrive at conclusions which are not completely wrong, it is nevertheless clear that he arrived at them for the wrong reasons.

It is not easy in a few paragraphs to delineate the various faults in the Marshallian reasoning. In the first place, his exposition in Book V, chapter xiii, is extremely sketchy, and, in the second place, it is impossible to avoid the somewhat extraneous difficulties arising from the admittedly unsatisfactory treatment of decreasing cost by Marshall. However, the latter is simply the most dramatic exemplification of the paradox that Marshall, with whom the doctrines of partial equilibrium and industry analysis are inseparably associated, nowhere presents a complete or satisfactory theory of the industry in its relationship to the firms which make it up. If anyone doubts this, he need only compare the treatment of these problems by Pigou, Marshall's shining pupil, in his 1912 *Wealth and Welfare* with his treatment in the late editions of the *Economics of Welfare* or with that of Viner in the *Zeitschrift* article cited in chapter iii.

Another inadequacy, but one that can be easily remedied, lies in the fact that Marshall neglects producers' surplus instead of treating this symmetrically with consumers' surplus, so that it is possible by the reasoning of page 468, footnote 2, to arrive at the curious conclusion that industries of increasing costs should in many cases be contracted even if there are no decreasing cost industries to expand.

There seems to be no point in discussing the Marshallian reasoning at greater length except to note that Pigou nowhere makes essential use of the concept of consumers' surplus in his welfare analysis.   He originally enunciated essentially the Marshallian conditions with respect to increasing and decreasing cost industries, but as a result of the criticisms of Allyn Young, Knight, and Robertson he seriously modified these conclusions.[5]   In its final form his doctrine holds that the equilibrium of a closed economy under competition is correct except where there are technological external economies or diseconomies.   Under these conditions, since each individual's actions have effects on others which he does not take into account in making his decision, there is a *prima facie* case for intervention.   But this holds only for technological factors (smoke nuisance, etc.); changes in factor prices resulting from the expansion of demand by firms in an industry represent transfers which are irrelevant for determination of ideal output.   (In all fairness it should be admitted that the correct use of consumers' surplus and producers' surplus might have helped to avoid error in this regard.)

There would be no reason to rake over these old ashes were it not for the fact that Professor Hicks has recently lent the weight of his authority to the view that the doctrine of consumers' surplus has a claim to importance in the welfare field.[6]   As I have indicated in chapter vii, careful perusal of his argument simply confirms my

[5] F. H. Knight, "Fallacies in the Interpretation of Social Cost," *Quarterly Journal of Economics* (1923).   Reprinted in *The Ethics of Competition* (New York: Harper, 1935), pp. 215–236.   Allyn Young, "Pigou's Wealth and Welfare," *Quarterly Journal of Economics*, XXVII (1913), 672–686.   D. H. Robertson, "Those Empty Boxes," *Economic Journal*, XXXIV (1924), 16–31.

[6] J. R. Hicks, "The Rehabilitation of Consumers' Surplus," *Review of Economic Studies*, VIII (1941), 108–116.

belief that the economist—mathematical, literary, beginner, expert
—had best dispense with consumers' surplus. It is a tool which
can be used only by one who can get along without its use, and
not by all such. As Hicks admits, it is not useful in the exposition
of the conditions of "equilibrium" or "optimum." And even in
the case of a Crusoe economy where the problems raised by many
individuals can be sidestepped, it is usually only devised to give
the loss in utility resulting from a deviation from the optimum in
the amount of one good.

In this connection its principal conclusion states that the
(second order) change in utility resulting from a deviation in the
amount of one commodity, other commodities continuing to be
optimally adjusted, depends upon the amount of the discrepancy
in that good times the discrepancy in the equilibrium condition.
This conclusion is no more plausibly derived from consumers' surplus than from simple intuition. And if one probes deeper, one
finds in any case that the theorem is incorrect even to the order of
infinitesimals (second) at which the argument is pitched.

Thus in the most favorable case to consumers' surplus where one
commodity, x_{n+1}, has literally constant marginal utility so that

$$U = L(x_1, x_2, \cdots, x_n) + mx_{n+1}, \tag{1}$$

and where the goods can be converted into each other at constant
technological rates as indicated by the relation

$$\sum_{1}^{n+1} b_i x_i = c, \tag{2}$$

for this conclusion to be correct it would be necessary that the
change in utility resulting from a small change in the amount
of x_1 be

$$\delta^2 U = 0 + \tfrac{1}{2} L_{11} \delta x_1^2. \tag{3}$$

Actually, by a simple extension of the reasoning in chapter iii, it is
given by

$$\delta^2 U = 0 + \tfrac{1}{2} \sum_{1}^{n} \sum_{1}^{n} L_{ij} \delta x_i \delta x_j. \tag{4}$$

If we proceed to higher orders of infinitesimals, the case is worse,
and the same can be said if we drop the unrealistic assumption

about the utility of the numeraire, and if the original position is not one of equilibrium.

Even if consumers' surplus did give a cardinal measure of the change in utility from a given change, it is hard to see what use this could serve. Only in the contemplation of alternative movements which begin or end in the same point could this cardinal measure have any significance, and then only because it is an indicator of ordinal preference. Such situations are comparatively rare as far as questions of social policy are concerned, being in the nature of the somewhat academic question as to whether the introduction of a little monopoly evil into one industry, all others being competitive before and after the change, is better or worse than introduction of some monopoly in another.

In connection with monopolistic competition the frequent occurrence of decreasing cost and indivisible initial costs inevitably raises problems of an "all or none" character. Waiving the difficulties arising from many individuals, we see that correct decisions necessitate reference to ordinal indifference curves and to nothing else. Certain difficulties connected with the determination of the optimal amount of differentiation of product were properly posed by Chamberlin, Cassels, and Kahn without the use of consumers' surplus.[7]

We may conclude from this lengthy digression that after making due allowances for external economies and for certain omissions in their expositions, the founders of neo-classical economics believed that perfect competition led to an optimum in "exchange and production" provided that the distribution of income was appropriate. But they did not believe that incomes imputed by the competitive process as of a given historical distribution of ownership of factors of production and personal abilities was in any sense the best one, and not subject to modification by appropriate mechanisms.

5. Before analyzing the problems encountered under the headings of optimum "production" and optimum "exchange," I should like to note briefly the existence of economists who attempted to

[7] E. H. Chamberlin, *The Theory of Monopolistic Competition* (3rd ed.; Cambridge: Harvard University Press, 1938), p. 94. J. M. Cassels, "Excess Capacity and Monopolistic Competition," *Quarterly Journal of Economics*, LI (1937), 426–443. R. F. Kahn, "Some Notes on Ideal Output," *Economic Journal*, XLV (1935), 1–35.

establish the stronger position that incomes imputed under competition were actually right and best. Thus at an earlier date, Bastiat, whose powers of analysis were hardly of the highest order even in his day, hoped to show that beneficent competition would lead to ". . . an amount of utility and enjoyment, always greater, and more and more equally distributed. . . ." [8]

Confronted with the undeniable fact of considerable inequality of income and possessing the latent Western European prejudice against inequality, writers had either to refer to a future day when competition would achieve better results, or attribute existing inequalities to the admittedly large institutional deviations from competition, or to look for inequalities among individuals' characteristics (including property ownership) to justify differences in income.

To anyone with knowledge of the world the perverse relationship between exertion and income made necessary a revision of the classical real cost doctrine in its simplest form, although the promotion by Senior of abstinence to the rank of a full-bodied real cost helped to bolster that doctrine. But ultimately refuge was found in the undeniable fact of differences in personal "ability" and the related doctrine of non-competing groups. This raised many questions as to the extent to which the relevant abilities were or were not "acquired characteristics" and the degree of correspondence between the distribution of abilities and income. That much of this discussion was meaningless and from most points of view irrelevant does not detract from its significance from the standpoint of the history of ideas.

Among analytical economists J. B. Clark [9] is best known for his belief that not only will factors of production have imputed to them their marginal productivity under competition, but that this is a "natural law" which is "morally justifiable" since this is their "actual," "specific" product. Indeed Clark himself considered that the principal way that his independently discovered marginal productivity doctrine represented an improvement upon von Thünen lay in his demonstration of its ethical fairness as compared to the latter's belief that the doctrine involved exploitation. That Clark, who clearly states the distinction between personal and

[8] F. Bastiat, *Harmonies of Political Economy* (2nd ed.; Edinburgh, 1880), p. 301.

[9] J. B. Clark, *The Distribution of Wealth* (New York, 1899).

functional income, should have thought that he had proved the ethical fairness of income determination under competition is simply a reflection of the fact that where emotional beliefs in right and wrong enter into analysis, it is usually not to the advantage of the latter.   As we shall see, even if all income resulted from personal services, Clark's proposition is not consistent with widely held ethical views; and if it is accepted as a definition rather than a theorem, it will be found to be consistent with *no* unambiguous ethical evaluation of different individuals' welfare.   Nevertheless, it has considerable appeal, especially in a frontier society, where each individual could be thought of as working by himself under conditions where "his" product could be identified.   Analytically, it is almost precisely in these terms that Clark first perceived his doctrine, going with painful slowness from the (broad) "zone of indifference" to the concept of the internal margin.

6. While Wicksell and Marshall held that competition would be optimal if the distribution of income were appropriate, it was left for Pareto [10] to take the stronger position that competition produces a *maximum d'utilité collective* regardless of the distribution of income, and indeed even if the utilities of different individuals were not considered to be comparable.   *An optimum position in this sense was defined by the requirement that there should not exist any possible variation or movement which would make everybody better off.*

His discussion is not easy to follow, and it has not received attention from economists commensurate with the importance which he attached to it.   Yet it forms the basis of many modern notions, and it led directly to the important contribution of Barone. Pareto also seems to have been one of the first to discuss criteria of planning under collectivism.

Pareto's exposition is complicated by the fact that he works with differentials or first order (infinitesimal) variations.   This was a very common practice with mathematicians and physicists of the nineteenth century, and because of its formal heuristic conveniences is still often used today.   And under proper qualifications this practice can be given a rigorous, unambiguous basis. Nevertheless, where delicate problems of interpretation are involved it often obscures more than it reveals, especially if the prob-

---

[10] V. Pareto, *Manuel D'Economie Politique* (1909), chap. vi; also the Mathematical Appendix, par. 89, *passim*.

lem arises as to whether any given differential expression is an "exact" differential.

Pareto is unwilling to add the utility or *ophelimite'* of different individuals together, either *in toto*, i.e. ($U^1 + U^2 + \cdots$), or for small variations ($\delta U^1 + \delta U^2 + \cdots$). For that would involve a comparison of different individuals' utility, and in addition it would depend upon the particular cardinal index of *ophelimite'* selected for each. But he was interested in comparing the summed variation in the utility of each, after these expressions have been divided by the marginal utility of any one good, *a*, selected as numeraire. For if we examine the dimensionality of the expression

$$\frac{1}{U_a{}^1} \delta U^1 + \frac{1}{U_a{}^2} \delta U^2 + \cdots, \tag{5}$$

where as usual subscripts represent partial differentiation, but where the superscript is taken to indicate different individuals, we shall see that this has the dimensionality of the good, *a*, and nothing else.

Pareto attempts to show that if the original position is one of equilibrium under perfect competition, then no possible variations, consistent with the fundamental scarcity of goods and given technology, can make the above expression positive. If it could, he says, it would be possible to arrange things so that each term in the expression could be made positive, and then everyone would be better off. But the expression *cannot* be made positive. Actually, regarded as a differential expression (of the first order), the above expression can be shown to be zero, in consequence of the fact that each commodity is sold at minimum unit cost (proportionality of marginal products, etc.,[11] and in consequence of the tangency of each individual's indifference curves to mutual price exchange loci. If recourse is had to differentials of higher order, the secondary maximum-minimum conditions of firms and individuals will guarantee that the expression (5) will be negative for all finite deviations from the competitive position, or so Pareto attempted to show.

Although Pareto's treatment is somewhat sketchy and in need of expansion, part of which Barone later provided, the main outlines are reasonably clear. But in connection with the funda-

[11] *Ibid.*, p. 646.

mentals of interpretation of the significance of his maximum, there do arise certain problems. First, can the differential expression of (5) be regarded as the exact differential of some expression? Actually, Pareto later gives a name to this expression, calling it δU; but is there an expression U (social utility?) of which this is an exact differential? Pareto does not tell us, but presumably he would answer, no, if he were on guard when the question was asked. As we shall see, Barone does work with an expression whose differential corresponds to (5), but he clearly recognizes that it is a construction, not involving the dimension of utility, but rather that of the numeraire good.

But the most important objection to Pareto's exposition is his lack of emphasis upon the fact that an optimum point, in his sense, is not a unique point.[12]   If transfers of income from one individual to another are arbitrarily imposed, there will be a new optimum point, and there is absolutely no way of deciding whether the new point is better or worse than the old.   His optimum points constitute a manifold infinity of values.   This locus can be obtained under regimes quite different from perfect competition (e.g., by multilateral monopoly).   Within Pareto's system it is impossible to decide, by his differential criterion or otherwise, which of two points on what may be called the "generalized contract locus" are better, or even that a given movement off the contract locus and hence to a non-optimal point is good or bad.   Actually in terms of the wider reference schemes of ordinary economic thought, such a movement may be deemed eminently desirable.   But Pareto shows that however desirable such a move may be, there exists still a better move, which for the same (ordinal) amount of harm to those who "should" be harmed, will yield more benefit for the worthy ones who are to be benefited.   This is an important contribution.   ·

7. In a masterly article, written in 1908 in Italian, but not translated into English until 1935,[13] Barone developed further and in greater detail the Paretian conditions of optimum, especially as

---

[12] In his earlier *Cours* discussion, II, 90 ff., he explicitly assumes the distribution of income to be *"convenable,"* but in his later *Manuel* treatment the dependence of the optimum point on the initial distribution of income, and hence its lack of uniqueness, is not brought to the foreground.

[13] Reprinted as an Appendix in F. A. Hayek, ed., *Collectivist Economic Planning* (London: Routledge, 1935), pp. 245–290.

they relate to the planning of production under collectivism. By avoiding all mention of utility and indeed without introducing even the notion of indifference curves, Barone was able to break new ground along lines which have in recent years become associated with the economic theory of index numbers.

Unlike most of the writers discussed above, Barone is unsatisfied with the statement that free competition maximizes product, or sums of product, which can then be distributed in any given fashion. Heterogeneous products cannot be added. Furthermore, leisure may be preferred to the maximization of output. It is significant that those writers who do not explicitly introduce the equations of general equilibrium should gloss over the definition of "product" which is allegedly maximized. Thus, Wicksell [14] confines his demonstration to a case where the same product can be provided by different sources, and only in this case shows that various marginal conditions are optimal. The same is true of the very excellent treatment by Knight, in which the movement of goods over alternative roads is analyzed for optimum conditions.[15]

It is remarkable that Professor Pigou, who reaches substantially correct conclusions, never squarely meets the problem of the definition of social product. His index number discussion represents an important contribution in its own right, but it is offered at best as an approximate criterion or indicator of changes in individual and social welfare. He would not seriously suggest that the thing to be maximized is the money value of output deflated by an ideal index of prices. Nor will the more exact limits of index number theory such as are discussed in chapter vi avail.

Barone proposes to add different products after they have been weighted by their respective prices; it is usually taken to be convenient to express these prices as ratios to the numeraire good, a. For Barone, productive services can be treated simply as algebraically negative goods and services. Thus, decisions between more or less work can be included in his welfare system. Then if the sum total of each good consumed by all individuals together is written as

$$A = a^1 + a^2 + \cdots$$
$$B = b^1 + b^2 + \cdots \tag{6}$$
$$\text{etc.,}$$

[14] Wicksell, *op. cit.*, p. 140, *passim.*
[15] Knight, *op. cit.*, p. 219.

and recalling that

$$\delta U^i = U_a{}^i \delta a^i + U_b{}^i \delta b^i + \cdots, \tag{7}$$

we can write Pareto's equation (5) above in the equivalent form

$$1(\delta a^1 + \delta a^2 + \cdots) + p_b(\delta b^1 + \delta b^2 + \cdots) + \cdots$$
$$= \delta A + p_b \delta B + \cdots. \tag{8}$$

In passing from (4) to (8), use is made of the fact that the ratios of marginal utilities of two goods for each individual are equal to their price ratios. Barone himself does not use this terminology, but no doubt he would have to if the connection with Pareto were to be shown.

The expression in (8) can be regarded as the variation in the following expression when prices are regarded as constants:

$$\Phi = A + p_b B + \cdots. \tag{9}$$

If productive services were known to be constant so that they could be neglected, (9) would equal (except for dynamic factors involving capital which we can ignore) money value of national product. If all productive factors are included, it will represent the net difference between value of consumers' goods and the return to productive services. Under many assumptions this quantity must be zero under the full conditions of perfect competition.

Barone shows that perfect competition maximizes this expression, prices being taken as fixed parameters, i.e., any variation from a condition of price equal to minimum cost must make $\delta\Phi$ as given in (8) negative. Thus, if we are at conditions other than perfect competition, with (8) not equal to zero for all possible variations, it will be possible to specify a movement which will make $\delta\Phi$ positive. But we can think of $\delta\Phi$ as being made up of the sum of a similar expression referring to each individual

$$\delta\Phi = \delta\varphi^1 + \delta\varphi^2 + \cdots = (\delta a^1 + p_b \delta b^1 + \cdots)$$
$$+ (\delta a^2 + p_b \delta b^2 + \cdots) + \cdots. \tag{10}$$

If for any movement, the total $\delta\Phi$ is positive, it is not necessary that each and every one of the individual's $\delta\varphi$ be positive; but it is necessary that those which are positive should outweight those which are negative. Thus, those who are hurt could be compensated by those who are helped, and there would still be a net gain left to be parceled out among the individuals.

This is essentially the gist of the Barone argument. The one point which will occur to the critical reader is the fact that arbitrary prices are assumed in evaluating the expression to be maximized. Which prices are to be used? Barone employs the prices which prevailed before a contemplated break with the conditions of competition are made, and this suffices if one merely wishes to demonstrate that not all individuals can be improved by any departure from competition.[16]

Unlike Pareto, Barone satisfies himself with deriving optimal *production* conditions without going into the fact that under competition no additional individual exchanges of fixed amounts of goods would be mutually profitable. No doubt this oversight resulted from his wish to avoid the use of indifference curves and utility, but even without these constructions, by the use of the index number notions which he pioneered, the enlarged conditions of exchange could have been included. It is a tribute to this work that a third of a century after it was written there is no better statement of the problem in the English language to which the attention of students may be turned.

8. The next writer who deserves our attention is A. P. Lerner, who comparatively recently developed, presumably independently, the Paretian conditions which show that the marginal equivalences realized by perfect competition lead to an optimum of production and exchange in the special senses discussed above.[17] Actually, in the field of production his statement of the problem is slightly different from that of Pareto and Barone. They showed that a movement to conditions of perfect competition in the field of production and cost could make everyone better off because they could be given more of every good. But they still worked with individuals. Even in a collectivized state where the existence of the individual is not assumed, the Lerner formulation of the sense in which output is optimal would still hold: *the marginal equivalences of competition are such as to give a maximum of any one product for*

---

[16] Actually, Barone discusses varying prices in a passage which seems obscure to me. *Op. cit.*, p. 255.

[17] A. P. Lerner, "The Concept of Monopoly and the Measure of Monopoly Power," *Review of Economic Studies*, I (1934), 157–175. "Economic Theory and Socialist Economy," *Review of Economic Studies*, II (1934), 51–61.

given specified amounts of all others. This is almost identical with the Pareto-Barone production propositions, but not quite.

Professor Hotelling, also presumably independently, developed in two articles [18] conditions closely related to the Pareto production and exchange conditions of optimum. In particular, he has insisted upon the fact that marginal rather than average costs provide the appropriate basis for pricing, and he developed the dramatic applications of this to the problem of railroad rates and decreasing cost public utilities in general. On the analytic side each thing which he sets out to prove he does prove with great elegance and generality, but his fundamental primitive assumptions are only implicitly related to each other and to the equations of general equilibrium. Moreover, his welfare work really falls into two distinct headings; on the one hand, that of the first article cited and much of the second article, and on the other hand, that of the second section of his second article referring to the "fundamental theorem" (especially pp. 248–256). Roughly these two diverse contributions of Hotelling fall respectively under the headings of optimal *production* and optimal *exchange* conditions; or, on the analytic side, to the difference between firms with unlimited budgets and the consumer with limited budget, to each of which fields Professor Hotelling has contributed much in the way of demand analysis. This dualism explains why so discerning a reader as Professor Frisch should have been puzzled by the Hotelling proof.[19]

[18] H. Hotelling, "The General Welfare in Relation to Problems of Taxation and of Railway and Utility Rates," *Econometrica*, VI (1938), 242–269, "Edgeworth's Taxation Paradox and the Nature of Demand and Supply Functions," *Journal of Political Economy*, XL (1932), 577–616.

[19] Space cannot permit a detailed examination of the exact 'steps in the Hotelling reasoning, this being particularly unnecessary since it is clear that his conclusions are impeccable. In the original specification of his system Professor Hotelling essentially generalizes the Dupuit-Marshall partial equilibrium set-up to many interrelated industries. However, unless we confine ourselves to the production problem alone, this will not lead to the equations of general equilibrium. These require the addition of the special demand functions of consumers for goods and their supply functions of productive services. In the mixed consumer-firm system the integrability conditions which give meaning to Hotelling's line integral, dead loss, and price potential (equal to the Barone Φ function) are not satisfied. Nor when it came to interpretation would it matter for the validity of the Pareto-Barone-Lerner conditions if they were. While Hotelling gives separate consideration to consumers when discussing excises, the two treatments are never adequately integrated.

9. The last writer to be mentioned is Professor A. Bergson.[20] He is the first who understands the contributions of all previous contributors, and who is able to form a synthesis of them. In addition, he is the first to develop explicitly the notion of an ordinal social welfare function in terms of which all the various schools of thought can be interpreted, and in terms of which they for the first time assume significance. In view of his own very generous acknowledgments of the work of others, even where he himself had independently rediscovered many basic theorems in an improved form, it is regrettable that his contribution has received so little notice. No doubt this stems in part from the mathematical character of his exposition, and to the fact that he uses the rather difficult notation of differentials throughout. The analysis that follows is simply an enlargement and development of his important work.[21]

THE SOCIAL WELFARE FUNCTION

It is fashionable for the modern economist to insist that ethical value judgments have no place in scientific analysis. Professor Robbins in particular has insisted upon this point,[22] and today it is customary to make a distinction between the pure analysis of

[20] A. Bergson, "A Reformulation of Certain Aspects of Welfare Economics," *Quarterly Journal of Economics*, LII (1938), 310–334.

[21] In recent years Kaldor and Hicks have given an exposition of certain aspects of welfare economics. N. Kaldor, "Welfare Propositions in Economics," *Economic Journal*, XLIX (1939), 549–552. J. R. Hicks, "Foundations of Welfare Economics," *Economic Journal*, XLIX (1939), 696–712. Mention should also be made of an important article which indicates the modification in the Pigouvian analysis necessitated by the considerations of monopolistic competition. R. F. Kahn, "Some Notes on Ideal Output," *Economic Journal*, XLV (1935), 1–35. A convenient compact summary of welfare economics is provided by O. Lange, "The Foundations of Welfare Economics," *Econometrica*, X (1942), 215–228. An advance in the discussion is represented by T. Scitovsky, "A Note on Welfare Propositions in Economics," *Review of Economic Studies*, IX (1941), 77–88. Because discussions of Free Trade illuminate the beliefs of economists upon these matters, and because this subject provides a convenient illustration, it would be desirable to review its literature. However, reference can only be made here to the survey in J. Viner, *Studies in the Theory of International Trade* (New York: Harper, 1937); to T. Scitovsky, "A Reconsideration of the Theory of Tariffs," *Review of Economic Studies*, IX (1942), 89–110; P. A. Samuelson, "Welfare Economics and International Trade," *American Economic Review*, XXVIII (1938), 261–266; "The Gains from International Trade," *Canadian Journal of Economics and Political Science*, V (1939), 195–205.

[22] L. Robbins, *An Essay on the Nature and Significance of Economic Science* (London, 1932).

Robbins *qua* economist and his propaganda, condemnations, and policy recommendations *qua* citizen. In practice, if pushed to extremes, this somewhat schizophrenic rule becomes difficult to adhere to, and it leads to rather tedious circumlocutions. But in essence Robbins is undoubtedly correct. Wishful thinking is a powerful deterrent of good analysis and description, and ethical conclusions cannot be derived in the same way that scientific hypotheses are inferred or verified.

But it is not valid to conclude from this that there is no room in economics for what goes under the name of "welfare economics." It is a legitimate exercise of economic analysis to examine the consequences of various value judgments, whether or not they are shared by the theorist, just as the study of comparative ethics is itself a science like any other branch of anthropology. If it is appropriate for the economist to analyze the way Robinson Crusoe directs production so as to maximize his (curious) preferences, the economist does not thereby commit himself to those tastes or inquire concerning the manner in which they were or ought to have been formed. No more does the astronomer, who enunciates the principle that the paths of planets are such as to minimize certain integrals, care whether or not these should be minimized; neither for all we know do the stars care. Our above historical review should show that there is meaty and weighty content to the field of welfare economics, without invoking new methods in economic thought. In saying this, I do not mean to imply that the field of welfare economics has scientific content because a number of its theorems do *not* require inter-personal comparisons of utility; this after all is a mere detail. That part which *does* involve inter-personal comparisons of utility also has real content and interest for the scientific analyst, even though the scientist does not consider it any part of his task to deduce or verify (except on the anthropological level) the value judgments whose implications he grinds out. In the same way, the mathematical theory of probability accepts as a primitive undefined assumption whose validity is not its concern the initial specification of "equally likely" events, the measure of various "classes" or the "collective," and it then proceeds to grind out the mathematical implications of these and subsidiary hypotheses. It is only fair to point out, however, that the theorems enunciated under the heading of welfare economics are not meaningful propositions or hypotheses in the technical sense. For they represent the deductive implications of assumptions which are not themselves meaningful refutable hypotheses about reality.

Without inquiring into its origins, we take as a starting point for our discussion a function of all the economic magnitudes of a system which is supposed to characterize some ethical belief—that of a benevolent despot, or a complete egotist, or "all men of good will," a misanthrope, the state, race, or group mind, God, etc. Any possible opinion is admissible, including my own, although it is best in the first instance, in view of human frailty where one's own beliefs are involved, to omit the latter. We only require that the belief be such as to admit of an unequivocal answer as to whether one configuration of the economic system is "better" or "worse" than any other or "indifferent," and that these relationships are transitive; i.e., A better than B, B better than C, implies A better than C, etc. The function need only be ordinally defined, and it may or may not be convenient to work with (any) one cardinal index or indicator. There is no need to assume any particular curvature of the loci (in hyper-space) of indifference of this function. Utilizing one out of an infinity of possible indicators or cardinal indices, we may write this function in the form

$$W = W(z_1, z_2, \cdots), \qquad (11)$$

where the z's represent all possible variables, many of them non-economic in character.

Between these z's there will be a number of "technological" relations limiting our freedom to vary the z's independently. Just what the content of these technological relations will be depends upon the level of abstraction at which the specifier of the value judgments wishes to work. If he is an out and out Utopian he may wish to ignore various institutional relations regardless of their empirical importance; indeed, he may go all out and repeal the laws of conservation of energy and widen greatly the technological productivities of the system. On the other hand, he may wish to take as fixed and immutable all social and economic institutions except those relating to the Central Bank. (Indeed those of fatalistic temperament may regard the restraints to be so numerous as to leave no problem of choice.) In other words, the auxiliary constraints imposed upon the variables are not themselves the proper subject matter of welfare economics but must be taken as givens.

Subject to these constraints, which may be written in the most general way as

$$g^i(z_1, z_2, \cdots) = 0, \tag{12}$$

there will presumably be an upper bound to W (even though no unique value of the z's need correspond to this maximum level). If certain assumptions of regularity are made, it would be possible to indicate formal conditions for the maximum, involving Lagrangean multipliers, matrices, rank, and quadratic forms definite under constraint, etc. However, there is no particular point in developing this formalism.

The subject could end with these banalities were it not for the fact that numerous individuals find it of interest to specialize the form of W, the nature of the variables, z, and the nature of the constraints.

(1) For one thing, prices are not usually included in the welfare function itself, except very indirectly through the effects of different prices and wages upon the quantities of consumption, work, etc.

(2) Also certain of the variables can be thought of as referring to a particular individual or family; e.g., one of the z's may be the amount of tea consumed by John Jones, or the amount of unskilled labor which he provides.

(3) It is often further assumed that the quantities of a given commodity consumed by one individual are of the same type as those consumed by another; technically, this means that certain of the variables enter in the technical side-conditions in sums, which relate the total amount produced of a commodity to input, regardless of the ultimate distribution of that output. Whatever may be said about the admissibility of this, the matter is still worse when a similar assumption is made concerning the homogeneity of the various services provided by different individuals. However, even if in the most rigorous sense each individual's talents are unique, society rarely has the time or patience to learn to appreciate the flavor of each man, and, in the absence of perfect "screening" of different individuals, it does treat them as if they were perfectly substitutable; thus for our purposes the   may be assumed to be so in many cases. This does not mean that we work with a single

grade of labor; on the contrary, the number of grades may be very large and the classification minute, but it is assumed that there are many individuals in each grade, actually or potentially.

(4) Not infrequently it is assumed that a given grade of productive service may be used indifferently in a number of uses. Technically this means that certain of the z's enter into the welfare function only as certain sums. As Bergson has pointed out, this involves implicit value judgments, so that Robbins when he discusses the problem of allocating resources as between alternative uses so as to maximize (in some sense) output or personal utility is not able even on the Robinson Crusoe level to avoid these notions; or rather, if resources are not assumed indifferent between at least two uses, few interesting marginal conditions can be deduced.

(5) A more extreme assumption, which stems from the individualist philosophy of modern Western Civilization, states that individuals' preferences are to "count." If any movement leaves an individual on the same indifference curve, then the social welfare function is unchanged, and similarly for an increase or decrease. Actually, an examination of the principles of jurisprudence, the folkways and mores, shows that in its extreme form this assumption is rarely seriously proposed. Even "sane" adults are not permitted to eat and drink what they think best, individuals cannot sell themselves in order to consume more in the present, milk ration tickets cannot be exchanged for beer at the will of the owner, etc.

But economists in the orthodox tradition have tended to consider the above cases as exceptions.[23] However, in recent years many economists, Frank Knight being a notable example, have

[23] Consider, however, the following interesting quotation from Edwin Cannan who was very much in the classical tradition: "We shall never decide whether to put a penny on beer or to further steepen the super-tax on incomes by considering how much the loss of a penny pinches the beer-drinker and the duke: we shall, and we do, decide it by making some rough estimate of the aggregate advantage in the long run of the two methods to society at large. For example, if we find that cheaper beer means better food for underfed children while less super-tax means more training of horses to run fast for a short distance with a very light burden, we incline to the super-tax: but if we find cheaper beer means more beer for drunkards and less super-tax means more houses for the people to inhabit in comfort and health, we incline to the beer tax." From an *Economic Journal* review of Sir Josiah Stamp's *Fundamental Principles of Taxation in the Light of Modern Developments*, reprinted in *An Economist's Protest* (London, 1927), p. 279.

insisted upon the degree to which individual tastes and wants are socially conditioned by advertising and custom so that they can hardly be said to belong to him in any ultimate sense. All this is recognized in the witticism of the soap box speaker who said to the recalcitrant listener, "When the revolution comes, you will eat strawberries and cream, and like it!" Attention should also be called to the fact that even the classical economist does not literally have the individual in mind, so much as the family; of course, some hardy souls will pursue the will-o'-the-wisp of sovereignty within the family so as to reduce even these collective indifference curves to an individualistic basis.

(6) One does not have to be a John Donne then to find fault with the above assumption, especially if we consider the closely related assumption that an individual's preference depends only upon the things which *he* consumes and not upon what others consume. As Veblen characteristically pointed out, much of the motivation for consumption is related to the fact that others do or do not have the same thing. Conspicuous expenditure, "keeping up with the Joneses," snob appeal, maintenance of face, are important in any realistic appraisal of consumption habits; and if we turn to the field of power analysis, it is not only on the national scale that "satisfactions" are relative and dog-in-the-manger tactics are rational.

If this sixth assumption is not made, many of the conclusions of welfare economics will remain valid, but they will require modifications to allow for certain "external" consumption economies not dissimilar analytically to the external technological economies and diseconomies of the Marshall-Pigou type.

(7) All of the above assumptions are more or less tacitly accepted by extremely divergent schools of thought. The next assumption involves a more controversial value judgment, but one which has been characteristic of much of modern thought of the last century, and which is especially typical of the beliefs of the classical and neo-classical economists. *It is that the welfare function is completely (or very nearly) symmetrical with respect to the consumption of all individuals.*

Taken in connection with previous assumptions, in its strict form it is not consistent with the patent fact of considerable differences in individuals' overt preference patterns. Thus, in addition to involving a very significant value judgment, it also involves a very definite assumption of fact. This was not appreciated by economists, who tended to believe in the desirability of an equality of income, leaving it to the individual to determine the exact form of his consumption. However, it is easy to show that the rule of equality of income (measured in dollars, numeraire, abstract purchasing power) applied to individuals of different tastes, but made to hold in all circumstances, is actually inconsistent with any determinate, definite W function. Equality becomes a fetish or shibboleth, albeit a useful one, in that the means becomes the end, and the letter of the law takes precedence over the spirit.

For the decision of equal incomes as optimal in one situation implies a certain relative well-being as between vegetarians and non-vegetarians; at different relative prices between vegetables and non-vegetables an equal distribution of income can no longer be optimal. Actually this does not render invalid the reasoning based upon this seventh premise since the adherents of this view implicitly held that individuals were very much alike, and if given equality of treatment would develop the same want patterns. Moreover, they could in all logic take the milder position that a great deal less inequality than existed in real life would be desirable even if one did not believe in complete equality.[24]

In a similar way, the belief that the individual should rightfully receive his imputed productivities is not consistent with a W function having properties (1) through (6). A change in the technological situation will alter individuals' fortunes so that the final result cannot be optimal if the initial situation was deemed so. Perhaps the bourgeois penchant for laissez-faire is the only case on record where a substantial number of individuals have made idols of partial derivatives, i.e., imputed marginal productivities.

One could similarly multiply expressions and beliefs which are part of everyday parlance, which upon examination turn out to be inconsistent and meaningless. The slogan, "the greatest good for the greatest number," was shown by Edgeworth to be one such;

[24] It is not the purport of the above lines that the use of a welfare function leads to a belief in inequality as compared to equality. It merely shows that equality of money income where there is diversity of tastes involves the equality of nothing important. It is in lesser degree like the Anatole France aphorism concerning the equality of the law in its treatment of rich and poor. Before Bergson's treatment one could have sensed, but not analyzed definitively, this subtlety.

and we might add the dictum, "each to count for one and only one." As Professor Knight has ceaselessly insisted, Western Man is a hodgepodge of beliefs stemming from diverse and inconsistent sources. Fortunately his life is sufficiently compartmentalized so that he can assume his various roles with a tolerable amount of ambiguity in each; and only the most introspective worry about this enough to become disorganized.

(8) A final essentially unnecessary assumption, which was especially characteristic of the last generation of economists, was *the definition of the welfare function, which was to be maximized, as the sum of cardinal utilities experienced by each individual.* Before the time of Bergson this was not uncommonly met even in the advanced literature, and vestiges can be found today. It stemmed from the main Utilitarian stream of economic thought, when utility was used interchangeably in a behavioristic, in a psychological, in a physiological, in an ethical sense.

It was not uncommon for older writers to ponder over the question as to whether utility was being maximized or whether pain was being minimized; whether by and large man was operating "in the red" below absolute zero, but making the best of a bad lot. The answer depended upon the author's theology and endocrine glands at the moment. Paley, Sidgwick, and others could seriously ask whether it was better to have a tremendous population, each contributing a little to a vast amount of Social Utility, or whether it was better to have less Social Utility, provided its average amount per head was maximized.

In the field of Public Finance the assumption of additive individual utilities plus the law of diminishing utility were used to justify the imposition of progressive taxes. In its most sweeping form this doctrine set up minimum aggregate sacrifice or maximum total utility as appropriate goals of action. This goal can be obtained only if the marginal utility of income (after taxes) is equal for all individuals; or if individuals are essentially alike, only with equal incomes for all.[25] On the other hand, the criterion that a given sum of taxes should be raised so as to lead to *equal sacrifice* for all is a much more conservative doctrine; following it we can

[25] F. Y. Edgeworth, "The Pure Theory of Taxation," *Economic Journal*, VII (1897), 550–571.

only be sure that taxes should increase with income, but not necessarily in proportion with income.[26]

Today such arguments are not very fashionable since it is as easy to assume one's conclusions with respect to appropriate policy as to assume the premises of these arguments. Not only is the former more direct, but it is more honest. Nevertheless, some of the considerations which enter into the above arguments are latent in much of modern discussion and thought. In the distribution of war burden the moderately well-to-do tend to point to their rather large sacrifices and to call upon the lower classes to share in these and make new ones. The relatively poorer farmers and laborers concentrate upon how much the rich have left after they have made substantial sacrifices, and how little they themselves have in any case, not in comparison with what they had before the war, but compared to what they consider fair. Whether war times are the appropriate times to redress ancient wrongs or not, it is too much to expect that the bargaining advantages which the war brings will not be used for this purpose.

In connection with this eighth assumption it was implicitly assumed that real income could be treated as a homogeneous quantity to be distributed among individuals. This could be literally true only in a one-commodity world, or in a world where all relative prices were fixed constants. Actually prices will vary depending how money income is distributed. Strictly speaking, therefore, the real judgments embodied in the welfare function must be judgments concerning a multitude of diverse goods. This would be

---

[26] The condition of equality of sacrifice is satisfied at each level of income if

$$U(X) - U(X - t) = \text{constant for all } X.$$

Differentiating this so as to determine the explicit change in t with respect to X,

$$\frac{dt}{dX} = \frac{U'(X - t) - U'(X)}{U'(X - t)}.$$

Because of diminishing marginal utility this is positive. But if we wish to have progressive taxation, the elasticity of *income after taxes* against income before taxes must be less than one. But

$$\frac{X}{X - t} \frac{d(X - t)}{dX} = \frac{X U'(X)}{(X - t) U'(X - t)},$$

which is less than one if, and only if, the elasticity of the marginal utility curve is less than unity. Thus, for Bernoulli's law of utility, equality of sacrifice would imply proportional rather than progressive taxation.

quite a problem even for a man with definite opinions and great preoccupation with value judgments. If, however, he takes refuge in assumption (5) that individual preferences are to count, the individual can be left to decide for himself how he will spend his money at given prices. Our ethical observer need only decide then what his preferences are as between the given levels of satisfaction of different individuals.

It might be thought that our ethical observer, even if the individuals themselves had no unique cardinal indexes of utility, would have to find cardinal indicators. But this would be quite incorrect. Of course, if utilities are to be added, one would have to catch hold of them first, but there is no need to add utilities.[27] The cardinal utilities enter into the W function as independent variables if assumption (5) is made. But the W function is itself only ordinally determinable so that there are an infinity of equally good indicators of it which can be used. Thus, if one of these is written as

$$W = F(U^1, U^2, \cdots), \tag{13}$$

and if we were to change from one set of cardinal indexes of individual utility to another set $(V^1, V^2, \cdots)$, we should simply change the form of the function F so as to leave all social decisions invariant. Thus, let us move from one configuration of goods going to the different individuals to another configuration which leaves W unchanged or which is socially indifferent. Then no redefinition of the U's or of F can change this fact: the social indifference loci are independent of cardinal numbering. And in this terminology the significance of assumption (5) that individual tastes shall count is contained in the requirement that the social indifference slopes between two goods *going to the same individual* are exactly the same as the individual's indifference ratios. Assumption (6) adds that these curves are unaffected by changes in the goods going to other individuals.

---

[27] Even if one wished to add utilities, it would seem silly from any ethical viewpoint to have one's opinions as to correct taxation influenced by how consumers spend their income on goods. Yet that is what the recent attempts to measure marginal utility must imply if they have any pretensions to relevance for policy. R. Frisch, *New Methods of Measuring Marginal Utility* (Tübingen, 1932). I. Fisher, "A Statistical Method for Measuring 'Marginal Utility' and Testing the Justice of a Progressive Income Tax," in *Economic Essays Contributed in Honor of John Bates Clark* (New York, 1927).

MATHEMATICAL ANALYSIS

The assumptions discussed above can be given mathematical formulation. Thus, assumptions (2) and (3) imply that the important variables of our system can be regarded as a number of commodities and productive services $(X_1, X_2, \cdots, X_n, V_1, V_2, \cdots, V_m)$. These totals can be distributed among s individuals of the system; the amounts going to each can be written with a superscript which identifies the individual and a subscript identifying the commodity or service. (While productive services could be written as negative commodities, I have chosen to conform to the more common procedure encountered in the literature.)

$$X_i = \sum_{k=1}^{s} x_i^k, \qquad (i = 1, \cdots, n)$$

$$V_j = \sum_{k=1}^{s} v_j^k. \qquad (j = 1, \cdots, m)$$

(14)

The social welfare function involves only the amounts going to each individual, not prices or totals. Therefore, equation (11) is specialized to

$$W = W(x_1^1, \cdots, x_n^1; \cdots; x_1^s, \cdots, x_n^s; \\ v_1^1, \cdots, v_m^1; \cdots; v_1^s, \cdots, v_m^s). \quad (15)$$

This exhausts the implications of the first four assumptions.

Assumptions (5) and (6) further specialize (11) so that the welfare function can be written as

$$W = W[U^1(x_1^1, \cdots, x_n^1; v_1^1, \cdots, v_m^1), \cdots, \\ U^s(x_1^s, \cdots, x_n^s; v_1^s, \cdots, v_m^s)], \quad (16)$$

where the cardinal forms of the U's and the W are arbitrary. Assumption (7) is meaningless unless the respective U's can be made identical; but if this can be done, W must then be a symmetric function of the U's. Assumption (8) requires that there exist a cardinal W and cardinal U's such that W is a summation of the U's. On the anthropological level this involves (aside from its arbitrariness) definite restrictions on the social rates of indifference between the commodities and services of the same and different individuals. These are similar to the empirical restrictions of independent individual utility as discussed in chapter vii.

In the previous section it was noted that the "technical" restraints must be assumed with the same arbitrariness as the welfare function itself. However, since the formulation of general equilibrium by Walras, it has been customary to take as given by the engineer the fundamental relationships between inputs and outputs and that production itself takes place in firms or industries which are distinct from the individuals, having no value in and of themselves. Under modern industrial conditions this is not unrealistic. But even here many interesting alternatives can arise. What one calls economics, economic engineering, engineering, etc., is to a considerable degree a matter of choice. One can assume that all production decisions involving relative marginal productivities are the concern of the engineer, or economic engineer, and that the economist can take as already derived a transformation relationship between the X's and V's of the form

$$T(X_1, X_2, \cdots, X_n; V_1, V_2, \cdots, V_m) = 0. \qquad (17)$$

This implicit relation is interpreted to give the maximum amount of any one output as of given amounts of all inputs and all other outputs, or the minimum amount of any one input as of given amounts of all outputs and all other inputs.

But if one starts from more primitive technological assumptions, such as the production functions of each commodity, the transformation locus is a derived theorem and not an axiom. Behind it lie many interesting optimal production conditions involving marginal productivities and other magnitudes usually thought of as economic rather than engineering.

PRODUCTION CONDITIONS

In a synthesis of welfare economics we can derive first a set of production conditions which require for their validity the weakest of all ethical assumptions: *simply that more of any one output, other commodities or services being constant, is desirable; similarly, less input for the same outputs is desirable.*

Under the simplest technological conditions we can take as given the production function relating each output to the inputs devoted to it.

$$X_i = X^i(v_{1i}, v_{2i}, \cdots, v_{mi}), \qquad (i = 1, \cdots, n) \qquad (18)$$

where the first subscript indicates the kind of productive factor and the second subscript the commodity to which it is applied. Of course, the total applied to all commodities is given by

$$V_j = v_{j1} + v_{j2} + \cdots + v_{jn}. \qquad (j = 1, \cdots, m) \qquad (19)$$

Ordinarily it is assumed that the production function possesses partial derivatives (marginal productivities), but the above formulation includes the case of so-called fixed proportions or fixed coefficients where the production function has contour lines with corners.

Equations (18) and (19) represent $(n + m)$ relations. If we specify arbitrarily all but one output (service), we can maximize (minimize) the remaining one. This is an extremum problem in which there are auxiliary constraints. The first order partial derivative conditions can be expressed directly as proportionalities and rank properties of the matrix of first partial derivatives of our functions. But it is illuminating to express these directly by means of the artifice of Lagrangean undetermined multipliers. To do this we set up the function

$$\Phi = \pi_1 X_1 + \pi_2 X_2 + \cdots$$
$$+ \pi_n X_n + \lambda_1 V_1 + \lambda_2 V_2 + \cdots + \lambda_m V_m \qquad (20)$$

and *pretend* to maximize it treating all the variables *as if* they were independent, and treating the π's and λ's as (undetermined) constants. If the correct secondary extremum conditions are written out in full, it will be seen that they are quite different from those that would have to hold if the Φ function were really to be maximized. *Only by accident* would these secondary conditions coincide; only by accident would Φ not be at a minimum or would it be at an extremum rather than simply at a stationary value.

This may seem to be an esoteric and recondite point of little practical significance. It is the primary contention of the present work that *everything* interesting is contained in the inequalities associated with an extremum position, rather than in the equalities. This is no less true of the field of welfare economics. From a deeper point of view *market prices, regarded as parameters by perfect competitors, are nothing more nor less than Lagrangean multipliers.* The Langrangean expression Φ corresponds to Barone's Φ function or to Hotelling's price potential and can be regarded as the value of output or national product, expressed in terms of money or any numeraire, and generalized by the subtraction of factor costs.

If the *game* of competition leads to optimal conditions, it does so partly by accident. For it is precisely under the conditions favorable to the maintenance of atomistic competition (briefly absence of decreasing costs) that the secondary conditions of the correct maximum problem agree with those guaranteeing the maximization of the money value of output as of fixed prices. Where there are substantial technological increasing returns, competition as an empirical phenomenon breaks down. It is in such conditions that collectivism is likely to be considered seriously as a social policy. If then a socialist regime should insist upon mechanically playing the game of competition with prices regarded as parameters à la Lange,[28] its managers would rush away from the minimization of Φ, even though this *minimization* may be precisely what is required under decreasing cost if welfare is to be *maximized*.

The moral is not that prices should cease to be related to marginal cost, or that planning under socialism is impossible. It is simply that the decentralized operators in a planned society should refrain from a literal aping of atomistic, passive, parametric price behavior. Instead of pretending that demand curves are infinitely elastic when they are not, the correct shape of the curve is to be taken into account. This does not mean that the decentralized operators should take account of their influence on price as a monopolist would.[29]

After the elimination of Lagrangean multipliers, the first order maximum conditions take the form

$$\frac{\dfrac{\partial X_i}{\partial v_{1i}}}{\dfrac{\partial X_k}{\partial v_{1k}}} = \cdots = \frac{\dfrac{\partial X_i}{\partial v_{mi}}}{\dfrac{\partial X_k}{\partial v_{mk}}} = \frac{T_{X_k}}{T_{X_i}}, \qquad (i, k = 1, \cdots, n) \qquad (21)$$

[28] O. Lange, article in *On the Economic Theory of Socialism*, B. E. Lippincott, ed. (Minneapolis: University of Minnesota Press, 1938), pp. 55–142.

[29] When we come to the full statement of welfare conditions, it will be seen that unusual difficulties do arise in the decreasing cost case in determining whether a given maximum position represents a *maximum maximorum* or whether the number of differentiated products should be reduced.

or the equivalent form

$$\frac{\dfrac{\partial X_1}{\partial v_{j1}}}{\dfrac{\partial X_1}{\partial v_{r1}}} = \cdots = \frac{\dfrac{\partial X_n}{\partial v_{jn}}}{\dfrac{\partial X_n}{\partial v_{rn}}} = \frac{T_{vj}}{T_{vr}}. \qquad (j, r = 1, \cdots, m) \qquad (22)$$

In words this takes the form: *productive factors are correctly allocated if the marginal productivity of a given factor in one line is to the marginal productivity of the same factor in a second line as the marginal productivity of any other factor in the first line is to its marginal productivity in the second line. The value of the common factor of proportionality can be shown to be equal to the marginal cost of the first good in terms of the (displaced amount of the) second good.*[30]

Geometrically these conditions can be easily derived in the two good, two factor case by means of a Jevons-Edgeworth-Bowley-Lerner diagram consisting of a box whose respective sides are equal to the available total amounts of the two factors. Any point within the box, if oriented with respect to the lower left-hand corner, can be thought of as representing the amounts of the two factors used in the production of the first good, and the iso-product contour lines can be sketched in. The same point when referred to the upper right-hand corner represents the allocation to the second good, whose contour lines can also be superimposed on the same diagram.

If we specify the amount of one of the goods and restrict movements to one of these contour lines, the optimum position is reached only when we have touched the highest output line of the other good, or at a point of tangency of the opposing iso-product lines. The geometrical diagram indicates the correct secondary conditions which are quite different from conventional diminishing returns. The locus of all such points of tangency, which can appropriately be called a "generalized contract" curve, represents the infinity of optimum positions. If along this locus we read off the amounts of the respective products, and plot one of these magni-

---

[30] By introducing as variables inputs and outputs of different dates optimal behavior over time can be included in the above formulation. However, when this is done, it will be seen that contrary to the belief of most economists since the time of Böhm-Bawerk, no single real interest rate is implied for a capitalist or socialist state. Equality would be a necessity only in the highly unusual case where relative prices of all goods remain the same over time.

tudes against the other, the resulting locus is the substitution, transformation, or opportunity cost curve, T. The slope of this curve at any point represents the marginal cost of one of the goods in terms of the other, or the ratio of marginal costs expressed in terms of some third magnitude.[31]

The substitution curve is drawn up as of given amounts of the factors of production and will shift with any changes in the latter. For a given transformation curve to be of any relevance, the factors of production must be regarded as being indifferent as between different uses.[32]

If constant returns to scale and only one factor (perhaps equal to a composite dose) are assumed, we have the classical case of a straight line transformation curve. If the first of these assumptions is made, but there is more than one factor of production, unless the goods should just happen to use the factors in the same proportion, the transformation curve will be concave to the origin because of the law of diminishing returns to varying proportions. The curve can also assume this shape for other reasons relating to returns to scale. In the decreasing cost case, however this arises, the curve will be convex to the origin.

In all of these cases let the firms or planners really take prices as given and attempt to maximize value of output or Φ. In the constant returns case there will be complete specialization on one of the goods (the one with comparative advantage) or complete indifference at the critical price ratio equal to the cost transformation ratio. If both goods are consumed, and if the economy is a closed one, the latter critical price ratio is sure to be the only relevant one.

In the increasing cost case at given price ratios the firm will

---

[31] For the geometrical picture see W. F. Stolper and P. A. Samuelson, "Protection and Real Wages," *Review of Economic Studies*, IX (1941), 58–74.

[32] It is only when the last two unnecessary and unrealistic assumptions are made that the so-called opportunity cost doctrine is even formally valid. Even under these conditions the usual formulation is rather a mumbo jumbo of high sounding gibberish, which does not state the conditions of equilibrium in a very direct way. All this is further complicated by the fact that most enunciations of the opportunity cost doctrine are purely verbal: leisure is treated as a displaced good! Inevitably, therefore, when the opportunity cost doctrine is carefully stated and qualified, it degenerates into the full conditions of general equilibrium in which factor supply and preference equations must be introduced if only as inequalities. This is not to imply that one must accept the dubious psychological language and interpretations of classical real cost theorists.

come into equilibrium at the levels of output which make prices proportional to marginal (transformation or factor) costs. However, in the decreasing cost case the planners in a socialist state attempting to maximize at fixed prices would concentrate on one or the other of the two commodities. But this would be optimal only in an open economy which could really trade with the outside world (in unlimited amounts) at the given price ratio. In a closed planned state it might be desirable to produce something of both, to have price ratios equal to marginal cost ratios even if that meant a minimization of Φ. If we regard the passive approach of the decentralized planners as an equilibrium process, it is clear that the correct optimum, being a minimum and not a maximum, would not be an equilibrium point at all. Or if the planners acted like Balaam's ass, it could be regarded as a highly unstable equilibrium point from which they would rush at the slightest disturbance.

Thus it is only accidentally—the first two cases—that competition is optimal. For it is in those cases that the Lagrangean expression (20) is at a maximum when we are at the correct maximum of (18). In these accidental cases, if we like, we may think of our production decisions as being independent of preferences, in the sense that they are *uniformly* best with respect to the most extreme weightings of the commodities. Under increasing returns we may even never settle on society's best transformation curve.

Actually our production conditions might have been introduced in more complex form than as single, isolated production functions of the form (18). It is to a certain extent arbitrary as to how much preliminary maximizing behavior we consider as being done by the engineer and how much by the economist. Under competitive conditions the relevance of prices to the decision is taken as the dividing line; but for welfare purposes we may dispense with prices completely. However, it would seem somewhat awkward then to term the problem one of engineering; still some economists might prefer to begin with the transformation function, T.

If we examine production possibilities more closely, it will be apparent that in many cases it will not be possible to end up with a single transformation function, T. Thus suppose that commodities divide up into two or more groups such that no productive factor is used in more than one group. Then there will be at least as many independent transformation curves as there are groups.

Of course, formally these can be combined into a single implicit equation, e.g., by equating their summed squares to zero, but this is trivial. No indeterminacy arises, however, from the multiplicity of transformation curves; we have fewer choices to make and therefore fewer marginal conditions.

PURE EXCHANGE CONDITIONS

The production conditions of the previous section were derivable on the basis of rather mild assumptions by virtue of the fact that more of all goods, however they are to be divided, would seem better than less. These conditions are still only *necessary*. They are not *sufficient*, since decisions must still be made as to how to divide up given available goods, and as to which of the available amounts of production will actually be used.

Even if the last of these two decisions is made, there remains the problem of dividing up a given total of all commodities and services among individuals. Once there has been specified a clearly defined W function, the final optimum point can be easily determined. But at this point after assuming, if only implicitly, the first six serious assumptions, the modern welfare economist becomes timid and hesitates to make assumption (7) or indeed any other specific welfare function. He has been conditioned against making ethical assumptions. If possible, therefore, he would like to develop further optimum conditions which are within broad limits independent of the form of the W specified. In fact, as has been known since the time of Pareto at least, it is possible to gratify this wish and to specify still another set of *necessary*, but not *sufficient*, conditions which must prevail as between individuals.

Here the simple assumption is made that W is undefined, or unspecified, except to the extent that it is a monotonic increasing function of the individual U's. We are not able to plot in the (U^1, U^2) plane a locus of points along which W is constant. We know only that a movement in the northeast direction of the plane increases W and is good, a movement in the southwest direction decreases W and is bad; a movement into either of the other two quadrants taken around a given point is indeterminate.

In words, the simple assumption is made that only if all individuals are made better (worse) off can we definitely state that a given movement is good (bad). Otherwise we must reserve judgment. Mathematically it is clear that for the levels of utility of all but one individual being arbitrarily specified, it is a necessary condition of equilibrium that the utility of the remaining individual be at a maximum, subject to the condition that there be fixed totals of all goods. For

$$\sum_{j=1}^{s} x_i{}^j = \bar{X}_i, \qquad \sum_{j=1}^{s} v_r{}^j = \bar{V}_r, \tag{23}$$

$$U^j(x_1{}^j, \cdots, x_n{}^j, v_1{}^j, \cdots, v_m{}^j) = \bar{U}^j, \qquad (j \neq k)$$

we must maximize

$$U^k = U^k(x_1{}^k, \cdots, x_n{}^k, v_1{}^k, \cdots, v_m{}^k). \tag{24}$$

By using Lagrangean multipliers or by direct methods, it can be easily shown that in equilibrium the ratio between marginal utilities of two goods consumed by one individual must be the same as the ratio of marginal utilities of the same goods to any other individual who consumes the same goods. If one or more of the goods is absent from the consumption of an individual, certain inequalities can be introduced to generalize the above conditions. We may write the first order conditions of equilibrium in the form

$$\frac{U_i{}^1}{U_j{}^1} = \frac{U_i{}^2}{U_j{}^2} = \cdots = \frac{U_i{}^s}{U_j{}^s}. \tag{25}$$

It will be noted that only ratios of marginal utilities for the same individuals are ever involved.[33] Thus, there is no need for numerical utility even for a single individual and no need to compare the utilities of different individuals.

Graphically the equilibrium may be represented by the same box-type diagram as was mentioned in the last section. The dimensions of the box represent the fixed totals of the commodities in existence. Any interior point oriented with respect to the lower left-hand corner represents the amount of consumption of the first individual, and the contour lines are now to be interpreted as indifference curves. Referred to the upper right-hand corner, a point represents the second individual's consumption, and his contour lines may be superimposed on the other. Specifying the

[33] Equilibrium conditions regarding the factors of production need not be indicated separately if it is remembered that they may be treated as negative commodities.

utility of the second individual, we maximize that of the first by moving along the given indifference line of the second individual until we reach (at a point of tangency) the highest indifference curve of the first. Because the original specification of the second man's utility was arbitrary, the final equilibrium is also arbitrary and not unique. The locus of all such arbitrary points is, of course, the familiar Edgeworthian contract curve and represents the set of points satisfying necessary exchange conditions.

After the discussion of the previous section it will not be necessary to reiterate at length the contention that the equality of the various ratios can be expressed without Lagrangean multipliers and without price ratios; moreover, in by no means impossible cases, even playing the game of competition would lead away from rather than toward the correct optimal position. As before, this is because the secondary conditions for a constrained maximum are not the same as the secondary conditions necessary literally to bring the Lagrangean expression to an extremum.

It will be noted that from any point off the contract curve there exists a movement toward it which would be beneficial to both individuals. This is not the same thing as to say, with Edgeworth, that exchange will in fact necessarily cease somewhere on the contract curve; for in many types of bilateral monopoly a final equilibrium may be reached off the contract curve. Nor is it the same as to say that points on the contract curve are better than points off the contract curve. Later I shall discuss the correct formulation of the significance of this condition.

But first it is well to write down the full first order conditions of equilibrium which must hold if we are to have an optimum of both production and exchange, that is, if we combine with the conditions of this section the conditions of the last section. *Then (1) we must have a common marginal rate of indifference between any two goods for every individual; this common indifference ratio must, moreover, be equal to the ratio at which one of these goods can be transformed into the other in a production sense, the transformation to come about as the result of transferring any resource from one good's production to the other's. (2) We must have for all individuals a common ratio of indifference between supplying more of any factor of production and enjoying more consumption of a given good; this common ratio must be equal to the rate at which supplying more of that factor results in greater production of the good in question.*

Mathematically, as Lange has shown,

$$
\begin{aligned}
\frac{U_{x_i}^1}{U_{x_j}^1} &= \cdots = \frac{U_{x_i}^s}{U_{x_j}^s} = \frac{T_{x_i}}{T_{x_j}}, & (i, j = 1, \cdots, n) \\
\frac{U_{v_k}^1}{U_{x_i}^1} &= \cdots = \frac{U_{v_k}^s}{U_{x_i}^s} = \frac{\partial X_i}{\partial v_{ki}} = \frac{T_{V_k}}{T_{x_i}}. & \begin{array}{l}(i = 1, \cdots, n) \\ (k = 1, \cdots, m)\end{array}
\end{aligned}
\tag{26}
$$

These conditions may be rewritten in a variety of ways but only being (at the first order level) necessary conditions rather than sufficient conditions, they are necessarily less in number than the number of the unknowns of the system. This is after taking account of the fact that the total of factors used in every use and the total of commodities consumed must equal the sums of these magnitudes over all individuals, i.e., even after taking into account equations (14). We are still short $(s - 1)$ equations. These can only be supplied on the basis of definite assumptions concerning how different individuals enter into the W function. This will be discussed in detail in the next section.

Returning to the combined production and exchange conditions of equations (26), I should like to point out various alternative formulations of them. First, it is easy to derive from them the conditions that the ratios of indifference between any two factors must be uniform for all individuals, and equal to the relative marginal productivities of the two factors in any line of production.

Second, it is sometimes convenient to interpret the first of these equilibrium conditions as specifying the equality of price and marginal utility ratios to the *ratios* of marginal cost. There is occasionally some uncertainty in the literature as to whether prices should *equal* marginal costs or just bear the same percentage discrepancy in every line. The distinction is especially important if decreasing costs are very prevalent, for then it is impossible for capitalistic monopolies or socialistic bureaus to recover their full costs of production if they charge only prices equal to marginal costs. Recourse must be had to direct taxation to cover the difference or to the imputed revenues accruing to state-owned factors of production, revenue which in a world of constant returns to scale would be available for distribution to the citizens of the state.

So long as only price ratios are used it is not necessary to state the units in which costs are measured, dollars, labor, fertilizer, or opportunity-substitution costs. In the usual exposition partial equilibrium conditions are implicitly assumed, and costs, wages, and prices are expressed in terms of dollars. In these conditions must prices be equal to marginal costs, or just proportional? The answer is *equality* if we take into account the conditions relating to factors of production such as are embodied in the second part of equations (26). If all factors of production were indifferent between different uses and completely fixed in amount (the pure Austrian case), then we could dispense with these conditions, and proportionality of prices and marginal cost would be sufficient. But if we drop these highly special assumptions, for which there is not in any case empirical or theoretical warrant, then if all prices were proportional to (say double) marginal costs, we should not have an optimum situation. By working a little more or less everybody could be made better off since in the described situation the preferred terms at which they exchange leisure and goods are not equal to the true productivity terms at which they can be transformed into each other.

I need not remind the reader that first order conditions are really of secondary importance as compared to the full inequalities implied by an optimum position. Also it should not be necessary to show in detail that the above conditions hold only if every factor of production is actually used in every line of production, and if something is produced of every good, and if all production and indifference functions have continuous partial derivatives. If any of these conditions fail, the number of equalities may be diminished, but in every case the correct general inequalities will prevent there being any essential ambiguities in the characterization of the optimum position. A closely related problem arises when there are multiple positions of equilibrium. With strongly convex indifference fields and strongly concave cost functions such cannot occur. But there is no reason why human nature should display the simple, regular properties which the observer-economist finds convenient. And it is the essence of the decreasing cost, increasing returns, lumpiness, indivisibility phenomena that improper curvature on the cost side should enter the picture.

Especially where differentiation of product arises as a result of monopolistic competition or as its cause, there arises the problem as to whether or not a commodity should be produced at all. If it is produced, the marginal cost conditions of (26) should be realized, but there may be a better maximum where none is produced. Here the extremum position is of the corner type, and the conventional equalities must be replaced by inequalities. This involves decision making at a distance; we cannot feel our way to the optimum, step by step, but must boldly experiment with diverse combinations. Where such "all or none" phenomena are concerned, things often get worse before they get better, and so decisions *im kleinen* will not suffice. Even aside from the difficulties of the paragraph after next, we cannot decide that a thing should be produced if a perfectly discriminating monopolist or government bureau could recover its total cost by some sort of a take-it-or-leave-it offer. In these cases involving finite decisions we must ask consumers (or Robinson Crusoe) whether a given abundance of fewer commodities is preferred to an alternative scarcity of a greater range of commodities.[34] At this point there will inevitably arise questions concerning the rationality of individual choice, questions which had been summarily suppressed by a cavalier acceptance of the validity of assumptions five and six set out in the third section back. But these questions, whatever their importance, cannot be settled by deductive analysis.

The equality of price to marginal cost creates confusions in the minds of many concerning the question as to whether or not costs which are fixed in the short run are not variable in the long run and hence should be covered by price. They ask whether price should not exceed short run marginal cost since the latter excludes elements of long range variable costs. There are two confusions revealed by this question. First, marginal cost is sometimes treated as a part of total unit costs, which it is not. Marginal cost is the difference between costs in two situations and cannot be identified in general with given components of cost, labor, materials, etc. Symptomatic of this confusion is the statement that competition tends to drive price down to prime or variable costs so that full costs are not recovered. Of course, pure competition (which is not really im-

[34] In certain special cases consumer's surplus may be employed to describe finite inequalities. But these cases are rare, and in any case we are rather better off if we use direct methods.

plied in the previous sentence) involves price equal to marginal cost, which may far exceed full unit costs depending upon the scale of output and the level of price. Not only did Alfred Marshall speak loosely on this matter, but so great a contribution as J. M. Clark's *Economics of Overhead Costs* errs, at least in exposition, in its diagnosis of the role of overhead costs in the breakdown of competitive theory. An examination of the character of agriculture, the last stronghold of pure competition, would show a high level of overhead costs with no tendency toward the breakdown of competition. Aside from non-imitable differentiation of product the principal cause of disintegration of competition is decreasing long run unit costs of each firm at levels representing large fractions of total demand for the product; this would be true even if all goods could be produced to order.

Marginal cost is not part of cost which must be met, and the equality of price and marginal cost has nothing to do with a recovery of full costs, determination of fair return on investments, correct imputation of factor shares, etc. Its purpose is to secure correct factor allocation, and avoid anomalous product allocation. This is accented if one considers a wavy cost curve or a cost curve showing a corner at the point of capacity (long run or short run). At the latter point marginal cost is undefined, or, if you prefer, it is anywhere from a finite amount to infinity. There is no clue as to proper price determination, but this is of no consequence so long as production does actually take place at the capacity point. Similarly, as demand fluctuates for a commodity whose cost curve shows waves because of lumpiness, etc., the correct price charged will vary greatly; rather than let a train set out with a single empty seat, the price should fall to zero. It is no argument against this statement that such pricing may not recover full costs, or that passengers will tend to wait until trains are least crowded. What could be more desirable socially than the evening out of traffic? Does not a railroad company which gives out passes to its own employees often follow the sound principle that they may ride as they please so long as they add nothing to costs? Incidentally, it will be seen from this discussion that where small changes in demand create great changes in social cost, posted, administered, relatively stable prices are *not* optimal devices.

The second and less important confusion involved in the statement that price should exceed short run marginal cost stems from the fallacious belief that long run marginal cost "inclusive of changes in long run variable factors" is greater than short run marginal cost. Actually, we know from the Wong-Viner-Harrod envelope theorem that they are equal for instantaneous rates of change if production is taking place at the anticipated level. For an actual, finite, forward movement from this point, short run marginal cost "exclusive of the fixed factors" is of course *greater* not smaller than marginal cost when all factors are varied optimally. Whether or not output is at the anticipated level, price equal to short run marginal cost is necessary in order that the existing plant be used optimally; the relationship between price and long run marginal cost is relevant to a decision as to whether to change the size of plant, when that decision arises. It one dropped the first order statement of optimum conditions and replaced them by the general inequalities which must be satisfied, it would be obvious that the optimum position must satisfy a different maximum condition (inequality) for every alternative which can be contemplated. Thus, it must not pay to make a small step forward or backward, a middling step, a sizable step, a huge step, to shut down completely or open a new line, etc., etc. Each of these implies a relationship between price or revenue and entirely different measures of marginal or differential cost.[35]

INTERPERSONAL OPTIMAL CONDITIONS

In the last two sections an attempt was made to derive as general conditions as possible with a minimum of controversial assumptions. Nevertheless, we have seen that it is not possible to deduce a unique equilibrium unless we have more to build upon. This is only as it should be, for intuition assures us that there cannot be an optimum position which is independent of the exact form of the W function. Even if all of the necessary conditions of production and exchange are satisfied, we are short as many equations as there are individuals in excess of unity. In a Robinson Crusoe world where there is but one individual (*pace* Friday!) there

---

[35] Once this fact is mastered, the whole question of "allocation of perfectly joint costs" is seen to be a false and irrelevant problem for either a firm or society. It derives its present day empirical importance from the intrusion, not necessarily irrationally, of "full cost" considerations into price formation, and to problems of government regulation, e.g., T.V.A., Tariff Commission, etc.

are no individuals in excess of unity, and the equilibrium is unique. But as soon as we have more than one individual, our previous conditions simply assure us that we are on the "generalized contract locus" from which there are no possible movements which are advantageous to each and every individual.

An infinity of such positions exists ranging from a situation in which all of the advantage is enjoyed by one individual, through some sort of compromise position, to one in which another individual has all the advantage. Without a well-defined W function, i.e., without assumptions concerning interpersonal comparisons of utility, it is impossible to decide which of these points is best. In terms of a given set of ethical notions which define a *Welfare function* the best point on the generalized contract locus can be determined, and only then.

All of this may be formulated mathematically as follows. The optimal conditions of production and exchange as given in equations (26) which summarize the argument of the previous two sections permit us to reduce the level of indeterminacy of the system to an implicit equation between the levels of well-being of the different individuals in the system. This may be written as

$$P(U^1, U^2, \cdots, U^s) = 0. \tag{27}$$

This says that we may specify at will the levels of well-being of all but one of the individuals, and the last one's well-being is uniquely determined. The essential shape of this *Possibility function* depends of course upon the technological and other assumed restraints of the system as well as upon the tastes of the different individuals. Notationally, the same implicit function can be written in many different ways, but the locus in question is invariant under these purely terminological changes. One should note, however, that since the exact numerical form of each U is arbitrary, no importance attaches to the curvature properties of this locus.

If we have a given definite welfare function, then we are to maximize

$$W = W(U^1, \cdots, U^s) \tag{28}$$

subject to the above constraint. The first order condition of equilibrium takes the form

$$\frac{W_i}{W_j} = \frac{P_i}{P_j}. \qquad (i, j = 1, \cdots, s) \tag{29}$$

These conditions, like the correct secondary conditions which need not be written explicitly, are independent of purely notational ambiguities involved in the welfare function, the possibility function, and the selection of particular cardinal indices of individual utility.

Equations (29) give us the missing $(s - 1)$ conditions of equilibrium, and our equilibrium is seen to be finally determinate. It is not at all necessary to take the expositional path followed above. Thus, Professor Pigou, who does not hesitate from the very beginning to make inter-individual comparisons of utility, moves directly via a maximization of (11) subject to (12) to the same equilibrium which Pareto-Barone-Lerner reach after they have admitted into their systems interpersonal comparisons of utility. And as will be discussed at greater length below, they end up with no optimum and no final definite conclusions if they are unwilling to permit others to introduce such ethical considerations.

The real significance of their analysis lies in the fact that they provide a relatively easy opening for the introduction of ethical notions. For it follows from their analysis that all of the action necessary to achieve a given ethical *desideratum* may take the form of *lump-sum taxes* or *bounties*. These may be given in the form of abstract purchasing power or in kind, it being necessary, however, that the latter should be freely exchangeable against other goods. Thus, instead of having to decide how much to allocate of each and every good to each individual, the ethical authority need only decide on the allocation of final incomes between individuals.

Working directly from a well-defined (ordinal) welfare function, we require that W be maximized subject to the physical constraints of the system. We may express the final conditions in many different forms, with or without Lagrangean multipliers. One such compact method which avoids as far as possible duplicating the exact form (but not the substance) of the conditions of the previous section is given as follows:

$$
\begin{aligned}
\frac{\partial W}{\partial x_i^1} &= \cdots = \frac{\partial W}{\partial x_i^s} = \frac{\partial W}{\partial X_i}, & (i &= 1, \cdots, n) \\
& & (j &= 1, \cdots, m) \\
\frac{\partial W}{\partial v_j^1} &= \cdots = \frac{\partial W}{\partial v_j^s} = \frac{\partial W}{\partial V_j} = \frac{\partial W}{\partial X_1}\frac{\partial X_1}{\partial v_{j1}} = \cdots = \frac{\partial W}{\partial X_n}\frac{\partial X_n}{\partial v_{jn}}.
\end{aligned}
\tag{30}
$$

Not only are these equations very similar to the famous Note XIV which summarizes much of what is best in Marshall's *Principles*, but they are cast almost exactly in the form followed by Professor Pigou in his *Economics of Welfare.* In words, two conditions are implied: *first, the marginal social utility (disutility) of the same good (service) must be equal for each individual; second, each factor of production must be divided among different possible uses so that its indirect, derived marginal social utility must be the same in every use and equal to its marginal social disutility.*

We may leave to the reader the task of showing the necessary modifications if the supply of a factor is inelastic, if a factor of production is not indifferent between different uses, if there is joint production, if there are external technological economies or diseconomies (so that the production function of a good contains in it factors of production devoted to other uses), etc. By dividing the above equations through by any single partial derivative, they may be thrown into a form which is independent of the particular cardinal representation of W.

While the Lerner production conditions are contained in the above set of equations, the exchange conditions are not. However, if we make the individualistic assumptions five and six above so that the welfare function takes on the special form given in equation (13), then in virtue of the identities

$$\frac{\partial W}{\partial x_i^r} = \frac{\partial W}{\partial U^r}\frac{\partial U^r}{\partial x_i^r} \tag{31}$$

the exchange conditions of the previous section are also included in these equations. Thus, the production and exchange conditions which constitute the "new welfare economics" are included in the old, but are themselves incomplete.

If we substitute the last identities in the fundamental equations (30), they can easily be thrown into the production and exchange conditions given in (26) plus the new interpersonal element guaranteeing us that the distribution of incomes and lump-sum allowances is optimal. This takes the mathematical form of equality of marginal social utility of income (expressed in terms of any good) for all individuals.

$$\frac{\partial W}{\partial x_i^1} = \frac{\partial W}{\partial x_i^2} = \cdots = \frac{\partial W}{\partial x_i^s}. \tag{32}$$

The statement that any "individualistic" ethical optimum can be effected by lump-sum taxes is a theorem, not an axiom. For its proof we require only that the individual indifference curves be such that they can be swung into final equilibrium by operating upon their incomes, letting them trade mechanically at fixed prices. The vast importance of this theorem for social policy in a planned or free enterprise economy is deserving of the greatest emphasis. Yet its greatest significance is in the realm of administration and tactics. From the standpoint of the logic of welfare analysis it is not fundamental. In fact it is not universally true.

First, the indifference curves of one or more individuals may have curvature properties such that the individual who believes or pretends to believe that prices are parameters beyond his control will rush away from rather than toward the correct optimum position. The remarks in the section above dealing with production which discuss the analogy between prices and Lagrangean multipliers and secondary conditions may be referred to here.

Second, and of more practical importance, the optimum position may be reached by means of discriminating all or none offers, sliding scales, etc., rather than by trading at uniform prices. The important thing is the realization of appropriate marginal conditions rather than what happens to the intra-marginal units. (Compare on this point the discussion above of recovery of full cost as a goal of pricing.) In a regime such as this, lump-sum allowances may not suffice to realize the optimum point.

Third, it is not really easy to devise in practice a tax or subsidy which is of a purely lump-sum character. A tax upon income affects marginal decisions with respect to effort and risk-taking. This is obvious. Less conspicuous is the fact that the usual ethical notions compel us to set our allowances according to a man's "circumstances," which are partially the result of his own actions and decisions. Analytically, the problem resembles that of determining fair piece rates or of setting a fair "handicap" for golfers of different ability. We wish to equalize opportunity for all contestants, but we do not want them to hold back from playing their best because of a fear of losing their favorable handicap. Ideally, the social managers would have to know the potentialities of every individual; and to remedy the distortions of imperfect lump-sum taxes, they would have to set a system of quotas and penalties based upon potentialities rather than upon performance.

Thus, we might decide that everyone should have at least a minimum income, that Society will make up the deficiency between what the less fortunate can earn and this minimum. Once this is realized by those who fall below the minimum, there is no longer an incentive for them to work at the margin, at least in pecuniary material terms. This is clearly bad social policy, not because I have a vulgar prejudice in favor of work and against leisure. On the contrary, the increases in real income in the years ahead probably will be spent in considerable degree on leisure. It is wrong because it forces the rest of society to give up leisure. Its fault lies in the fact that the individual's allowance is not a lump-sum one. It varies inversely with his effort, and thus penalizes effort. It would be tolerable only if a small percentage of the population were below the minimum, or if we could rely upon new motivations in the Utopia of the future. I, myself, put considerable stock in the possibility of changing conventional patterns of motivation. However, this will not provide comfort to those who wish to utilize a parametric pricing system with algebraic lump-sum allowances, since these same considerations undermine the "individualistic" assumptions upon which their analysis is based.[36]

Fourth, because decisions need only be made concerning incomes, the problem of formulating political slogans and beliefs which will command wide approbation is simplified. However desirable this may be from a political point of view, it must never be forgotten that from a consistent ethical point of view decisions should be made concerning the welfare function itself. Beliefs concerning the distribution of income are derivative rather than fundamental. Except in the admittedly unrealistic case where all tastes are identical, setting up such beliefs as goals is equivalent to accepting a "shibboleth" and to embracing an ambiguous, undefin-

---

[36] The clash between equity and incentive is not unimportant for the present stage of modern capitalism. To an important first approximation the adverse effects of high marginal rates of taxation stem not from the level of the rates, provided they are less than 100 per cent, but from the "curvature" of the tax formula whereby gains increase tax liability more than equivalent losses reduce tax liability. But the essence of "progression" in taxation and in income redistribution is curvature. The only solution lies in pooling risks, and in drafting tax legislation so as to produce a maximum of averaging over time. If this does not suffice, equity may still be worth considerable unavoidable costs.

able welfare function. Among other things such a procedure involves making a shibboleth of the existing distribution of relative technological scarcities of goods. (Of course, whether this is a bad practice is not in itself part of the content of welfare economics, which does not presume to deduce appropriate beliefs. However, welfare economics can legitimately point out the implications of different ethical propositions.)

NEW VERSUS OLD WELFARE ECONOMICS

While in a real sense there is only one all-inclusive welfare economics, which reaches its most complete formulation in the writings of Bergson, it is possible to distinguish between the New Welfare Economics, which involves roughly the contents of the sections on production and exchange and which makes no assumptions concerning interpersonal comparability of utility, and the Old Welfare Economics which starts out with such assumptions. Roughly it is the distinction between Pareto and Pigou. From our above discussion it will be clear that the former is included in the latter, but not vice versa.

Strictly speaking there is no opposition between the two points of view. However, it is not uncommon for expositors of the "new" set of doctrines to imagine that their results have significance even if one is unwilling to make any ethical assumptions. In fact this belief is almost a necessity for anyone who has taken seriously Robbins' dicta concerning the inadmissibility of welfare economics in the body of economic theory. Once it is apprehended that the latter notion is a delusion, the need to believe in the significance of the production and exchange conditions divorced from the interpersonal conditions will disappear. Nevertheless, it may be desirable to appraise their significance taken by themselves.

I pass over as being obvious from our discussion of the first six assumptions about the W function that it is not literally true that the new welfare economics is devoid of *any* ethical assumptions. Admittedly, however, its assumptions are more general and less controversial, and it is for this reason that it gives incomplete necessary conditions, whose full significance emerges only after one has made interpersonal assumptions. To refuse to take the last step renders the first two steps nugatory; like pouring out a glass of water and then refusing to drink. To say that the first two conditions should be realized, but that the third is meaningless, is like saying that it does not matter whether or not a man has hair, so long as it is curly!

A limited significance remains for the new welfare economics if we hold that a welfare function is definable but undefined, and if we look for conditions which hold true uniformly for all possible definitions. It cannot tell us which of *any* two situations is better, but it can occasionally rule out one given situation as being worse than another in the sense that everyone is worse off. It cannot tell us when society really has a choice between two given situations. Most important of all it cannot tell us that a movement about which it can give a determinate answer is better than a movement about which it cannot give an answer. If we are at a point not on the Possibility Function, it assures us that there exists a still better point. But it cannot assert that a given point on the Possibility Function is better than all, or many, points not on the Possibility locus.

Concretely, the new welfare economics is supposed to be able to throw light on such questions as to whether the Corn Laws should have been repealed. This act would help many individuals, but hurt landowners. It is usually assumed, although not necessarily quite rigorously, that free trade can be expected to lead to a new "situation" in which those who are benefited can afford to bribe those who are hurt. It is thought that this constitutes a "case" for free trade. Actually, this leads to no positive guide to action. For the new welfare economics cannot state definitely: "The Corn Laws should be repealed, and the landowners should be compensated." Occasionally such a statement is implicit in a writer's formulation, but it is clear that this involves an unwarranted assumption as to the adequacy of the *status quo*, an assumption which the new welfare economics holds to be neither right nor wrong, but meaningless.

On the other hand, the new welfare economics cannot make the definite statement: "The Corn Laws should be repealed, and the owners should *not* be compensated." It can only assert in a negative way: " 'Twere better that the Corn Laws be repealed, and compensation be paid, *if necessary*." It gives no real guide to action. Nor does our experience with man as a social animal suggest that one can safely predict, as a factual matter, that "educated and intelligent men of goodwill" in point of fact tend to move to the generalized contract locus. As an empirical statement of fact we cannot agree with the assertion of Edgeworth that bilateral monopolists must end up somewhere on the contract curve. They may end up elsewhere, because one or both is unwilling to discuss the possibility of making a mutually favorable movement for fear that the discussion may imperil the existing tolerable *status quo*.

Scitovsky [37] has attempted to remedy certain deficiencies in the usual statement of the new welfare economists by developing a double test of the desirability of two situations, in which the distribution of income of the new situation is treated symmetrically with that of the old situation. While his is an improvement on certain earlier statements, it is so primarily in a negative way, to the extent that it delimits the scope of the new welfare economics. His own positive formulation is also a " 'twere better" statement, and not a positive guide to action. Such statements are not without value, but they are not at all substitutes for the policy dictates which stemmed from the old welfare economics.

Within the limited scope of the " 'twere better" statements there is an ambiguity which Scitovsky alone seems to have sensed. The term "situation" can mean a number of different things. It can refer to an actual position reached by every individual prior to the repeal of a tariff, and to the new situation which would actually be attained by each individual after new action is taken, i.e., repeal with varying or no amounts of compensation. Or it can mean the totality of all possible positions available with the Corn Laws unrepealed, and the totality of all possible positions with the Corn Laws repealed. The latter is the more significant sense, and can be given significance in terms of the Possibility Function developed above. Thus, a perfectly legitimate " 'twere better" statement can be made as follows: "Technological change can make everybody better off in the sense that it will shift the Possibility Function outwards." [38] We cannot deduce from this the dictum: "Technological change is a good thing," since the introduction of technological change will in fact mean a vector movement from the old

[37] T. Scitovsky, "A Note on Welfare Propositions in Economics," and "A Reconsideration of the Theory of Tariffs," *Review of Economic Studies*, IX (1941–42), 77–88 and 89–110.
[38] In effect Scitovsky recognizes the case where the Possibility Function is given a twist rather than everywhere being shifted outward.

positions of every individual to their new positions which can hardly bode good to all.

At this point the new welfare economist will fall back on the vague statement that "probably technological change will result in good on balance." Not only is this argument on its probability side based upon ignorance rather than knowledge, but it is meaningless as well unless the admissibility of a W function is admitted.

In closing I should like to point out that the point of view which I have been calling the new welfare economics is really only a caricature. On the whole, Pareto, Barone, Hotelling, and Lerner sidestepped interpersonal judgments rather than denied them. Bergson synthesizes the various aspects, as does Lange. Whether Kaldor and Hicks are open to the criticism along the lines which Stigler has recently advanced,[39] the reader must decide.

CONCLUSION

In the present chapter I have attempted to give a brief but fairly complete survey of the whole field of welfare economics. It would be possible to develop the subject further in many respects and to consider a number of related problems. However, limitations of space preclude this, and I shall content myself with two final remarks.

First, what is the best procedure if for some reason a number of the optimum conditions are *not* realized? What shall we do about the remaining ones which are in our power? Shall we argue that "two wrongs do not make a right" and attempt to satisfy those we can? Or is it possible that failure of a number of the conditions necessitates modifying the rest? Clearly the latter alternative is the correct one. A given divergence in a subset of the optimum conditions necessitates alterations in the remaining ones. Thus, in a world where almost all industries are producing at marginal social cost less than price (either because of monopoly or external economies) it would not be desirable for the rest to

[39] N. Kaldor, "Welfare Propositions in Economics," *Economic Journal*, XLIX (1939), 549–552; J. R. Hicks, "Foundations of Welfare Economics," *Economic Journal*, XLIX (1939), 696–712; G. J. Stigler, "The New Welfare Economics," *American Economic Review*, XXXIII (1943), 355–359; P. A. Samuelson, "Further Commentary on Welfare Economics," *American Economic Review*, XXXIII (1943), 604–607. See also P. A. Samuelson, "Welfare Economics and International Trade," *American Economic Review*, XXVIII (1938), 261–266.

produce up to the point where marginal cost equals price. Neither would it be quite correct to seek the same percentage or absolute divergence from the optimum conditions in each case; although in this particular example, if the elasticity of the supplies of the factors of production were zero, the proportionality of prices to marginal cost would be as good as the exact equality. Still another example to show that failure of some conditions necessitates alteration of the rest is provided by the possibility of increasing welfare by deliberately selling below marginal costs to groups with a high marginal (social) utility of income. Given a faulty distribution of income, this can improve the situation, although it would be still better to have the full optimal conditions realized.

The last point consists of the warning that the introduction of dynamic conditions into our analysis necessitates a considerable change in the statement of optimal conditions.[40] The difference is not one of principle, but it is nevertheless important. Judged purely on statical grounds, monopolies or a patent system may appear as unmitigated evils, and certainly inferior to atomistic competition and free trade. But in a dynamical world these judgments may have to be reversed; viz. the infant industry argument for protection, the stimulus to large scale research which only a monopolist can afford, the (alleged) necessity to hold out incentives to inventors, etc. Indeed the measure of support which capitalism commands is most importantly related to precisely these factors of development.

In admitting the superiority of monopoly to atomistic competition in certain respects, we do not imply that it is the best possible organization of an industry. There necessarily exists a still better third alternative, which may or may not be less Utopian than the restoration and maintenance of atomistic competition.

[40] Arguments which allege that individuals, under capitalism or socialism, decide what goods they shall consume, but are not capable of making a correct decision with respect to saving seem to suggest that there is a qualitative difference introduced by dynamics. I refer to the argument that wealthy men are necessary in order to provide for saving and capital formation, and that in a socialist state the government should decide what the appropriate amounts of capital formation should be. If one specifies a W function satisfying the first six assumptions and includes in it as separate variables future goods and services, both of these views are wrong whether there is capitalism or socialism. However, especially where problems of the present and future are concerned, modern philosophers balk at the assumption that what people think is best for them really is. Naturally, when the individualistic assumption six is dropped, our conditions are altered. But the same would be true if we denied this assumption in a statical world.

Part Two

CHAPTER IX

THE STABILITY OF EQUILIBRIUM: COMPARATIVE STATICS AND DYNAMICS

INTRODUCTION

IT WAS AN achievement of the first magnitude for the older mathematical economists to have shown that the number of independent and consistent economic relations was in a wide variety of cases sufficient to determine the equilibrium values of unknown economic prices and quantities. Since their life spans were only of finite duration, it was natural that they should have stopped short at this stage of counting equations and unknowns. It remains to be explained, however, why in the first quarter of the twentieth century economists should have been content with what was after all only preliminary spade work containing in itself (at least explicitly) few *meaningful* theorems of observational significance such as could even ideally be empirically refuted under any conceivable circumstances.

It is the task of comparative statics to show the determination of the equilibrium values of given variables (unknowns) under postulated conditions (functional relationships) with various data (parameters) being specified. Thus, in the simplest case of a partial-equilibrium market for a single commodity, the two independent relations of supply and demand, each drawn up with other prices and institutional data being taken as given, determine by their intersection the equilibrium quantities of the unknown price and quantity sold. If no more than this could be said, the economist would be truly vulnerable to the gibe that he is only a parrot taught to say "supply and demand." Simply to know that there are efficacious "laws" determining equilibrium tells us nothing of the character of these laws. In order for the analysis to be useful it must provide information concerning the way in which our equilibrium quantities will change as a result of changes in the parameters taken as independent data.

In the above illustration let us consider "tastes" as a changing parameter influencing only the demand curve. Will an increase in demand raise or lower price? Clearly the statement that, before and after the assumed change, price is determined by the intersection of supply and demand gives us no answer to the problem. Nothing can be said concerning the movement of the intersection point of *any* two plane curves as one of them shifts. And yet most economists would argue that in a wide variety of circumstances this question can be given a definite answer—namely that price will increase.

How is this conclusion derived? For few commodities have we detailed quantitative empirical information concerning the exact forms of the supply and demand curves even in the neighborhood of the equilibrium point. Not only would large amounts of time and money be necessary to get such information, but in many cases it is practically impossible to derive useful empirical information concerning what would happen if virtual changes in price confronted the demanders or the suppliers.

This is a typical problem confronting the economist: in the absence of precise quantitative data he must infer analytically the qualitative direction of movement of a complex system. What little success he has hitherto achieved can be classified in large part under two headings: (1) theorems proceeding from the assumption of maximizing behavior on the part of firms or individuals, and (2) stability conditions relating to the interaction between economic units. Although inadequately explored until comparatively recently, the first type of conditions is best known and will not be dealt with here except incidentally. As will become evident later, however, from certain points of view they can be fitted in as special cases of the second set. It is the central task of this chapter to show how the problem of stability of equilibrium is intimately tied up with the problem of deriving fruitful theorems in comparative statics. This duality constitutes what I have called the *correspondence principle*.

Comparative Statics

The problem may be approached in full generality by considering n unknown variables $(x_1, \cdots, x_n)$ whose equilibrium values are to be determined for preassigned values of a parameter, α. We assume n independent and consistent, continuously differentiable implicit relations involving some or all of the unknowns and the parameter α; or

$$f^i(x_1, \cdots, x_n, \alpha) = 0. \qquad (i = 1, \cdots, n) \qquad (1)$$

These determine a set of equilibrium values [1]

$$x_i^o = g_i(\alpha). \qquad (2)$$

We wish to determine the sign of

$$\frac{dx_i^o}{d\alpha} = g_i'(\alpha). \qquad (3)$$

Differentiating (1) totally with respect to α, we can express this as

$$\frac{dx_i^o}{d\alpha} = -\frac{\sum_{j=1}^{n} f_\alpha^j \, \Delta_{ji}}{\Delta}, \qquad (4)$$

where the subscripts indicate partial differentiation,

$$\Delta = \begin{vmatrix} f_1^1 & f_2^1 & \cdots & f_n^1 \\ f_1^2 & f_2^2 & \cdots & f_n^2 \\ \cdots\cdots\cdots\cdots\cdots\cdots \\ f_1^n & f_2^n & \cdots & f_n^n \end{vmatrix} = |f_i^j|,$$

and Δ_{ji} is the cofactor of the element in the jth row and ith column of Δ.

Unless some *a priori* restrictions are placed upon the nature of the elements involved in these determinants, no useful theorems can be derived. Each unknown derivative depends upon an $n(n + 1)$ infinity of possible values. If the various determinants were expanded out, a sum of $n!$ terms would appear in the denominator and in the numerator. Regarded simply as chance drawings taken at random from a hat, the probability that the signs of these would all agree would go rapidly to zero as the number of variables increased. Fortunately, as will be shown, the analysis of the stability of equilibrium will aid in evaluating these complicated expressions.

---

[1] If for a given value of $\alpha = \alpha_1$, there exists a solution $(x_1^o, \cdots, x_n^o)$, and if the matrix $[\partial f^i/\partial x_j]$ is of rank n in a neighborhood of (x^o), then by the implicit-function theorem equations (2) represent single-valued continuously differentiable functions in a sufficiently small neighborhood of (α_1, x^o).

In the simple example of supply and demand alluded to above our unknowns are (p, q), and our equilibrium system can be written:

$$\begin{cases} q - D(p, \alpha) = 0, & (D_\alpha > 0, D_p < 0) \\ q - S(p) = 0, \end{cases} \tag{5}$$

where α is a parameter of shift representing "taste" and D_p is usually assumed to be less than zero. Also

$$\frac{dp^o}{d\alpha} = D_\alpha^o \frac{1}{S_p^o - D_p^o}, \tag{6}$$

$$\frac{dq^o}{d\alpha} = D_\alpha^o \frac{S_p^o}{S_p^o - D_p^o}. \tag{7}$$

Whether or not price will increase when demand increases is seen to depend upon the algebraic difference between the slopes (referred to the price axis) of the demand and supply curves at the equilibrium point. Quantity will increase only if the slope of the supply curve is of the same sign as this algebraic difference. If the system is stable in the sense of Walras, it can be shown that the supply curve must have a greater algebraic slope than the demand curve so that price will necessarily increase; the change in quantity is necessarily of ambiguous sign depending upon whether the supply curve is positively inclined or so-called "backward-rising." [2]

STABILITY AND DYNAMICS

Before deriving explicitly the Walrasian stability conditions referred to above, I turn to a discussion of the meaning of a stable equilibrium. This will be found to presuppose a theory of dynamics, namely a theory which determines the behavior through time of all variables from arbitrary initial conditions. If we have given n variables $[x_1(t), \cdots, x_n(t)]$, and n functional equations of

[2] The distinction suggested by Mr. Kahn between "forward-falling" and "backward-rising" negatively inclined supply curves while suggestive does not rest upon a dynamic analysis of the attainment of equilibrium and so does not adequately come to grips with the problem in all its complexity. Cf. R. F. Kahn, "The Elasticity of Substitution and the Relative Share of a Factor," *Review of Economic Studies*, I (1933), 72–78; also N. Kaldor, "A Classifactory Note on the Determinateness of Equilibrium," *Review of Economic Studies*, I (1933), 122–136.

The suggestion of Professor Viner that the latter type of curve gives the maximum amount forthcoming at a given price while the former does not will receive amplification in the course of this argument.

the general form

$$F^i[\underset{-\infty}{\overset{t}{x_1}}(\tau), \underset{-\infty}{\overset{t}{x_2}}(\tau), \cdots, \underset{-\infty}{\overset{t}{x_n}}(\tau), t] = 0, \qquad (i = 1, \cdots, n) \qquad (8)$$

then their behavior is determined once certain initial conditions are specified.[3] Examples of functional equation systems are given by sets of differential, difference, mixed differential-difference, integral, integro-differential, and still more general systems. Following the excellent terminology of Professor Frisch,[4] stationary or equilibrium values of the variables are given by the set of constants $(x_1{}^o, \cdots, x_n{}^o)$ which satisfy these equations identically, or

$$F^i[\underset{-\infty}{\overset{t}{x_1{}^o}}, \underset{-\infty}{\overset{t}{x_2{}^o}}, \cdots, \underset{-\infty}{\overset{t}{x_n{}^o}}, t] = 0.[5] \qquad (i = 1, \cdots, n) \qquad (9)$$

If the system has *always* been in equilibrium up until time t^o, it will subsequently continue in equilibrium. However, the equilibrium values $(x_1{}^o, \cdots, x_n{}^o)$ may be attained or even be maintained for a finite period of time, and yet because of generalized dynamical "inertia" it need not (and in general will not) remain in equilibrium subsequently, but may well "overshoot" the mark.

The equilibrium position possesses *perfect stability of the first kind* if from any initial conditions all the variables approach their equilibrium values in the limit as time becomes infinite; i.e., if

$$\lim_{t \to \infty} x_i(t) = x_i{}^o, \qquad (10)$$

regardless of the initial conditions. Alternatively, it is sometimes stated that an equilibrium is stable if a displacement from equi-

---

[3] What constitute initial conditions depends upon the nature of the functional equations. For differential systems only values of the coördinates, velocities, and higher derivatives at some initial time need be specified. For difference equations defined only for integral values of t the same is true, where differences replace derivatives. In the general case values of the variables over a continuous time interval, possibly stretching back to $-\infty$, are required to constitute a complete set of initial conditions.

[4] R. Frisch, "On the Notion of Equilibrium and Disequilibrium," *Review of Economic Studies*, III (1936), 100–105.

[5] Of course, such a set need not exist. Thus, the simple system

$$\frac{dx}{dt} = e^x - x$$

has no stationary equilibrium values since $e^x - x = 0$ has no real roots. Similarly, $dx/dt = 1$ defines no stationary equilibrium position.

librium is followed by a return to equilibrium.   A displacement is equivalent to an arbitrary change in the initial conditions and is possible only if some of our functional equations are momentarily relaxed or if our system is enlarged to include impressed forces or shocks.

Stability of the first kind *in the small* exists if for sufficiently small displacements the equilibrium is stable.   Stability in the small is contained within perfect stability but not vice versa.   A system may be stable for small finite displacements but not for large displacements.   Nevertheless, stability in the small is a necessary condition for perfect stability and will be analyzed here in greatest detail.

It should be pointed out that no conservative dynamical system of the type met in theoretical physics possesses stability of the first kind.   If one displaces a frictionless pendulum, it will oscillate endlessly around the position of stable equilibrium.[6]   Its motion is bounded, however, and it never remains on one side of the equilibrium position for more than a finite time interval.   Such behavior may be characterized as *stability of the second kind* or as stability in the second sense.   As before, a distinction can be made between stability of the second kind in the small and complete stability of the second kind.   For the most part in the present investigation I shall be concerned with the problem of stability of the first kind.

The equations of comparative statics are then a special case of the general dynamic analysis.   They can indeed be discussed abstracting completely from dynamical analysis.   In the history of mechanics, the theory of statics was developed before the dynamical problem was even formulated.   But the problem of stability of equilibrium cannot be discussed except with reference to dynamical considerations, however implicit and rudimentary.[7]   We find ourselves confronted with this paradox: in order for the comparative-statics analysis to yield fruitful results, we must first

---

[6] A dynamical system into which friction is introduced via a dissipation function may enjoy stability of the first kind.   On these and kindred matters see G. D. Birkhoff, *Dynamical Systems* (New York, 1927).

[7] This is seen to be involved in the virtual-work analysis and in the minimum-potential-energy condition characteristic of a stable statical ("stationary") equilibrium position.

develop a theory of dynamics.[8] This is completely aside from the
other uses of dynamic analysis as in the studies of fluctuations,
trends, etc.   I turn now to some illustrations of these propositions.

I. In the literary explanations of the process by which supply
and demand are equated, the assumption is usually made that if
at any price demand exceeds supply, price will rise; if supply exceeds demand, price will fall.   Let us state this more precisely as
follows:

$$\dot{p} = \frac{dp}{dt} = H(q_D - q_S) = H[D(p, \alpha) - S(p)], \qquad (11)$$

where $H(0) = 0$, and $H' > 0$.

In the neighborhood of the equilibrium point this can be expanded in the form

$$\dot{p} = \lambda(D_p{}^o - S_p{}^o)(p - p^o) + \cdots, \qquad (12)$$

where $\lambda = (H')^o > 0$, and where terms involving higher powers of
$(p - p^o)$ are omitted.   The solution of this simple differential
equation for initial price $\bar{p}$ at time zero can be written at sight:

$$p(t) = p^o + (\bar{p} - p^o)e^{\lambda(D_p{}^o - S_p{}^o)t}. \qquad (13)$$

If the equilibrium is to be stable,

$$\lim_{t \to \infty} p(t) = p^o. \qquad (14)$$

This is possible if, and only if,

$$D_p{}^o - S_p{}^o \leqq 0. \qquad (15)$$

If in what follows we rule out neutral equilibrium in the large and
in the small, the equality sign may be omitted so that

$$D_p{}^o - S_p{}^o < 0. \qquad (16)$$

If the supply curve is positively inclined, this will be realized.   If
it is negatively inclined, it must be less steep (referred to the price
axis) than the demand curve.   If our stability conditions are
realized, the problem originally proposed is answered.   Price must
rise when demand increases.

---

[8] The point made here is not to be confused with the commonplace criticism of
comparative statics that it does not do what it is not aimed to do, namely describe
the transition paths between equilibria.

II. These so-called Walrasian stability conditions are not neces-sarily the only ones.[9] If alternative dynamic models are postu-lated, completely different conditions are deduced, which in turn lead to alternative theorems in comparative statics.

Thus, in Marshall's long-run theory of normal price the quan-tity supplied is assumed to adjust itself comparatively slowly. If "demand price" exceeds "supply price," the quantity supplied will increase. Preserving our notation of equations (5), remembering that quantity rather than price is regarded as the independent variable, and neglecting higher-order terms, we have the following differential equation

$$\dot{q} = k \left(\frac{1}{D_{p^o}} - \frac{1}{S_{p^o}} \right) (q - q^o), \qquad (k > 0) \qquad (17)$$

whose solution is

$$q(t) = q^o + (\bar{q} - q^o)e^{k(1/D_{p^o} - 1/S_{p^o})t}. \qquad (18)$$

If the equilibrium is to be stable,

$$\frac{1}{D_{p^o}} - \frac{1}{S_{p^o}} = \frac{1}{D_{p^o}} \frac{S_{p^o} - D_{p^o}}{S_{p^o}} < 0, \qquad (19)$$

i.e., the demand-curve slope referred to the quantity axis is less algebraically than that of the supply curve. Since the demand curve is negatively inclined,

$$\frac{S_{p^o}}{S_{p^o} - D_{p^o}} > 0. \qquad (20)$$

Referring back to equations (7), we see that Marshallian stability conditions require that quantity increases when demand increases in every case, while the change in price is necessarily ambiguous depending upon the algebraic sign of the supply curve's slope.

It is to be pointed out that this forward-falling supply curve is not a true supply curve in the sense of the amount forthcoming at each hypothetical price, although it is a true supply curve in the sense of being the locus of price-quantity points traced out by fluctuations in *sufficiently steep* demand curves. As such it is a reversible long-run relation.

[9] A historical error is involved in the identification of the above stability conditions with Walras in alleged contrast to those of Marshall which are shortly to be discussed. Actually as far back as in the *Pure Theory of Foreign Trade* Marshall defined stable equilibrium, in which a so-called backward rising supply curve was involved, much like the Walrasian case.

III. Still another dynamic model may be considered. It has been held that for some commodities supply reacts to price only after a given time lag, while price adjusts itself almost instantaneously. This leads to the familiar cobweb phenomenon. Using the same notation, our dynamic model takes the form of the following difference equations,

$$q_t = S(p_{t-1}),$$
$$q_t = D(p_t, \alpha). \tag{21}$$

In the neighborhood of equilibrium

$$(q_t - q^0) = \left(\frac{S_p{}^o}{D_p{}^o}\right)(q_{t-1} - q^o) \tag{22}$$

with the solution

$$q_t = q^o + (\bar{q} - q^o)\left(\frac{S_p{}^o}{D_p{}^o}\right)^t. \tag{23}$$

Stability requires that

$$\left|\frac{S_p{}^o}{D_p{}^o}\right| < 1. \tag{24}$$

If the supply curve is positively inclined, it must be steeper absolutely than is the demand curve, reference being made to the quantity axis. In this case the approach to equilibrium is of a damped oscillatory nature, every other observation being on one side of the equilibrium value.

If the supply curve is negatively inclined, it must be steeper referred to the quantity axis than is the demand curve, precisely as in the case of Walrasian stability. The approach to equilibrium is asymptotic. As in the Walrasian case, we can deduce the theorem in comparative statics that price will necessarily increase even though the change in quantity is indefinite.

It is to be noted that a first-order difference equation is richer in solution that the corresponding first-order differential equation. Not only does it admit of oscillatory solutions, but the stability conditions relate to the absolute value of the root of an equation, implying two distinct inequalities. Remembering that $D_p{}^o$ is negative, the inequality of (24) can be written

$$D_p{}^o < S_p{}^o < -D_p{}^o.$$

The new inequality tells us that any increase in output as a result of an increase in demand cannot be so large as the increase in output resulting from an "equivalent" increase in supply.

IV. Still a fourth dynamical model that has been considered is that of Marshall in the *Pure Theory of Foreign Trade.* Let Figure 2 represent the familiar offer curves of two trading bodies (suppliers and demanders) respectively. Equilibrium is attained at the intersection (not necessarily unique) of two such curves. If equi-

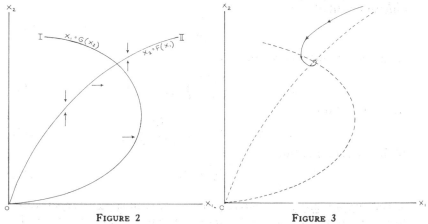

FIGURE 2   FIGURE 3

librium is displaced, country I is to act in such a way as to change the amount of x_1 in the horizontal direction of its offer curve (as indicated by the pointed horizontal arrows). Similarly country II adjusts x_2 vertically in the direction of its offer curve. Mathematically,

$$\dot{x}_1 = H_1[G(x_2) - x_1],$$
$$\dot{x}_2 = H_2[F(x_1) - x_2], \tag{25}$$

where $H_i' > 0$, $H_i(0) = 0$, and $G(x_2) - x_1 = 0$, $F(x_1) - x_2 = 0$ represent the statical offer curves of countries I and II respectively. For $H_1' = H_2'$ and proper units, the following system of differential equations will hold in the neighborhood of equilibrium,

$$\dot{x}_1 = -(x_1 - x_1^\circ) + (G')^\circ(x_2 - x_2^\circ),$$
$$\dot{x}_2 = (F')^\circ(x_1 - x_1^\circ) - (x_2 - x_2^\circ). \tag{26}$$

The solution takes the form:

$$x_1(t) = x_1^\circ + k_{11}e^{\lambda_1 t} + k_{12}e^{\lambda_2 t},$$
$$x_2(t) = x_2^\circ + k_{21}e^{\lambda_1 t} + k_{22}e^{\lambda_2 t}, \tag{27}$$

where the k's depend upon the initial values $(\bar{x}_1, \bar{x}_2)$ and the λ's are roots of the characteristic equation

$$D(\lambda) = \begin{vmatrix} -1 - \lambda & (G')^o \\ (F')^o & -1 - \lambda \end{vmatrix} = 0. \tag{28}$$

Clearly

$$\lambda = -1 \pm \sqrt{(G')^o(F')^o}. \tag{29}$$

The equilibrium will be stable if the real part of λ is necessarily negative, or

$$R(\lambda) < 0. \tag{30}$$

If both $(G')^o$ and $(F')^o$ are of opposite sign (e.g., if one has an elastic demand, the other an inelastic demand), this condition will necessarily be satisfied. The solution will be oscillatory, but damped, approaching equilibrium in a spiral as shown above in Figure 3, and obeying an equation of the form

$$x_i = x_i^o + e^{-t}(a_i \sin \theta t + b_i \cos \theta t). \qquad (i = 1, 2) \tag{31}$$

If both are positive, however (each with elastic demands), then

$$\sqrt{(G')^o(F')^o} < 1, \tag{32}$$

$$(G')^o(F')^o < 1, \tag{33}$$

and

$$(G')^o < \frac{1}{(F')^o}. \tag{34}$$

In terms of the slopes of both offer curves referred to the x_1 axis

$$\left(\frac{dx_2}{dx_1}\right)_{\mathrm{I}} > \left(\frac{dx_2}{dx_1}\right)_{\mathrm{II}}. \tag{35}$$

The equilibrium is approached asymptotically.

If both curves are negatively inclined, stability requires

$$\left(\frac{dx_2}{dx_1}\right)_{\mathrm{I}} < \left(\frac{dx_2}{dx_1}\right)_{\mathrm{II}}. \tag{36}$$

Clearly, the general condition when the curves are of like sign can be written

$$\left|\frac{dx_2}{dx_1}\right|_{\mathrm{I}} > \left|\frac{dx_2}{dx_1}\right|_{\mathrm{II}}, \tag{37}$$

and the approach to equilibrium will in every case be asymptotic.[10]

---

[10] Somewhat paradoxically, in this case positions of stable equilibrium need not be separated by positions of unstable equilibrium because of the possibility of complex roots.

The stability conditions derived here will be found, if translated into terms of supply and demand curves rather than offer curves, to imply differing and inconsistent conditions from those of the preceding cases.

V. In the four cases considered I have been concerned with problems of stability of the first kind. Following a suggestion of Dr. Francis Dresch of the University of California, let us suppose that price falls not when the instantaneous supply exceeds demand, but only when accumulated stocks exceed some normal value, Q^o, or

$$\dot{p} = \lambda(Q^o - Q) + \cdots = \lambda Q^o - \lambda \int_0^t (q_S - q_D)dt, \quad (? > 0) \quad (38)$$

since the stock equals the accumulated difference between the amount produced and the amount consumed. Differentiating with respect to t, neglecting terms of higher power, and redefining our time units so as to suppress the dimensional constant λ we would have

$$\ddot{p} = (D_{p^o} - S_{p^o})(p - p^o), \quad (39)$$

whose solution is

$$p(t) = p^o + c_1 e^{(\sqrt{D_{p^o} - S_{p^o}})t} + c_2 e^{-(\sqrt{D_{p^o} - S_{p^o}})t}, \quad (40)$$

the c's depending upon the initial price and price change.

Only if

$$D_{p^o} - S_{p^o} < 0, \quad (41)$$

can explosive behavior be avoided. If the above inequality is realized, however, the square root will be a pure imaginary number so that the solution takes the form of an undamped harmonic:

$$p(t) = b_1 \cos \sqrt{S_{p^o} - D_{p^o}} \, t + b_2 \sin \sqrt{S_{p^o} - D_{p^o}} \, t + p^o. \quad (42)$$

Thus, if we require our second-order differential equation to have at least stability of the second kind, we come to the same theorems in comparative statics as in case I.

There is at least one serious objection to assuming a nondamped system of this kind. If there are superimposed upon our system random shocks or errors, these will tend to accumulate so that the expected amplitude of the cycles will increase with time. This is well illustrated by the familiar Brownian movement of large molecules under the impact of random collisions. The molecule "takes a random walk," and its mean variance increases with the observation time.[11] Before adopting a similar hypothesis in economic analysis, some statistical evidence of its possible validity should be adduced.[12]

We have now surveyed five different dynamic setups and related stability conditions, all referring to a simple one-commodity market. Except possibly for cases IV and V, all are mathematically trivial. Unaided intuition or simple geometrical methods serve to reveal sufficient conditions for stability. They are of significance, however, because each has played an important part in the history of economic science; and precisely because of their simplicity they provide a useful illustration of the general principle involved. In the following sections I shall be concerned with more complex problems.

THE STABILITY OF MULTIPLE MARKETS

While it might be more elegant at this stage to develop formally for general systems the fundamental principles illustrated thus far, our foregoing discussion provides a very convenient opening for an examination of a problem which has received considerable attention lately at the hands of Professor Hicks. In *Value and*

---

[11] Random shocks are not necessarily to be regarded as a nuisance. In their absence friction might imprison the system at some fixed level other than the "true" equilibrium level (friction being disregarded). Often random shocks serve to insure the realization of *average* values nearly equal to the equilibrium ones, just as iron filings placed upon a piece of paper over a magnet assume the lines of force of the magnetic field when gently tapped.

[12] One can avoid an undamped system by assuming that price tends to fall not only when stocks are large, but also when current supply exceeds current demand; i.e., when stocks tend to accumulate. Then we have

$$\dot{p} = \alpha \left[Q^o - \int_0^t (q_S - q_D)dt \right] - \beta(q_S - q_D)$$

or, for price deviations

$$\ddot{p} = \alpha(D_p^o - S_p^o)p + \beta(D_p^o - S_p^o)\dot{p}. \qquad (\alpha, \beta > 0)$$

The equilibrium is stable only if

$$R(\lambda) < 0,$$

or if

$$\lambda^2 - \beta (D_p^o - S_p^o)\lambda - \alpha (D_p^o - S_p^o) = 0,$$

$$D_p^o - S_p^o < 0.$$

This agrees with the condition of case I and the one just derived. In fact, each of these is a special case when one of the coefficients vanishes. For intermediate values, the solutions range continuously between damped harmonic motion and exponential approach to equilibrium.

Capital, Chapter VIII and Mathematical Appendix, §21, he has attempted to generalize to any number of markets the stability conditions of a single market. The method of approach is postulational; stability conditions are not deduced from a dynamic model except implicitly.[13] Propositions which are deduced here as theorems are assumed as definitions of stability.

For a single market, according to Professor Hicks, equilibrium is stable if an increase in demand raises price. (This rules out in the beginning cases II and IV.) For multiple markets equilibrium is *imperfectly* stable if an increase in demand for a single good raises its price after all other prices have adjusted themselves; the equilibrium is *perfectly* stable if an increased demand for a good raises its price even when *any* subset of other prices is arbitrarily held constant (by means of a relaxation of other equilibrium conditions).

To test the necessity or sufficiency of these criteria in terms of a more fundamental definition of stability of equilibrium let us make a natural generalization of the Walrasian conditions of the following form: the price of any good will fall if its supply exceeds its demand, *these each being regarded as functions of all other prices.*

Mathematically,

$$\dot{p}_i = - H_i(q_s{}^i - q_D{}^i)$$
$$= - H_i[q_s{}^i(p_1, \cdots, p_n) - q_D{}^i(p_1, \cdots, p_n)]$$
$$= H_i{}' \sum_{j=1}^{n} a_{ij}{}^o(p_j - p_j{}^o) + \cdots, \qquad (43)$$

where

$$0 = q_s{}^i(p_1, \cdots, p_n) - q_D{}^i(p_1, \cdots, p_n) = - q_i(p_1, \cdots, p_n) \quad (44)$$

represent statical equations of supply and demand, $a_{ij}{}^o$ represents the partial derivative of q_i with respect to the jth price evaluated at the equilibrium set of prices. In general, $a_{ij}{}^o \neq a_{ji}{}^o$.[14] It is

---

[13] It is true that on page 70 a hint of a dynamical process creeps into the discussion. The approach to equilibrium seems to be regarded as taking place in finite steps at discrete intervals of time; i.e., in accordance with certain difference equations. Correctly stated, this argument would not lead to essentially different stability conditions from my system of differential equations discussed below, as the later general discussion will disclose.

[14] If the demand and supply were each drawn up with reference to firms maximizing profit, well-known integrability conditions would guarantee this equivalence. On the consumer's side there need be no such equivalence, and if we consider a consumer whose total purchases balance his total sale of productive services, such an equality for every

instructive to consider first, however, the symmetrical case (such as characterizes markets made up exclusively of entrepreneurs); and let the speeds of adjustments, H_i', be set equal to one. The solution of equations (43) can be written

$$p_i(t) = p_i^o + \sum_{j=1}^{n} k_{ij} e^{\lambda_j t}, \tag{45}$$

where $(\lambda_1, \cdots, \lambda_n)$ are latent roots of the characteristic equation and

$$f(\lambda) = \begin{vmatrix} a_{11}^o - \lambda & a_{12}^o & \cdots & a_{1n}^o \\ a_{21}^o & a_{22}^o - \lambda & & a_{2n}^o \\ \cdots\cdots\cdots\cdots\cdots\cdots\cdots\cdots\cdots\cdots\cdots \\ a_{n1}^o & a_{n2}^o & \cdots & a_{nn}^o - \lambda \end{vmatrix} \tag{46}$$

$$= |a - \lambda I| = |a_{ij}^o - \lambda \delta_{ij}| = 0,$$

the k's depend upon the matrix a and upon the initial conditions.[15] As before, stability requires $R(\lambda_j) < 0$.

By a well-known theorem of Hermitian matrices, in the symmetrical case all the roots are necessarily real. If the equilibrium is to be stable, they must all be negative. According to a classical theorem, this is possible if and only if a is the matrix of a negative definite quadratic form; i.e., only if all principal minors alternate in sign as follows:

$$|a_{ii}^o| < 0; \quad \begin{vmatrix} a_{ii}^o & a_{ij}^o \\ a_{ji}^o & a_{jj}^o \end{vmatrix} > 0; \quad \begin{vmatrix} a_{ii}^o & a_{ij}^o & a_{ik}^o \\ a_{ji}^o & a_{jj}^o & a_{jk}^o \\ a_{ki}^o & a_{kj}^o & a_{kk}^o \end{vmatrix} < 0,$$

$$i \neq j \neq k \neq i. \tag{47}$$

combination of goods and services would, strictly interpreted, lead to an absurdity; it would imply expenditure proportionality and, hence, zero consumption of every good and zero offering of every service! For the general demand or supply function we need not expect a canceling off of "income effects" since individuals usually face firms in consumption and factor markets.

[15] If the roots are not distinct, polynomial terms of the form $t e^{\lambda t}$, $t^2 e^{\lambda t}$, $\cdots$, $t^s e^{\lambda t}$ appear where $(s + 1)$ is the multiplicity of a repeated root. In any case the problem of stability depends only upon the λ's and is unaffected by such multipliers since the exponential always governs the asymptotic behavior of the solution whenever dampening does occur.

Any ratio of the form

$$\frac{\begin{vmatrix} 1 & 0 & \cdots & 0 \\ 0 & a_{jj}{}^o & \cdots & a_{jk}{}^o \\ \cdots\cdots\cdots\cdots\cdots\cdots \\ 0 & a_{kj}{}^o & \cdots & a_{kk}{}^o \end{vmatrix}}{\begin{vmatrix} a_{ii}{}^o & a_{ij}{}^o & \cdots & a_{ik}{}^o \\ a_{ji}{}^o & a_{jj}{}^o & \cdots & a_{jk}{}^o \\ \cdots\cdots\cdots\cdots\cdots\cdots \\ a_{ki}{}^o & a_{kj}{}^o & \cdots & a_{kk}{}^o \end{vmatrix}} \qquad (48)$$

is necessarily negative in sign.   But such ratios are precisely equal
to the change in the price of the ith good with respect to a unit
increase in its net supply when appropriate subsets of other prices
are held constant, so that for this case the stability criteria of Professor Hicks are seen to be correct theorems.

Where perfect symmetry is not present (and in business-cycle
analysis it is almost always absent), the Hicks criteria are not at
all necessary conditions and in many cases not sufficient.[16]   A
system may possess stability of the first kind even though neither
perfectly nor *imperfectly* stable in Hicks's sense.   I long suspected
that perfect stability is a sufficient condition for stability of the
first kind.   But this conjecture proved to be false.   Perfect stability, like imperfect stability, is neither a necessary nor sufficient

[16] A word of warning may be in order concerning the indiscriminate use of either
prices or quantities as independent variables.   This leads to contradictory definitions of
complementarity in the literary discussion on page 44 and the mathematical definitions
on page 311, the inconsistency between which can lead to opposite signs.   Such an
interchange of independent variables (as between the literary definition of stability on
page 63 and the mathematical conditions on 315 and 325) is particularly important
where nonsymmetrical matrices are concerned.   Does

$$\frac{dx_i}{dp_i} < 0, \qquad \begin{vmatrix} \dfrac{dx_i}{dp_i} & \dfrac{dx_i}{dp_j} \\[2mm] \dfrac{dx_j}{dp_i} & \dfrac{dx_j}{dp_j} \end{vmatrix} > 0, \cdots \qquad \text{where} \qquad \frac{dx_i}{dp_j} \neq \frac{dx_j}{dp_i},$$

imply

$$\frac{dp_i}{dx_i} < 0, \qquad \begin{vmatrix} \dfrac{dp_i}{dx_i} & \dfrac{dp_i}{dx_j} \\[2mm] \dfrac{dp_j}{dx_i} & \dfrac{dp_j}{dx_j} \end{vmatrix} > 0, \cdots ?$$

The answer is yes, but the proof is not simple.   Even with symmetry the product
$(dp_i/dx_i)(dx_i/dp_i)$ need not be of positive sign if more than two variables are involved.

condition.[17]   In any case it is too strict a condition, while the requirement of imperfect stability is not strict enough; only in the case of symmetry do these limits converge.   Why any system should be expected to possess *perfect* stability, or why an economist should be interested in this property is by no means clear.   Not working with an explicit dynamical model, Professor Hicks probably argued by analogy from well-known maximum conditions, whereby a maximum must hold for arbitrary displacements and through any transformation of variables.   As a result, some variables may be made constants, and with respect to the remaining arbitrary subsets the definiteness of various quadratic forms must be insured.   On the other hand, in terms of a truly dynamic process the equilibrium must be stable for arbitrary initial conditions or displacements and for arbitrary nonsingular transformations of variables, but *not* necessarily for arbitrary modifications of the dynamic equations of motion such as are involved in the Hicks procedure of holding subsets of other prices constant (by violating or relaxing true dynamical relations).   In principle the Hicks procedure is clearly wrong, although in some empirical cases it may be useful to make the hypothesis that the equilibrium is stable even without the "equilibrating" action of some variable which may be arbitrarily held constant.   (In connection with the Keynesian model later discussed, an example of this is presented.)

To summarize: for every case true necessary and sufficient stability conditions are that $R(\lambda_j) < 0$, where λ_j represents the

[17] The matrix

$$\begin{bmatrix} \epsilon & 1 & 0 & 0 \\ 0 & \epsilon & 1 & 0 \\ 0 & 0 & \epsilon & 1 \\ -1 & +1 & -1 & 1+\epsilon \end{bmatrix}$$

for sufficiently small ϵ's has all principal minors positive and yet has some roots whose real parts are negative. This shows that even Hicksian *perfect* stability does not guarantee dynamic stability. See P. A. Samuelson, "The Relation between Hicksian Stability and True Dynamic Stability," *Econometrica*, XII (1944), 256–257. Also, as Metzler has recently shown, the Hicksian conditions are necessary (but not sufficient) if the system is to be stable for all possible (positive) rates of adjustment in different markets; and if all off-diagonal terms are non-negative, the Hicks conditions are both necessary and sufficient for stability. L. A. Metzler, "Stability of Multiple Markets: The Hicks Conditions," *Econometrica*, XIII (1945), 272–292. For a proof that the inverse of the last matrix must consist of all elements of the same sign, see J. Mosak, *General Equilibrium Theory in International Trade* (Bloomington, Indiana: Principia Press, 1944), p. 49. Sometimes "positive" must be replaced by "non-negative" in these matters.

latent roots of the matrix a. This is not equivalent to the Hicks conditions.[18]

In an address before the Econometric Society Professor Lange [19] suggested that the speed of reaction might be different in every market so that instead of writing

$$\dot{p}_i = H'q_i + \cdots \tag{49}$$

as in (43), we write

$$\dot{p}_i = H_iq_i + \cdots, \tag{50}$$

where $H_i = H_i'(0)$ is the (positive) coefficient appropriate to the ith market.

Even this is not sufficiently general unless a particular commodity classification is to be favored, and if our formulation is to be invariant under linear transformations of commodities and prices. We have no choice but to admit that the rate of adjustment in one market may depend on the excess demand in *other* markets; so that in matrix terms

$$\dot{p} = Hq + \cdots = Hap + \cdots, \tag{51}$$

where q is the column of q_i's; a the square matrix a_{ij}^o; and where H need not now be a positive diagonal matrix. It would seem reasonable at first to require H to be positive definite, or at least to be positive quasi-definite, as the latter expression was defined in chapter vi. But if we apply the contragredient transformation c as given in equation (47) of chapter vi,

$$\begin{aligned} q &= c\bar{q}; & \bar{q} &= c^{-1}q \\ p &= c'^{-1}\bar{p}; & \bar{p} &= c'p, \end{aligned} \tag{52}$$

[18] The following illustrations bear this out: The system
$$\begin{aligned} \dot{p}_1 &= -2p_1 + 4p_2, \\ \dot{p}_2 &= -p_1 + p_2, \end{aligned}$$
possesses stability of the first kind, but is neither perfectly nor imperfectly stable. The system
$$\begin{aligned} \dot{p}_1 &= p_1 - p_2, \\ \dot{p}_2 &= -2p_1 + p_2, \end{aligned}$$
is imperfectly stable, but departs ever further from equilibrium.

[19] O. Lange, Abstract of "The Stability of Economic Equilibrium," *Econometrica*, X (1942), 176–177; *Price Flexibility and Employment* (Bloomington, Indiana: Principia Press, 1944), appendix.

then it can be verified that

$$\dot{p} = \bar{H}\bar{q} + \cdots = c'H\bar{q} + \cdots = \bar{H}\bar{a}\bar{p} + \cdots = (c'Hac'^{-1})\bar{p} + \cdots. \quad (53)$$

It follows that our restrictions cannot be placed upon H alone, but only upon the product of H and a; that is, the results depend upon the statical matrix a and upon the dynamical reaction-speed matrix H. It is sufficient for stability that in some coördinate system H^{-1} be positive quasi-definite and a negative quasi-definite, but these conditions are by no means necessary.

Before leaving the problem of stable multiple markets, I should like to sketch the effect of the introduction of stocks and its relevance to stability of the second kind. Let price fall not when current supply exceeds current demand, but when existing stocks (accumulated over time from the divergence of current production and consumption) exceed an equilibrium amount. Then for proper time units and equal speeds of adjustment

$$\dot{p}_i = Q_i^\circ - \int_0^t (q_S - q_D)d\tau = Q_i^\circ + \int_0^t \sum_{j=1}^n a_{ij}^\circ(p_j - p_j^\circ)d\tau + \cdots$$

or

$$\ddot{p}_i = \sum_{j=1}^n a_{ij}^\circ(p_j - p_j^\circ) + \cdots, \quad (54)$$

whose solution takes the form

$$p_i(t) = p_i^\circ + \sum_{j=1}^n (k_{ij}e^{\sqrt{\lambda_j}\,t} + h_{ij}e^{-\sqrt{\lambda_j}\,t}), \quad (55)$$

where $|a_{ij}^\circ - \lambda_j\delta_{ij}| = 0$, and where for unrepeated roots the k's and the h's are constant depending upon initial conditions. Clearly the motion will be explosive and undamped unless $\sqrt{\lambda_j}$ are all pure imaginary numbers; i.e., unless λ_j is real and negative.

If the system is symmetrical, this clearly leads to the same conditions as those for stability of the first kind. If not symmetrical, the substitution of second derivatives everywhere for first derivatives (through the hypothesis of dependence upon accumulated stocks rather than instantaneous flows) implies more rigid conditions upon the coefficients to insure stability of the second kind than were previously required to insure stability of the first kind. This is of course because of the requirement that the roots be real as well as negative.[20]

ANALYSIS OF THE KEYNESIAN SYSTEM

Up until now I have considered examples drawn from the field of economic theory. The techniques used there are of even more fruitful applicability to problems of business cycles. To illustrate this I shall analyze in some detail the simple Keynesian model as outlined in the *General Theory*. Various writers, such as Meade, Hicks, and Lange, have developed explicitly in mathematical form the meaning of the Keynesian system.[21] The three fundamental relationships stressed by Keynes are (1) *the consumption function* relating consumption (and hence savings-investment) to income, and for generality to the interest rate as well; (2) *the marginal efficiency of capital* relating *net* investment to the interest rate and to the level of income (as of a fixed level of capital equipment, fixed for the short period under investigation); (3) *the schedule of liquidity preference* relating the existing amount of money to the interest rate and the level of income.

Mathematically, these may be written as follows:

$$C(i, Y) - Y + I = -\alpha, \tag{56}$$

$$F(i, Y) - I = -\beta, \tag{57}$$

$$L(i, Y) = M, \tag{58}$$

where i, Y, I stand respectively for the interest rate, income, and investment; C, F, L stand respectively for the consumption function, the marginal-efficiency-of-capital schedule, and the schedule of liquidity preference. M stands for the existing amount of money, taken as a parameter; α is a general parameter representing

---

[20] One could consider the generalization of the intermediate hypothesis of footnote 12 where price change depends upon stocks and flows, namely,

$$\ddot{p}_i = \sum_{j=1}^{n} a_{ij}{}^o [\alpha \dot{p}_i + \beta (p_i - p_i{}^o)]. \qquad \begin{pmatrix} \alpha > 0 \\ \beta > 0 \end{pmatrix}$$

If stable for $\beta > 0$, $\alpha = 0$, and also for $\beta = 0$, $\alpha > 0$, it can perhaps be proved to be stable for all intermediate cases.

[21] J. E. Meade, "A Simplified Model of Mr. Keynes' System," *Review of Economic Studies*, IV (1937), 98–107; J. R. Hicks, "Mr. Keynes and the 'Classics'; A Suggested Interpretation," *Econometrica*, V (1937), 147–159; Oskar Lange, "The Rate of Interest and the Optimum Propensity to Consume," *Economica*, V (1938), 12–32.

an upward shift in the propensity-to-consume schedule; similarly as the parameter β increases, the marginal-efficiency schedule shifts upward.

We have three relations to determine the three unknowns in terms of three parameters, viz.:

$$i = i(\alpha, \beta, M),$$
$$Y = Y(\alpha, \beta, M), \qquad (59)$$
$$I = I(\alpha, \beta, M).$$

As explained in the first section of this part, the usefulness of the Keynesian equilibrium system lies in the light it throws upon the way our unknowns will change as a result of changes in data. More specifically, what are the signs of

$$\frac{di}{d\alpha}, \quad \frac{dY}{d\alpha}, \quad \frac{dI}{d\alpha},$$
$$\frac{di}{d\beta}, \quad \frac{dY}{d\beta}, \quad \frac{dI}{d\beta},$$
$$\frac{di}{dM}, \quad \frac{dY}{dM}, \quad \frac{dI}{dM}?$$

Differentiating totally with respect to our parameters and evaluating the resulting linear equations, we find

$$\frac{di}{d\alpha} = \frac{-L_Y}{\Delta}, \quad \frac{dY}{d\alpha} = \frac{L_i}{\Delta}, \quad \frac{dI}{d\alpha} = \frac{F_Y L_i - F_i L_Y}{\Delta},$$

$$\frac{di}{d\beta} = \frac{-L_Y}{\Delta}, \quad \frac{dY}{d\beta} = \frac{L_i}{\Delta}, \quad \frac{dI}{d\beta} = \frac{(1 - C_Y)L_i + C_i L_Y}{\Delta},$$

$$\frac{di}{dM} = \frac{1 - C_Y - F_Y}{\Delta}, \quad \frac{dY}{dM} = \frac{F_i + C_i}{\Delta}, \qquad (60)$$

$$\frac{dI}{dM} = \frac{F_Y(F_i + C_i) + (1 - C_Y - F_Y)F_i}{\Delta},$$

where

$$\Delta = \begin{vmatrix} C_i & C_Y - 1 & 1 \\ F_i & F_Y & -1 \\ L_i & L_Y & 0 \end{vmatrix} = L_Y(F_i + C_i) + L_i(1 - C_Y - F_Y). \quad (61)$$

On the basis of a priori, intuitive, empirical experience the following assumptions are usually made:

$$C_Y > 0, \quad F_Y > 0, \quad F_i < 0, \quad L_Y > 0, \quad L_i < 0, \qquad (62)$$

while
$$C_i \gtreqless 0$$
and is usually assumed in modern discussions to be of minor quantitative importance.

In order to evaluate our nine derivatives we must be able to determine unambiguously the signs of all numerators as well as the common denominator, Δ. Δ consists of five terms, two of which are of positive sign, two of negative sign, and one ambiguous. On the basis of deductive analysis along strictly statical lines nothing can be inferred concerning its sign. Moreover, even if the sign of Δ were determined, all but four of the nine would be found to have numerators of indeterminable sign.

This is a typical case. If we are to derive useful theorems, we must clearly proceed to a consideration of a more general dynamic system which includes the stationary Keynesian analysis as a special case. This can be done in a variety of alternative ways. I shall consider two, the first of which is based upon a differential system and yields quite definite results.

Case 1. Let us assume as before that the second and third relations of marginal efficiency and liquidity preference work themselves out in so short a time that they can be regarded as holding instantaneously. Let us assume, however, that I now represents "intended" investment, and this magnitude equals savings-investment only in equilibrium, i.e., when all the variables take on stationary values. If, however, because of some change, consumption (say) should suddenly increase, national income not having a chance to change, actual savings-investment would fall short of "intended" investment because of inventory reduction, etc. Consequently, income would tend to rise. Similarly an excess of actual savings-investment over intended investment would tend to make income fall. Mathematically, this hypothesis may be stated as follows: *the rate of change of income is proportional to the difference between intended savings-investment and actual savings-investment.* The discussion here is unrelated to the controversy over the equality of savings and investment despite possible appearances to the contrary. The superficial resemblance between my formulation and the Robertsonian identities whereby the difference between investment and savings is the time difference of income should not mislead the careful reader.

Equations (56), (57), and (58) are replaced by the dynamical ones:

$$\dot{Y} = I - [Y - C(i, Y) - \alpha], \tag{63}$$

$$0 = F(i, Y) - I + \beta, \tag{64}$$

$$0 = L(i, Y) - M. \tag{65}$$

The solution of these is of the form:

$$Y = Y^o + a_1 e^{\lambda t},$$

$$i = i^o + a_2 e^{\lambda t}, \tag{66}$$

$$I = I^o + a_3 e^{\lambda t},$$

where

$$\Delta(\lambda) = \begin{vmatrix} C_i & C_Y - 1 - \lambda & 1 \\ F_i & F_Y & -1 \\ L_i & L_Y & 0 \end{vmatrix} = \Delta + \lambda L_i = 0. \tag{67}$$

The equilibrium is stable only if

$$\lambda = -\frac{\Delta}{L_i} < 0. \tag{68}$$

But $L_i < 0$; therefore,

$$\Delta < 0 \tag{69}$$

unambiguously.

This establishes four theorems: an increased marginal efficiency of capital will (1) raise interest rates and (2) raise income; an increased propensity to consume will (3) raise interest rates and (4) raise income. But how will the creation of new money affect interest rates? This can be answered by considering more stringent stability conditions. Let us suppose that the interest rate were kept constant (say) by appropriate central bank action. This assumption is equivalent to dropping the liquidity preference equation (65) and treating i as a constant in the remaining equations. If the equilibrium is stable under these conditions, we must have

$$\begin{vmatrix} C_Y - 1 - \lambda & 1 \\ F_Y & -1 \end{vmatrix} = 0 = (1 - C_Y - F_Y) + \lambda, \tag{70}$$

or

$$-\lambda = (1 - F_Y - C_Y) > 0. \tag{71}$$

This leads to another important theorem: (5) *the marginal propensity to consume plus the marginal propensity to invest cannot exceed unity or the system will be unstable* (as of a fixed interest rate).[22] It also tells us (6) that an increase in the amount of money must, *ceteris paribus*, lower interest rates.

We are left with four ambiguities of sign. Two of them depend upon the fact that savings may vary in any direction with respect to a change in interest rates. If we assume that normally savings out of a given income increase with the interest rate, or, if they do decrease, do so not so much as does investment, then three more theorems become true: an increase in the amount of money (7) increases income and (8) increases investment; (9) an increase in the marginal-efficiency schedule increases investment. There remains a final ambiguous term. What is the effect upon investment of an increased propensity to consume? This is seen to be essentially ambiguous depending upon the quantitative strengths of the liquidity-preference slopes and the marginal-efficiency slopes. As income increases, money becomes tight because of the need for financing more transactions. This tends to depress investment. As an offset, the increase in income tends to increase investment through the marginal propensity to invest. Which effect will be the stronger cannot be decided on *a priori* grounds.

I have prepared a 3 × 3 classification indicating the signs of the nine terms. All but four have definite signs. Of these four, one is essentially ambiguous as indicated by a question mark. The remaining three show under question marks their normal, presumptive signs.

	i	Y	I
Increase in propensity to consume	α	$+$	$+$	$?$
Increase in marginal efficiency of capital	β	$+$	$+$	$\overset{?}{+}$
Increase in amount of money	M	$-$	$\overset{?}{+}$	$\overset{?}{+}$

[22] If we take investment also as an independent parameter (say through government action), we lose equation (57) and have for stability the condition

$$|C_Y - 1 - \lambda| = (C_Y - 1) - \lambda = 0,$$

$$\lambda = C_Y - 1 < 0,$$

or that *the marginal propensity to consume must be less than one.* But this is weaker than the previous condition in view of the fact that the marginal propensity to invest is assumed positive.

Case 2. I now turn to a system based on a difference equation. It is founded upon considerations similar to those underlying the Kahn-Clark multiplier block diagrams, and for this reason alone is worth consideration. In addition, the analytical contrasts between differential and difference systems is brought out. Reversing the order of the previous exposition, let us take investment as an independent parameter and the interest rate as a constant. Let consumption be a given function of income during the preceding period of time:

$$C_t = C(\bar{\imath}, Y_{t-1}) = C(Y_{t-1}). \qquad (72)$$

What properties must this function satisfy if the equilibrium is to be stable? Income clearly equals consumption plus investment:

$$Y_t = C_t + I_t. \qquad (73)$$

Recalling that investment is treated as a constant, $\bar{I}$, and using the consumption relation, we find

$$Y_t = C(Y_{t-1}) + \bar{I}, \qquad (74)$$

or, to a first approximation,

$$(Y_t - Y^o) = C_{Y^o}(Y_{t-1} - Y^o), \qquad (75)$$

where

$$Y^o = C(Y^o) + \bar{I} \qquad (76)$$

is the equilibrium level of income for investment equal to $\bar{I}$.

The solution of this difference equation takes the form

$$Y_t = Y^o + K(C_{Y^o})^t \qquad (77)$$

and is stable only if

$$|C_{Y^o}| < 1 \qquad (78)$$

or

$$-1 < C_{Y^o} < 1.^{23} \qquad (79)$$

While the marginal propensity to consume is usually assumed to be positive, it need not be so, and still the equilibrium can be a

---

[23] This inequality is in effect the formal justification of Keynes' reply to those criticizing his fundamental law, that the burden of proof lay upon them to explain why, if their allegations were correct, the economic system was not hopelessly unstable. See the passages quoted from a letter of Keynes in E. W. Gilboy, "The Propensity to Consume: Reply," *Quarterly Journal of Economics*, LIII (1939), 634. While fundamentally correct, Keynes does overlook the possibility of other stabilizers such as the marginal propensity to invest, interest rate, etc.

stable one.   Even if it lies between zero and minus one, it is interesting to observe that the "multiplier" is positive since

$$\frac{dY^o}{d\bar{I}} = \frac{1}{1 - C_{Y^o}} > 0, \tag{80}$$

but less than unity because of negative "secondary" effects.

Let us now drop the assumption that investment is a datum,
although keeping the interest rate constant.   Our dynamic system
is of the form

$$C(\bar{\imath}, Y_{t-1}) - Y_t + I_t = 0, \tag{81}$$

$$F(\bar{\imath}, Y_t) - I_t = 0, \tag{82}$$

and the equilibrium is stable only if

$$|\lambda| = \left| \frac{C_Y}{1 - F_Y} \right| < 1, \tag{83}$$

or

$$-|1 - F_Y| < C_Y < |1 - F_Y|. \tag{84}$$

Now if the marginal propensity to invest is less than unity
$(1 - F_Y > 0)$,[24] this leads to essentially the same stability conditions as before, namely, the marginal propensity to consume
plus the marginal propensity to invest must be less than unity
$(C_Y + F_Y < 1)$.   But, and this is paradoxical, if the marginal
propensity to invest is sufficiently large, i.e., greater than $+2$, the
marginal propensity to consume may exceed unity, and yet the
equilibrium will be stable!   Moreover, beyond a certain critical
value the larger the marginal propensity to invest, the more stable
is the system.   This comes from neglecting the lag between Y and I.

If we now consider the system in which none of the variables
are taken as given, namely,

$$\begin{aligned}
C(i_t, Y_{t-1}) - Y_t + I_t &= 0, \\
F(i_t, Y_t) - I_t &= 0, \\
L(i_t, Y_t) - M &= 0,
\end{aligned} \tag{85}$$

[24] In the marginal-efficiency relation I have made investment depend upon income,
which itself includes investment.   Other writers, notably Lange (*op. cit.*), have made
it depend only upon consumption.   The result is indifferent since they can be shown
to be equivalent.   If, however, it is assumed that $dI/dC > 0$, the marginal propensity
to invest, $dI/dY = (dI/dC)/[1 + (dI/dC)]$, cannot exceed unity.   If a one-period lag
is put in (82), then the sum of the consumption and investment propensities must be
less than one.

stability requires that

$$|\lambda| = \left| \frac{L_i C_Y}{\Delta + L_i C_Y} \right| < 1. \tag{86}$$

In what may be termed the normal case, where the marginal propensity to invest is less than unity, this requires as before that

$$\Delta < 0, \tag{87}$$

and immediately all the eight determinations of sign of Case I become correct.

In the unusual, but possible, case where

$$1 - F_Y < 0 < C_Y < (F_Y - 1) - \frac{L_Y}{L_i}(F_i + C_i), \tag{88}$$

the equilibrium will be stable, but the signs of our 3 × 3 table now are as follows:

	i	Y	I
α	—	—	?
β	—	—	?
M	—	?	?

In words, the only theorem which remains true under all circumstances is that an increase in the amount of money must lower interest rates if the equilibrium is stable.

This example illustrates the additional complexities which systems based upon difference equations involve. Later some of the reasons for this will be explained.

The examples here adduced serve, I hope, to illustrate the light which dynamical analysis sheds upon comparative statics. Problems in theory and business cycles of any complexity will almost surely require similar analytic treatment if useful and meaningful theorems are to be derived.

CHAPTER X

THE STABILITY OF EQUILIBRIUM: LINEAR AND NONLINEAR SYSTEMS

INTRODUCTION

IN THE PREVIOUS CHAPTER it was pointed out that there exists an intimate formal dependence between comparative statics and dynamics. To my knowledge this had not previously been explicitly enunciated in the economic literature, and for lack of a better name I shall refer to it as the *Correspondence Principle*. It is the purpose here to probe more deeply into its analytical character, and also to show its two-way nature: not only can the investigation of the dynamic stability of a system yield fruitful theorems in statical analysis, but also known properties of a (comparative) statical system can be utilized to derive information concerning the dynamic properties of a system.

An understanding of this principle is all the more important at a time when pure economic theory has undergone a revolution of thought—from statical to dynamical modes. While many earlier foreshadowings can be found in the literature, we may date this upheaval from the publication of Ragnar Frisch's Cassel Volume essay of only a decade ago.[1] The resulting change in outlook can be compared to that of the transition from classical to quantum mechanics. And just as in the field of physics it was well that the relationship between the old and the new theories could be in part clarified, so in our field a similar investigation seems in order.

Before entering, however, upon these unavoidably technical matters, a few *obiter dicta* concerning the fundamental differences between statical and dynamical systems may be in order. Conceived broadly, a dynamical system might be regarded as any set of functional equations which together with initial conditions (in the most general sense) determine as solutions certain unknowns in function of time. According to this definition timeless, statical

---

[1] Ragnar Frisch, "Propagation Problems and Impulse Problems in Dynamic Eocnomics," *Economic Essays in Honor of Gustav Cassel* (London, 1933), pp. 171–205.

systems are simply degenerate special cases in which the functional equations take on simple forms and determine as solutions functions of time which are identically constants. We may, however, define a dynamical system more narrowly so that it will not be regarded as truly dynamic if the functional equations involve only variables "of the same instant of time," containing time, if at all, only as a parameter.[2] This excludes the customary statical systems of the "historical" as well as the timeless variety.[3] It is possible, however, that certain subsets of the solutions of the dynamical equations are defined by equations which are structurally identical with those which define a statical system. (Thus the stationary solution of a time-sequence analysis, say of the multiplier-block-diagram variety, may be determined by a formula exactly like that of a timeless, instantaneous system.) This constitutes a second possible mutual orientation of statical and dynamical systems.

From still a third point of view a statical system can be looked upon as *the limiting case of a heavily damped dynamical system.* Thus any statical equation

$$f(x) = 0$$

which admits a unique solution x^o can be related to a dynamical system of the form

$$f\{x_t + \Delta(x_t - x^o)\} = 0.$$

This yields directly the equivalent linear difference equation

$$x_t + \Delta(x_t - x^o) = x^o,$$

or

$$x_{t+1} = x^o.$$

Thus, whatever the initial magnitude of x, at the next "instant" the system always takes on its correct statical value. This generalizes easily to systems of more than one variable.

In the following I deal with interrelationships between statics and dynamics which largely fall under the second of the three headings here discussed.

---

[2] Ragnar Frisch, "On the Notion of Equilibrium and Disequilibrium," *Review of Economic Studies*, III, February, 1936, 100–105.

[3] In chapter xi I deal at some length with the distinction between complete causal systems and historical or incomplete causal ones, also with the closely related topic of the generalization of the notion of stationary equilibrium to systems involving time explicitly.

FUNCTIONAL EQUATIONS AND STATIONARY SOLUTIONS

Starting out with n functional equations which constitute a dynamical system involving n unknown functions $\{x_1(t), \cdots, x_n(t)\}$, but not time explicitly,

$$F^i\{\underset{-\infty}{\overset{t}{x_1}}(\tau), \underset{-\infty}{\overset{t}{x_2}}(\tau), \cdots, \underset{-\infty}{\overset{t}{x_n}}(\tau)\} \equiv 0, \qquad (i = 1, \cdots, n) \qquad (1)$$

we define a stationary solution $(x_1^o, \cdots, x_n^o)$ as one for which

$$F^i\{\underset{-\infty}{\overset{t}{x_1^o}}, \underset{-\infty}{\overset{t}{x_2^o}}, \cdots, \underset{-\infty}{\overset{t}{x_n^o}}\} \equiv 0. \qquad (2)$$

These last equations correspond to a set of ordinary statical functions in n variables $(x_1, \cdots, x_n)$:

$$f^i(x_1, \cdots, x_n) = 0, \qquad (i = 1, \cdots, n) \qquad (3)$$

where of course

$$f^i(x_1^o, \cdots, x_n^o) = 0. \qquad (i = 1, \cdots, n) \qquad (4)$$

The types of functional equations which have been most studied are those defined by differential equations, difference equations, and integral equations, and mixed varieties. The first of these possesses the most highly developed theory and provides valuable examples of various principles. Since economic observations consist essentially of series defined for integral values of time, the second category of difference equations is perhaps of greatest interest to the theoretical economist.

The above classes of functional equations have this much in common: they can all be written as the limit of an infinite set of equations in an infinite number of unknowns. However, it is not customary to write a system of differential equations in the form (1); but by use of the singular Dirac δ function defined to make the following identity formally true,

$$f(x) = \int_{-\infty}^{\infty} \delta(a - x)f(a)da, \qquad (5)$$

any linear differential equation can be written as an integral equation. Similarly any integral equation of the form

$$B(t) + \int_0^{\infty} k(a)B(t - a)da = 0, \qquad (6)$$

where B is analytic and k possesses finite moments of all orders, can be written as a differential equation of infinite order, namely,

$$B(t) + \sum_0^\infty c_i B^i(t) = 0, \tag{7}$$

where

$$c_i = \frac{(-1)^i \int_0^\infty k(a)a^i da}{i!}. \tag{8}$$

Difference equations and mixed types can also be regarded as differential equations of infinite order; by the use of the Dirac function or by extension of the definition of integration, they can equally well be represented as integral equations. In the following treatment I shall investigate formal identities, being little concerned with problems of convergence, and omitting rigorous proofs. There is ample precedent and pragmatic justification for this procedure in all applied sciences.

The greatest attention will be paid to systems of differential equations and systems of difference equations. Without loss of generality these can be written in the following *normal* form:

$$\frac{dx_i}{dt} = f^i(x_1, \cdots, x_n), \qquad (i = 1, \cdots, n) \tag{9}$$

and

$$\Delta x_i(t) = g^i\{x_1(t), \cdots, x_n(t)\}, \tag{10}$$

or

$$x_i(t+1) = G^i\{x_1(t), \cdots, x_n(t)\} = x_i + g^i. \tag{11}$$

If not already in this form they can be so transformed by the introduction of new variables.

For the stationary solutions,

$$\frac{dx_i}{dt} = 0 = f^i(x_1, \cdots, x_n), \qquad (i = 1, \cdots, n) \tag{12}$$

or

$$\Delta x_i = 0 = g^i(x_1, \cdots, x_n) = G^i - x_i. \qquad (i = 1, \cdots, n) \tag{13}$$

Systems of Volterra linear integral equations with Poisson kernels of the form

$$x_i(t) = \phi_i(t) + \sum_1^n \int_{-\infty}^t K_{ij}(t - \epsilon)x_j(\epsilon)d\epsilon, \qquad (i = 1, \cdots, n) \tag{14}$$

are also of interest. Unfortunately, the theory of nonlinear integral equations is only fragmentary.

LINEAR AND NONLINEAR SYSTEMS

Up until now most economists have concerned themselves with linear systems, not because of any belief that the facts were so simple, but rather because of the mathematical difficulties involved in nonlinear systems. This is understandable and excusable since all thought advances in small steps. Nevertheless, from the standpoint of a study of industrial fluctuations this can be a rather seriouts limitation. Thus, in a linear system the amplitude of fluctuation depends upon the initial displacement; no intrinsic amplitude —as between full employment and zero employment—is involved. The attempt to introduce such a fixed amplitude in a linear system by the device of determining coefficients so that there will be neither dampened nor explosive solutions appears to be misdirected. As pointed out in the previous chapter, page 268, the stochastical dispersion of the system increases indefinitely. Related to this is the fact that this does not yield a unique amplitude, but one which depends linearly upon initial conditions.

If we insist that a system be linear and that it do not involve time explicitly, then for differential and difference systems we are restricted to the case of constant coefficients. This type is mathematically simple, and exact solutions are known. But a high price is paid for this simplicity in terms of special assumptions which must be made.

THE NONLINEAR DIFFERENTIAL EQUATION IN ONE VARIABLE

Nevertheless, I shall show that the problem of stability of equilibrium, if not that of macrodynamic business-cycle analysis, depends formally in an important way upon the solution of linear systems. This may be illustrated by a simple differential equation in one variable.

$$\frac{dX}{dt} = \dot{X} = f(X) = A_0 + A_1 X + A_2 X^2 + \cdots, \qquad (15)$$

where f is analytic and expressible as a power series. This equation presents no difficulties of solution since by a single quadrature it may be solved; namely,

$$l - l_0 = \int_h^x \frac{dX}{f(X)} = F(X). \tag{16}$$

Let us suppose a "simple" stationary solution $X = X^o$ exists so that

$$\begin{aligned} f(X^o) &= 0, \\ f'(X^o) &\neq 0. \end{aligned} \tag{17}$$

Then the transformation of variables

$$x = X - X^o \tag{18}$$

transforms (15) into the form

$$\dot{x} = f(x + X^o) = \frac{\sum\limits_0^\infty f^i(X^o)x^i}{i!} = 0 + a_1 x + a_2 x^2 + \cdots, \tag{19}$$

where a constant term is no longer involved, and a_1 does not vanish.

Then we can assert:

THEOREM I: *A formal solution of the differential equation (19) can be written as an infinite power series in the solution of the simple linear system*

$$\dot{x} = a_1 x, \tag{20}$$

or

$$x(t) = \sum_1^\infty c_i \{g_1(\alpha, t)\}^i = \sum_1^\infty c_i \{\alpha e^{a_1 t}\}^i, \tag{21}$$

where α is a constant depending upon initial conditions.[4]

That this holds formally (i.e., without regard to the question of convergence) can be shown by substitution. Thus,

$$\dot{x} = a_1 \sum_1^\infty i c_i g_1{}^i = \sum_1^\infty a_j \{ \sum_1^\infty c_k g_1{}^k \}^j. \tag{22}$$

Expanding out and equating coefficients of the same degree in g_1, we find that each c can be determined in succession from the a's

[4] E. Picard, *Traité d'Analyse*, III, 185; G. D. Birkhoff, *Dynamical Systems* (New York, 1927), chapter iii.

and all previous c's.

$$c_1 = \text{arbitrary,}$$

$$c_2 = \frac{a_2 c_1^2}{a_1},$$

$$\cdots \cdots \cdots,$$
$$\cdots \cdots \cdots, \tag{23}$$
$$\cdots \cdots \cdots,$$

$$c_n = M(c_{n-1}, \cdots, c_1).$$

Equation (15) before transformation to the form not involving a constant term can in a similar fashion be formally solved by an infinite power series in the solution of the equation

$$\dot{x} = a_0, \tag{24}$$

or

$$x = \sum_1^\infty K_i g_0^i(t, \alpha) = \sum_1^\infty K_i \{a_0 t + \alpha\}^i. \tag{25}$$

But this is only the conventional power-series solution in t and tells us nothing about the stability of the system; every term taken by itself goes to infinity regardless of the a's, although the infinite sum need not.

It is well known that such a series as that in the exponentials is convergent for absolute values of α sufficiently small in a time interval sufficiently small. But if the system possesses first-order stability,[5] i.e., if $a_1 < 0$, then the series will converge for all values of t between t_0 and $+ \infty$ since $|e^{a_1 t_i}|$ is decreasing with time, approaching zero in the limit. Since each term approaches this limit, then

$$\lim_{t \to \infty} x(t, \alpha) = 0. \tag{26}$$

Therefore, if the system possesses first-order stability, it necessarily possesses stability in the small. It is to be emphasized that this is an *exact* solution in which no terms are considered to be of an order of smallness and ignorable. Likewise, if the system possesses first-order instability, it must be unstable in the small. However, the system may be in neutral first-order equilibrium, and possess either stability or instability in the small. In this case a_1 vanishes, and we must consider the stability of the nonvanishing term of lowest

---

[5] Not to be confused with stability of the first kind, a concept employed in the previous chapter.

degree. This will be done later. We may state our results as
follows:

THEOREM II: (*a*) *First-order stability is a sufficient condition for
stability in the small.* (*b*) *The absence of first-order instability is a
necessary condition for stability in the small.*

EXAMPLE: LOGISTIC LAW

We may illustrate the above principles by considering the
simplest nonlinear system

$$\dot{X} = A_0 + A_1 X + A_2 X^2, \tag{27}$$

where

$$A_1^2 - 4A_0 A_2 > 0, \tag{28}$$

if there are to be any "simple" stationary solutions.

Without essential loss of generality, we may by linear transformation of X involving only translation and scale change, and
by scale change in t, bring the above system into the form

$$\dot{x} = x(1 - x). \tag{29}$$

The equation

$$x - x^2 = 0 \tag{30}$$

has roots 0 and 1, each of which represents a stationary state. The
above differential equation will be recognized as one which is satisfied by the Verhulst-Pearl-Reed logistic law, according to which
percentage changes in a variable fall off linearly with the magnitude
of that variable, approaching a limit asymptotically. The above
equation, however, is slightly more general since it admits of solutions which are not S-shaped.

By quadrature its general solution is found to be of the form

$$x = \frac{1}{1 + Ke^{-t}}, \tag{31}$$

where K is a parameter determined by the initial value of x at time
zero according to the formula

$$K = \frac{1}{x(0)} - 1. \tag{32}$$

For $K = 0$ we have the stationary solution

$$x(t) \equiv 1, \tag{33}$$

and for $K = \infty$ we have the stationary solution

$$x(t) \equiv 0. \tag{34}$$

It can be easily verified that the latter stationary level is unstable, while the stationary level of unity is approached asymptotically by all adjacent motions. We may classify all possible initial conditions as follows:

$$\left. \begin{array}{ll} + 1 \leqq x(0) \leqq \infty, & - 1 < K \leqq 0, \\ 0 < x(0) \leqq 1, & 0 \leqq K < + \infty, \end{array} \right\} \quad \lim_{t \to \infty} x(t) = 1;$$

$$x(0) = 0, \qquad K = \infty, \qquad x \equiv 0; \tag{35}$$

$$- \infty < x(0) < 0, \quad - \infty < K < - 1, \qquad \lim_{t \to \infty} x(t) = - \infty.$$

Let us now apply our expansion theorem to this problem.[6] Expanding around the zero equilibrium point, and determining the c coefficients, we readily find

$$x = \alpha e^t - \{\alpha e^t\}^2 + \{\alpha e^t\}^3 - \{\alpha e^t\}^4 + \cdots = \sum_{1}^{\infty} (-1)^{i-1} \{\alpha e^t\}^i. \tag{36}$$

For given values of t and sufficiently small values of α this is readily seen to be a convergent series equal to the geometric series expansion of

$$\frac{\alpha e^t}{1 + \alpha e^t} = \frac{1}{1 + \dfrac{1}{\alpha} e^{-t}}. \tag{37}$$

But for large values of t

$$|\alpha e^t| > 1, \tag{38}$$

and the series diverges. This confirms our expectation that the zero equilibrium level is unstable.

The transformation

$$y = x - 1 \tag{39}$$

enables us to apply our expansion theorem to the determination of the stability of the other equilibrium level. Our differential equation becomes

$$\dot{y} = - y - y^2, \tag{40}$$

and in the new variable the equilibrium level equals zero. De-

---

[6] Cf. A. J. Lotka, *Elements of Physical Biology* (Baltimore, 1925), pp. 64–68.

termining the c's by substitution as before, we find

$$y(t) = - \{Ke^{-t}\} + \{Ke^{-t}\}^2 - \{Ke^{-t}\}^3 + \{Ke^{-t}\}^4 - \cdots \quad (41)$$

$$= \sum_{1}^{\infty} (-1)^i \{Ke^{-t}\}^i.$$

This will be recognized as the formal expansion of

$$y = \frac{1}{1 + Ke^{-t}} - 1. \quad (42)$$

For small values of K and nonnegative values of t, this converges uniformly, and each term goes to zero as time becomes infinite. Thus, the equilibrium is stable in the small.

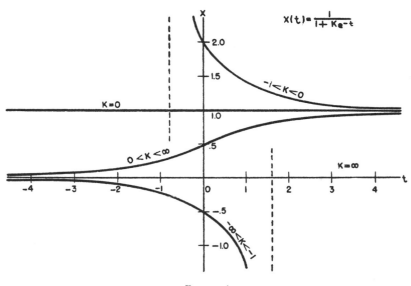

FIGURE 4

This example also throws light on the domain of convergence of the series of exponentials. It is easy to see from the exact solution of (31) that the stationary level ($y = 0$, $x = 1$) is stable for all positive displacements from equilibrium, i.e., $y(0) > 0$, $x(0) > 1$, and also for all negative displacements which are less than unity in absolute value ($-1 < y(0) < 0$, $0 < x(0) < 1$). But the series expansion of (41) is convergent only for $|K| < 1$, or for

$(-\frac{1}{2} < y(0) < +\infty, \frac{1}{2} < x(0) < \infty)$.[7] Thus, its domain of convergence is smaller than the region of true stability. It provides only a lower limit which is not generally at the same time an upper limit to the region of stability.

In Figure 4 is depicted the solution of this equation for all possible initial conditions $x(0)$. The stationary level of unity is seen to be stable; that of zero unstable. The diagram brings out one feature not yet mentioned. The lower and upper branches each approach an asymptote for finite values of t. This means that for negative displacements around the zero level the system recedes from equilibrium at an infinite rate of speed after some finite time has elapsed. For the upper branch it may be loosely said that the system approaches equilibrium after "coming in from infinity at an infinite velocity."

This example also suggests what is doubtless a valid "separation" theorem. *Points of stable equilibrium (in the small) are separated by points of definitely unstable equilibrium; and vice versa.* (In the interpretation of this, stable or unstable equilibrium may be of higher order so long as positions of one-sided stability-instability are ignored.)

THE PROBLEM OF HIGHER-ORDER STABILITY

Thus far I have considered only "simple" stationary states; i.e., those with power-series expressions in which the first-degree term does not vanish. I now turn to "degenerate" stationary states, those corresponding to multiple roots of the equation

$$\dot{X} = 0 = f(X), \tag{43}$$

where

$$\frac{d^i f(X^o)}{dX^i} = 0. \qquad (i = 0, \cdots, n-1; n \geqq 2) \tag{44}$$

In the neighborhood of such a root the differential equation takes the form

$$\dot{x} = a_n x^n + a_{n+1} x^{n+1} + \cdots, \tag{45}$$

[7] The expansion breaks down at the level at which the curve has an inflection point; i.e., where

$$\ddot{y}(t) = 0 = f'\{y(t)\}\dot{y}.$$

I venture the conjecture, completely unverified, that this may be a general phenomenon.

where

$$n \geq 2.$$

The solution of the equation

$$\dot{x} = a_n x^n, \tag{46}$$

where higher powers are neglected, can be expected by analogy with the previous case to dominate the remaining terms for sufficiently small initial displacements of equilibrium. In the investigation of simple systems this was analytically deduced (viz., Theorems I and II); for higher-order systems this conjecture has not been verified, but is doubtless true. We wish to investigate, therefore, the stability of solutions of equation (46). If they are all stable (unstable), we shall say that the equilibrium position in question possesses nth-order stability (instability).

By elementary methods of integration we can find the exact solution to (46); thus

$$
\begin{aligned}
x^{-n}dx &= a_n dt, \\
x^{1-n} &= (1 - n)a_n t + x(0)^{1-n}.
\end{aligned} \tag{47}
$$

To solve explicitly for x two cases arise depending upon whether n is odd or even.

$$
\begin{aligned}
x(t) &= \frac{1}{\{a_n(1 - n)t + x(0)^{1-n}\}^{1/(n-1)}} \qquad \text{for } n \text{ even};\\[2mm]
x(t) &= \pm \frac{1}{\{a_n(1 - n)t + x(0)^{1-n}\}^{1/(n-1)}}, \qquad \text{for } n \text{ odd};
\end{aligned} \tag{48}
$$

where the appropriate sign is to be taken so that x satisfies the initial condition $x = x(0)$. Both cases may be subsumed under the heading

$$x(t) = \{\operatorname{sgn} x(0)\}^n \frac{1}{\{a_n(1 - n)t + x(0)^{1-n}\}^{1/(n-1)}}. \tag{49}$$

Clearly if n is even, $(n - 1)$ is odd. Therefore, the second term within the brackets takes on either sign depending upon whether the initial displacement is plus or minus. Consequently, regardless of the sign of a_n, for some value of t, and for some displacement, the denominator will vanish, which means that x becomes infinite, and the equilibrium is not stable. Actually for n even the equilibrium possesses one-sided stability-instability. If

$x(0)$ is of the same sign as a_n, the motion will be unstable; if $x(0)$ is of opposite sign to a_n, it will be stable.   Thus, we have one-sided stability-instability.

If n is odd, then the second term of the denominator is always positive.   If, and only if, a_n is negative (so that the first term is positive) will the denominator stay of the same sign and approach infinity as t approaches infinity.   Hence, we have the following:

THEOREM III : *If the first nonvanishing coefficient is odd and negative, the system is stable in the small; if the first nonvanishing coefficient is odd and positive, the system is unstable.   If the first nonvanishing term is even, the system possesses one-sided stability-instability.*

This presents a strong analogy to the necessary secondary conditions for a maximum.   Write the differential equation

$$\dot{X} = f(X) = F'(X), \tag{50}$$

where

$$F(X) = \int_a^X f(X)dX.$$

Then the following sums up the results achieved:

THEOREM IV: (*a*) *If $F(X^o)$ affords a relative maximum to F, then X^o is a stationary solution of the differential equation and possesses stability in the small; and conversely.*

(*b*) *If $F(X^o)$ affords a relative minimum to F, then X^o is an unstable equilibrium level.*

(*c*) *If X^o is a stationary value of $F(X^o)$ which is not an extremum, then the system possesses one-sided stability-instability.   Alternatively, if F assumes a stationary value, and $F' = f$ assumes an extremum value, the equilibrium is stable-unstable.*

(*d*) *If $F'(X)$ vanishes identically, the equilibrium is neutral.*

This possibility of linking up the problem of stability with a statical maximum problem is but one special aspect of the *Correspondence Principle*, and one to which we shall have occasion to refer again.

An Example of One-Sided Stability-Instability: Malthusian and Optimum Population Theories

The meaning of one-sided stability-instability may not be intuitively obvious; fortunately a simple well-known economic example may be used to illustrate it.   According to Malthus population would increase, decrease, or remain stationary depending upon the per capita level of subsistence (real income, food, etc.). Let X = total population, S = per capita real income. Then the percentage rate of growth of the population is an increasing function of the level of subsistence, passing from negative values to positive values at some "minimum level of subsistence," S^o. Mathematically,

$$\frac{1}{X}\frac{dX}{dt} = \psi(S), \tag{51}$$

where

$$\psi'(S) > 0, \psi(S^o) = 0.$$

But the level of income (production) depends itself upon the level of population (labor) as of given capital, land, and technology. Moreover, Malthus implicitly and explicitly assumed the law of diminishing (per capita) returns. Thus,

$$S = \phi(X), \phi'(X) < 0. \tag{52}$$

This last relationship enables us to eliminate S as a variable and to express the rate of growth of the population in terms of itself.

$$\frac{1}{X}\frac{dX}{dt} = \psi\{\phi(X)\} = f(X), \tag{53}$$

where

$$f' = \psi'\phi' < 0,$$

and a stationary level X^o corresponds to

$$f(X^o) = \psi(S^o) = 0. \tag{54}$$

The equilibrium is stable because $f'(X^o) < 0$. If the population exceeds the equilibrium level, each family will receive less than the subsistence level, and the population will decline. If it falls below the equilibrium level (through war, etc.), the average income will be high, and the population will increase. In Figure 5 the minimum level of subsistence is shown by MM'. Below this level population will decrease as shown by the long arrow; above this level it will increase as shown by the other long arrow. $R'R$ is the returns curve, and the intersection E_1 represents a position of stable equilibrium as shown by the short directed arrows.

More modern theory suggests the possibility that there may be increasing returns in the early stages. In this case there may be two intersections between the returns curve and the minimum subsistence level, yielding two points of equilibrium.   In the diagram the new returns curve is $R''R$, and the new intersection point is E_2. The new equilibrium point is unstable since here

$$f' = \psi'\phi' > 0. \tag{55}$$

If population falls below this level, it will become extinct since as returns fall off, so does population, etc., etc.

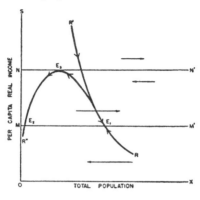

FIGURE 5

About a decade ago the theory of an optimum population achieved a certain vogue.   According to one form of this theory, at some intermediate point average returns would be at a maximum.   If by education one could raise the minimum standard of comfort insisted upon by all families to this maximum level, then population would reach this optimum equilibrium level.   Without entering upon the merits or demerits of the scheme, I should like to point out that such an equilibrium level possesses one-sided stability-instability.   For displacements from equilibrium towards a larger population it is stable, since such a movement lowers returns and causes population to decrease towards equilibrium.   But for negative displacements of population it is unstable, since these also lower returns and cause population to decrease still more until the point of extinction is reached.   In Figure 5 the minimum level of subsistence (comfort) is irreversibly pushed up by education exactly to NN' so that its intersection, E_3, with $R''R$ represents a maximum of per capita real income.   The arrows indicate the one-sided nature of the equilibrium point.

Analytically,

$$f' = 0, \qquad (56)$$

and the first nonvanishing derivative is even and negative. Thus, f is at an extremum, and Theorem IV, (c), applies. The equilibrium is one-sided.[8]

Systems of Equations in "n" Variables

Definition: The system of n differential equations

$$\dot{x}_i = f^i(x_1, \cdots, x_n) = \sum_j a_{ij}x_j + \sum_{j,k} a_{ijk}x_jx_k + \cdots,$$

$$(i = 1, \cdots, n) \quad (57)$$

where all summations range from 1 to n, will be said to possess a *simple* stationary solution $(0, \cdots, 0)$ providing that the matrix (a_{ij}) possesses n (distinct, nonvanishing) roots $(\lambda_1, \cdots, \lambda_n)$, which are *not* connected by a linear commensurability relation of the form

$$i_1\lambda_1 + i_2\lambda_2 + \cdots + i_n\lambda_n = 0 \qquad (58)$$

for any set of integers $i_1, \cdots, i_n$, not all zero.

In this case a fundamental set of solutions of the equations involving only linear terms

$$\dot{x}_i = \sum_{j=1}^{n} a_{ij}x_j \qquad (59)$$

can be written in the form

$$\alpha_1 e^{\lambda_1 t}, \ \alpha_2 e^{\lambda_2 t}, \ \cdots, \ \alpha_n e^{\lambda_n t}, \qquad (60)$$

where the λ's are the latent roots of the matrix (a_{ij}) or roots of the secular equation

$$D(\lambda) = \begin{vmatrix} a_{11}-\lambda & a_{12} & \cdots & a_{1n} \\ a_{21} & a_{22}-\lambda & \cdots & a_{2n} \\ \cdot & \cdot & & \cdot \\ \cdot & \cdot & & \cdot \\ \cdot & \cdot & & \cdot \\ a_{n1} & a_{n2} & \cdots & a_{nn}-\lambda \end{vmatrix} = (\lambda_1-\lambda)(\lambda_2-\lambda)\cdots(\lambda_n-\lambda).$$

$$(61)$$

[8] I need not warn the reader against the lack of realism of the above theories in light of modern demographic trends. For large parts of Western Europe and North American where *net and gross reproduction rates* are low, perhaps no level of real income can lead to a stationary population. Moreover, these rates may fall with increasing real income; this, however, is presumably an irreversible effect.

Then we have the following theorem: [9]

THEOREM V: *A formal solution of the set of differential equations is provided by a power series in the solutions of the first-order equations; i.e.,*

$$y_i = G^i(\alpha_1 e^{\lambda_1 t}, \alpha_2 e^{\lambda_2 t}, \cdots, \alpha_n e^{\lambda_n t})$$
$$= \sum_j c_{ij}(\alpha_j e^{\lambda_j t}) + \sum_{j,k} c_{ijk}\alpha_k\alpha_j e^{(\lambda_j + \lambda_k)t} + \cdots. \tag{62}$$

By formal substitution this can be verified, remembering that the noncommensurability relationship (58) is satisfied. Each set of c's can be determined in terms of previous sets and the known a's.

The matrix a may have (pairs of) complex roots, corresponding for linear systems to damped or undamped sine-cosine terms. The system will be said to have first-order stability if the real parts of all roots, real or complex, are all negative, since this will imply damped motion (exponential or harmonic) of the linear system. An important part of the stability problem is the determination of necessary or sufficient conditions that all real parts are negative, and this will be dealt with in Mathematical Appendix B.

Here I should like to mention the generalization of Theorem II.

THEOREM VI: *(a) First-order stability is a sufficient condition for stability in the small; (b) the absence of first-order instability is a necessary condition for stability in the small.*

This follows because the series (62) can be shown to converge for all values of t and values of α sufficiently small if all the real parts are negative. Since it converges for limited values of α and t, and since all terms are decreasing in absolute magnitude, it consequently never ceases to converge.

A stationary equilibrium position is not "simple" if a commensurability relationship of the form mentioned holds. Even if such a relationship does exist, the above theorem is valid providing there are no zero roots. If no roots vanish, linear commensurability relations introduce into the infinite power series terms of the form

$$p_n(t)e^{(i_1\lambda_1 + \cdots + i_k\lambda_k + \cdots)t}, \tag{63}$$

where $p_n(t)$ is a polynomial. If the real parts of all λ's are negative, the exponential will dominate, and the solution will still be stable.

[9] Cf. Picard, *op. cit.*; Birkhoff, *op. cit.*

Zero roots or ones whose real parts are zero, i.e., pure imaginaries, cause greater difficulties since stability in the small becomes dependent upon terms of higher degree. I am not aware that this has been completely analyzed in the mathematical literature except for special cases. I shall not, therefore, enter upon the problem except to prove a *general* theorem relating to those many variable systems associated with the maximum of some function.

Before doing so I may summarize briefly the results achieved so far as follows: Stability in the small of a nonlinear system of differential equations depends except in singular cases upon the stability of a linear system. This dependence can be rigorously defined and does *not* involve a dubious neglect of the squares of small quantities, etc.

THE STABILITY OF A STATIONARY POSITION
WHICH IS ALSO A MAXIMUM

If $(X_1^o, \cdots, X_n^o)$ yields an isolated relative maximum to a twice differentiable function $F(X_1, \cdots, X_n)$, then it is not hard to show by the theorem of the mean that

$$\frac{\partial F}{\partial X_i} = F_i(X_1^o, \cdots, X_n^o) = 0, \qquad (i = 1, \cdots, n) \qquad (64)$$

and, assuming we have an isolated stationary value,

$$F_1(X_1, \cdots, X_n)(X_1 - X_1^o)$$
$$+ F_2(X_1, \cdots, X_n)(X_2 - X_2^o) + \cdots < 0 \quad (65)$$

for values of X sufficiently close to X^o, but distinct from it.

Suppose we are given a system of differential equations

$$\frac{dX_i}{dt} = f^i(X_1, \cdots, X_n) = F_i(X_1, \cdots, X_n). \qquad (66)$$

Only special differential systems can be so written. Unfortunately space does not permit a discussion of necessary and sufficient conditions satisfied by such special systems.

THEOREM VII: $(X_1^o, \cdots, X_n^o)$ *is a stationary solution for the above system, and it is stable in the small.*

Transforming the equilibrium point to the origin $(0, \cdots, 0)$, we have

$$\frac{dx_i}{dt} = F_i(X_1^o + x_1, \cdots, X_n^o + x_n), \qquad (67)$$

and $\sum_1^n F_i x_i < 0$ for sufficiently small nonzero values of x.

Multiplying the first equation of (67) by x_1, the second by x_2, etc., and summing we find

$$\sum_1^n x_i \frac{dx_i}{dt} = \frac{d}{dt}\left\{ \sum_1^n \frac{x_i^2}{2} \right\} = \sum_1^n F_i x_i < 0. \qquad (68)$$

For sufficiently small values of x, the sum of squares is decreasing. Hence, as t goes to infinity, it approaches a limit which cannot be different from zero. If

$$\lim_{t \to \infty} (x_1^2 + x_2^2 + \cdots + x_n^2) = 0, \qquad (69)$$

then

$$\lim_{t \to \infty} x_1 = 0, \qquad \lim_{t \to \infty} x_2 = 0, \qquad \cdots, \qquad \lim_{t \to \infty} x_n = 0. \qquad (70)$$

Hence, the equilibrium is stable. A relative proper minimum yields definitely unstable equilibrium, while a nonextremum stationary value yields stability-instability.

This theorem, while not applicable to all differential equations, is nevertheless very important for economic systems. Within its scope it is exceedingly general since it does not require that the f's be analytic, and it covers simultaneously the stability of first and higher orders. Economically it says that the system is always climbing a hill and will approach the top.

THE DIFFERENCE EQUATION IN ONE VARIABLE

The problem of differential systems has been analyzed in a fairly complete manner, and we must now turn to systems of difference equations, which are perhaps of even greater importance for economic theory. The simplest case is provided by the general nonlinear difference equation in one variable

$$X(t + 1) = f\{X(t)\}, \qquad (71)$$

or

$$\Delta X(t) = g\{X(t)\} = f - X(t). \tag{72}$$

So simple is this equation that we can indicate its solution graphically, showing on one diagram all possible types of qualitative behavior in the neighborhood of an equilibrium position. In Figure 6 two functions are plotted—one relating the succeeding

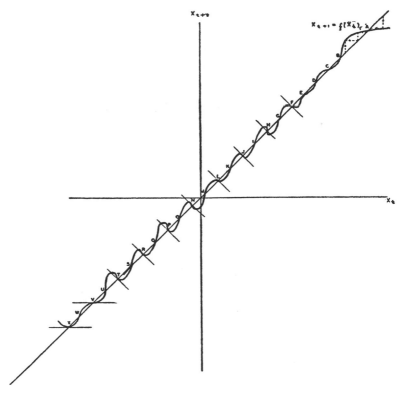

FIGURE 6

value of X (vertical axis) to the given value of X (horizontal axis); the other is simply a 45° line.

The solution of our equation for any initial condition is shown by broken lines running between these two functions in the indicated fashion. Any initial value $X(t)$ leads to a new value $X(t + 1)$ indicated by running up vertically to the curve $f\{X(t)\}$; this new value must be transferred to the abscissa in order to derive its successor. This is effected by moving horizontally to the 45° line; a vertical movement yields the next value, and so the process goes. Stationary equilibrium positions are defined by the intersection of the f function and the 45° line, or analytically by roots of the equation

$$f(X) - X = 0. \tag{73}$$

The diagram illustrates what are essentially all possible types of equilibria. Twenty-four points of equilibrium are indicated, but only sixteen represent qualitatively different kinds of equilibrium, eight being duplicates. Point A represents a position of equilibrium, stable in the small. Displacement in either direction results in an asymptotic return to equilibrium. Point B represents unstable equilibrium; displacement is followed by an ever-increasing one-way disequilibrating movement. C represents a position of stable equilibrium, differing from A in that it has first-order neutrality and has only high-order stability. D possesses first-order neutrality, but high-order instability; therefore, it is unstable in the small, and the recession from equilibrium is monotonic. E has first-order neutrality, but its next nonvanishing derivative is even. Consequently, it has one-sided stability-instability.

Thus far we have met only equilibria like those of the one-variable differential system. That the single difference equation is richer in types of equilibria is illustrated by the variety still to come. F possesses first-order stability, and hence is stable in the small. Unlike A the approach to equilibrium is not monotonic, but rather by means of damped oscillations of period two. G represents simply a position of neutral equilibrium in the small, possessing first- and high-order neutrality. The system stays wherever it is put. H differs from F only in that the equilibrium is unstable, the divergence from equilibrium being along explosive oscillations; I is simply a duplication of B, as are K, M, O, Q, S, U, and W.

J represents a position of neutral equilibrium. The system oscillates with constant amplitude around this position. (In physics this would be called stable equilibrium. In the terminology of the previous chapter, it has stability of the second kind—not to be confused with second- or high-order stability.) *L* like *J* possesses first-order neutrality, but unlike *J* has high-order stability. Equilibrium is approached by damped oscillations. *N* also has first-order neutrality, but possesses high-order instability of an oscillatory nature. *P* and *R* like *L* and *N* possess high-order, oscillatory stability and instability, respectively, but analytically differ slightly. *T* possesses oscillatory neutrality of all orders, and hence is neutral in the small. It can be thought of as including *J* as a special case. Finally, *V* and *X*, while they possess first-order stability, are analytically of singular type and should be differentiated. The former has monotonic stability, the latter oscillatory stability.

The following classification may clarify the possible types.

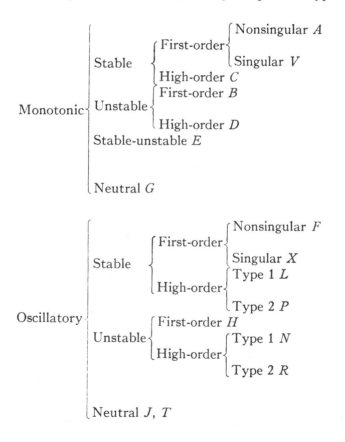

We discriminate analytically between the sixteen cases depending upon the first and higher derivatives of $f(X)$. The first subdivision between monotonic and oscillatory hinges upon whether $f'(X)$ is positive or negative. Within the monotonic classification we have first-order stability if f' is less than unity, and first-order instability if f' is greater than unity. If f' equals unity, we have first-order neutrality and must proceed to higher derivatives. If all these derivatives vanish, we have true neutrality in the small. If the first nonvanishing derivative is odd and positive, we have high-order stability; if odd and negative, we have high-order instability. If the first nonvanishing higher derivative is even, we have one-sided stability-instability.

Within the oscillatory classification things are even more complicated. If f' is less than unity in absolute value, we have first-order stability; if greater than unity in absolute value, we have first-order instability. If $f' = -1$, then we must proceed to higher derivatives. Should all of these vanish, we have neutral oscillatory equilibrium (J). More generally, if all odd higher derivatives vanish, the equilibrium is neutral and oscillatory as in T. When $f' = -1$, and the first nonvanishing derivative is odd and positive, the equilibrium possesses high-order oscillatory stability; if odd and negative, the equilibrium possesses high-order oscillatory instability. When $f' = -1$, and the first nonvanishing derivative is even, then we go on to consider the first nonvanishing odd derivative. As in the previous cases, we have stability or instability depending upon whether this is negative or positive.

Finally, we are confronted with the singular cases when $f' = 0$. If the next nonvanishing derivative is odd and positive, we have monotonic stability; if odd and negative, or if even and of any sign, we have stable oscillatory equilibrium. If all derivatives vanish, the equilibrium is perfectly stable as indicated in the first section of this chapter; when displaced, the system returns "instantly" to equilibrium and does not merely approach equilibrium asymptotically.

A few remarks may be in order concerning the qualitative behavior of a first-order system from any initial condition. It could no doubt be shown that it must do one of the following: (a) go off to infinity; (b) approach an equilibrium level; or (c) approach a periodic motion of some finite period. If it is reversible, that is, if $f(X)$ is not only single-valued but admits of a single-valued inverse, then the only periodic motion possible under heading (c) is one of period two. It is not appropriate to investigate here the meaning of the stability of motions more general than stationary equilibrium levels. When this is done, it will be found no doubt that there exist valid "separation" theorems concerning the ordering of stable and unstable periodic motions. The necessity because of continuity (Rolle's theorem, etc.) of duplicating certain equilibrium points in the above diagram provides a hint at such relationships.

ANALYTIC SOLUTION

As with the differential equation systems an exact solution of the general nonlinear analytic difference equation can be indicated. Let

$$x(t + 1) = a_1x(t) + a_2x(t)^2 + a_3x(t)^3 + \cdots, \tag{74}$$

or

$$\Delta x(t) = (a_1 - 1)x(t) + a_2x(t)^2 + a_3x(t)^3 + \cdots. \tag{75}$$

We rule out cases where the first-degree term vanishes in either of these expressions; and we rule out all cases of singular and neutral first-order equilibrium so that $a_1 \neq 1, 0$, or -1.

A formal solution of this is given by a power series in the solution of the simpler linear equation

$$\begin{aligned} x(t + 1) &= a_1x(t), \\ \Delta x(t) &= (a_1 - 1)x(t). \end{aligned} \tag{76}$$

Let

$$g_1(t) = \alpha a_1{}^t. \tag{77}$$

THEOREM VIII: *A formal solution to (74) is provided by*

$$x(t) = c_1\{\alpha a_1{}^t\} + c_2\{\alpha a_1{}^t\}^2 + c_3\{\alpha a_1{}^t\}^3 + \cdots. \tag{78}$$

This may be verified by formal substitution provided that $a_1 \neq 1, 0$, or -1. Each c is obtainable in terms of all previous c's and the known a's.

More generally, we are given n difference equations in normal form

$$x_i(t + 1) = \sum_j a_{ij}x_j(t) + \sum_{j,k} a_{ijk}x_j(t)x_k(t) + \cdots, \tag{79}$$

where the latent roots of a, $(\lambda_1, \cdots, \lambda_n)$, are never equal in absolute value to zero or one, and where there exist no linear commensurability relations of the form

$$m_1 \log \lambda_1 + m_2 \log \lambda_2 + \cdots + m_n \log \lambda_n = 0, \qquad (80)$$

for m's integers not all vanishing. Then

THEOREM IX: *A formal solution to the system of difference equations is given by an ascending power series in the solutions of the linear system*

$$x_i(t + 1) = \sum_j a_{ij} x_j(t), \qquad (81)$$

or

$$\begin{aligned}
x_i(t) &= \theta^i(\alpha_1\lambda_1{}^t, \cdots, \alpha_n\lambda_n{}^t) \\
&= \sum_j c_{ij}\{\alpha_j\lambda_j{}^t\} + \sum_{j,k} c_{ijk}\{\alpha_j\lambda_j{}^t\}\{\alpha_k\lambda_k{}^t\} + \cdots.
\end{aligned} \qquad (82)$$

Each set of c's can be determined by formal substitution from all previous sets and the known a's.   If some of the roots are multiple, or if a linear commensurability relation of type (80) does hold, there will probably exist a similar power-series solution augmented by terms with polynomial multipliers in t, provided always that the absolute value of all roots equals neither zero nor one.

All of the remarks of earlier sections concerning convergence of such series apply. We must remember, however, the first-order stability of a difference-equation system implies

$$|\lambda_i| < 1, \qquad (83)$$

and conversely.   The following theorem is easily derived along now familiar lines.

THEOREM X: *For a difference-equation system first-order stability is a sufficient condition for stability in the small, and the absence of first-order instability is a necessary condition.*

Space does not permit me to illustrate the above remarks with an economic example, such as would be provided by the familiar cobweb theorem applied to nonlinear supply and demand curves.

OTHER FUNCTIONAL EQUATIONS

While this has not been verified, one can hazard the conjecture that more general nonlinear functional equations can in the neighborhood of an equilibrium point be expressed as a power series in solutions of the simpler linear systems. Thus, under suitable assumptions functional equations can be written in the Taylor-like expansion

$$X_i(t) + F^i\{\underset{-\infty}{\overset{t}{X_1}}(\tau), \cdots, \underset{-\infty}{\overset{t}{X_n}}(\tau)\}$$

$$= \{X_i(t) - X_i{}^o\} + \sum_j \int_{-\infty}^t K_{ij}(t - \tau)\{X_j(\tau) - X_j{}^o\}d\tau \quad (84)$$

$$+ \sum_{j,s} \int_{-\infty}^t \int_{-\infty}^t K_{ijs}(t - \tau_1, t - \tau_2)\{X_j(\tau_1) - X_j{}^o\}$$

$$\{X_s(\tau_2) - X_s{}^o\}d\tau_1 d\tau_2 + \cdots,$$

where K_{ij}, K_{ijs} represent first and second functional derivatives respectively. The linear system

$$X_i(t) - X_i{}^o + \sum_j \int_{-\infty}^t K_{ij}(t - \tau)\{X_j(\tau) - X_j{}^o\}d\tau = 0 \quad (85)$$

is known to have solutions of the form

$$X_i(t) - X_i{}^o = \sum_1^\infty \alpha_{ij}e^{\lambda_j t}, \quad (86)$$

where the λ's are infinite roots of the transcendental equation

$$D(\lambda) = |\delta_{ij} + \int_0^\infty K_{ij}(v)e^{-\lambda v}dv| = 0. \quad (87)$$

In population analysis single integral equations of this type play an important part, and the solution in terms of an infinite number of exponentials has been called by A. J. Lotka [10] the Hertz-Herglotz solution of these equations. It can perhaps be shown that an infinite power series in the infinite solutions of the linear system will provide a solution for the nonlinear case.

Similarly mixed equations of the type

$$y'(t) = f\{y(t), y(t - \theta)\} \quad (88)$$

may be expressible in terms of the Frisch-Holme linear equation

$$y'(t) = ay(t) + by(t - \theta). \quad (89)$$

[10] For an excellent bibliography of applications see A. J. Lotka, "A Contribution to the Theory of Industrial Replacement," *Annals of Mathematical Statistics*, vol. X (1939).

As in the preceding integral equation, boundary or initial conditions for this equation necessarily involve an arbitrary function over an interval, and hence the exponential solutions must be infinite in number so that an arbitrary function can be expanded in terms of them. (The same would be true of difference equations not solely defined for integral values of t. Arbitrary periodic functions would enter into the solution, and these would be expressible in the Fourier infinite exponential series.) This raises problems of doubly infinite series and cannot be entered upon here.

CHAPTER XI

SOME FUNDAMENTALS OF DYNAMICAL THEORY

IN THE PREVIOUS two chapters I have examined a number of economic examples of historical interest drawn from the fields of theory and business cycles, and have attempted to suggest the importance of dynamical analysis not only for its own sake, but as an aid in arriving at useful theorems in the realm of comparative statics. Now with less use of illustrative economic material, I should like to examine analytically the formal aspects of this problem, at the same time indicating possible directions of generalization.

STATICS AND DYNAMICS [1]

Often in the writings of economists the words "dynamic" and "static" are used as nothing more than synonyms for good and bad, realistic and unrealistic, simple and complex. We damn another man's theory by terming it static, and advertise our own by calling it dynamic. Examples of this are too plentiful to require citation.

Some writers attempt to distinguish between statics and dynamics by analogy with what they understand to be the relationship in theoretical physics. That this is a fruitful and suggestive line of approach cannot be doubted. But it is too much to suppose that very many economists have the technical knowledge necessary to handle the formal properties of analytical dynamics. Consequently, they become bogged down in the search for economic concepts corresponding to mass, energy, inertia, momentum, force, and space. A case in point is Professor Frank Knight's otherwise stimulating essay on *Statics and Dynamics*.[2]

It is certainly true, notably in the writings of Marshall,[3] that economists have made use of biological as well as of mechanical

---

[1] With a few alterations the following section is taken from my article, "Dynamics, Statics, and the Stationary State," *Review of Economic Statistics*, XXV (1943), 58–61.

[2] Chap. vi of *The Ethics of Competition* (New York, 1935). This is an English translation of an article in *Zeitschrift für Nationalökonomie* for 1930.

[3] See the references to *statical method* and *biology* in the Index to the eighth edition of the *Principles*. In none of his writings does Marshall show more than a passing familiarity, such as might be expected of any intelligent layman, of the biological notions of his time. Therefore, he could not be expected to have discerned the lasting truths

analogies, in which evolution and organic growth is used as the antithesis to statical equilibrium analysis.   In general the results seem to have been disappointing; viz., the haziness involved in Marshall's treatment of decreasing cost.   And if one examines the more exact biological sciences, one looks in vain for any new weapon, secret or otherwise, for discovering scientific truths.   If the bloodstream is capable of a simple, abstract, rigorous description in terms of the usual laws of physical thermodynamics, so much the better; if not, one must be content with more complicated, unwieldy explanations.   Indeed, according to the late L. J. Henderson the very notion of a stable equilibrium, so characteristic of physical theory, was actually first observed empirically in connection with the resistance of the human body to disease, and formulated by the ancients as the well-known *vix medicatrix naturae*.[4]

Nor should the problems encountered in the biological field be considered necessarily more complex and less subject to simple formulation than those in the physical field.   Few biological sciences are less "exact" than meteorology, which must certainly be included in the physical sciences.[5]   Here, simple and abstract theories spun out from a few assumptions are likely to be inferior to the intuitive hunches of experienced practitioners, but this is only a reflection of the present primitive state of the subject.   New truths are ascertained in the same way as in more advanced subjects, and it is to be hoped that rule of thumb may be replaced by more exact and unambiguous formulations.[6]

from the fashions of the moment.   Nevertheless, writing at the time that he did, it was inevitable that he should have been influenced, if not convinced, by the Spencerian doctrines popular at the end of the nineteenth century.

[4] See J. A. Schumpeter, *The Theory of Economic Development* (Cambridge, Mass., 1934, English edition), Preface, p. xi, for Mill's notions of statics and dynamics and their intellectual origins.

[5] Of course, it can be said that experimentation is not possible in meteorology as in other physical sciences.   But what about astronomy, in some ways the most exact of all, in which no experimentation is possible?

[6] In discussing the limitations of mathematical methods in economics, Professor Viner expresses the belief that the biological character of the subject, so to speak, makes such methods of limited applicability.   By this I take him to mean that the subject is complex and difficult, not that any fundamentally different methods of investigation are required.   See "Marshall's Economics, the Man and His Times," *American Economic Review*, XXXI (1941), 223–236.

Gustav Cassel in his *Fundamental Thoughts in Economics* (New York, 1925), chap. i, considers Economic Dynamics to be a third stage of analysis, following a pure Static Economy and a "quasi-static" Uniformly Progressive Economy.

Leaving aside all analogies with other fields, there has necessarily been within the main corpus of economic theory a preoccupation with dynamics, if only implicitly. The Classical economists from Smith through Mill had theories of the long-run movements of population and accumulation.[7] J. B. Clark rigidly separated the static from the dynamic in his thought.[8] (Other examples could be multiplied.) Clark's celebrated static state and the "circular flow" of Professor Schumpeter raise a rather vexing point of terminology—the relation of static to stationary—now cleared up more or less to the satisfaction of everybody by Professor Frisch.

Stationary is a descriptive term characterizing the behavior of an economic variable over time; it usually implies constancy, but is occasionally generalized to include behavior periodically repetitive over time. Used in this sense, the motion of a dynamical system may be stationary: e.g., the behavior of a pendulum satisfying Newton's Laws of Motion, but subject to no disturbance and hence remaining at rest; or the behavior of national income after a change in investment has given rise to dwindling transient geometric progressions of the usual "block-diagram" character.

Statical then refers to the form and structure of the postulated laws determining the behavior of the system. An equilibrium defined as the intersection of a pair of curves would be statical. Ordinarily, it is "timeless" in that nothing is specified concerning the duration of the process, but it may very well be defined as holding over time. A simple statical system as defined above would also have the property of being stationary; but, as we shall see in a moment, statical systems can be devised which are not stationary over time.

In defining the term *dynamical*, at least two possibilities suggest themselves. First, it may be defined as a general term including statical as a special rather degenerate case. Or, on the other hand, it may be defined as the totality of all systems which are *not* statical. Much may be said for the first alternative; the second, however, brings out some points of controversy in the literature and will be

[7] See L. Robbins, "On a Certain Ambiguity in the Conception of Stationary Equilibrium," *Economic Journal*, XL (1930), 194–214.

[8] J. M. Clark has wished to carry on where his father left off, to construct a dynamics which would supplement statics. See J. M. Clark, *A Preface to Social Economics* (New York, 1936).

discussed here.   This decision involves no point of substance, since only verbal problems of definition are involved.

We may say that *a system is dynamical if its behavior over time is determined by functional equations in which "variables at different points of time" are involved in an "essential" way.*   This formulation is to be attributed to Professor Frisch.[9]   Special examples of such systems are those defined by *difference* equations, i.e., those involving a variable and its lagged values; integral equations in which the preceding values of the variable enter in a "continuous" way. By a liberal interpretation of the circumlocution "variable at a different point of time," we may bring differential equations under the definition, remembering that differential coefficients characterize the behavior of a function in the neighborhood of a point. Mixed types and more general functionals are included.

Attention is called to the fact that variables at different points of time must enter into the problem in an *essential* way.   Thus, a system involving a rate of production per unit time, i.e., a time derivative, may yet be statical.   This is because the variable of which the rate is the time derivative may have no economic significance.   It can be interpreted as the cumulated amount of production from the beginning of time or from an initial date; no significant economic process depends upon this variable.   The necessity for the present insistence may be apprehended if it is realized that every variable can be written as the derivative of something, namely its own integral.   Moreover, a system may be pseudodynamic in the sense that formal manipulation of it permits us to reduce it to statical form.   Unless, therefore, we reserve the designation dynamics for systems which involve economically significant variables at different points of time in an *irremovable* way, we shall find that no nondynamic systems exist.

According to the present definition the historical movement of a system may not be dynamical.   If one year the crop is high because of favorable weather, the next year low, and so forth, the system will be statical even though not stationary.   The same is true of a system showing continuous growth or trend, if the secular

[9] Ragnar Frisch, "On the Notion of Equilibrium and Disequilibrium," *Review of Economic Studies*, III (1935–36), 100–106.

movement is taken as a datum and if the system adapts itself instantaneously.[10]

On the other hand, a truly dynamical system may be completely nonhistorical or causal, in the sense that its behavior depends only upon its initial conditions *and the time which has elapsed,* the calendar date not entering into the process. For many purposes, it is necessary to work with systems which are both historical and dynamical. The impact of technological change upon the economic system is a case in point. Technological change may be taken as a historical datum, to which the economic system reacts noninstantaneously or in a dynamic fashion. Another instance is provided by a business cycle of a regular periodic character, which results from impressing an oscillatory outside force upon a mechanism with an intrinsic (damped) period of its own.

We may distinguish, then, four distinct cases made up of all possible combinations of static-dynamic and historical-causal:

1. Static and stationary
2. Static and historical
3. Dynamic and causal (nonhistorical) [11]
4. Dynamic and historical

Almost all systems can be placed in one of these categories; and, depending upon the point of view or purpose at hand, the analysis may be formulated so as to put a given system arbitrarily in one category rather than another. Thus, if a system is very heavily damped so that it approaches its equilibrium value extremely rapidly, its dynamic features may be passed over in order to simplify the analysis.

Or a system which is causal from a very broad viewpoint may be regarded as historical if certain movements are taken as unexplained data for purposes of the argument. (In fact, every historical system is to be regarded as an *incomplete* causal system.)

[10] I conceive Henry Moore's moving equilibrium to be of this statical type, although the movements around the secular trend are dynamic in character. H. L. Moore, *Synthetic Economics* (New York, 1929).

[11] The notion of causation in a closed interdependent system is exceedingly slippery and ambiguous. As used here, a system is said to be causal if from an initial configuration it determines its own behavior over time. While it is not appropriate to say that one subset of variables causes another to move, it is permissible to speak of a change in a given parameter or datum as causing changes in the system or in its behavior over time.

To a meteorologist-economist a business cycle caused by weather disturbances and sunspots would constitute a causal process. But ordinarily the economist is willing to regard the causation as unilateral and to adopt a division of labor in which he does not study astronomy but considers his job as done when he has pushed economic analysis to a "noneconomic" cause.[12] However, there is nothing sacred about the conventional boundaries of economics; if the cycle were meteorological in origin, economists would branch out in that direction, just as in our day a political theory of fiscal policy is necessary if one is to understand empirical economic phenomena.

An important class of phenomena cannot conveniently be brought under the above four categories. I refer to dynamical stochastic processes such as that realized if a damped pendulum is subjected to "random" shocks. We shall have reason to discuss such processes in connection with dynamical problems arising in the study of the business cycle.

For a given pattern of shocks, as determined by the particular workings of chance in the sequence of time under discussion, we have simply a dynamic historical system of type 4 above. But if we consider the totality of all possible shocks which may be expected to occur if they are regarded as random draws from a fixed universe, it is clear that calendar time is not really involved, but only the time which has elapsed since the beginning of the process. In this sense it is like type 3 rather than type 4, although the word causal may no longer seem appropriate.

It seems best, therefore, to specify two more categories:

5. Stochastical and nonhistorical
6. Stochastical and historical

The latter occurs when we have a dynamical system containing stochastical variables, and where either the structure of the system varies in an essential way with time, or where the universes characterizing the random variables change in an essential way with time. Simple examples of types 5 and 6 are provided by

$$X_{t+1} = \tfrac{1}{2}X_t + \{h_t\},$$
$$X_{t+1} = \tfrac{1}{2}X_t + t + \{m_t\}, \tag{1}$$

[12] J. A. Schumpeter, *Theory of Economic Development*, chap. i.

where in the first case the random variable h which may appear at any instant of time is drawn from an unchanging universe; and where in the second case the random variable m is drawn from a universe defined differently at each instant of time.[13]

In his recent book *Value and Capital*,[14] Professor Hicks has given an exceedingly simple definition of dynamics: "I call Economic Statics those parts of economic theory where we do not trouble about dating; Economic Dynamics those parts where every quantity must be dated" (p. 115).

In terms of the above six categories this definition is overly general and insufficiently precise. The second category consisting of historically moving static equilibria would certainly require dating of the variables; but it would not thereby become dynamic. My objection is to his definition, not to his practice, for many of the systems which he analyzes are in the strict sense dynamic.

CAUSAL SYSTEMS

By a *complete causally-determinate* system I shall mean one belonging to the third category of the above classification, whose behavior is determined by initial conditions (in the broadest sense) in such a way that its behavior depends only upon the time which has elapsed since the establishment of such initial conditions. That is to say, the specification of similar given initial conditions at a later period of time would result in a similar evolution of the system except at a constantly later time period. Mathematically, if $\bar{x}$ represents initial conditions at time t^o, our solution takes

---

[13] In the above form the initial formulation of stochastic processes seems to be due to G. U. Yule. See the references to the work of Yule, Slutsky, and Frisch in H. Wold, *A Study in the Analysis of Stationary Time Series* (Uppsala, Sweden, 1938). However, the notions of a Markoff Chain, a Brownian movement, etc., go far back in the literature of mathematics. See S. Chandrasekhar, "Stochastic Problems in Physics and Astronomy," *Reviews of Modern Physics*, XV (1943), 1–89.

As is noted later, many systems which involve stochastical processes can nevertheless be described *in part* by nonstochastical models of the first four types discussed above. Often probabilities and statistical parameters may themselves be treated as causally determined coördinates. Thus, if it is known that the first system described in equation (1) takes on the value k at time 0, and that the mean and standard deviation of h are respectively a, b, then the expected (mean value) of X_t is given by the solution of a causal dynamical equation like that of (1) with the stochastic term removed.

[14] J. R. Hicks, *Value and Capital* (Oxford, 1939).

the form

$$x = f[t - t^o; \bar{x}(t^o)], \tag{2}$$

where x and $\bar{x}$ stand for a finite or even infinite set of variables.

Without this restriction our system would be a *historical* one depending in an essential way upon the time at which the initial conditions are specified, and could only be written

$$x = f[t; t^o; \bar{x}(t^o)].^{15} \tag{3}$$

Thus, the differential equation

$$\dot{x} + x = 0 \tag{4}$$

does not contain time explicitly, and its solution is of the form

$$x(t) = \bar{x}(t^o)e^{-(t-t^o)}, \tag{5}$$

while

$$\dot{x} + x = t \tag{6}$$

has the solution

$$x(t) = (t - 1) + [\bar{x}(t^o) + 1 - t^o]e^{-(t-t^o)}. \tag{7}$$

The first is a complete causal system; the second is not. For the first a specification of the initial conditions (value of $\bar{x}$) and a knowledge of the time which has elapsed is sufficient to locate the quantity x; in the case of the second it is necessary as well to know the historical date at which the initial conditions are preassigned.[16]

---

[15] This represents a one parameter, not a two parameter, family of curves. A change in t^o introduces no new solutions, but simply alters the initial conditions $\bar{x}(t^o)$ which identify each.

[16] Complete causal systems are essentially unchanged by the transformation

$$t' = t + a,$$

but become historical ones in the time scale defined by the transformation

$$t' = h(t), \qquad h''(t) \not\equiv 0;$$

although for simple scale changes dimensional constants serve to maintain all essential invariances. Conversely, in special cases there may exist transformations (of time) which convert a historical system into a causal one; viz., the historical system

$$t \frac{dx}{dt} + x = 0$$

becomes after the transformation

$$t = e^{t'}, \qquad \text{where} \qquad t' = \log t,$$

a complete causal system in the new time t', namely,

$$\frac{dx}{dt'} + x(t') = 0.$$

It should perhaps be explicitly mentioned that no metaphysical significance attaches to this definition. Not only is an arbitrary time scale involved, but also any historical system may be regarded, as we shall later see, as an "incomplete" causal one. Furthermore, the elements of our system may very well be probabilities, which are themselves determinate although the value of certain variates may be uncertain.

Merely from the definition of a causal system certain interesting properties become obvious. If within a finite period of time a system returns to exactly the same initial conditions from which it started, its motion must be perfectly periodic, since it must again do the same, etc.[17] Then again, a determinate economic system cannot on the downswing pass through precisely the same configuration as it did on the upswing. Some of the relevant variables (costs, prices, etc.) must present a different pattern or else relevant *dynamic* aspects of them must (time derivatives, lagged values, etc.).

Let us now consider some definite causal determinate systems. An investigator interested in only certain aspects may wish to concentrate upon a particular subset of variables, neglecting their mutual interdependence with the totality of all. To a first approximation the excluded ones may be assumed to be arbitrarily given functions of time. The system studied is essentially an "incomplete" causal one and as such is indistinguishable from any other historical one. Thus, given three bodies, one of large mass compared to the other two and of great distance from them, it is often convenient to analyze the behavior of the two smaller ones on the assumption that they are in a gravitational field changing with respect to time (as the external body pursues its "relatively" independent path); although in fact the three bodies together form a gravitational field independent of time.

Which variables will be taken as data, and which as unknowns to be analyzed, will depend in each case upon the purpose at hand and upon a diagnosis of the particular interrelations present. Often the economist takes as data certain traditionally noneconomic variables such as technology, tastes, social and institutional conditions, etc.; although to the students of other disciplines these are processes to be explained and analyzed, and are not merely

[17] G. D. Birkhoff and D. C. Lewis, Jr., "Stability in Causal Systems," *Philosophy of Science*, II (1935), 304–333.

history.[18]   On the other hand, one may limit the scope of one's inquiry within the economic sphere.   Thus, in studying a hypothetical short inventory cycle one might take longer waves as given.   Then again, it is often necessary to go beyond the realm of traditional economic variables in throwing light upon a particular process; especially often, for example, into the political sphere.   The world rarely fits into the taxonomic classifications of pedagogues.

Among the numerous reasons for electing to regard certain variables as independent or arbitrary parameters, one in particular deserves attention in connection with dynamic analysis.   Certain processes are conceived to move slowly as compared to others.   Thus, we distinguish long run tendencies from shorter run tendencies, and so forth in infinite regression.   The interplay of these processes will be given in more detail later.

Stationary States and their Generalization

In chapter ix a stationary or equilibrium state of a dynamic system of n variables defined by n functional equations of the general form

$$F^i\left[\underset{-\infty}{\overset{t}{x_1(\tau)}}, \cdots, \underset{-\infty}{\overset{t}{x_n(\tau)}}, t\right] = 0 \qquad (i = 1, \cdots, n) \qquad (8)$$

was provided by a set of constants $(x_1^o, \cdots, x_n^o)$ for which

$$F^i(\underset{-\infty}{\overset{t}{x_1^o}}, \cdots, \underset{-\infty}{\overset{t}{x_n^o}}, t) \equiv 0. \qquad (9)$$

Even if the system is not a complete causal one, i.e., if it involves time explicitly, it may still possess one or more stationary equilibrium levels.   Thus, the system described in footnote 16, p. 318, is historical, but has the stationary equilibrium level $x \equiv 0$.   However, only in exceptional cases will a historical system possess stationary equilibrium positions; and as pointed out in chapter ix, even complete causal ones may lack such positions.   It is desirable, therefore, to consider the manner in which a stationary equilibrium can be generalized.

If the variables of our system are "dated," and involve time explicitly, but are not truly dynamic in the Frisch sense of involving variables at different points of time (derivatives, integrals, and

[18] See J. A. Schumpeter, *The Theory of Economic Development*, chap. i.

more complicated functionals), the manner of generalization is obvious. Our historic (but Frisch-static) system is of the form

$$F(X, t) = F^i(x_1, \cdots, x_n, t) = 0.^{19} \qquad (i = 1, \cdots, n) \qquad (10)$$

A solution of this system

$$X = X^o(t) \qquad (11)$$

such that

$$F[X^o(t), t] = 0 \qquad (12)$$

may be termed the *moving equilibrium*. However, this is almost trivial since the moving equilibrium is the only possible evolution of the system.[20] Let us turn, therefore, to truly dynamic historical systems.

For definiteness, let us contemplate the dynamical system assumed by H. L. Moore in his pioneering attempt to determine empirical supply and demand elasticities. While he adopted a general equilibrium approach in which the quantity of each good depends upon all prices, the formal difficulties of the problem will be lessened if we concentrate upon a partial equilibrium market involving only one good q and its price p.

The demand for the good is a functional relationship between its quantity, its price, and time,

$$q_t = D(p_t, t). \qquad (13)$$

Quite inadvertently, and probably for the purely statistical purpose of deriving the elasticity of supply simultaneously with the demand elasticity, Moore assumed that the quantity supplied depended upon time and *price at a previous period of time*,

$$q_t = S(p_{t-1}, t). \qquad (14)$$

The two equations together form a dynamical system which determines the evolution of (p, q) for given initial values of p or q;

[19] I shall have frequent recourse to matrix notation whereby a set of variables $(x_1, \cdots, x_n)$ will be represented by (X), a set of functions $[f^1(x_1, \cdots, x_n), \cdots, f^n(x_1, \cdots, x_n)]$ by $f(X)$, etc. Thus, $f(X) = 0$ implies $f^i(x_1, \cdots, x_n) = 0$, where $(i = 1, \cdots, n)$.

[20] Quite possibly one might imagine random or chance errors causing deviations from the equilibrium defined by the equations (10) so that the moving equilibrium represents a smoothed out trend of the actual observations. One might have $f(x + \epsilon, t) = 0$, where ϵ is a random variable.

namely,

$$p_t = f[t, \bar{p}(t^o)],$$
$$q_t = g[t, \bar{p}(t^o)]. \tag{15}$$

There exists a one parameter family of motions; each motion is determined by efficacious forces, but not all can be termed moving equilibria or the term loses significance.

If time did not enter explicitly into our equations, i.e., if neither the demand curve nor the supply curve were shifting, the stationary equilibrium would clearly be defined by

$$D(p^o) - q^o = 0,$$
$$S(p^o) - q^o = 0. \tag{16}$$

For this steady motion, and here defining $\Delta p_t = p_t - p_{t-1}$

$$p_t = p_{t-1} = \cdots = p^o,$$
$$q_t = q_{t-1} = \cdots = q^o, \tag{17}$$
$$\Delta p_t \equiv \Delta q_t \equiv 0.$$

When time is explicitly involved, what is the analogous position of moving equilibrium? Let us consider the following alternative definitions which have been advanced: (1) the definition which Moore seemed to urge whereby the position of moving equilibrium is to be represented as a statistical trend; (2) the moving equilibrium defined by the "equality" of supply and demand; (3) the moving equilibrium defined by the "Frisch barring process," to be described later.

1. The representation of equilibrium as simply a statistically fitted trend has apparently no universal validity. In particular, if this method is applied to the causal case (especially where the approach to equilibrium is nonoscillatory), it need not lead to the correct equilibrium level, nor necessarily to any stationary level. Probably its apparent acceptance by Moore rested in part upon its supposed relation to the criterion to be described next. For stochastical systems, discussed later, trend-fitting is more defensible, but still not optimal.

2. The criterion that moving equilibrium be defined by equilibrium of supply and demand seems on first sight a natural generalization of the stationary case. But, upon examination, ambiguities appear in this formulation. Given any price, demand reacts in-

stantaneously, supply after one year. What sense is there in equating the two? (Of course, each year in the shortest run price is determined by the equality of demand and short run supply for all possible motions.) Nevertheless, if the shifts are very "slow," one might as a first approximation disregard the differences between p_t and p_{t-1} and equate

$$D(p_t, t) = S(p_{t-1}, t) = S(p_t - \Delta p_t, t) \doteq S(p_t, t) \qquad (18)$$

on the assumption that $\Delta p_t \doteq 0$. Solving

$$D(p_t, t) - S(p_t - 0, t) = 0, \qquad (19)$$

we get

$$p_t = p_1(t), \qquad (20)$$

and this might be termed the moving equilibrium for price. Paradoxically, on the assumption that price is not changing, we derive a moving equilibrium path for price! But this is characteristic of the method of successive approximation. Assumptions known to be in error are made, later to be corrected. A second approximation would be derived by making

$$\Delta p_t = \Delta p_1(t) \qquad (21)$$

and equating

$$D[p_2(t), t] - S[p_2(t) - \Delta p_1(t), t] = 0, \qquad (22)$$

and the nth approximation by the relation

$$D[p_n(t), t] - S[p_n(t) - \Delta p_{n-1}(t), t] = 0. \qquad (23)$$

If the sequence of functions $[p_i(t)]$ converges uniformly to a limit function $\bar{p}(t)$, then $\bar{p}(t)$ is *a* solution of our original system.

The method outlined above is essentially identical with the moving equilibrium of a biological or chemical system undergoing slow changes.[21] If the system is defined by

$$\dot{x} = f(x, t), \qquad (24)$$

where f_t is small, the moving equilibrium (first approximation), $x_1(t)$, is defined by

$$\frac{d(x_0)}{dt} = 0 = f(x_1, t); \qquad x_0 = \text{constant}; \qquad (25)$$

[21] See A. J. Lotka, *Elements of Physical Biology* (Baltimore, 1925), chap. xxi. This contains numerous references.

the second approximation, $x_2(t)$, by

$$\dot{x}_1 = f(x_2, t); \tag{26}$$

and the nth by

$$\dot{x}_{n-1} = f(x_n, t). \tag{27}$$

The sequence of functions $[x_i(t)]$ may or may not converge uniformly to a limit function; if it does converge, the limit function is one solution of the original. (Instead of a single variable any number could be involved without affecting the argument.)

The above definition has the following advantages in its favor. For nonhistorical causal systems not involving time explicitly, it does yield the correct positions of stationary equilibrium at the first approximation. Also the successive approximations are invariant under changes of variables of the form

$$y = f(x); \qquad x = f^{-1}(y),$$

and changes of time

$$t' = g(t); \qquad t = g^{-1}(t').$$

Nevertheless, these advantages do not outweigh the overwhelming shortcomings involved in this definition. What after all is being approximated? Suppose all solutions of equation (24) were known exactly to be of the form

$$x = \psi(t, \bar{x}). \tag{28}$$

There would then be no need for approximations at all. Which of these solutions could legitimately be termed *the* moving equilibrium? The particular method of successive approximation outlined above, if it converges at all, selects out arbitrarily and mysteriously the particular solution to be dignified by this title.[22] I reject, therefore, the above method of approximation as defining a unique moving equilibrium, although it may be appropriate for arriving at particular solutions.

For a linear differential equation of the form

$$\dot{x} - a(t)x = b(t), \tag{29}$$

the general solution equals any particular solution plus the general

---

[22] The successive functions in the approximation sequence, $x_i(t)$, do not in general satisfy the same initial conditions so that only in the limit can one determine which initial conditions the final solution attained will satisfy.

solution of the reduced homogeneous equation

$$\dot{x} - a(t)x = 0. \tag{30}$$

Let

$$x = cu(t) \tag{31}$$

represent the general solution of (30), where c is a parameter specified by initial conditions. Let $v_1(t)$ be a particular solution of (29). Then

$$v_1(t) + cu(t) \tag{32}$$

is the general solution of (29). Clearly also

$$[v_1(t) + au(t)] + ku(t) \tag{33}$$

is a general solution since the expression in brackets is a particular solution for a specific a.

In some fields (electrical network theory, etc.) special significance is attached to that particular solution which "contains" no terms of the form $[au(t)]$, and it might be thought that this might be an acceptable definition of moving equilibrium. Where the functions involved are not the simple elementary ones, the above criterion does not specify unambiguously a unique function. But it can often be modified to do so. In fact, the limit function defined by convergent approximation sequences of the type described in the previous section often represents this particular solution. I am not aware, however, of any useful purpose to be served by embracing this definition.[23]

There is one interesting interpretation of the first approximation which deserves detailed attention. One often encounters the notion of an equilibrium which, before it is reached, recedes because of historical perturbing forces. Imagine a boy carrying a stone at the end of a piece of string. If he were standing still, equilibrium would be attained when it hung vertically at rest. But as he walks the stationary equilibrium is never attained, the position in which

---

[23] In linear systems (electrical, etc.) where there is an impressed periodic force, the general solution of the differential equations can be written as the sum of a purely periodic motion and a transient. In the case of damped systems the transient necessarily goes to zero in the limit, and the motion necessarily approaches the purely periodic function. For some purposes it might be convenient to define the purely periodic function as a "moving equilibrium" and give it privileged treatment, particularly if the periodic function is a pure sine wave.

equilibrium might be possible if his motion were to stop being constantly displaced.

We have here what may be termed *receding* equilibrium. For the time i, it is the position of stationary equilibrium which *might* be attained if subsequent to i all historical changes were suspended. That is to say, in all our functional equations a bar is placed over t wherever it occurs explicitly for times subsequent to i.   The result is a hypothetical or virtual complete causal system.   For a new i, we have a corresponding virtual equilibrium, and thus is defined our receding equilibrium as a function of time.

Let us examine a simple example to illuminate this concept. Let

$$\dot{x} + x = t \tag{34}$$

be a historical system.   At t equal to i, the receding equilibrium is the stationary equilibrium corresponding to the causal system

$$\frac{dx}{dt} + x(t) = i, \tag{35}$$

where the right-hand member is treated as a constant.   Clearly, such a position is given by

$$0 + x = i. \tag{36}$$

But this is precisely the first approximation $x_1(t)$ of equation (25), specifically in this case

$$\frac{dx_0}{dt} = 0 = t - x_1. \tag{37}$$

The virtual path of the system after the freezing of historical change is only one possible solution.   For other initial conditions at time i, different solutions will be defined.   In particular, let us consider initial conditions $u(i, \bar{x})$, where u is a true solution of the historical system (34).   The corresponding virtual path may be written

$$x = v[t, u(i, \bar{x})]. \tag{38}$$

For the specific system defined by (34)

$$u(t, \bar{x}) = t - 1 + (\bar{x} + 1)e^{-t}, \tag{39}$$

$$v[t, u(i, \bar{x})] = (-e^{i} + \bar{x} + 1)e^{-t} + i. \tag{40}$$

The actual solution of the historical system is seen to be an envelope to the family of virtual solutions $v[t, u(t, \bar{x})]$. The virtual movement for short times approximates closely the true movement in that they are mutually tangent. That is, if the boy were suddenly to stop walking, the pendulum would change its motion; but the new motion would be tangential to the old, and for short intervals they would not diverge much.

The virtual curves approach asymptotes or hypothetical stationary equilibria. These equilibrium values plotted against time form the curve of receding equilibria. This function of time is not in general a solution of the true dynamical equations.[24] The stability of the hypothetical equilibrium can, however, be determined, and, as will be seen later, bears some relation to the stability of the actual motions.

3. I turn now briefly to the "normal" values or "equilibrium" values defined by Professor Frisch.[25] This is defined by relaxing a subset m of our n functional equations

$$f^i[\underset{-\infty}{\overset{t}{x_1(\tau)}}, \cdots, \underset{-\infty}{x_n{}'(\tau)}, t\,] = 0, \qquad (i = 1, \cdots, n) \tag{41}$$

and replacing them by a set of m hypothetical equations

$$g^i(\underset{-\infty}{\overset{t}{x_1}}, \cdots, \underset{-\infty}{\overset{t}{x_n}}, t) = 0. \tag{42}$$

In the new set of n equations the instantaneous forms of the variables (at least in some of the places where they occur) are barred and regarded as unknowns. Everywhere else (in all dynamic forms of the variables and possibly in some places where the instantaneous forms appear) is substituted *one solution of the original set of functional equations defined for a particular set of initial conditions*. This yields n historical equations of the special form (10)

[24] It is possible for the receding equilibrium to be one solution as, for example, in the system

$$\ddot{y} + y = t.$$

$y = t$ is the receding equilibrium and at the same time an actual motion of the system. If the boy has always been walking at a steady pace, the pendulum may be hanging vertically.

[25] R. Frisch, "On the Notion of Equilibrium and Disequilibrium," *Review of Economic Studies*, III (1936), 100–105.

in the barred variables, $(\bar{x}_1, \cdots, \bar{x}_n)$. This defines the moving equilibrium.

Professor Frisch is well aware that this definition does not correspond in the stationary case to the concept of equilibrium; he even thinks that the former will eventually replace the latter "as the tendency to formulate the economic reasoning in exact dynamic mathematical terms gains ground." [26] But this concept, he believes, is what many modern writers have in mind.

Whether or not this last conjecture is true, I do not know, particularly since I am unacquainted with the original Scandinavian writings.[27] But for the present purpose this is irrelevant; it is only important to point out the differences between this concept of a "normal" and the moving equilibrium for which we are looking.

Some of the salient properties of the "normal" movement are:

(1) It is in general *not* a solution of the original set. There exists no set of initial conditions which would produce it in actuality.

(2) It is not unique, but depends upon as many parameters as are necessary to specify initial conditions for the original set of equations. This is because it depends upon the particular solution —out of an infinity of possible solutions—inserted in the modified set of equations f and g. (See the italicized sentence above.)

(3) Being defined by essentially static, albeit possibly historical equations, there is no sense in asking questions concerning its stability.

For all these reasons it is unsatisfactory as a representation of moving equilibrium for our present purposes.[28]

---

[26] *Ibid.*, p. 102.

[27] Professor Frisch illustrates this concept by referring to the Wicksellian relation between the actual and natural rate of interest. In so rationalizing the arguments of some neo-Wicksellians he is, I fear, over charitable, ascribing to them an undeserved degree of sophistication. Actually, Wicksell himself considered for the most part a system of implicit dynamic relations not involving time explicitly, i.e., without historical change. (Witness, for example, his controversy with Professor Davidson on the equilibrium requirement of stable prices in a system undergoing output expansion because of irreversible technological change.) Within a nonhistorical framework it is possible to construct dynamic models of the Wicksellian system in which the natural rate of interest represents the stationary equilibrium level of the system and *not* the solution of a hypothetical alternative system. If this be granted, what is the corresponding condition for a system in which elements of historical change have been introduced? This brings us back to our original query.

[28] Still another notion of moving equilibrium is suggested by an explosive exponential

Resolution of the Problem

We have examined in turn alternative definitions of moving equilibrium and found good reasons for rejecting each one. This suggests a reëxamination of the purpose for which it is desirable to find a concept of moving equilibrium.

It will be remembered that in the case of nonhistorical causal systems there was found to be no ambiguity in the definition of a stationary equilibrium state; in fact, it was the hope of generalizing the notion of a stationary state for historical systems that motivated the search for moving equilibria.

Let us go back a step and ask why we were interested in a position of stationary equilibrium. Clearly it is only one out of an infinity of possible motions of the dynamical system in question. But, and this suggests the answer to our question, *if the stationary equilibrium is stable, all motions approach it in the limit.*[29]

We were concerned then with the behavior of all the motions of the dynamical system; and it was simply in the nature of a co-

---

solution of a causal system such as
$$\dot{y} - y = 0.$$
This has solutions of the form
$$y = ke^t.$$
On the above definition every motion but the stationary equilibrium one would be a moving equilibrium. By definition all the moving equilibria would be unstable. The effect of small shocks would be multiplied through time. On the other hand, the variable $(\dot{y}/y)$ would be relatively stable.

The above concept which applies, for example, to a population with constant specific fertility and mortality is in contrast to the moving equilibrium represented by the growth curve of an infant. Given a small shock (measles, etc.), the child's weight will deviate from "normal" growth, but afterwards will catch up so that no evidence of the interruption will remain in the later progress of the child. Similarly, an economy recovers from the effect of (say) a war and continues on its secular path. But the population referred to above is forever different in absolute numbers after a shock (war, etc.) even though its relative age distribution and other features may again approach stable form.

[29] Let $x^0(t) = x^0$ represent the equilibrium position of a system. Let $x^i(t)$ represent any other motion. Then, if stable,
$$\lim_{t \to \infty} x^i(t) = x^0;$$
i.e., for any given positive ϵ, however small, there exists a t^0 such that
$$|x^i(t) - x^0| < \epsilon, \qquad \text{for} \qquad t > t^0.$$
But this is symmetrical in $x^i(t)$ and x^0 so that the equilibrium position can be said to approach any motion, as well as vice versa. It easily follows that $x^i(t)$, any motion, approaches $x^1(t)$, a particular motion selected arbitrarily.

incidence that this problem could be studied by an examination of the properties of a single special one.   It will perhaps be enlightening to point out that even in the nonhistorical case we can just as well concentrate upon *any other* single motion than the equilibrium one.   For if they all approach the equilibrium motion, then they all approach each other.   And *every* motion must approach *any* one selected at random.

This suggests the following answer to our dilemma.   *We shall concern ourselves not with the stability of a particular motion of a historical system which can be given the privileged title of moving equilibrium, but rather with the stability of each and every motion of the system.*   This will not preclude our designating for special attention particular motions with special properties (as, for example, strictly periodic motions, steady motion in which some coördinate increases linearly, etc.).

This suggests how I would answer the purely verbal problem: what processes shall be designated as *equilibrium* processes?   Once we have stripped the equilibrium concept of normative and teleological connotations, it does not much matter how we apply the term.   The term may be applied to stationary values only.   From this narrow point of view a competitive industry would be in equilibrium only after all long run conditions had been satisfied, entry of firms, correct output for each firm, etc.

For other purposes we might apply the term to those intermediate short run situations in which each firm is producing at price equal to marginal cost (and above average variable cost), even if price diverges from average cost so that the number of firms is changing or is about to change.   It might be reserved for situations of the last described type where the further condition is realized that the number of firms is changing at a causally determined rate.   Still others may be willing to apply it to momentary conditions of supply and demand including variations in speculative stocks of the good in question.

I, myself, find it convenient to visualize equilibrium processes of quite different speed, some very slow compared to others. Within each long run there is a shorter run, and within each shorter run there is a still shorter run, and so forth in an infinite regression. For analytic purposes it is often convenient to treat slow processes as data and concentrate upon the processes of interest.   For example, in a short run study of the level of investment, income, and employment, it is often convenient to assume that the stock of capital is perfectly or sensibly fixed. Of course, the stock of capital from a longer run point of view is simply the cumulation of net investment, and the reciprocal influence between capital and the other variables of the system is worthy of study for its own sake, both with respect to a hypothetical final equilibrium and the simple course of growth of the system over time.

So to speak, we are able by *ceteris paribus* assumptions to disregard the changes in variables subject to motions much "slower" than the ones under consideration; this is nothing but the "perturbation" technique of classical mechanics. At the same time we are able to abstract from the behavior of processes much "faster" than the ones under consideration, either by the assumption that they are rapidly damped and can be supposed to have worked out their effects, or by inclusion of them in the dynamical equations (derivatives, differences, etc.) which determine the behavior of the system out of equilibrium.

The first of the above mentioned alternatives constitutes the justification for the use of comparative statics rather than explicit dynamics. If one can be sure that the system is stable and strongly damped, there is no great harm in neglecting to analyze the exact path from one equilibrium to another, and in taking refuge in a *mutatis mutandis* assumption. Of course, if one chooses to neglect certain dynamic processes, one may still retain others; e.g., in studying capital formation over two decades I may choose to neglect inventory fluctuations, but still may retain the acceleration principle in its secular aspects.

Under the second alternative where shorter run processes are contained in (say) the differential equations of the system, it is to be understood that these differential equations do not necessarily hold exactly at each instant of time. There may well be a still shorter run theory which explains how still higher differential equations lead to (rapidly) damped approaches to the postulated differential equation relations. And so forth in endless regression.

It may be argued that so general a connotation is at variance with traditional usage of the word equilibrium. Is it not straining language to think of a cannon ball as being at equilibrium, not only after it has fallen to the ground at rest, but also at every point in its flight, when it is on its mean trajectory as well as in its precession around this path? Perhaps such terminology may occasionally lead to confusion; however, with carefully stated qualifications it may be convenient.

To examine the stability of any motion $[u_1(t), \cdots, u_n)]$ simply substitute into the functional equations

$$x_i(t) = u_i(t) + \eta_i(t), \tag{43}$$

where the above equation is simply a definition for the η's. There result n functional equations in the η's since the u's are given functions. Because the u's constitute a solution of the original system, there exists a solution in the η's of the form $(0, 0, \cdots, 0)$. The original solution will be stable if for all possible initial conditions

$$\lim_{t \to \infty} \eta_i(t) = 0. \qquad (i = 1, \cdots, n) \tag{44}$$

Moreover, provided the original functional equations are of a very general class (differential equations, difference equations, integral equations, etc.), the resulting equations can for sufficiently small displacements be regarded as *linear* in the η's. They are not, however, independent of time, but ordinarily will involve it explicitly.

This is most easily seen for a single variable. Let our implicit functional equation be

$$f[u(\tau) \overset{t}{\underset{-\infty}{+}} \eta(\tau); t] = 0, \tag{45}$$

where

$$f[\overset{t}{\underset{-\infty}{u(\tau)}}; t] = 0, \tag{46}$$

because u is a solution. Providing certain assumptions are made concerning the continuity of the functional f and its functional derivatives of higher order, there exists an expansion very much like Taylor's expansion for ordinary functions of a point. This takes the form

$$f[u(\tau) \overset{t}{\underset{-\infty}{+}} \eta(\tau); t] = 0 + \int_{-\infty}^{t} K_1(t, \tau_1)\eta(\tau_1)d\tau_1 + \cdots, \tag{47}$$

where K_1 is the functional derivative of f. This seems to result only in linear integral equations, but by use of the Stieltjes integral or the Dirac operator $\delta(x)$ with the property that

$$\int_{-\infty}^{\infty} f(x)\delta(x - a)dx = f(a), \tag{48}$$

and

$$\int_{-\infty}^{\infty} f(x)\delta'(x - a)dx = - f'(a), \tag{49}$$

the general linear differential and difference equations can easily be written as linear integral equations. Thus,

$$\frac{dx}{dt} + x(t) = 0 \tag{50}$$

takes the form

$$\int_{-\infty}^{\infty} K(t, \tau)x(\tau)d\tau = 0, \tag{51}$$

where

$$K(t, \tau) = - \delta'(\tau - t) + \delta(\tau - t). \tag{52}$$

The convertibility of the problem of stability at least in its first order aspect into an examination of linear systems is of inestimable value since the largest part of existing mathematical knowledge relates to such systems.

CONCEPTS OF STABILITY

In chapter ix there was some discussion of various kinds of stability. Our treatment would not be complete without at least a cursory survey of the various senses in which this term has been used.

(a) It has sometimes been used in a very broad sense. Any position of equilibrium is stable if deviations from it remain bounded. If no motions go out to infinity, then each is stable. For many purposes this is unsatisfactory. Better names than *stability* can be suggested for this property. An egg balanced on its tip upon a level plain would be stable in the above sense.

(b) Poincaré implied still another definition when he coined the phrase *stability in the sense of Poisson*. "This means that, although the system may not exactly repeat itself starting from an arbitrary initial state, yet in general it will return to the vicinity of its initial state and nearly repeat its motion during a long interval of time." [30] This is quite different from the usual meaning of stability, and the term *recurrent* is perhaps more appropriate to systems employing this property.

(c) A very common use of stability in nonconservative physical systems is the one which I have termed *stability of the first kind*. It holds when every motion approaches in the limit the position of equilibrium (and every other motion). It is not reversible in time; going backwards, all stable systems become unstable. [31]

Subdivisions under this heading are of course possible. Thus, there is stability of the first kind *in the small* if in a sufficiently small neighborhood of a given motion all motions are stable. *First order stability of the first kind* prevails when certain sufficient conditions hold; namely, when the linear terms in the expansion of our functional equations taken by themselves yield a system which is perfectly stable. We have been concerned almost exclusively with this definition of stability.

(d) All conservative physical systems are reversible in time, and volumes are preserved in phase space. This rules out stability of the first kind. A conservative system free of the dampening dissipative force of friction, if displaced from stable equilibrium, never returns to rest at stationary equilibrium. A pendulum displaced from the perpendicular has higher total energy (equal to potential energy plus zero initial kinetic energy) than the equilibrium position since the latter represents a minimum. Total energy must be conserved, so, in passing through the equilibrium position, the system must possess motion in order to provide some kinetic energy to be added to the minimized potential energy.

(e) There remain still other notions such as *permanent* stability (the previous definition holding for all time between minus and plus infinity), *semi-permanent* stability in which the above properties hold for "long" periods of time, *complete* or *trigonometric* stability in which the motion can be approximated by certain harmonic sums, etc. [32]

[30] G. D. Birkhoff and D. C. Lewis, Jr., "Stability in Causal Systems," *Philosophy of Science*, II (1935), 310.

[31] This might be termed stability in the sense of Liapounoff. (See E. Picard, *Traité D'Analyse*, III, p. 200.) It is also shown there that instability of the first order rules out stability in this sense. Birkhoff has termed this unilateral stability.

[32] See G. D. Birkhoff, *Dynamical Systems* (New York, 1927), chap. iv, for more detailed discussion.

It is unnecessary to go further into this problem except to point out that unlike the greater part of the subjects treated here, the analysis of the concept of stability with the implied investigation of the qualitative behavior of generalized dynamical paths leads into some of the most difficult problems in higher mathematics.

Nature of the Business Cycle

We have seen that there are many interesting and fruitful aspects of dynamics which have nothing to do with the business cycle as such, but which are important for the understanding of processes usually classified under the heading of economic theory. However, of all branches of dynamics the one which has received the greatest attention is that dealing with the fluctuations in employment, income, and general business activity. Numerous explanations, associated with a variety of names, have been put forward. In fact, there have been so many different theories that it has been necessary to devise a number of different systems of classification in which to catalogue them (e.g., underconsumption, overinvestment, etc.; or frictional, institutional, monetary; exogenous versus endogenous; etc.). I should like to survey these in a brief way in order to isolate the analytical differences involved rather than to concentrate on the historical, institutional, and personal variations.

(1) It is a commonplace today to employ the terms *exogenous* and *endogenous* in describing cycle theories. The former refers to theories which find the origin of the cycle in some outside, non-economic datum which varies in a quasi-periodic manner, and by one way causation engenders a cycle in economic time series. A sunspot or meteorological theory is usually offered as the prototype of this class. Inasmuch as the economic fluctuations whose explanation we are seeking are not themselves strictly periodic, or more than quasi-oscillatory, it is not really necessary that the exogenous factors be any more regular in their periodicity and amplitude. Nor need the exogenous factors be completely independent of reciprocal influence from the economic system; strictly speaking, it is only necessary that lines of causation be *largely* one way in direction, from the outside in. Analytically the extreme exogenous theory is analogous to a "forced" periodic motion, where the economic system reacts instantly to the external driving im-

pulse. In terms of my earlier six categories, the system. is historical but static.

(2) At the other extreme there is the purely endogenous theory, or the so-called self-generating cycle. Various theories emphasizing monetary factors, inventories, the acceleration principle, psychology, etc., fall under this heading. The determinants of the system consist of dynamic equations involving different periods of time (lags, derivatives, etc.) which generate recurrent motions. Once the cycle is under way, boom gives way to depression, depression to revival, revival to boom, and so forth.

Some economists think that illegitimate circular reasoning is involved in this view: that it shows how the cycle, once started, perpetuates itself, but begs the question as to the original existence of the cycle. Even if valid, this would be an objection of no particular consequence since there are an infinity of exogenous and chance factors which could give rise to the initial cycle. Actually, as will be shown below, a cycle is not required to start off the process, but only an initial displacement from equilibrium, however small and noncyclic in character.

Endogenous Models

Analytically the pure endogenous cycle is usually likened to the motion of a frictionless pendulum which satisfies a simple Newtonian second order differential equation. Upon closer examination difficulties appear with this notion. In the first place, all dampening must be ruled out or else the cycle will come to an end; similarly, in most theories anti-dampening or explosive behavior is ruled out. Now in a physical system there are grand "conservation" laws of nature which guarantee that the system must fall on the thin line between dampening and anti-dampening, between stability and instability. But there is nothing in the economic world corresponding to these laws, and so it would seem infinitely improbable that the coefficients and structural relations of the system be just such as to lead to zero dampening.

There is still another difficulty. Even within an endogenous theory the economic system is not regarded as isolated. It is subject to outside disturbances, but these are not taken to be related to the business cycle in an important way. If we consider a system which taken by itself is on the border line between stability and instability, it may be said to be stable in the second sense discussed earlier. But if we now let random variations impinge on the system, it becomes unstable in the sense that the (expected) amplitude of its swings increases with time, and its variance approaches infinity in the limit.[33]

I think it ill-advised, therefore, that Kalecki [34] in an empirical determination of the coefficients of an assumed mixed difference-differential equation system should have imposed the conditions that the motion have zero damping. One can sympathize with his aim of deriving a system with constant amplitude of fluctuation, whatever one thinks of the empirical foundation for this hypothesis. But after imposing a highly improbable constraint, he did not achieve what he was looking for; namely, a system with constant amplitude of fluctuation.

Equally important, the purely endogenous analyses so far discussed are unable to provide an explanation for the exact or approximate *amplitude* of the cycle. Like the pendulum system they are essentially linear in character, and every linear system can take on any amplitude depending only upon the magnitude and sign of the original displacements. Thus, a pendulum can be made to swing in a small or large arc by means of a small or large initial displacement. To explain the observed level of oscillation of the cycle the economist with a linear endogenous theory must go back to the value of the original prehistoric disturbance, and must explain why succeeding shocks have not swelled the cycle.

There are two avenues of escape from the fundamental difficulties encountered in the simple, linear, purely endogenous models. The first, which has been widely discussed in the technical literature, involves dropping the assumption that the system possesses zero dampening, and placing reliance upon external shocks to keep fluctuations from dying down. This solution involves dropping the assumption of a purely endogenous system, but permits the retention of linearity assumptions. It is discussed in detail in later sections. It is to be stressed that the exogenous impulses which keep the cycle alive need not themselves be even quasi-oscillatory in character.

[33] On p. 343 below the sum of the A's will not converge nor will the sum of their squares, where there is zero dampening.

[34] M. Kalecki, "A Macrodynamic Theory of Business Cycles," *Econometrica*, III (1935), 327–352.

The other alternative is to drop the assumption of linearity even though this entails considerable mathematical difficulties. For the qualitative problem of stability, relations "in the small" were seen to have important implications as necessary conditions for stability or instability "in the large." In consequence, it was useful and permissible to work with linear relations as a first approximation even though that approximation was admittedly not exact. But in the realm of quantitative dynamics and economic fluctuations this approximation must be dropped if we are to get correct quantitative and qualitative results.

For linear systems are lacking in the qualitative richness of nonlinear systems. The former are either damped or undamped, stable or unstable, regardless of the size of initial displacement. *Nonlinear systems for the first time introduce a theory which accounts for fluctuations of a particular amplitude, independent of the initial displacement.* Thus, a nonlinear system may possess an unstable stationary level so that when the equilibrium position is displaced in the slightest, ever increasing swings are begun. But instead of oscillating to infinity, a particular amplitude is finally reached and maintained. This periodic motion may be stable in the sense that any further disturbance will result in a motion which approaches the given periodic motion from above or below.

As an example of such a nonlinear equation, consider the differential equation

$$\ddot{x} - \mu(1 - x^2)\dot{x} + x = 0. \tag{53}$$

While zero is a stationary equilibrium level of the system, an evaluation of the coefficients of the above equation for that level will show that the equilibrium is unstable. For small departures from equilibrium the system behaves like an explosively oscillatory linear system, but finally the nonlinearity asserts itself, and the motion settles down to a fixed amplitude. Geometrically, in the $(x, dx/dt)$ phase space the equilibrium point is given by the origin, out from which flow expanding spirals. However, each of these approaches a closed curve representing the periodic motion. If we begin initially from a point outside the closed curve, we have contracting spirals which approach the closed curve from without. The stability of the periodic motion in the small is verifiable by examining the solution of a variational linear differential equation of the second order with periodic coefficients, derived by evaluating the coefficients of (53) along the periodic motion in question. This equation of variation in turn is seen to be stable because its "characteristic exponents or multipliers" all have negative real parts.[35] The uniqueness of the periodic solution is more difficult to establish, but in the case cited it has been done.

Such nonlinear systems have received a certain amount of attention in theoretical mechanics under the headings of "self-exciting oscillations" or "relaxation oscillations."[36] Much still remains to be done in this field. In the field of economics one nonlinear system has received complete treatment. I refer to the so-called cobweb theorem in which supply lags one period. In general, this leads to a nonlinear difference equation of the first order, which is so simple as to permit of a complete graphical solution.

As we have seen in previous chapters, the linear cobweb case permits of only three possibilities: for *any* amplitude the system is either damped, anti-damped, or exactly in between. (Actually in real life, both in an economic or physical system, a movement to infinity is unthinkable. Therefore, if a linear system is unstable, its motion will grow until it no longer remains linear; its structure will "give," etc.) Dropping the assumption of linearity, we find that the system may possess special periodic motions other than that of stationary equilibrium. Thus, with the equilibrium point unstable, there will be a stable "box" approached by all near-by motions, the size of the box determining the unique amplitude of the cycle. There may, of course, be several such periodic motions, each being alternately stable and unstable. In real life the last one can in most cases be taken as stable.[37]

[35] See G. D. Birkhoff, *Dynamical Systems*, chap. iii.

[36] Equations of this type are sometimes known as Van der Pol equations after the name of the man who has devoted a good deal of attention to them. However, their history goes back into the 19th century at least. A partial bibliography can be found in T. Von Kármán, "The Engineer Grapples with Nonlinear Problems," *Bulletin of the American Mathematical Society*, XLVI (1940), 615–683. See also Norman Levinson and Oliver K. Smith, "A General Equation for Relaxation Oscillations," *Duke Mathematical Journal*, IX (1942), 382–403; B. Van der Pol, "Relaxation Oscillations," *Philosophical Magazine*, II (1926), 978–992.

[37] There is a vast literature on the cobweb theorem. The most complete treatment seems to be that of W. Leontief, "Verzögerte Angebotsanpassung und Partielles Gleichgewicht," *Zeitschrift für Nationalökonomie*, Band V (1934).

Elsewhere in economic analysis there are to be found suggestions of nonlinear dynamics.[38] However, the formal difficulties of solution are so great that very much remains to be done. This is all the more important since a careful analysis of various literary theories will show that some of the most simple of them depend in an essential way upon nonlinear elements. Among these is a wide class of what I have termed "billiard table" theories, which deduce a turning point of the cycle from such considerations as the fact that the system "hits the full employment ceiling and bounces back, so to speak." Another of this type is the Hawtreyan notion of the minimum reserve ratios of banks against which the system rebounds. Such notions are less successful in explaining the lower turning point since there is no (relevant) natural bottom to the economic system.[39]

It is not unexpected to find that the simplest empirical notions may lead to the most complicated mathematical problems. This is a fact to inspire humility in both literary and mathematical investigators, but should prove discouraging to neither.

MIXED EXOGENOUS-ENDOGENOUS THEORIES

It is not necessary to subscribe exclusively to one of these two polar types. Perhaps most economists are eclectic and prefer a combination of both. For example, an economist who believed in the reality of waves of different length might plausibly regard the long Kondratieff wave as being primarily exogenous in character, depending as it does upon wars, gold discoveries, and great technological upheavals. Its impact upon the system might involve endogenous, transient cyclical movements, but their movements might take place in a much shorter time period so that compared

---

[38] See Ph. Le Corbeiller, "Les Systemes Autoentretenus et les Oscillations de Relaxation," *Econometrica*, I (1933), 328–332. J. Tinbergen, *Statistical Testing of Business Cycle Theories* (Geneva: League of Nations, 1939).

[39] Professor A. H. Hansen, in his *Fiscal Policy and Business Cycles* (New York: Norton, 1941), chap. xiii, seems to regard the level at which the average propensity to consume is 100 per cent as such a natural bottom. I think this is putting the matter much too strongly, even though I agree that below this level certain upward tendencies are brought into play. R. F. Harrod's *The Trade Cycle* (Oxford, 1936) places considerable emphasis upon nonlinear factors in connection with his "dynamic determinants."

to the length of the Kondratieff cycle these might be regarded as "rapidly damped" and be neglected.[40]

On the other hand, the extremely short fluctuations, to the extent that they exist, might be explained almost wholly in endogenous terms with reference to the dynamics of inventories, the acceleration principle, speculation, etc. These short cycles would perhaps die down were it not for the random and systematic disturbances received from the longer movements in investment.

To illustrate the above remarks the reader may construct for himself a model in which there is superimposed a regular periodic movement of autonomous net investment upon a system in which both the multiplier and the acceleration principle are operating. The period oí the autonomous movement should be longer than the intrinsic period of the (damped) responding mechanism. Specifically, consider the equation

$$Y(t + 2) - \alpha(1 + \beta)Y(t + 1) + \alpha\beta Y(t) = P(t), \qquad (54)$$

where α is the marginal propensity to consume, β is the so-called "relation" of the acceleration principle, and $P(t)$ is a periodic movement, not necessarily a pure sine wave.[41]

If the process has been going along for a long time, it will finally approach a periodic motion of income in which autonomous investment shows a lead over income, and in which the amplitude of the final motion is proportional to that of $P(t)$, the exact factor of proportionality increasing with the nearness of the intrinsic period of the left-hand side to the postulated periodicity of the right-hand side, i.e., with the approach to resonance.

However, if we break in at an arbitrary point of time, there will be in addition to this motion a damped transient whose qualitative properties depend only on the endogenous response characteristic

[40] On the whole, we should rather expect greater irregularity in amplitude and periodicity in a cycle generated by exogenous factors than in one endogenous in character. This is in accord with the prevailing view that a diversity of factors is responsible for the few recorded "long waves" of economic history, and with the notion that there is much less predictability into the future of even the *qualitative features* of such a movement. On all these matters the reader may be referred to the well-known views of Schumpeter, Mitchell, Hansen, *et al.*

[41] Cf. P. A. Samuelson, "Interactions between the Multiplier Analysis and the Principle of Acceleration," *Review of Economic Statistics*, XXI (1939), 75–78. E. G. Bennion has worked out a number of interesting arithmetical models in which the agreement between theory and the model sequences is complete.

of the multiplier-relation system. This can give shorter cycles, brought into life so to speak by the shocks incident to the longer wave.[42]

Mixed Systems of a Linear Stochastic Type

Thus far I have been considering mixed exogenous-endogenous systems in which the exogenous forces are periodic in nature, or at least quasi-periodic. There is, however, a stochastical theory designed to explain the existence of quasi-periodic cycles by means of a damped system responding to random shocks. The latter serve to keep alive the fluctuations of the system in spite of dampening.[43] But in doing so they tend to displace the phase of the given motion so that ordinary periodogram analysis will not, in a long series, reveal a "significant" period in the vicinity of the intrinsic frequencies of the responding system. This is intuitively obvious if we think of ordinary periodogram analysis as Fourier analysis, and the latter as equivalent to fitting by least squares the best single harmonic to the time series in question. The ordinate of the usual periodogram is equal to that part of the total variance (in absolute or percentage terms) of the time series which can be explained by the best harmonic of that frequency. Because of the constant disturbance of phase, in a long series no sine wave will give a good fit.[44]

It remains an open question whether other of the usual methods of time series analysis (counting distances between peaks and troughs, etc.) will suffice to give back the known periods even in artificially constructed model sequences of the type of equation (1)

[42] If we drop the assumption of linearity, then the response of the system will show some differences. The amplitude of income will not be simply proportional to the amplitude of the function $P(t)$, nor will the final solution be a simple additive combination of periodic and transient components. Qualitatively, however, the result will be a final approach to a periodic motion with characteristic shorter waves in the transition period. Unless kept alive, these will die out.

[43] H. Wold, *A Study in the Analysis of Stationary Time Series* (Uppsala, Sweden, 1938).

[44] Cf. the reference given in footnote 43. See also the brilliant contribution of Professor Ragnar Frisch to the Cassel volume, "Propagation Problems and Impulse Problems in Dynamic Economics," *Economic Essays in Honor of Gustav Cassel* (London, 1933), pp. 171–205. While ordinary periodogram analysis will not do, the "Generalized Harmonic Analysis" of Norbert Wiener is designed precisely for problems of this type. See the references to his 1930 *Acta Mathematica* article in H. T. Davis, *The Analysis of Economic Time Series* (Bloomington, Indiana: Principia Press, 1942), and also the reference there to the 1935 article of Bartels, and the latter's suggestive concept of the "harmonic dial."

above. It is clear, however, from the work of Slutsky [45] and others that the time series generated by such sequences resemble qualitatively the usually encountered economic time series. [46]

By means of the analysis of the previous chapter it is clear that (except for terminal adjustments which become negligible in a long series) the solution of the damped dynamic stochastic system of the following type

$$L(Y) = Y(t) + a_1 Y(t-1) + \cdots + a_n Y(t-n) = \{z_t\}, \quad (55)$$

where z is a random variable serially uncorrelated in time and drawn from an unchanging universe whose first two moments $(0, \sigma_z^2)$ exist, takes the following form

$$Y(t) = A_0 Z(t) + A_1 Z(t-1) + \cdots + A_n Z(t-n) + \cdots. \quad (56)$$

As t grows the number of coefficients in this sequence becomes infinite, but in such a way as to leave their sum and the sum of their squares finite and equal respectively to $(1/\sum_0^n a_i, k)$. By the usual central limit theories it is easy to show that (except for terminal adjustments) the variance of $Y(t)$ is given by

$$V_t = (A_0^2 + A_1^2 + \cdots + A_t^2)\sigma_z^2, \quad (57)$$

or in the limit by

$$V_\infty = k\sigma_z^2, \quad (58)$$

where k is finite. The actual frequency distribution of $Y(t)$ tends to some limit with increasing t, with zero mean and variance equal to the last given expressions. This is usually true even if the original frequency distribution of z is not at all normal (i.e., Gaussian).

The interested reader can satisfy himself that the superposition of a random variable on to a periodic force leads to a forced motion

[45] Eugen Slutsky, "The Summation of Random Causes as the Source of Cyclic Processes," *Econometrica*, V (1937), 105–146.

[46] The article by Trygve Haavelmo, "The Probability Approach in Econometrics," *Econometrica*, vol. XII, Supplement (1944), deals with the problems of determining empirically such stochastical relations. The article by H. B. Mann and A. Wald, "On the Statistical Treatment of Linear Stochastic Difference Equations," *Econometrica*, XI (1943), 173–220, shows that the conventional least squares treatment of autocorrelation is (asymptotically) a "consistent" method of determining the a coefficients. It would be outside the scope of the present work to go into these problems. A number of articles in the *Annals of Mathematical Statistics* for 1942 deal with the sampling distribution of the autocorrelation coefficient.

just like that described above except that the mean of the asymptotically normal distribution fluctuates according to the periodic function described in the previous section. He can also work out the implications of having a stochastic variable z_t which is not serially independent.

NON-LINEAR STOCHASTIC SYSTEMS

A more difficult problem is that of developing for a non-linear system the stochastic theory which corresponds to that dealt with in the previous section. As far as the present writer is aware, this is almost completely unexplored ground. No more than a bird's-eye view of the problem can be attempted here.

We consider a non-linear system of the form

$$Y(t) - f[Y(t - 1), \cdots, Y(t - n), Z(t)] = 0, \qquad (59)$$

whose initial conditions may be written in the abbreviated matrix form

$$Y_0 = [Y(-i)], \qquad (60)$$

where i goes from zero to $(n - 1)$. If desired, the Y's and Z's may be considered as column matrices of many variables. As before, the Z refers to a random variable drawn from the same universe over time and without serial correlation. Formally, the solution may be written in the form

$$Y(t) = F_t[Z(t), Z(t - 1), \cdots, Z(0), Y_0], \qquad (61)$$

where the exact nature of F depends upon that of f. It has been shown in Mathematical Appendix B, Section 8, that with an appropriate redefinition of the variables Y and Z we may consider equations (59) to be of the first order, i.e., to depend only upon the value of Y one period ago. The new Z will now have zeros in some of its components, but as before there will be no serial correlation between successive Z's.

Under certain restrictions upon the partial derivatives of f, such as correspond to the economic reality of any relevant damped economic system, it should be possible to enunciate limit theorems not unlike those holding for linear systems. The fact that so many well-known non-linear statistics go to normality in the limit as the sample size becomes large suggests that many of these limit theorems would actually be of Gaussian form.[47] It would be a task of some delicacy to establish conditions under which this must certainly be so. However, it is not to be thought that in most cases the limiting distributions must be of Gaussian form. In a moment I shall specify a non-linear system which approaches a limiting distribution *not* of Gaussian form; in fact, an example will be given of one which remains bounded but approaches no stationary (probability) state, but oscillates indefinitely in a simple periodic fashion.

The key to a successful analysis of the difficult non-linear case lies in shifting our attack from the study of any one particular motion as it is bombarded by a particular set of random shocks to the analysis of the probability states corresponding to all possible shock patterns weighted in accordance with their likelihood. These contrasting approaches are to a certain extent similar to the contrast between the motion of a single molecule, the totality of motions of an ensemble of molecules as in statistical mechanics, and the kinetic theory of gases which describes macroscopic states of a system. However, the analogy is not perfectly complete and should not be pressed too far.

First, let us assume that the initial conditions at time t are known. Then from our knowledge of the probability universe of Z_t we may write down immediately the conditional probability description of Y_{t+1}, given Y_t, namely,

$$P(Y_{t+1}, Y_t) = H(Y_{t+1}, Y_t), \tag{62}$$

where the exact form of H can be easily specified as soon as f and the probability distribution of Z_t are given.

Now if we assume that the exact probability distribution of Y_t is known, and equal to $P_t(Y_t)$, it is possible to write down the distribution of Y_{t+1} in the form

$$P_{t+1}(Y_{t+1}) = \int_{-\infty}^{\infty} H(Y_{t+1}, Y_t)P_t(Y_t)dY_t. \tag{63}$$

It is to be noted that even in the non-linear case the probabilities at different instants of time are related by a recursive *linear* functional.

---

[47] Unlike most statistics computed from a sample, the F operations on the Z's are definitely not symmetric functions.

For concreteness we may show what form the H takes in the simplest case of a one variable first order system of the form

$$y_{t+1} = ay_t + Z_t \qquad (64)$$

with probability density for Z given by $R(Z)$. Then corresponding to equation (63) we have the relation

$$P_{t+1}(Y_{t+1}) = \int_{-\infty}^{\infty} R(y_{t+1} - ay_t)P_t(y_t)dy_t. \qquad (65)$$

To see whether or not P_t approaches a limiting distribution it is natural to put the same P in both sides of the above equation and solve the resulting equation for the form of the unknown distribution. This is an integral equation of the Fredholm type but with infinite limits. For the special type of R given above, and for a less than unity, the existence of a limit is assured.

For absolute a greater than unity we know that the variance increases without limit, and that there cannot be a limiting form other than the trivial zero solution. We may state this in another manner. If we put a parameter λ in front of the integral in (63) and ask for a function P which satisfies both sides, such will exist only if λ is a characteristic value or eigen-value of the kernel H. For undamped linear systems $\lambda = 1$ will not be a characteristic value. It would be a task of some considerable mathematical difficulty to indicate just when the integral equation arising from a non-linear system had an eigen-value equal to unity and to derive the corresponding eigen-function $P(t)$.

The problem would be simplified if we could assume that our non-linear f gives bounded values, whatever the value of previous Y's. This is obviously possible only for non-linear systems; earlier discussion of the physical limitations of full employment and zero income suggest that it is often realistic to assume barriers which guarantee this fact. With this assumption the absolute value of Y must be less than some number M, and we have $-M$ and $+M$ as the limits in the integrals instead of the infinite limits. This removes the singularity in the Fredholm equation. It is to be hoped that this continuous but bounded case will be fully analyzed by mathematicians and economists.

I shall confine myself to the simpler case where Y is a discrete rather than a continuous variable. By making the classification fine enough, we can reach any empirical degree of approximation to reality so there is no essential loss of generality involved. By replacing the above integrals by Stieltjes integrals, both cases can be handled simultaneously. However, in the simpler case under discussion, the integrals can be described by sums. But in this case Y takes on only integral values, and the probability functions for Y and Z are at each time denumerable sequences of numbers. Corresponding to the kernel H we now have a matrix H whose properties depend upon the f function and the probability sequence $R(Z)$.

However, to make the problem manageable there are other difficulties to be taken care of. Even in the simple linear case, with Z taking on integral values and the initial Y's taking on integral values, the Y's at a later stage will not be confined to integral values unless the coefficients of the integral equation are themselves integers. Let us satisfy this requirement in our simple linear example of equation (64) by setting a equal to unity. Our H matrix is then seen to consist of an infinite number of rows and columns, each column consisting of the R sequence of probabilities referring to the different Z values, with $R(0)$ centered in the diagonal of the matrix as follows:

$$
\begin{array}{cccc}
\cdots\cdots\cdots\cdots\cdots\cdots\cdots\cdots\cdots\cdots\cdots \\
\cdots R(0) & R(-1) & R(-2)\cdots \\
\cdots R(1) & R(0) & R(-1)\cdots \\
\cdots R(2) & R(1) & R(0)\ \cdots \\
\cdots R(3) & R(2) & R(1)\ \cdots \\
\cdots\cdots\cdots\cdots\cdots\cdots\cdots\cdots\cdots\cdots\cdots
\end{array}
\tag{66}
$$

It is not an easy matter to work rigorously with infinite matrices and their latent roots and vectors. In this case we can be sure that there is a latent root of unity by virtue of the property that probabilities must add up to unity, but we cannot attach unambiguous meaning to this, nor solve for the corresponding latent vector.

It might be thought that the difficulty is of our own making in that the R sequence has been considered to be infinite. However, the assumption of a finite number of terms in R only introduces zeros in each column after one reaches a certain distance from the diagonal. The matrix must still be considered to be infinite in size, and, if we wait long enough, Y can take on any integral value, however large.

There is the further more serious difficulty that a damped system with leading coefficient equal to unity cannot have coefficients which are all integers. Clearly an equation whose roots are all less than unity in absolute value will have a product less than unity, and hence a coefficient which is not an integer.

Therefore, even in the discrete case I shall make the non-linear assumption that the difference equation which defines the dynamical path of the system is such as to yield bounded values of Y_t. It is convenient to assume that the Y's in addition to being discrete take on only a finite number of values in this bounded interval; i.e., we "round off" to some degree of accuracy. Because we make our classifications as fine as we wish, there is no serious loss of generality involved. In this case the probabilities at time t of the different values of Y, n in number, can be represented by the equation

$$P_{t+1} = HP_t, \tag{67}$$

where the P's are column matrices of n elements, and the H is a square n by n matrix, whose properties depend upon those of the non-linear system and on the probability distribution of Z. It will be noted that the sums of the columns of H are in every case unity. This follows from the consideration that if Y is *certainly* in position i at a given time (so that the P vector has zeros everywhere except for a unity in the ith element), then it must certainly be *somewhere* one period later. But its probability of being in each of the n positions one period later is under these conditions nothing but the ith column, whose sum must therefore add up to unity. Note also that all of the elements of H must be positive in virtue of their interpretation as conditional probabilities.

Because the columns add up to unity we place a minus one in each diagonal and add each row to the first row. The result is a singular matrix with zeros in the first row. This shows that unity is a latent root. Similarly the fact that all elements are positive and add up to unity guarantees that there are no latent roots which exceed unity in absolute value. For if there were, we could select initial conditions for which a given element in P would grow exponentially without limit. This contradicts the assumption that no (probability) element of P can exceed unity.

In most cases there will be one root of unity and all other roots less than unity in absolute value. Thus, whatever the original probability distribution of Y, it will gradually approach a stationary probability state given by the latent vector of H corresponding to the unit latent root. It will satisfy the equations

$$HP = P, \tag{68}$$

where the P is normalized so that its elements (and not their squares) add up to unity. The exact values of the P's can be derived by solving $(n - 1)$ linear equations. It will be noted that the solution secured will have nothing to do with the limiting Gaussian form.

In special cases the unit latent root may not be simple so that no unique stationary probability distribution is reached. In still other cases there may be another latent root whose absolute value is equal to unity, and which is either complex or equal to minus one. In either case for "most" initial probability states there will be no approach to a stationary probability state; instead there will be periodic oscillation. A simple example is provided by a 2 by 2 H matrix of the form

$$\begin{bmatrix} 0 & 1 \\ 1 & 0 \end{bmatrix}. \tag{69}$$

If we start out with a probability vector (a, b), it gives rise, because of the negative latent root, to the oscillatory sequence (b, a), (a, b), (b, a), etc., without ever approaching a limit.[48]

---

[48] See W. Feller, *An Introduction to Mathematical Probability and Its Applications* (New York: Wiley, 1950) for discussion of Markoff processes.

CHAPTER XII

CONCLUSION

ECONOMICS is a growing subject in which very much is left to be done. It is only appropriate, therefore, in bringing this work to a close, to indicate a few of the important unsolved problems crying out for further investigation.

In the first and second chapters I outlined the general problem of *comparative statics:* how from a knowledge of the qualitative and quantitative properties of our equilibrium conditions we can hope to deduce meaningful theorems concerning the direction and magnitude of changes in our variables when certain data change. In chapter iii it was shown that in a large class of cases the economist derives definite theorems by means of the hypothesis that the equilibrium position represents a maximum or minimum position. The *inequalities* associated with the definition of an extremum position were seen to be the source of fruitful theorems in comparative statics.

Chapter iv represented an application of this analysis to the cost and production theory of the firm, just as chapter v gave a treatment of constrained maxima as required by the theory of consumer's behavior. Special aspects of the latter subject received treatment in chapters vi and vii. And finally the study of static maxima and minima was brought to completion in the analysis of welfare economics given in chapter viii.

In the first chapter of Part II it was shown that simply from the standpoint of fruitful comparative statics *dynamic analysis* is useful and necessary. Indeed, the *correspondence principle*, enunciating the relationship between the stability conditions of dynamics and the evaluation of displacements in comparative statics, provides the second great weapon in the arsenal of the economist interested in deriving definite, meaningful theorems.

In chapter x dynamical systems are studied for their own sake, particularly in their stability aspects, while in chapter xi I have discussed various fundamentals of dynamical analysis including formal problems arising out of the study of business cycles.

Broadly speaking, the development of analytical economics has proceeded in a natural evolutionary order. First, in Walras we have the final culmination of the notion of *determinateness* of equilibrium on the *statical* level. This has received further elaboration in the hands of Pareto and others.

However, Pareto took a second, further step. He laid the basis for a theory of *comparative statics* by showing how a change in a datum would displace the position of equilibrium. Even earlier Cournot had pioneered in this "infinitesimal" analysis, although with reference to a narrower set of problems.

While Pareto laid the basis for *comparative statics*, his own work was not rich in definite theorems in this subject, precisely because he rarely concerned himself with the secondary inequalities relevant to maximum positions. On the few occasions when he did do so, he came to grief because of mathematical errors in their statement. It was left for W. E. Johnson, Slutsky, Hicks and Allen, Georgescu-Roegen, Hotelling, and other modern writers to begin to make progress along this third line.

However, only a part of economic theory is concerned with the maximizing action within an economic unit. Where the interactions between individuals are concerned, the scope of fruitful *comparative statics* may be greatly extended by a fourth advance, the apprehension of the *correspondence principle*, whereby the comparative statical behavior of a system is seen to be closely related to its dynamical stability properties.

A natural fifth step to take after we have investigated the response of a system to change in given parameters is to investigate its behavior as a result of the passage of time. Thus, we cultivate *dynamics* for its own sake, especially with respect to the qualitative properties of the respective motions.

The usefulness of any theoretical structure lies in the light which it throws upon the way economic variables will change when there is a change in some datum or parameter. This commonplace holds as well in the realm of dynamics as in statics. It is a logical next step, therefore, to begin to create a theory of *comparative dynamics*. This will include the theory of comparative statics as a special case, and indeed all of the earlier five subjects, but it will cover a much richer terrain.

The central notion of *comparative dynamics* is simple enough.

We change something (just *what* need not concern us at the moment), and we investigate the effect of this change on the whole motion or behavior over time of the economic system under investigation. It will be seen that comparative statics involves the special case where a "permanent" change is made, and only the effects upon final levels of stationary equilibrium are in question.

In *comparative dynamics* we consider a much broader class of changes. (a) We may make a change in *initial conditions*. By definition this alters the immediate behavior of the system in a known way. By the assumption of continuity we may infer that the position of the system for some region adjacent to the initial conditions is also altered in the same direction. For intermediate lapses of time a separate investigation is necessary to determine what happens to the system. However, for a *stable* system it is clear by virtue of the definition of stability that for sufficiently long time periods there will be no final alteration in the behavior of the system.

(b) We may make a change in some *force* acting on the system. Thus, we may cause autonomous investment to vary. Actually, there are a variety of cases which must be considered. The change in force may be permanent; it may be intermittent; it may be transient or instantaneous. In this very last case the analysis may be subsumed under the heading of a shift in initial conditions. In the case of stable systems the response to a permanent alteration gives us a description of the actual path followed by a system in going from one "comparative static level" to another.

For linear dynamic systems, but only for these, the most general of the above variations can be thought of as made up of the cumulated effect of unit impulses, or of changes in the instantaneous initial conditions of the system. This follows from the basic *superposition theorem* which underlies much of applied mathematical analysis.

(c) Finally, there may be a change in some internal parameter of the system. We may ask, for example, what the effect of a change in the marginal propensity to consume or in the "relation" may have on the behavior of a system. Again, the change in question may be permanent, varying, transient, etc.

The rich variety of forms which the change in data may take is matched by the numerous ways in which we can choose to describe the "resulting effects on the behavior of the system." Except in the most simple cases we shall find it necessary to summarize in various ways the information contained in the resulting changes in the system at each and every instant of time.

From a short run point of view interest will center on the immediate reaction on the system. The answer to this question can often be secured by a method which is formally like that of comparative statics with the significant difference that some of the variables treated are really dynamic in character.

This may be illustrated by the important case in the Keynesian analysis where investment is taken to be a variable whose value is to be determined by a system of relations like those discussed at the end of chapter ix. For the usual Keynesian theory, in the short run at least, the stock of capital is taken to be constant. By "solving" such a system we can finally reduce our relations down to a single equation between the amount of investment, I, and the stock of capital, K, and the value of some parameter, α. This parameter might well be the amount of thriftiness in the system. Now if we are interested in the effect upon the stock of capital in the immediate future of a change in this parameter, the answer can be given by treating investment as if it were an ordinary statical variable and solving, as in chapter ii, our equilibrium equations to determine the direction of change of investment with respect to the parameter, α.

However, to answer our question in comparative dynamics we must introduce the fact that investment, which we have previously been treating as an ordinary statical variable, is really the rate of change of the stock of capital, or equal to dK/dt. If the comparative statical analysis tells us that investment is reduced by an increase in thriftiness, we can be sure that in some sufficiently short run the amount of capital in existence will be less than it would otherwise have been. For if two curves start out from the same point with differing rates of increase, we can be sure that the one with the greatest rate of increase will exceed the other for some small region at least.

As it happens, a similar statement can be given in this case to the wider problem as to what happens to capital *in the long run* as a result of a change in thriftiness. Thus, if instead of simply asking what level of consumption maximizes current investment, we widen Professor Lange's question [1] and seek the levels of consumption leading to the most capital *at each instant of time*, we shall find that capital formation in a run of any length is only maximized if at each instant the Lange criteria are met.

However, when the problems of comparative dynamics are posed in general and realistic form, it turns out that the above identity results almost by chance. Thus, consider a system of two or n dynamical equations

$$\frac{dx_i}{dt} = g^i(x_1, \cdots, x_n, \alpha). \qquad (i = 1, \cdots, n) \qquad (1)$$

Suppose, furthermore, that an increase in α always increases dx_1/dt, or that g_α^1 is always positive. Does it follow that an increase in α always results in a higher x_1 at each subsequent instant of time? The answer is no. For some sufficiently small instant of time, starting out from given initial conditions, this must of course be true, but it need not continue to be true. In the one variable case to which I reduced the Keynes-Lange system, the stronger theorem is true. For in this case we may solve explicitly our differential equation in the form

$$t - t^o - \int_{x_1^o}^{x_1} \frac{du}{g^1(u; \alpha)} = 0, \qquad (2)$$

and by partial differentiation of the above implicit relation between t, x_1, and α, it is easy to show that the change in x_1 with respect to α, t being fixed, must be of the same sign as the definitely known coefficient g_α^1. The reader can work out the geometrical reason for this.

Not only is the direct solution of the system impossible in the multi-variable case, but the corresponding theorem is definitely untrue. Economically this is not hard to visualize. If the parameter, α, has a pronounced effect upon the growth of a second variable, after a sufficiently long period of time this indirect influence may outweigh the direct favorable influence on the first variable. The reader may wish to work out an even more complicated model than the above in which α enters as a dynamic parameter. Thus, it is not difficult to construct a model in which deficit financing has a favorable effect upon the growth of capital in the short run, but the accumulated bad effects of the growing debt are adverse to capital growth. I do not wish to pass judgment upon the reality of the above assumptions, but simply wish to point out the possible occurrence in economic systems of the common medical phenomena whereby short term remedies may have long term deleterious effects.

Of course, if we confine our attention to the behavior of long period stationary equilibrium positions, the methods of comparative statics come into their own again. All time derivatives, differences, etc., are set equal to zero and the resulting system solved like any statical system of chapter ii.

Finally, the economist will often be interested in the effect upon some characteristic of the motion of the system. How will a change in the "relation" affect the average level of a fluctuating trendless system, its periodicity, its dampening, and its amplitude? Nor need we confine ourselves to simple stable systems. Thus, it is of the greatest interest to know how a change in age-specific mortality will affect the net-reproductive-rate; or how the period of delay in the expenditure of income will affect the rate of inflation under a given defined inflationary gap.

The further development of analytical economics along the lines of comparative dynamics must rest with the future. It is to be hoped that it will aid in the attack upon diverse problems—from the trivial behavior of a single small commodity, to the fluctuations of important components of the business cycle, and even to the majestic problems of economic development.

MATHEMATICAL APPENDIX A

Many mathematical theorems of importance to the economist are not to be found collected in any one convenient place. Without striving for rigor, I have gathered together some of those most relevant to the matters under discussion in the present work.

I. Maximum Conditions for a Single-Variable Function

Let

$$z = f(t)$$

be a defined function with a continuous second derivative everywhere on an interval

$$a \leqq t \leqq b.$$

z will enjoy a relative maximum at the point t^0, providing

$$f(t) \leqq f(t^0), \qquad a < t^0 < b \tag{1}$$

for neighboring values of t.

It is necessary in order that this condition be satisfied that

$$f'(t^0) = 0, \tag{2}$$

and

$$f''(t^0) \leqq 0. \tag{3}$$

The first of these conditions is derived in the following manner. By the Theorem of the Mean,

$$f(t) - f(t^0) = (t - t^0)f'[t^0 + \theta(t - t^0)]. \qquad 0 < \theta < 1$$

Suppose

$$f'(t^0) > 0.$$

Then from our continuity assumptions there exists an interval

$$|t - t^0| < m$$

within which the following inequality holds everywhere

$$f'(t) > 0.$$

Hence, for all such neighboring values of t larger than t^0, we have

$$f(t) - f(t^0) > 0,$$

which contradicts our hypothesis.   Similarly,

$$f'(t^0) < 0$$

would lead to a contradiction.   Therefore,

$$f'(t^0) = 0.$$

The second necessary condition is derived in a similar manner. From Taylor's expansion with a remainder we have

$$f(t) - f(t^0) = (t - t^0)f'(t^0) + \frac{(t - t^0)^2}{2} f''[t^0 + \theta'(t - t^0)].$$

$$0 < \theta' < 1$$

But

$$f'(t^0) = 0,$$

and so this becomes

$$f(t) - f(t^0) = \frac{(t - t^0)^2}{2} f''[t^0 + \theta'(t - t^0)].   \qquad 0 < \theta' < 1$$

Suppose

$$f''(t^0) > 0.$$

Then by assumed continuity

$$f''(t) > 0$$

on an interval

$$|t - t^0| < m'.$$

In consequence,

$$f(t) - f(t^0) > 0$$

on this interval.   But this is a contradiction.   Therefore,

$$f''(t^0) \leqq 0.$$

Actually, it can be shown under conditions of proper continuity that the first non-vanishing derivative must be even and negative for a relative maximum.

I define a *regular* maximum as one for which the equality sign in equation (3) is excluded.   It is necessary and sufficient in order that z enjoy a regular maximum at t^0 that

$$f'(t^0) = 0,$$

and

$$f''(t^0) < 0.   \qquad (4)$$

Similarly, necessary conditions for a relative minimum under our assumed conditions are

$$f'(t^0) = 0,$$

and

$$f''(t^0) \geqq 0. \tag{5}$$

Necessary and sufficient conditions for a regular minimum are

$$f'(t^0) = 0,$$

and

$$f''(t^0) > 0. \tag{6}$$

II. Maximum Conditions for a Function of Many Variables

Let

$$z = f(x_1, \cdots, x_n)$$

be a defined function with continuous second order partial derivatives of all kinds in an open region S. Then a point (X^0) in S affords a relative maximum to z provided that

$$f(x_1, \cdots, x_n) \leqq f(x_1^0, \cdots, x_n^0)$$

for sufficiently close values of (X).

It is necessary in order for this to be true that

$$\frac{\partial f(x_1^0, \cdots, x_n^0)}{\partial x_1} = 0$$

$$\frac{\partial f(x_1^0, \cdots, x_n^0)}{\partial x_2} = 0$$

$$\cdot$$
$$\cdot$$
$$\cdot$$

$$\frac{\partial f(x_1^0, \cdots, x_n^0)}{\partial x_n} = 0$$

and

$$0 \geqq \frac{\partial^2 f}{\partial x_1 \partial x_1} h_1{}^2 + 2 \frac{\partial^2 f}{\partial x_1 \partial x_2} h_1 h_2 + 2 \frac{\partial^2 f}{\partial x_1 \partial x_3} h_1 h_3 + \cdots + 2 \frac{\partial^2 f}{\partial x_1 \partial x_n} h_1 h_n$$

$$+ \frac{\partial^2 f}{\partial x_2 \partial x_2} h_2{}^2 + 2 \frac{\partial^2 f}{\partial x_2 \partial x_3} h_2 h_3 + \cdots + 2 \frac{\partial^2 f}{\partial x_2 \partial x_n} h_2 h_n$$

$$+ \cdots \cdots \cdots \cdots \cdots \cdots$$

$$+ \cdots \cdots \cdots \cdots \cdots$$

$$\frac{\partial^2 f}{\partial x_n \partial x_n} h_n{}^2,$$

where $(h_1, h_2, \cdots, h_n)$ are arbitrary numbers, and the partial derivatives are evaluated at the point (X^0).

If we adopt the following notation

$$f_i^0 = f_i^0(x_1^0, \cdots, x_n^0) = \frac{\partial f(x_1^0, \cdots, x_n^0)}{\partial x_i}, \qquad (i = 1, \cdots, n)$$

and

$$f_{ij}^0 = \frac{\partial^2 f(x_1^0, \cdots, x_n^0)}{\partial x_i \partial x_j},$$

then our necessary conditions can be written symbolically

$$f_i^0 = 0, \qquad (i = 1, \cdots, n) \tag{7}$$

and

$$\sum_1^n \sum_1^n f_{ij}^0 h_i h_j \leqq 0. \tag{8}$$

It is necessary and sufficient for a regular relative maximum that

$$f_i^0 = 0, \qquad (i = 1, \cdots, n)$$

and

$$\sum_1^n \sum_1^n f_{ij}^0 h_i h_j < 0 \tag{9}$$

for not all h's equal to zero.   In addition to the vanishing of all first partial derivatives, a regular relative maximum requires that the quadratic form whose coefficients are the second partial derivatives be negative definite.   This last condition is the generalization to many variables of the single-variable condition that the second derivative be negative for a regular relative simple maximum.   Its meaning will be amplified in a later section.

The proof of these necessary conditions can be easily demonstrated by the use of a device which enables us to convert our problem into that of a single-variable one, upon which we can bring to bear the results of the previous section.

Let

$$x_i = x_i^0 + th_i, \qquad (i = 1, \cdots, n)$$

where the h's take on arbitrary values.   Clearly for a relative maximum we must have

$$f(x_1^0 + th_1, x_2^0 + th_2, \cdots, x_n^0 + th_n) \leqq f(x_1^0, \cdots, x_n^0).$$

For given values of the h's, not all equal to zero, f can be regarded as a function of the single variable t, and the above condition can be written

$$f(t) \leqq f(0).$$

From the previous section we know that this requires that

$$f'(0) = 0,$$

and

$$f''(0) \leqq 0.$$

But, by performing the indicated differentiation, we find

$$f'(0) = \sum_1^n f_i^0 h_i = 0, \tag{10}$$

and

$$f''(0) = \sum_1^n \sum_1^n f_{ij}^0 h_i h_j \leqq 0.$$

In order that (10) be satisfied for arbitrary values of the h's, each partial derivative must vanish, or

$$f_i^0 = 0. \qquad (i = 1, \cdots, n)$$

For a regular relative maximum, we get by this method

$$f_i^0 = 0, \qquad (i = 1, \cdots, n)$$

and

$$\sum_1^n \sum_1^n f_{ij}^0 h_i h_j < 0, \qquad \text{not all } h\text{'s} = 0,$$

these conditions being both necessary and sufficient.

Similarly, a regular relative minimum requires that

$$f_i^0 = 0, \qquad (i = 1, \cdots, n)$$

and

$$\sum_1^n \sum_1^n f_{ij}^0 h_i h_j > 0, \qquad \text{not all } h\text{'s} = 0. \tag{11}$$

The appropriate quadratic form must be in this last case *positive definite*.

III. Conditions for a Constrained Maximum

As before, let

$$z = f(x_1, \cdots, x_n)$$

be a defined function with continuous second partial derivatives in an open region S. In addition, we impose subsidiary conditions on the admissible values of our variables in the form of the following m implicit functions of the n variables, defined in S with continuous second partial derivatives,

$$G^1(x_1, \cdots, x_n) = 0,$$
$$G^2(x_1, \cdots, x_n) = 0,$$
$$\qquad \cdot \qquad\qquad (m < n)$$
$$\qquad \cdot$$
$$\qquad \cdot$$
$$G^m(x_1, \cdots, x_n) = 0.$$

Under what conditions will a point (X^0) in S afford a relative maximum to z, and satisfy the subsidiary conditions? Such a point is defined as follows:

$$f(x_1, \cdots, x_n) \leqq f(x_1{}^0, \cdots, x_n{}^0),$$

where

$$G^k(x_1, \cdots, x_n) = G^k(x_1{}^0, \cdots, x_n{}^0) = 0, \qquad (k = 1, \cdots, m)$$

and (X) sufficiently close to (X^0).

The way to solve this problem which would suggest itself most naturally would be to use our m subsidiary conditions to eliminate m of our variables by expressing them in terms of the remaining $(n - m)$ variables. We assume that the rank of the matrix

$$\begin{bmatrix} \dfrac{\partial G^1}{\partial x_1} & \dfrac{\partial G^1}{\partial x_2} & \cdots & \dfrac{\partial G^1}{\partial x_n} \\ \dfrac{\partial G^2}{\partial x_1} & \dfrac{\partial G^2}{\partial x_2} & \cdots & \dfrac{\partial G^2}{\partial x_n} \\ \cdot & \cdot & & \cdot \\ \cdot & \cdot & & \cdot \\ \dfrac{\partial G^m}{\partial x_1} & \dfrac{\partial G^m}{\partial x_2} & \cdots & \dfrac{\partial G^m}{\partial x_n} \end{bmatrix}, \quad \text{or} \quad [G_i{}^k] \quad \begin{array}{l} (k = 1, \cdots, m) \\ (i = 1, \cdots, n) \end{array}$$

is of order m so that at least one m^2 determinant does not vanish.

This insures us that we can in fact uniquely solve our subsidiary conditions for m variables in terms of the remaining $(n - m)$. Since the numbering of our variables is arbitrary, we may write this without loss of generality as

$$x_i = \pi^i(x_{m+1}, x_{m+2}, \cdots, x_n). \qquad (i = 1, \cdots, m)$$

By substitution in our original expression, z can now be expressed in terms of the variables $(x_{m+1}, x_{m+2}, \cdots, x_n)$ with no conditions of constraint, and the analysis of the previous section can be applied.

However, there is a great loss of symmetry in such a procedure since not all our variables are treated alike. Fortunately, by the use of an artifice which can be rigorously justified, it is possible to derive a more symmetrical set of conditions.

Consider the Lagrangean-multiplier expression

$$\begin{aligned} H = H(x_1, \cdots, x_n) &= f(x_1, \cdots, x_n) \\ &+ \lambda_1 G^1(x_1, \cdots, x_n) + \cdots + \lambda_m G^m(x_1, \cdots, x_n), \end{aligned}$$

where the λ's are constants, not all zero, whose values will be determined later. Obviously for values of (X) satisfying the subsidiary conditions indicated above, all terms after the first must vanish, making our new expression equivalent to z. This suggests that for a maximum at (X^0)

$$\frac{\partial H^0}{\partial x_i} = H_i^0 = \frac{\partial f^0}{\partial x_i} + \lambda_1 \frac{\partial G^{10}}{\partial x_i} + \cdots + \lambda_m \frac{\partial G^{m0}}{\partial x_i} = 0,$$

$$(i = 1, \cdots, n) \quad (12)$$

subject to

$$G^k(x_1^0, \cdots, x_n^0) = 0. \qquad (k = 1, \cdots, m)$$

It is unnecessary for our purposes to indicate explicitly the rigorous proof of this statement.[1]

The last two sets together constitute $(n + m)$ equations in the $(n + m)$ unknowns $(x_1, \cdots, x_n, \lambda_1, \cdots, \lambda_m)$. Under the proper restrictions the values of all the x's and λ's are uniquely determined.

[1] See Carathéodory, *Variationsrechnung und Partielle Differentialgleichungen Erster Ordnung* (Leipzig und Berlin, 1935), pp. 164–189. The conditions of (12) are identical to those of (13) which follow. Carathéodory shows that if some minor of (13) greater than m were non-vanishing, then one could—by the implicit function theorem—solve for some x in terms of f, where f is both greater and less than the extremum value, f^0. This is a contradiction.

The above first necessary conditions can be expressed independently of the λ's. Consider the matrix

$$
\begin{bmatrix}
\dfrac{\partial f}{\partial x_1} & \dfrac{\partial G^1}{\partial x_1} & \dfrac{\partial G^2}{\partial x_1} & \cdots & \dfrac{\partial G^m}{\partial x_1} \\[2mm]
\dfrac{\partial f}{\partial x_2} & \dfrac{\partial G^1}{\partial x_2} & \dfrac{\partial G^2}{\partial x_2} & \cdots & \dfrac{\partial G^m}{\partial x_2} \\[2mm]
\cdot & \cdot & \cdot & & \cdot \\
\cdot & & \cdot & & \cdot \\
\cdot & \cdot & \cdot & & \cdot \\[2mm]
\dfrac{\partial f}{\partial x_n} & \dfrac{\partial G^1}{\partial x_n} & \dfrac{\partial G^2}{\partial x_n} & \cdots & \dfrac{\partial G^m}{\partial x_n}
\end{bmatrix}, \quad \text{or} \quad \left[\dfrac{\partial f}{\partial x_i} ; \dfrac{\partial G^k}{\partial x_i} \right] \quad \begin{array}{l} (i = 1, \cdots, n) \\ (k = 1, \cdots, m) \end{array}
$$

The rank of this matrix must be equal to m; i.e., every $(m + 1)^2$ determinant must vanish. Thus,

$$
\left| \frac{\partial f}{\partial x_i} ; \frac{\partial G^k}{\partial x_i} \right| = 0, \qquad \begin{array}{l} (i = 1, \cdots, m + 1) \\ (k = 1, \cdots, m) \end{array} \tag{13}
$$

and so forth for all possible combinations of (n) variables taken $(m + 1)$ at a time. These will yield $(n - m)$ *independent* conditions on the partial derivatives of f and the G's.

For concreteness consider the case of a many variable function to be maximized as of one subsidiary condition of restraint. According to the conditions indicated above there will result at an extremum tangency between the locus of restraint and a contour locus of z, $(n - 1)$ conditions familiar in many branches of economic theory.

In addition to the first necessary conditions upon first partial derivatives, there are as in the previous sections certain added secondary conditions on the second partial derivatives. The following must hold:

$$
\sum_1^n \sum_1^n H_{ij}{}^0 h_i h_j
$$

$$
= \sum_1^n \sum_1^n \left(\frac{\partial^2 f^0}{\partial x_i \partial x_j} + \lambda_1 \frac{\partial^2 G^{10}}{\partial x_i \partial x_j} + \cdots + \lambda_m \frac{\partial^2 G^{m0}}{\partial x_i \partial x_j} \right) h_i h_j \leqq 0 \tag{14}
$$

for

$$
\sum_1^n \frac{\partial G^{k0}}{\partial x_i} h_i = 0. \qquad (k = 1, \cdots, m)
$$

In summary, it is necessary and sufficient for a regular relative constrained maximum that

$$H_i^0 = 0, \qquad (i = 1, \cdots, n)$$

and

$$\sum_1^n \sum_1^n H_{ij}^0 h_i h_j < 0$$

for

$$\sum_1^n \frac{\partial G^{k^0}}{\partial x_i} h_i = 0, \qquad \text{not all } h\text{'s} = 0.$$

The meaning of these secondary conditions requiring the definiteness of certain quadratic forms under linear restrictions will be dealt with later.

IV. QUADRATIC FORMS

A real (homogeneous) quadratic form in n variables $(h_1, \cdots, h_n)$ is defined as follows:

$$\begin{aligned}
Q(h_1, \cdots, h_n) = {} & a_{11}h_1^2 + a_{12}h_1h_2 + \cdots + a_{1n}h_1h_n + \\
& a_{21}h_2h_1 + a_{22}h_2^2 + \cdots + a_{2n}h_2h_n + \\
& \quad\cdot \qquad\quad \cdot \qquad\qquad\quad \cdot \\
& \quad\cdot \qquad\quad \cdot \qquad\qquad\quad \cdot \\
& \quad\cdot \qquad\quad \cdot \qquad\qquad\quad \cdot \\
& a_{n1}h_nh_1 + a_{n2}h_nh_2 + \cdots + a_{nn}h_n^2 ,
\end{aligned} \qquad (16)$$

where the a's are real constants. A quadratic form in the single variable x would take the form

$$Q(x) = ax^2;$$

in two variables (x, y) it would be written

$$ax^2 + 2bxy + cy^2.$$

Since the order of multiplication is indifferent, it is clear that any quadratic form can be made symmetrical, i.e.,

$$a_{ij} = a_{ji}; \qquad a = a'. \qquad (17)$$

For if not already symmetrical, we may rewrite it without affecting its value as

$$\sum_1^n \sum_1^n \frac{a_{ij} + a_{ji}}{2} h_i h_j$$

which is symmetrical.   Unless otherwise specified we shall deal
only with symmetrical quadratic forms.

A *positive definite* quadratic form is one which is always positive
except when all the variables equal zero (at which point all quadratic forms vanish).   A *negative definite* quadratic form is one
which is always negative except at the origin.   A definite form is
positive definite or negative definite.   A *semi-definite* form is one
which never changes sign but may be zero at a set of points other
than the origin.   Thus, a *positive semi-definite* form could more
appropriately be called a *non-negative* form.   All forms which are
neither definite nor semi-definite are called *indefinite*.

A quadratic form in n variables is singular if the rank of its
matrix [2]

$$a = [a_{ij}],$$

is less than n; i.e., if the determinant

$$|a_{ij}| = 0.$$

It may be observed that all *semi-definite* forms are singular.

Forms in less than three variables

In the case of a single variable, it is easy to determine the
definiteness of

$$Q(x) = ax^2.$$

The form is (1) positive definite, (2) semi-definite and singular, or
(3) negative definite depending upon whether

$$a \gtreqless 0.$$

It is more difficult to ascertain whether a form in two variables
is positive definite.   If

$$Q = ax^2 + 2bxy + cy^2$$

is to be always positive except at the origin $(0, 0)$, it must clearly
be positive for $(1, 0)$.   But

$$Q(1, 0) = a, \tag{18}$$

and so a necessary condition is

$$a > 0. \tag{19}$$

---

[2] A matrix is of rank r if all its determinants of order $(r + 1)$ vanish.   All determinants of a still higher order will be found also to vanish.

Similarly, it can be proved that

$$c > 0. \tag{20}$$

These conditions are necessary but not sufficient. To derive still another necessary condition and determine complete sufficient conditions, let us consider the form as a quadratic equation in x with parameter y,

$$f(x) = ax^2 + (2by)x + (cy^2) = 0.$$

If the form is positive definite, x must not vanish for any non-vanishing y. Solving by the familiar rule for extracting the roots of a quadratic, we have

$$x = -\frac{2by \pm \sqrt{4b^2y^2 - 4acy^2}}{2a} = \left[\frac{-b \pm \sqrt{b^2 - ac}}{a}\right] y.$$

But this must yield no real value of x or the form would not be positive definite. Hence, the expression under the radical must be negative, and we have as an additional necessary condition

$$ac - b^2 > 0. \tag{21}$$

However, our three necessary conditions (19), (20), and (21) are not all independent. The last of them in conjunction with either of the first two implies all three. The sufficiency of these conditions is implied by the fact that the form is positive for the values $(1, 0)$, zero only for $(0, 0)$, and never changes sign; consequently, it is *positive definite*.

These conditions may be given a more convenient form. The matrix of the form in two variables is obviously

$$\begin{bmatrix} a & b \\ b & c \end{bmatrix}.$$

If we define a <u>principal minor of a determinant</u> as a subdeterminant formed by <u>crossing out the same rows and columns so</u> that the diagonal elements of the minor are contained in the diagonal elements of the original matrices, then our necessary and sufficient conditions are implied in the statement: <u>*all principal minors must be positive*</u>. These are three in number, but not being all independent, a complete set may be specified by making successive principal minors positive starting with the upper left-hand corner and adding successively corresponding rows and columns. (In this case there is only one row and one column to add.)

For the form to be negative definite it could be shown along similar lines that

$$a < 0,$$

$$\begin{vmatrix} a & b \\ b & c \end{vmatrix} > 0; \tag{22}$$

or that the first principal minor is negative, and the successive ones alternate in sign; those of odd order being negative, and those of even order being positive. This is because $[a_{ij}]$ is negative definite only if $[-a_{ij}]$ is positive definite.

Forms in any number of variables

The special methods applicable to forms of few variables cannot be applied in the general case. We must therefore seek more general methods. A non-singular transformation of variables of the type

$$h_i = \sum_1^n b_{ij}p_j; \qquad (i = 1, \cdots, n)$$

or using matrix notation,

$$h = bp, \qquad p = b^{-1}h,$$

leaves the quadratic form positive definite if originally positive definite. This is made plausible from the recognition that the origin goes into the origin, and that every point in the h space is uniquely related to every point in the p space. Consequently, Q after the transformation takes on only the values taken on before.

$$Q(h) = Q(bp) = \hat{Q}(p).$$

In particular, let the transformation b be such as to take Q into a sum of squares of the form [3]

$$Q(bp) = \hat{a}_1 p_1{}^2 + \hat{a}_2 p_2{}^2 + \cdots + \hat{a}_n p_n{}^2. \tag{23}$$

It is well known that an infinity of transformations exist which will do this.

[3] In matrix notation

$$Q = h'ah,$$
$$= p'(b'ab)p, \qquad \text{where} \qquad h = bp.$$

b must be chosen so that

$$b'ab = \begin{bmatrix} \hat{a}_1 & 0 & \cdots & 0 \\ 0 & \hat{a}_2 & \cdots & 0 \\ \cdot & \cdot & & \cdot \\ \cdot & \cdot & & \cdot \\ \cdot & \cdot & & \cdot \\ 0 & 0 & \cdots & \hat{a}_n \end{bmatrix} = [\hat{a}_i \delta_{ij}], \qquad \text{where} \qquad \delta_{ij} = \begin{cases} 1 \text{ for } i = j \\ 0 \text{ for } i \neq j \end{cases}.$$

Our problem is for the moment reduced to the simpler one of determining the definiteness of a quadratic form which is a sum of squares. Clearly this is positive definite, if and only if

$$\hat{a}_j > 0. \qquad (j = 1, \cdots, n) \qquad (24)$$

By the famous *Sylvester's Law of Inertia* it is known that the number of plus and minus coefficients in the a's is independent of the transformation employed. Clearly, therefore, the $\hat{a}$'s, if all positive after a particular transformation, are all positive for any possible transformation.

Transformation into a sum of squares

Two out of the infinity of possible transformations are of particular interest since they show definitely what conditions upon the matrix a are implied by its being positive definite. First, there exists a transformation b—gotten by an extension of the method of "completing the square"—such that

$$\hat{a}_1 = a_{11}$$

$$\hat{a}_2 = \frac{\begin{vmatrix} a_{11} & a_{12} \\ a_{21} & a_{22} \end{vmatrix}}{a_{11}} = \frac{A^2}{A^1}$$

$$\hat{a}_3 = \frac{\begin{vmatrix} a_{11} & a_{12} & a_{13} \\ a_{21} & a_{22} & a_{23} \\ a_{31} & a_{32} & a_{33} \end{vmatrix}}{\begin{vmatrix} a_{11} & a_{12} \\ a_{21} & a_{22} \end{vmatrix}} = \frac{A^3}{A^2}$$

$$\cdots \qquad (25)$$

$$\hat{a}_n = \frac{\begin{vmatrix} a_{11} & a_{12} & \cdots & a_{1n} \\ a_{21} & a_{22} & \cdots & a_{2n} \\ & & & \\ & & & \\ a_{n1} & a_{n2} & \cdots & a_{nn} \end{vmatrix}}{\begin{vmatrix} a_{11} & a_{12} & \cdots & a_{1,n-1} \\ a_{21} & a_{22} & \cdots & a_{2,n-1} \\ & & & \\ & & & \\ a_{n-1,1} & a_{n-1,2} & \cdots & a_{n-1,n-1} \end{vmatrix}} = \frac{A^n}{A^{n-1}}$$

It is necessary and sufficient, therefore, that these ratios are all positive.[4]   But

$$A^1 = a_{11} = Q(1, 0, \cdots, 0) > 0.$$

Hence, a necessary and sufficient condition that a quadratic form be positive definite is that the principal minors $(A^1, \cdots, A^n)$ must be positive.

Minimum properties of Q

Some preliminary observations are in order before discussing explicitly the second transformation.   Because a quadratic form is homogeneous of the second degree in the h's, if its sign is always positive on the unit hypersphere defined by

$$h_1{}^2 + h_2{}^2 + \cdots + h_n{}^2 = 1, \tag{26}$$

it is positive everywhere except at the origin.[5]   There is no loss in generality, therefore, in considering the sign of Q subject to the side condition (26).

Since Q is everywhere continuous with continuous derivatives, it necessarily attains a minimum on the closed hypersphere.   *For the form to be positive it is necessary and sufficient that the minimum of Q on the unit hypersphere be positive;* because then, and only then, is it positive everywhere except at the origin.

This minimum can be calculated explicitly.   Consider

$$Q = \sum_1^n \sum_1^n a_{ij} h_i h_j$$

[4] Cf. H. Hancock, *Theory of Maxima and Minima*, pp. 89–91.

[5] This is to be seen as follows.   If Q were negative for any value of $h (= \bar{h})$ not necessarily on the unit hypersphere, it would be negative for some value on the hypersphere.   Suppose

$$\sum_1^n h_i{}^2 = r^2.$$

Then the point $(\bar{h}_1/r, \cdots, \bar{h}_n/r)$ is on the unit hypersphere and

$$Q\left(\frac{\bar{h}}{r}\right) = \frac{1}{r^2} Q(\bar{h})$$

so that their signs agree.

subject to

$$\sum_1^n h_i^2 - 1 = 0.$$

Form the expression

$$H = \sum_1^n \sum_1^n a_{ij}h_ih_j - \lambda(\sum_1^n h_i^2 - 1).$$

According to the previous section it is necessary for a minimum that

$$2 \sum_1^n a_{ij}h_j - 2\lambda h_i = 0, \qquad (i = 1, \cdots, n)$$

or

$$\sum_1^n (a_{ij} - \lambda\delta_{ij})h_j = 0. \qquad (i = 1, \cdots, n) \tag{27}$$

These are linear homogeneous equations which possess a non-vanishing solution if, and only if, the determinant

$$D(\lambda) = |a_{ij} - \lambda\delta_{ij}| = 0.\text{[6]} \tag{28}$$

This is an nth degree equation in λ and will possess n roots, some of which may be repeated. For simplicity, we assume them to be distinct. Let us indicate these by

$$\lambda_1 < \lambda_2 < \cdots < \lambda_n.$$

At least one must be real since a real minimum does exist. Actually, by a well-known theorem of Hermitian matrices of which our symmetrical real matrix is a special case, all are necessarily real.[7] Corresponding to any λ_k, there exists a unique solution $(h_1{}^k, \cdots, h_n{}^k)$ satisfying equations (27) and lying on the unit hypersphere defined by (26).

Also, multiplying the first equation of (27) by $h_1{}^k$, the second by $h_2{}^k$, etc., and adding we find

$$\lambda_k = \sum_1^n \sum_1^n a_{ij}h_i{}^kh_j{}^k = Q(h^k). \qquad (k = 1, \cdots, n) \tag{29}$$

It follows that the smallest of the λ's, λ_1, equals the minimum of

[6] This is called a *secular equation*, a *determinantal equation*, and the *characteristic equation* of the matrix a. Its roots are the latent roots of the matrix a.

[7] H. Hancock, *Theory of Maxima and Minima*, pp. 107–109. See also the discussion on orthogonality in footnote 9 below.

the quadratic form.   *Hence, a necessary and sufficient condition that a quadratic form be positive definite is that all the latent roots of its matrix be positive:*[8]

Similarly, a form is positive semi-definite if none of the λ's is negative, although one or more is zero.   *A form is negative definite if, and only if, all the λ's are negative.*

Second transformation into a sum of squares

This can be proved in still another way.   Consider the transformation

$$p_k = \sum_1^n h_i{}^k h_i. \qquad (k = 1, \cdots, n) \qquad (30)$$

It is orthogonal, i.e.,[9]

$$\sum_1^n p_i{}^2 = \sum_1^n h_i{}^2, \qquad (31)$$

$$\sum_1^n h_i{}^k h_i{}^m = \delta_{km}.$$

---

[8] It can be shown that λ_2 is the minimum of Q on the set of points lying on the unit hypersphere and satisfying the constraint defined by

$$h_1{}^1 h_1 + h_2{}^1 h_2 + \cdots + h_n{}^1 h_n = 0.$$

If we adjoin still another constraint,

$$h_1{}^2 h_1 + h_2{}^2 h_2 + \cdots + h_n{}^2 h_n = 0,$$

λ_3 minimizes Q.   Generally, λ_r minimizes Q subject to

$$\sum_1^n h_i{}^2 = 1,$$

$$\sum_1^n h_i{}^j h_i = 0. \qquad (j = 1, \cdots, r - 1)$$

[9] In matrix notation

$$b = [h_i{}^k].$$

Orthogonality is defined by

$$bb' = I; \qquad \text{therefore,} \qquad b' = b^{-1}.$$

Therefore, $p = bh$ implies $h = b'p$.

To show that any two different h columns are orthogonal, note that

$$ah^k = \lambda_k h^k, \qquad ah^j = \lambda_j h^j,$$

and that

$$0 = (h^j)'ah^k - (h^k)'ah^j = (\lambda_k - \lambda_j)(h^k)'h^j.$$

If the two roots are unequal, the very last product must vanish and the h's are orthogonal.

Because two vectors consisting of conjugate complex numbers cannot be orthogonal, this shows the truth of the previous assertion that all roots of a symmetrical matrix must be real.

Hence,

$$h_i = \sum_1^n h_i{}^k p_k, \qquad (i = 1, \cdots, n) \tag{32}$$

and

$$Q(p) = \sum_1^n \sum_1^n a_{ij} \sum_1^n \sum_1^n h_i{}^k p_k h_j{}^m p_m$$

$$= \sum_1^n \sum_1^n \left(\sum_1^n \sum_1^n a_{ij} h_i{}^k h_j{}^m \right) p_k p_m {}^{10}$$

$$= \sum_1^n \lambda_k p_k{}^2. \tag{33}$$

This shows that the original quadratic form can be transformed into a sum of squares whose coefficients are the latent roots of the matrix a. This furnishes a second proof *that the λ's must all be positive if the quadratic form is positive definite, and conversely.*[11]

Characteristic equation of a matrix

Let us consider in more detail the nth degree determinantal equation

$$D(\lambda) = |a_{ij} - \lambda \delta_{ij}| = (\lambda_1 - \lambda)(\lambda_2 - \lambda) \cdots (\lambda_n - \lambda). \tag{34}$$

Expanding out the determinant, this becomes

$$(-\lambda)^n + c_1(-\lambda)^{n-1} + \cdots + c_{n-1}(-\lambda) + c_n = 0, \tag{35}$$

---

[10] Proof that the expression in parentheses above equals λ_k is derived by multiplying the ith equation of (27) by $h_i{}^m$ and summing. This gives

$$\sum_1^n \sum_1^n a_{ij} h_j{}^k h_i{}^m = \lambda_k \sum_1^n h_i{}^k h_i{}^m = \lambda_k \delta_{km}$$

because of the orthogonality property of the transformation b.

[11] The above discussion implicitly assumes that all latent roots are distinct. If they are not, the matrix a can still, because of its symmetry and linear divisors, be transformed into a diagonal matrix whose elements are the latent roots, but not by a *unique orthogonal* transformation.

where

$c_1 = a_{11} + a_{22} + \cdots + a_{nn} = $ sum of all n principal minors of the first order.

$$c_2 = \begin{vmatrix} a_{11} & a_{12} \\ a_{21} & a_{22} \end{vmatrix} + \begin{vmatrix} a_{11} & a_{13} \\ a_{31} & a_{33} \end{vmatrix} + \cdots = \begin{array}{l} \text{sum of all } n(n-1)/2 \\ \text{principal minors of the} \\ \text{second order.} \end{array}$$

.
.   (36)
.

$c_r = $ sum of all $n!/r!(n-r)!$ principal minors of the rth order.

.
.
.

$c_n = |a_{ij}| = D(0).$

From the familiar relationship between the roots and coefficients of a polynomial we have

$$\begin{aligned} c_1 &= \lambda_1 + \lambda_2 + \cdots + \lambda_n = a_{11} + a_{22} + \cdots + a_{nn} \\ c_2 &= \lambda_1\lambda_2 + \lambda_1\lambda_3 + \cdots + \lambda_1\lambda_n \\ &\quad + \lambda_2\lambda_3 + \cdots + \lambda_2\lambda_n \\ &\quad + \cdots + \lambda_{n-1}\lambda_n \end{aligned}$$

.
.   (37)
.

$c_r = $ sum of all possible products of $(\lambda_1, \cdots, \lambda_n)$ taken r at a time.

.
.
.

$c_n = |a_{ij}| = D(0) = \lambda_1\lambda_2 \cdots \lambda_n > 0.$

Descartes' rule of signs requires that all the c's be positive if all the λ's are to be positive, and conversely. It is clearly sufficient that all principal minors be positive.

It is obvious that definiteness of the quadratic form Q implies definiteness of all quadratic forms made up of subsets of the variables, for these are simply special cases when some of the h's are set equal to zero. The latent roots of the matrices of all such subsets must be positive. From a consideration of the minimum properties of the λ's given in footnote 8, it follows that any such latent root λ^* satisfies the relation

$$\lambda_1 \leqq \lambda^* \leqq \lambda_n. \tag{38}$$

From this fact we have another proof of the necessity that all principal minors must be positive since the product of the latent roots of a submatrix equals a corresponding principal minor.

Definiteness of inverse matrix

Repeatedly in economic problems it is important to be able to evaluate the principal minors of the reciprocal or inverse matrix a^{-1} when a is known to be definite.[12] The following theorem is, therefore, very useful. *If a is the matrix of a positive definite form, then a^{-1} is the matrix of a positive definite form.* Let

$$Q = h'ah.$$

Perform the transformation

$$h = a^{-1}p, \tag{39}$$

where $a = a'$ because of the symmetry of the matrix a. Then

$$Q = p'a^{-1\prime}aa^{-1}p = p'a^{-1\prime}Ip = p'a^{-1}p. \tag{40}$$

This shows that the original quadratic form can be transformed into one whose matrix is the inverse of the original matrix. From our previous discussion this must be definite.[13]

[12]

$$a^{-1} = \begin{bmatrix} \dfrac{A_{11}}{A} & \cdots & \dfrac{A_{1n}}{A} \\ \cdot & & \cdot \\ \cdot & & \cdot \\ \cdot & & \cdot \\ \dfrac{A_{n1}}{A} & \cdots & \dfrac{A_{nn}}{A} \end{bmatrix}$$

where A is the determinant of the matrix a, and A_{ij} is the cofactor of the element in the ith row and jth column of the determinant $A = |a_{ij}| \cdot a^{-1}$ is termed the inverse of a because the transformation a^{-1} following the transformation a is equivalent to the identity transformation I because of the property

$$aa^{-1} = a^{-1}a = I.$$

Only non-singular matrices have inverses.

[13] Sylvester's *Law of Latency* states a more general relationship. The latent roots of $f(a)$ are equal to $f(\lambda)$ where the λ's are the latent roots of a. This follows from the

V. Quadratic Forms Definite under Constraints

Let us now derive necessary and sufficient conditions that a quadratic form

$$Q = \sum_1^n \sum_1^n a_{ij} h_i h_j$$

is positive definite for values of h satisfying $m(< n)$ linear conditions of constraint

$$\sum_1^n g_j{}^\alpha h_j = 0, \qquad (\alpha = 1, \cdots, m) \tag{41}$$

where $|g_j{}^\alpha|$ is of rank m.[14] It would be possible of course to eliminate m variables by use of the equations of constraint, substitute in Q, and apply the theory of the previous section to a quadratic form in $(n - m)$ variables. But this is lacking in symmetry.

following identities:

$$ax = \lambda Ix$$
$$f(a)x = f(\lambda I)x$$
$$= f(\lambda)Ix.$$

Where $f(a) = a^{-1}$, the theorem above emerges as a special case. In the above theorem f must be a rational function.

[14] It is, of course, sufficient that a be the matrix of a positive definite quadratic form, since, if it is positive everywhere, it is clearly positive for the subset of values satisfying the m conditions of constraint. But this is not a necessary condition. The failure to recognize this was responsible for technical errors in economists' treatment of utility theory up until Slutsky's classic treatment of the subject.

The maximum of

$$U = \varphi(x_1, \cdots, x_n)$$

subject to the side condition

$$\sum_1^n p_i x_i = I$$

does not require as secondary conditions that the matrix of the Hessian

$$[\varphi_{ij}]$$

be a negative definite form. In fact, the definiteness of this matrix is *not* invariant under a general monotonic transformation of the utility index of the form

$$F = F(\varphi)$$
$$F_i = F' \varphi_i$$
$$F_{ij} = F' \varphi_{ij} + F'' \varphi_i \varphi_j,$$

whereas the correct conditions later to be developed are invariant.

As in the previous section, there is no loss of generality in considering the behavior of Q on the unit hypersphere defined by

$$\sum_1^n h_i^2 - 1 = 0. \tag{42}$$

This additional side condition is adjoined to the m equations of (41), and Q is to be minimized. Form the expression

$$H = \sum_1^n \sum_1^n a_{ij}h_ih_j + 2\sum_1^m \mu_\alpha \sum_1^n g_i^\alpha h_j - \lambda(\sum_1^n h_j^2 - 1), \tag{43}$$

where λ and the μ's are Lagrangean multipliers. At a minimum we must have

$$H_i = 2(\sum_1^n a_{ij}h_j + \sum_1^m \mu_\alpha g_i^\alpha - \lambda h_i) = 0, \qquad (i = 1, \cdots, n) \tag{44}$$

or

$$\sum_1^n (a_{ij} - \lambda\delta_{ij})h_j + \sum_1^m \mu_\alpha g_i^\alpha = 0, \qquad (i = 1, \cdots, n)$$

$$\sum_1^n g_j^\alpha h_j = 0, \qquad (\alpha = 1, \cdots, m) \tag{45}$$

$$\sum_1^n h_j^2 - 1 = 0.$$

A non-vanishing solution of these equations exists if, and only if, the following bordered determinant vanishes,

$$D_m(\lambda) = \begin{vmatrix} a_{ij} - \lambda\delta_{ij} & g_i^\alpha \\ g_j^\alpha & 0 \end{vmatrix}$$
$$= (-1)^n A(\lambda - \lambda_1)(\lambda - \lambda_2) \cdots (\lambda - \lambda_{n-m}) \tag{46}$$

where $A > 0$. The roots of this $(n - m)$th degree equation are all real because of the symmetry of the determinant. Let them be written in algebraic order

$$\lambda_1 \leqq \lambda_2 \leqq \cdots \leqq \lambda_{n-m}.$$

Then if the form is to be positive definite under the above constraint, the smallest root, λ_1, easily shown to be equal to the absolute minimum of Q under constraint, must be positive, and conversely. *Hence, it is necessary and sufficient in order for a form to be positive definite that all roots of the above bordered determinant equation be positive.*[16]

Recalling that the roots are all real and applying Descartes' rule of signs, it can be shown as in the previous section that the following bordered principal minors must all be of sign $(-1)^m$.

$$0 < (-1)^m B^r = (-1)^m \begin{vmatrix} a_{ij} & g_i{}^\beta \\ g_j{}^\alpha & 0 \end{vmatrix}. \qquad \begin{aligned} (i, j &= 1, \cdots, r) \\ (\alpha, \beta &= 1, \cdots, m) \\ m + 1 &\leqq r \leqq n \end{aligned} \qquad (47)$$

These $(n - m)$ conditions are both necessary and sufficient.

If the form is to be negative definite under constraint, the determinants B^r must alternate in sign, the first one being of sign $(-1)^{m+1}$, the second of opposite sign, etc., i.e.,

$$(-1)^r B^r > 0, \qquad m + 1 \leqq r \leqq n. \qquad (48)$$

The inverse of the bordered matrix

It is of considerable importance for many economic problems to know what is implied with respect to the inverse or reciprocal of our matrix. The latter can be written in matrix notation

$$R = \begin{bmatrix} a_{11} & \cdots & a_{1n} & g_1{}^1 & \cdots & g_1{}^m \\ \cdot & & \cdot & \cdot & & \cdot \\ \cdot & & \cdot & \cdot & & \cdot \\ \cdot & & \cdot & \cdot & & \cdot \\ a_{n1} & \cdots & a_{nn} & g_n{}^1 & \cdots & g_n{}^m \\ g_1{}^1 & \cdots & g_n{}^1 & 0 & \cdots & 0 \\ \cdot & & \cdot & \cdot & & \cdot \\ \cdot & & \cdot & \cdot & & \cdot \\ g_1{}^m & \cdots & g_n{}^m & 0 & \cdots & 0 \end{bmatrix} = \left[\begin{array}{c|c} a & g \\ \hline g' & 0 \end{array} \right] \qquad (49)$$

The matrix has been partitioned into four submatrices; one is n by n, another m by n, still another n by m, and the last m by m. The matrix is symmetrical, i.e.,

$$R = R'. \qquad (50)$$

[16] The form is *negative definite* if, and only if, all are negative. If the roots differ in sign, it is *indefinite*. If one or more are zero, but the rest are of the same sign, it is *semi-definite*.

The inverse or reciprocal matrix is defined by

$$RR^{-1} = I = \text{identity matrix.}$$

It can be written

$$\left[\begin{array}{c|c} a & g \\ \hline g' & 0 \end{array}\right]\left[\begin{array}{c|c} \hat{a} & \hat{g} \\ \hline \hat{g}' & q \end{array}\right] = I. \tag{51}$$

Performing the operation of matrix multiplication, we find

$$\left[\begin{array}{c|c} a\hat{a} + g\hat{g}' & a\hat{g} + gq \\ \hline g'\hat{a} + 0 & g'\hat{g} + 0 \end{array}\right] = \left[\begin{array}{c|c} I & 0 \\ \hline 0 & I \end{array}\right] = I. \tag{52}$$

This implies the following four matrix identities:

$$\begin{aligned} a\hat{a} + g\hat{g}' &= I, \\ a\hat{g} + gq &= 0, \\ g'\hat{a} &= 0, \\ g'\hat{g} &= I. \end{aligned} \tag{53}$$

It can be shown that $\hat{a}$ is the matrix of a positive semi-definite form provided Q is positive definite under constraint. It is only of rank $(n - m)$; i.e., all determinants of higher order than $(n - m)$ vanish.

MATHEMATICAL APPENDIX B

THE THEORY OF DIFFERENCE AND OTHER FUNCTIONAL EQUATIONS

1. IN THE FIRST mathematical appendix I have included a very brief summary of such theorems as play an important role in economic analysis. However, it seems desirable to give a fuller treatment of difference equations and other functional equations. First, although in many ways the theory of simple difference equations is more elementary than that of differential equations, it is not customarily taught in mathematics courses, and no convenient expositions of the subject from the standpoint of the economist are to be found.[1] Second, just as differential equations are of cardinal interest to the physicist, so difference equations are of the greatest importance to the dynamic economist, and hence their exposition deserves a prominent place.

A SINGLE EQUATION

2. A difference equation can be written as an implicit relation of the following form

$$f[y(t + n), y(t + n - 1), \cdots, y(t), t] = 0. \tag{1}$$

This will be said to be of the nth order because it involves the variable y at n different (equally spaced!) periods of time. It may be noted that the fact that the y values are defined for t values differing by an integer does not really imply any restriction; for if the *equally spaced* values differ by any quantity, we may redefine our time variable so as to make this difference equal to unity. Although the values of t differ by an integer, it is not necessary that t take on only integral values. However, for purposes of eco-

---

[1] The economist may consult with profit G. Boole, *Treatise on the Calculus of Finite Differences* (London, 1880); L. M. Milne-Thomson, *The Calculus of Finite Differences* (London, 1933); P. M. Batchelder, *An Introduction to Linear Difference Equations* (Cambridge, Massachusetts, 1927); N. E. Nörlund, *Vorlesungen über Differenzenrechnung* (Berlin, 1924) for a more advanced treatment and bibliography.

nomics it is usually only necessary to consider the values of y for integral values of time. By breaking up our time into small enough units we can keep the error involved in this procedure down to any requisite level. As we shall see, this greatly simplifies the mathematical theory and makes it resemble very closely the theory of differential equations.

Equation (1) is an identity in t. The reader will see from this that it may be written in very many ways, e.g., as a single relation not between $[y(t + n), \cdots, y(t)]$, but as a single relation between $[y(t), \cdots, y(t - n)]$, etc. However, because equation (1) contains as its last factor the explicit term t, rewriting our difference equation in the manner suggested will involve a slight modification of the form of the f function. Non-historical systems, which are of the greatest interest in dynamic economics, do *not* involve time explicitly and therefore omit the last t in equation (1).

3. Difference equations receive their name because they involve the value of a variable at different points of time. As written in equation (1), however, there is no direct use made of the notion of finite differences $\Delta^n y$, defined in books [2] on interpolation as follows:

$$\Delta y(t) = y(t + 1) - y(t),$$
$$\Delta^2 y(t) = \Delta y(t + 1) - \Delta y(t) = \{y(t + 2) - y(t + 1)\}$$
$$- \{y(t + 1) - y(t)\}$$
$$= y(t + 2) - 2y(t + 1) + y(t),$$

$$\vdots \tag{2}$$

$$\Delta^n y(t) = \Delta^{n-1} y(t + 1) - \Delta^{n-1} y(t)$$
$$= \sum_0^n \frac{n!}{(n - i)!i!} (-1)^i y(t + n - i)$$
$$\Delta^0 y(t) = y(t).$$

It will be intuitively clear that a knowledge of n adjacent values of y will permit us to calculate the value of y and of its first $(n - 1)$ differences. (See equation 6 below.) Therefore, by substitution into equation (1) we can always write it in the following form:

$$F[\Delta^n y(t), \Delta^{n-1} y(t), \cdots, \Delta y(t), y(t), t] = 0, \tag{3}$$

[2] See E. T. Whittaker and G. Robinson, *The Calculus of Observations* (3rd ed., London: Blackie, 1940), chaps. i–iv.

where F is related to f as follows

$$F[\Delta^n y, \cdots, \Delta y, y, t] = f[y + n\Delta y$$
$$+ \frac{n(n-1)}{2} \Delta^2 y + \cdots + \Delta^n y, \cdots, y + \Delta y, y, t]. \quad (4)$$

Not only can every difference equation like (1) be written as (3), but also conversely, because of the relations given in (2), every equation of form (3) can be written as form (1). Thus, the two forms are completely equivalent, and we can choose between them on the basis of convenience. Actually, the form of equation (1) is most frequently encountered in the literature, although later it will be shown how either may be handled.

4. Their relationship to each other may be further revealed if we examine briefly the notion of an operator. Thus, Δ may be thought of as a difference operator defined by the first equation of (2). In a similar way we may define the differential operator $D(=d/dt)$ by the relation

$$Dy(t) = y'(t), \qquad D^2 y(t) = Dy'(t) = y''(t), \quad \text{etc.}$$

In the last century the English mathematician Boole, following up the earlier fruitful suggestion of Leibnitz, employed the shifting operator E defined as follows

$$Ey(t) = y(t+1), \qquad E^2 y(t) = y(t+2), \quad \text{etc.}$$

The success of the operator method stems from the recognition that these may be treated *as if* they were algebraic quantities. Thus, leaving out the y function completely, we may write out the operator identity

$$E = 1 + \Delta. \quad (5)$$

Treating these as algebraical expressions subject to the usual binomial theorem we derive immediately the relations

$$E^n = (1 + \Delta)^n = 1 + n\Delta + \frac{n(n-1)}{2} \Delta^2 + \cdots$$
$$+ \frac{n!}{(n-i)!\,i!} \Delta^i + \cdots,$$
$$\Delta^n = (E - 1)^n = E^n - nE^{n-1} + \frac{n(n-1)}{2} E^{n-2} + \cdots$$
$$+ (-1)^i \frac{n!}{(n-i)!\,i!} E^{n-i} + \cdots. \quad (6)$$

Note the agreement of the second of these with equation (2), and the use of the first of these in connection with equation (4).

Exercises:

1. The algebraic deviation of the price of hogs from the equilibrium value is in any year $\frac{3}{4}$ the deviation of the previous year, but of opposite sign. Set up a difference equation for the price of hogs. Intuitively is the process stable or unstable? (Hint: Use as your variable the deviation of price from the equilibrium value.) Write out the first few terms of the sequence.

2. Form a difference table of the numbers 2, 4, 8, 16, 32. How many difference columns can you fill in with the given numbers? What is the general rule relating the number of columns of the difference table which can be derived from a given set of numbers? Note the triangular form.

3. Write the difference equation of the first exercise in the form of equation (3) rather than (1).

4. Write the difference equation $y(t + 2) - \alpha(1 + \beta)y(t + 1) + \alpha\beta y(t) = 0$ in terms of the E notation and also in terms of the Δ notation.

5. What is the meaning of E^{-1}?

6. The receding difference operator ∇ is defined by $\nabla y(t) = y(t) - y(t - 1)$. Give its relationship to E^{-1}, corresponding to the relations of equation (5).

7. Write out the usual Taylor's expansion for $y(t + 1)$ in terms of $y(t)$ using the D notation. Verify the relation $e^D = E$. (Hint: Use the series expansion $e^x = 1 + x/1! + x^2/2! + \cdots$.) What would seem to be meant by sine D? by $1/(1 - \Delta)$?

8. What is the first difference of t^2? the second and third differences? What is the third difference of any second degree polynomial? What is the nth difference of any nth degree polynomial? the $(n + 1)$th difference of an nth degree polynomial?

9. Write out the difference equation satisfied by the numbers in exercise 2.

10. Let us define ascending factorial polynomials as follows: $x^{(n)} = x(x - 1) \cdots (x - n + 1)$. Verify that $\Delta x^{(n)} = n x^{(n-1)}$. Of what does this remind you?

Systems of Equations

5. Up until now we have been concerned only with a single variable. In most applications to an economic system many variables are involved. Hence, we must introduce the notion of a system of difference equations in m variables $(y_1, \cdots, y_m)$. These consist of a set of difference equations in the variables in question. Just as a static system can only hope to be determinate if it consists of as many equations as unknowns, a dynamic system must contain as many independent, consistent equations as there are unknowns. Thus, our system takes the form

$$f^1[y_1(t + n), y_2(t + n), \cdots, y_m(t + n); \cdots;$$
$$y_1(t), y_2(t), \cdots, y_m(t); t] = 0,$$

$$\vdots \tag{7}$$

$$f^m[y_1(t + n), y_2(t + n), \cdots, y_m(t + n); \cdots;$$
$$y_1(t), y_2(t), \cdots, y_m(t); t] = 0,$$

As before, if desired this can be written in finite difference form by making use of the relationships between Δ and E. It is not necessary that each of the equations in the above set should involve the same number of lags; it is often convenient as a matter of notation to write each as if it contained the same number of lags as the greatest number, n, which occurs in any of the equations. From the discussion at the end of section 2 of this appendix it will be clear that we can shift our time reference point so that some $y_i(t + n)$ appears in each equation.

6. A difference equation system such as is defined in equation (7) can be thought of as an identity which holds for each value of t. It is equivalent then to an infinite number of implicit relations. This does not lead to overdeterminateness because each new time period defines as many new variables as there are equations. In fact, if we confine t to a finite number of consecutive values, we shall always find that we have less equations than we have unknowns. Thus, the system is formally indeterminate unless we adjoin certain so-called "initial conditions" or "boundary conditions."

This may be illustrated by a sum of money growing at six per cent interest per annum. Its behavior over time follows a simple difference equation, but the process is completely unambiguous only if we specify how much money there was to begin with; or alternatively, if we specify to what value the principal will have grown by any given date.

In the above example of a first order difference equation involving a single variable only one initial condition can be arbitrarily specified. Therefore, one is said to be the order of the system. If we had a system consisting of two difference equations each of the third order (i.e., each involves three lags), then the number of initial values which can be arbitrarily prescribed would be seen to be two times three. In general, where there are m difference equations in m variables, and each involves n lags, the number of arbitrarily assignable initial conditions will be seen to be m times n, and this number will be termed the maximum order of the system.[3]

7. Adding initial conditions equal to the order of the system in effect supplies us with the missing equations discussed in the pre-

---

[3] In the interests of expositional convenience and uniformity I have departed from the usual mathematical custom of saying that in this case the order of the system is *at most* n times m. By adopting the convention described at the end of section 5 I have insured that the order will be exactly n times m.

vious section so that our unknowns no longer exceed the number of our relations. Actually, it is well known that a system of implicit equations equal to a specified number of variables may not determine a unique solution because of inconsistency, dependence, multiplicity of roots, etc. However, in any relevant, empirical economic system it is the task of the economist and not of the mathematician to specify an adequate number of relations to make the system determinate. Moreover, in causal dynamic systems it is natural to think of causation as taking place unilaterally in time, from past to present rather than from future to present. Therefore, it is convenient to concentrate upon the case where the specified boundary conditions are truly *initial* conditions sufficient to start the system off, after which it determines its own behavior at each step. This means that the implicit equations of (7) can be solved explicitly for values of $y_i(t + n)$ as single-valued functions of "previous" y's.

$$y_i(t + n) = J^i[y_1(t + n - 1), \cdots, y_m(t + n - 1); \cdots;$$
$$y_1(t), \cdots, y_m(t); t]. \qquad (i = 1, \cdots, m) \quad (8)$$

Under these conditions, if we specify any initial conditions of the form

$$\begin{bmatrix} y_1(0) & y_2(0) & \cdots & y_m(0) \\ \cdot & \cdot & \cdots & \cdot \\ \cdot & \cdot & \cdots & \cdot \\ \cdot & \cdot & \cdots & \cdot \\ y_1(n - 1) & y_2(n - 1) & \cdots & y_m(n - 1) \end{bmatrix}, \quad (9)$$

then we can clearly determine from equations (8) the quantities $[y_1(n), \cdots, y_m(n)]$. Adding these to the previously prescribed variables, we are in a position to determine the y's at the next instant of time, and so forth *ad infinitum*. In other words, by the use of the familiar principle of mathematical induction we can state an important *existence* and *uniqueness* theorem: *a system of difference equations of the type indicated in (8), subject to prescribed initial conditions as given in (9), possesses a solution for all positive values of t. The solution is unique.*

This theorem is valuable, not because it tells us how to find a convenient solution, but because it assures us that once we have found a solution, and verified it by substitution in the difference equation and initial conditions, then we can rest assured that it is the only possible solution.

8. In this section it will be shown that any system of order S, whatever be the values of m and n, can be replaced by a system of S first order difference equations in S variables. This reduction to what may be called *normal* form is always possible by means of redefining $S = nm$ new variables, $Y_{11}, \cdots, Y_{nm}$, as follows:

$$
\begin{aligned}
Y_{1i} &= y_i \\
Y_{2i} &= Ey_i \\
&\ \cdot \\
&\ \cdot \\
Y_{ni} &= E^{n-1}y_i.
\end{aligned}
\qquad (i = 1, \cdots, m) \qquad (10)
$$

In terms of the new variables the reader can show that the system defined by (8) becomes

$$
\begin{aligned}
EY_{1i} &= Y_{2i} \\
EY_{2i} &= Y_{3i} \\
&\ \cdot \\
&\ \cdot \\
&\ \cdot \\
EY_{n-1,i} &= Y_{ni} \\
EY_{ni} &= J^i.
\end{aligned}
\qquad (i = 1, \cdots, m) \qquad (11)
$$

Our initial conditions are written simply as

$$
[Y_{ji}(0)] = [Y_i(j - 1)]. \qquad (12)
$$

By way of illustration let us consider a system consisting of one second order equation in one variable.

$$
y(t + 2) + a_1 y(t + 1) + a_2 y(t) = \sin t; \ y(0) = b_0, \ y(1) = b_1. \quad (13)
$$

The order of this system is clearly two. Defining new variables as follows

$$
\begin{aligned}
Y_1(t) &= y(t), \\
Y_2(t) &= Ey(t),
\end{aligned}
\qquad (14)
$$

we can write the above system in the normal form

$$
\begin{aligned}
EY_2(t) &= -a_1 Y_2(t) - a_2 Y_1(t) + \sin t, \\
EY_1(t) &= Y_2(t), \\
Y_1(0) &= b_0, \\
Y_2(0) &= b_1.
\end{aligned}
\qquad (15)
$$

The reader should work out several examples, such as that of exercise 4, section 4 above.

It is to be noted that equations (7) can by a similar definition of variables be written as S first order *implicit* equations. Indeed, an indeterminate system, involving more unknowns than equations, can always be converted into an (equally indeterminate) first order system.

9. We have seen that a single high order equation can be transformed into a number of first order equations. Is the reverse possible? Can a first order system (and, therefore, any system) be transformed into a single equation, whose maximum order is equal to the maximum order of the normal system? Usually the answer is yes, although the reduction is easier to indicate than actually to perform, and in singular cases, where certain conditions on the partial derivatives of the f's fail, the reduction may be impossible. Also, a well-determined explicit system may *after reduction* be expressible only as an ambiguous implicit high order relation in one variable. Thus, the well-determined system

$$Ey_2 = y_1{}^2; \qquad Ey_1 = y_2 + y_1 \qquad (16)$$

can be reduced to the well-determined second order equation in y_1

$$E^2y_1 - Ey_1 = y_1{}^2, \qquad (17)$$

but in y_2 we get only the *ambiguous* implicit equation

$$(E^2y_2 - Ey_2 - y_2{}^2)^2 = 4y_2{}^2Ey_2. \qquad (18)$$

Let us suppose that we have a normal system of order S,

$$y_i(t + 1) = J_i[y_1(t), \cdots, y_s(t), t], \qquad (i = 1, \cdots, s) \quad (19)$$

or, in abbreviated notation,

$$EY = J(Y, t).$$

It will necessarily involve $2S$ variables, namely the y's at two instants of time. Given S equations in $2S$ variables, it is not possible to eliminate all but one of the y's and be left with a difference equation involving only that y. If we write down the identities

$$E^2Y = J(EY, t + 1)$$
$$E^3Y = J(E^2Y, t + 2)$$
$$\cdot$$
$$\cdot \qquad\qquad\qquad\qquad\qquad\qquad (20)$$
$$\cdot$$
$$E^sY = J(E^{s-1}Y, t + S - 1),$$

we shall have introduced as many new variables as we have equations. But not all of these need be eliminated; only those involving all variables except the one in question. All together we have S^2 equations in $S^2 + S$ variables, and we seek to eliminate $(S - 1)(S + 1)$ variables. Our number of equations exceeds this by one, so we can hope to perform the elimination, the remaining equation being the desired S order equation in a single variable.[4]

10. Everything said about difference equations applies with very little modification to differential equations. The reader should write out a single differential equation corresponding to the single difference equation (1) by writing out the latter using the operator E, and then substituting for E the operator D. Similarly, he should write out the system of equations (7) in terms of E, and then derive a system of differential equations by the substitution of D for E. The same applies to initial conditions and to the notion of the *order* of a system. The argument showing how a system of equations can always be reduced to first order normal form also applies directly to differential equations. He may check his reasoning by referring to the first chapter of the Moulton book just cited.

Exercises:

1. The national income of each of two countries equals domestic investment plus domestic consumers' goods production plus exports. The consumption and imports of each country are respectively determinate functions of income in that country in the previous period. Set up the *system* of difference equations describing the behavior of each national income over time. Specialize these by assuming constant marginal propensities to consume and import.

2. Use the 45° line graphical method of chapter x to analyze whether or not the equation, $Y_{t+1}^2 + Y_t^2 = 9$, defines a unique causal system. If necessary, modify the definition of the equation slightly so as to remove all ambiguity. Can the initial value, Y_0, be assigned *completely* at pleasure? (Hint: try a few arithmetical examples.)

3. The system, $Ey(t) = z(t)$; $Ez(t) = .5\,y(t) + 2\,z(t)$, was converted to normal form from a single equation in y. What was the exact form of that equation, and what definitions were used in converting it to normal form?

4. Given the system, $Ey_1 = y_2$; $Ey_2 = y_1$, derive a second order equation in each of the variables alone.

[4] The reader may consult F. R. Moulton, *Differential Equations* (New York, 1930), pp. 6–9, for a more complete discussion of this problem taken with special reference to differential equations. For linear equations this is worked out in some detail in P. A. Samuelson, "A Method of Determining Explicitly the Coefficients of the Characteristic Equation," *The Annals of Mathematical Statistics*, XIII (1942), 424–429.

5. A body falling in the earth's gravitational field satisfies the equation, $d^2x/dt^2 = -g$. Convert into normal form.

6. Write out a system of difference equations in Δ form. Define the concepts of order, normal form, etc.

11. If only numerical answers are desired, one may simply use the difference equation at each instant of time to calculate successively the new values of the variables, and so forth for as long a time interval as is desired. However, this may be tedious in practice, and inevitably there must be rounding off at each stage so that the accuracy of the solution deteriorates with its length. (For a stable system if the errors of rounding off remain within a certain limit, the errors of the solution will remain bounded.)

The method of actual numerical examples has had considerable use in economics, and is valuable from the standpoint of providing illustrations.[5] Still one can never be sure that another arithmetical example might not contradict the principles inferred from this one, so that the method is of limited usefulness even for the purpose of providing qualitative information concerning solutions. After all, life is not long enough for us to complete even one sequence, nor to try all possible initial conditions, nor to vary the form of the structural relations.

Unfortunately, if we simply consider difference equations in all generality, there is no simple analytical way to write out explicit solutions. The same is true of differential equations. The beginning student may be taught a variety of *ad hoc* tricks which may work on particular equations, but the advanced student must rest content with his existence theorem which tells him that there exists a unique solution; often the proof of the existence theorem tells him how he may (painfully) approximate to that solution.

In both of these lines much more complete results may be achieved if we restrict ourselves to linear systems. That this may be a serious limitation, especially for business cycle purposes, is shown in chapter xi. However, in chapter x it is shown how the assumption of linearity is not seriously limiting if we are primarily interested in stability, especially in the small.

In much of what follows, therefore, we shall confine our attention to systems which have two properties. First, they are to be linear. There is the added advantage that most mathematical

[5] E. Lundberg, *Studies in the Theory of Economic Expansion* (London, 1937).

expositions are concerned with these.   Second, they are not to involve time explicitly.   Most economic systems of interest are causal rather than historical in nature and satisfy this requirement, thereby simplifying our task and enhancing mathematical tractibility.

In fact, if we insist that a system be timeless and at the same time linear, we are left with the exceedingly simple case of *constant coefficients*, whose theory is perfectly complete and elementary. We shall see that exactly the same thing is true of differential equations so that one who has mastered either of these branches has little difficulty with the other.   From a more fundamental point of view, each of these is simply the exemplification of a more general theory of linear operational equations.

12.   There is, however, one *non-linear* case where a more or less complete solution can always be indicated.   That is the case of the first order equation of the form

$$y_{t+1} = f(y_t). \tag{21}$$

The 45° diagram of chapter x pictures the various types of equilibrium solutions, $y_t = a$, with the property, $a - f(a) = 0$.   It is also clear from that diagram that a motion which remains bounded need not approach an equilibrium position, but may approach a periodic motion (one of the boxes of the cobweb theorem).   Some of these boxes are stable and some are unstable.   We may test the stability of a motion which repeats itself every S periods by the method which Professor Leontief [6] has suggested.   Let us define

$$\begin{aligned} f_1(x) &= f(x) \\ f_2(x) &= f[f(x)] \\ &\quad\cdot \\ &\quad\cdot \\ &\quad\cdot \\ f_s(x) &= f[f_{s-1}(x)] = f\left[f\{f_{s-2}(x)\}\right] \text{ etc.} \end{aligned} \tag{22}$$

It is then true that the solution of equation (21) at any time t, for given initial condition, y_0, is given by

$$y(t) = f_t(y_0). \tag{23}$$

[6] W. Leontief, "Verzögerte Angebotsanpassung und Partielles Gleichgewicht," *Zeitschrift für Nationalökonomie*, Band V (1934).

However, this is more an indication of a solution than a solution itself since the f's in question may be very complicated functions.

Suppose that $(a_1, a_2, \cdots, a_s)$ represents a periodic solution of the original equation. This will be true if, and only if, the new difference equation

$$y_{i+1} = f_s(y_i) \tag{24}$$

is such that

$$f_s(a_i) = a_i. \qquad (i = 1, \cdots, s) \tag{25}$$

The motion will be stable if, and only if, the above equilibrium points of the new single difference equations are stable. This can be tested by means of the methods developed in chapter x.

Exercise:

Show that the stability of the periodic motion depends upon

$$|f'(a_1)f'(a_2) \cdots f'(a_s)| \gtreqless 1.$$

[Hint: What is $f_s'(a_i)$ equal to?]

13. The case of the *first order differential equation* which does not involve time explicitly,

$$dy/dt = f(y), \tag{26}$$

is one which admits of an immediate solution by quadrature, as indicated in chapter x. Its richness of solution is limited, every motion being monotonic. Hence, if bounded, the motion must approach an equilibrium point. There may, of course, be a number of equilibrium points alternately stable and unstable.

Exercises:

1. Let $f(x) = x^i$. What is the general expression for $f_k(x)$?
2. Show that every equilibrium value of $f(x)$ is an equilibrium value of $f_2(x)$. Is the converse true? What about the stability of the common equilibrium points, will they agree?

LINEAR SYSTEMS

14. A linear system is one which involves the dependent variables in expressions of the first degree, i.e., without higher powers, cross-products, nonelementary functions, etc. For the purpose of this section it is not necessary that time be excluded or that it enter the problem linearly. We may write our linear system in the form

$$L[y(t)] = f(t), \tag{27}$$

where L stands for any general operation upon a whole system of variables, and f represents a known function or set of functions. For the discussion of this section it is not even necessary that L represent difference equations rather than differential equations. Rather, it may represent an implicit functional of y over the whole t interval, and in the notation of chapter ix, page 261, it could be written as

$$L[y(t)] = F[y(\tau); t].$$

The fundamental linear property which L must satisfy is as follows:

$$L(y_1 + y_2) = L(y_1) + L(y_2), \tag{28}$$

from which follows immediately the general relation,

$$L(a_1y_1 + a_2y_2 + \cdots + a_ny_n)$$
$$= a_1L(y_1) + a_2L(y_2) + \cdots + a_nL(y_n). \tag{29}$$

From this general definition of a linear system there follow immediately two important general theorems.

Superposition theorem: *The solution of* (27) *when f is made up of the sum of two different f's is equal to the sum of the solutions appropriate to each.*   Mathematically, this may be written in slightly more general form:

$$L(y_i) = f_i \qquad \text{implies} \qquad L(\textstyle\sum a_iy_i) = \sum a_if_i. \tag{30}$$

The proof follows immediately from (29).

This means that the solution of a system with many forces acting on it is equal to the sum of the separate effects of each. Even where this is not strictly true, the economic situation may approximate to this condition.

For many linear systems it may be possible to give the solution for a fundamental set of f's into which any f can be decomposed. If this is the case, our problem is immediately solvable.

Our second theorem states: *The difference between any two solutions of* (27) *must satisfy the reduced (or homogeneous) equation*

$$L(y) = 0. \tag{31}$$

This follows immediately if we substitute each of the solutions in (27), and then subtract one expression from the other.   The right-hand function will cancel out, and according to (29) we may regroup the terms on the left-hand side to achieve the desired result.

A most important corollary of this theorem is derived simply by rearranging terms. *The most general solution (i.e., any solution) of (27) may be written as the sum of some one particular solution and the general solution of the reduced equation (31).*

This permits us to concentrate upon the more easily manageable reduced equation in order to determine the uniqueness, multiplicity, boundary conditions, etc., of the solutions. It is often possible by ingenuity, good luck, or intuition to arrive at a particular solution of the unreduced case, and the present corollary tells us how to transform it into the general solution, if only we can find the general solution of the reduced case.

Exercises:

1. Except that there are no boundary conditions, show that the above remarks apply to a single linear algebraic equation of the form, $ax = b$. Show that when the reduced equation, $ax = 0$, has but a single solution, the full equation has but a single solution. Can the converse be stated? Can you state that the uniqueness of either equation guarantees the uniqueness of the other? (Hint: Distinguish three possible cases, neither a nor b equal to zero, both equal to zero, only one equal to zero.)

2. Consider two (or more) linear algebraic equations. Show that uniqueness of either the reduced or unreduced equations implies uniqueness of the other. Show, however, that the reduced equation can have many solutions, when the unreduced has none. Enumerate all the possibilities, and with the aid of a textbook on algebra show how one can recognize each case. (Hint: The terminology of matrices and determinants will be found useful.)

3. Show that the following integral, and mixed difference-differential equations are respectively linear:

$$y(t) + \int_{-\infty}^{t} k(t - a)y(a)da = f(t),$$

$$y'(t) + ay(t - 1) = f(t).$$

Do they involve time *explicitly?*

15. In view of the importance of the reduced or homogeneous system of the form

$$L(y) = 0, \tag{32}$$

we shall devote a number of sections to it. Most of our analysis will apply to *systems* of equations, but occasionally it will be desirable to confine attention to a single high order equation in one variable. Where difference equations are concerned, this may be written in the form

$$a_0(t)y(t + n) + a_1(t)y(t + n - 1) + \cdots + a_n(t)y(t) = 0. \quad (33)$$

Much of the mathematical theory of difference equations is concerned with the case where the a's are simple polynomials or analytic functions, just as much of the classical theory of ordinary differential equations is concerned with the case

$$a_0(t)y^n(t) + a_1(t)y^{n-1}(t) + \cdots + a_n(t)y(t) = 0, \quad (34)$$

where the a's are of the same simple type.

However, if we insist that the economic system be nonhistorical, i.e., independent of calendar time, and if we also insist that it be linear, then the a's must be constants, and we have the case of constant coefficients.

16. Whether or not time enters explicitly, it is easy to derive from equation (29) the theorem: *A linear combination of a number of solutions of the reduced equation (32) is itself a solution;* i.e.,

$$L(c_1y_1 + c_2y_2 + \cdots + c_sy_s) = 0 \quad \text{if} \quad L(y_i) = 0. \quad (35)$$

Since the difference between two solutions is a linear combination, we have the immediate corollary:

$$L(0) = 0. \quad (36)$$

If the y stands for a whole set of variables, the zero must of course stand for a whole set of variables equal to zero.

Usually, in the analysis of differential equations and difference equations as well, the mathematician looks for a *basic set* of special solutions in terms of which any solution can be written by linear combination.   This linear combination, written with undetermined coefficients, is called the *general solution* of the reduced system.

If there is an existence theorem which guarantees a unique solution of the reduced system satisfying certain initial conditions, we should of course expect the number of undetermined constants in the general solution to be equal to the number of arbitrarily assignable, initial or boundary conditions, or equal to the order of the system, S.

The reader should note that not every set of S distinct special solutions of the reduced system will form the *basis* for a general solution.   Thus, if one or more of the given S solutions can be written identically in t as a linear combination of the others, the set of particular solutions is said to be *linearly dependent* and cannot form a basis for the general solution. For a linear combination of all S solutions can in this case be regarded as a linear combination of less than S linearly independent solutions; the number of constants in such an expression is necessarily less than S, and hence we cannot hope to satisfy S arbitrary initial conditions.

17. However, the reverse is not necessarily true. If we find S solutions which are linearly independent (i.e., which are not linearly dependent), it does not follow from our existence theorem that they form a basis for the general solution. Indeed, there may exist no general solution in the sense in which we have been using the word. This is perhaps inadequately emphasized in the mathematical texts because of their preoccupation with the special case of differential equations where a stronger theorem can be enunciated. Thus,

$$D^2 y(t) = 0 \tag{37}$$

has linearly independent solutions $(1, t)$ which form a basis for a general solution, in terms of which any solution can be written. But

$$E^2 y(t) = 0 \tag{38}$$

has two linearly independent solutions,

$$
\begin{aligned}
y_1(t) &= 1, & t &= 0; & y_2(t) &= 1, & t &= 1, \\
y_1(t) &= 0, & t &\geq 0; & y_2(t) &= 0, & t &\geq 1,
\end{aligned}
\tag{39}
$$

which do not provide such a basis. For the function

$$
\begin{aligned}
y_3(t) &= 1, & t &= 2, \\
y_3(t) &= 0, & t &\geq 2,
\end{aligned}
\tag{40}
$$

is a solution of (38) for appropriate initial conditions, and yet it cannot be written as a linear combination of the two linearly independent solutions.[7]

---

[7] It may be objected that $y_3(t)$ does not satisfy the difference equation (33) for all values of t, particularly for t equal to zero. However, a solution is to be thought of as satisfying a difference equation if for given *arbitrary* initial conditions it is in accord with the prescribed law. To help clear up the present paradox, it should be pointed out that solutions which are linearly independent on one interval of t may be linearly dependent on another interval. It is also to be pointed out that the example cited is one in which the solution of the difference equation is unique to the right of the initial conditions but not to the left. It is also one in which the irreversibility in time disappears if the difference equation is replaced by an "equivalent" one of lower order.

The absence of a general solution does not mean that we cannot find the solution, for given initial conditions. Our existence theorem guarantees us that we can find such a solution. Actually, such a solution can be written as a linear combination of basic solutions. However, the above example shows us that the linearly independent basic solutions may have to be different sets for every initial point; there need not exist a set of basic solutions which will serve uniformly for all initial times.

Linear Operator Equations with Constant Coefficients

18. I turn now to the case of difference or differential equations with constant coefficients. Since it will be shown later that the solution for equations of any order can be written in terms of solutions of the first order case, I shall consider this simplest of all cases. In the first order case our difference equation becomes

$$\begin{aligned} (E - q)y(t) &= f(t), \\ y(t_0) &= b, \end{aligned} \tag{41}$$

and the corresponding differential equation becomes

$$\begin{aligned} (D - q)y(t) &= f(t), \\ y(t_0) &= b. \end{aligned} \tag{42}$$

Each of these may be considered as special exemplifications of a general first order equation in a simple operator, h,

$$\begin{aligned} (h - q)y(t) &= f(t), \\ y(t_0) &= b. \end{aligned} \tag{43}$$

For h to be an *admissible* operator it is only necessary that there be an existence theorem guaranteeing that the above equation has a unique solution for the arbitrarily specified initial condition. How this existence theorem is established need not concern us at this point; we have seen how it can be done for difference equations, and the reader may refer to any work on differential equations for the corresponding proof. In addition to E and D, examples of h are Δ, tD, $E + 5$, etc. On the other hand, such an operator as D^2 would not be an admissible h, because the system corresponding to (43) would not have a unique solution. This is because two initial conditions are necessary, rather than one, to satisfy a second order differential equation.

We may suppose the solution of the above system to be written as a linear functional of f, with q and b as parameters, or as $F(t, q, b; f)_h$, where F has the fundamental linear property

$$F(t, q, c_1b_1 + \cdots + c_sb_s; c_1f_1 + \cdots + c_sf_s)_h$$
$$= c_1F(f, q, b_1; f_1)_h + \cdots + c_sF(t, q, b_s; f_s)_h. \quad (44)$$

From this fact it is easy to verify that h is a linear operator with the properties

$$h(c_1y_1 + c_2y_2) = c_1hy_1 + c_2hy_2,$$
$$h^2y = h(hy),$$
$$\cdot$$
$$\cdot$$
$$\cdot \quad (45)$$
$$h^ny = hh^{n-1}y,$$
$$h^0y = 1y,$$
$$h0 = 0,$$
$$P(h)Q(h)y = Q(h)P(h)y,$$

where P and Q are polynomials.

19. So far we have not defined h raised to a negative power. It would be natural to define

$$y = h^{-1}f(t)$$

as the solution of

$$hy = f(t).$$

However, it is clear from our existence theorem that this cannot have an unambiguous meaning unless we specify some initial condition. This corresponds to the familiar indeterminacy of the indefinite integral of a function, $D^{-1}f$. We need a constant of integration or a definite lower limit of integration before there can be a determinate answer. We shall not have occasion to use negative powers of h even though readers familiar with the Heaviside operational methods will realize the mnemonic advantages to be derived from such a procedure. These advantages are counterbalanced by the aura of mystery which surrounds some of the usual expositions of this method. In general, the methods here outlined will be of "classical type," albeit in somewhat amplified form. It is the present writer's conviction, which need not be sustained here, that a careful examination of the Heaviside-Cauchy operational calculus, of Bromwich-Wagner contour integrals, of Laplace transforms, etc., will show that where these differ from the classical methods the advantages are in favor of the latter. These remarks are intended to apply to ordinary differential equations of finite order with constant coefficients and do not refer to the use of the Laplace transform in connection with partial differential equations, nor in connection with integral equations of *faltung* type, etc.[8]

20. Being first concerned with the reduced equation, where $f(t)$ vanishes, we concentrate upon solutions of the form $F(t, q, b; 0)_h$. Because of the linear properties of h given in (45), this can be written in the special form $bF(t, q, 1; 0)_h$. Hence, peculiar importance attaches to the solution of the reduced first order equation with initial condition equal to unity. Let us determine, therefore, the exact form of the F function for h equal to E and for h equal to D.

Clearly if
$$Ey = qy, \qquad y(t_0) = 1,$$
then
$$y(t_0 + 1) = qy(t_0) = q,$$
$$\vdots \tag{46}$$
$$y(t_0 + t) = qy(t_0 + t - 1) = qqy(t_0 + t - 2) = \cdots = q^t,$$
$$y(t) = q^{t-t_0},$$
or
$$F(t, q, 1; 0)_E = q^{t-t_0}. \qquad (t \geqq t_0)$$

Of course, the final proof of the above relation is to be found in the fact that when substituted into the difference equation, q^{t-t_0} satisfies it and the boundary condition in question. Our existence theorem guarantees that it is the only solution.

We may rewrite the differential equation (42) in the form
$$dy/y = qdt. \tag{47}$$

Integrating each side, taking antilogs and inserting the appropriate constant of integration so as to satisfy the initial condition of unity at t equal to t_0, we easily find the solution to be
$$F(t, q, 1; 0)_D = e^{q(t-t_0)}. \qquad (t \geqq t_0) \tag{48}$$

[8] G. Doetch, *Theorie und Anwendung der Laplace Transformation* (Berlin, 1937).

The reader may verify that the operators Δ and tD have respectively the fundamental solutions

$$F(t, q, 1; 0)_\Delta = (1 + q)^{t-t_0}, \qquad (t \geqq t_0) \qquad (49)$$

and

$$F(t, q, 1; 0)_{tD} = (t/t_0)^q. \qquad (t \geqq t_0) \qquad (50)$$

Thus far, it has been implicitly assumed that q is a real variable. However, no detail of the procedure or proof would be essentially changed if q were assumed to be a complex number of the form $(a + ib)$. It may be argued that no real economic process need be described in terms of complex numbers. This can be readily admitted. However, when we come to equations of higher order, it will be shown that the solution can always be written in terms of purely algebraic combinations of the roots of higher order polynomials. In order that every polynomial have exactly as many roots as its degree, it is necessary to introduce complex numbers. Because these occur in conjugate pairs, it will always be possible to regroup terms at the end and express everything in terms of real numbers. But it is most convenient to work with complex numbers in the intermediate steps.

21. We may now inquire into the stability of this fundamental first order solution. It is clear that the initial condition enters only as a scale factor and cannot affect the problem of stability. Under what conditions will

$$\lim_{t \to \infty} F(t, q, 1; 0)_h = 0? \qquad (51)$$

If we examine each of the four specified F's corresponding to the four distinct operators, E, D, Δ, tD, it is clear that we have the following respective conditions:

E: absolute value of root must be less than one, or $|q| < 1$;

D: real part of q must be negative, or $R(q) < 0$;

Δ: absolute value of $(1 + q)$ must be less than one, or $|1 + q| < 1$;

tD: real part of q must be negative, or $R(q) < 0$.

In the complex plane the first of these is interpreted to mean that q must be inside the unit circle so that its absolute value or modulus will be less than unity. For the differential system the value of q must be in the left half of the complex plane. Later it will be shown that the stability of the reduced equation determines the stability of the system.

22. Having introduced a basic solution of the reduced equation, $F(t, q, 1; 0)_h$, I now introduce a basic special solution of the unreduced equation. By combining these two, the solution to the general first order system (43) can be written. Our special solution of the unreduced equation is that for which the initial condition, b, is zero. In accordance with our above notation, this can be written as $F(t, q, 0; f)_h$. How it is to be found for any given operator need not concern us here; our existence theorem assures us that it exists, and often suggests how it is to be found.

The reader can verify that the following do represent basic special solutions for the respective simple operators.

$$D: \int_0^{t-t_0} e^{q(t-t_0-a)} f(a) da;$$

$$E: \sum_0^{t-t_0-1} q^{t-t_0-1-i} f(i) \tag{52}$$

etc.

Because of our existence theorem, no proof other than verification is necessary.

Consider now the expression

$$y(t) = F(t, q, 0; f)_h + bF(t, q, 1; 0)_h. \tag{53}$$

Substitution shows that it is a solution of the general equation (43). Its initial value is

$$y(t_0) = F(t_0, q, 0; f)_h + bF(t_0, q, 1; 0)_h = 0 + b, \tag{54}$$

satisfying the correct initial condition, and thereby constituting the unique solution.

23. We shall show that the most general system *of any order* has a solution consisting of two parts: a special particular solution of the reduced equation with vanishing initial conditions, and a "general" solution of the reduced equation with assignable constants sufficient to satisfy the prescribed initial conditions.

In fact, once the first order case has been thoroughly analyzed, the general case yields to a *purely algebraic* treatment. In what follows, I shall try to bring to a completion the Heaviside program of "algebrizing" the treatment of simple operators. As far as I know, the mathematical literature, because of its principal preoccupation with special operators, stops short of such a complete program; at some stage the concept of integration or summation is introduced into the discussion. Moreover, the present fashion of thought introduces transcendental notions such as the Laplace transform even in the simplest cases of ordinary differential equations with constant coefficients. It will appear from what follows that the Laplace transform, however useful it may be to one who has grown accustomed to it, is neither necessary for rigor nor necessary for analytical and computational short cuts. In a fundamental sense it is an artifice which "cancels out of the problem," and aesthetically it represents an alien intrusion having no "natural" connection with the problem under discussion. Furthermore, the present treatment may throw light on the connection between so-called "classical" and "operational" methods, showing their complete equivalence and identity. Aside from the lamentable aura of mystery surrounding many discussions of operational methods, the literature abounds with diverse, contradictory claims and counterclaims as to the advantages of the alternative methods.

Despite the facts that simple operators are being discussed and that an algebraic treatment is being used, the present treatment is essentially classical, with one important addition: full use is made of the *specialized algebraic character* of the equations determining solution constants. When so amplified, the classical methods not only arrive at the same results as the operational methods, but actually go through the same intermediate steps. Wherever the two methods diverge, the advantage lies with the classical. For those who must have their Laplace transform, the concept is suitably generalized to any operator in section 29.

24. We may begin by enunciating what is a theorem and not an assumption: *If h is a simple operator such that the system*

$$(h - q)y = f(t), \qquad (t \geqq t_0)$$
$$y(t_0) = b \tag{55}$$

has a unique solution for suitably limited functions f, and for q an arbitrary complex number, then the general nth order equation

$$P_n(h)y = h^n y + a_1 h^{n-1} y + a_2 h^{n-2} y + \cdots + a_{n-1} hy + a_n y = f(t),$$
$$y(t_0) = b_0,$$
$$hy(t)]_{t=t_0} = b_1,$$
$$\cdot$$
$$\cdot$$
$$\cdot$$
$$h^{n-1}y(t)]_{t=t_0} = b_{n-1},[9] \tag{56}$$

has a solution, and the solution is unique.

To prove the first part, I shall specify one solution, leaving its uniqueness to later discussion.   First, let us note the algebraic fact that every nth degree polynomial has exactly n roots if we count each with its appropriate multiplicity.   If q_i denotes the ith root, we may write our polynomial in the form

$$P_n(x) = (x - q_1)(x - q_2) \cdots (x - q_n). \tag{57}$$

Let us define n new polynomials as follows:

$$P_{n-1}(x) = P_n(x)/(x - q_1) = \sum_0^{n-1} a_{i,n-1} x^{n-1-i},$$

$$P_{n-2}(x) = P_{n-1}(x)/(x - q_2) = \sum_0^{n-2} a_{i,n-2} x^{n-2-i},$$

$$\cdot$$
$$\cdot$$
$$\cdot$$

$$P_r(x) = P_{r+1}(x)/(x - q_{n-r}) = \sum_0^{r} a_{i,r} x^{r-i}, \tag{58}$$

$$\cdot$$
$$\cdot$$
$$\cdot$$

$$P_1(x) = P_2(x)/(x - q_{n-1}) = \sum_0^{1} a_{i,1} x^{1-i} = x - q_n,$$

$$P_0(x) = P_1(x)/(x - q_n) = 1.$$

[9] For brevity we shall write $h^k y(t)]_{t=t_0}$ as $h^k y(t_0)$, where there is no possibility of confusion.

Also, let us define some new functions as follows:

$$Z_0(t) = f(t),$$
$$(h - q_1)Z_1(t) = Z_0(t),$$
$$(h - q_2)Z_2(t) = Z_1(t),$$

$$\cdot$$
$$\cdot$$
$$\cdot$$

$$(h - q_n)Z_n(t) = Z_{n-1}(t). \tag{59}$$

By our hypothesis on a first order system, each of these is determinable once we specify initial values $[Z_1(t_0), Z_2(t_0), \cdots, Z_n(t_0)]$. In a moment these will be prescribed.

By virtue of the definitions of $Z_k(t)$ in (59), it will be clear that

$$
\begin{aligned}
f(t) &= Z_0(t) \\
&= (h - q_1)Z_1(t) \\
&= (h - q_1)(h - q_2)Z_2(t) \\
&\qquad \cdots \\
&= (h - q_1) \cdots (h - q_n)Z_n(t).
\end{aligned} \tag{60}
$$

Thus, $Z_n(t)$ is a solution of our equation, and it remains only to make certain that we pick the $Z_i(t_0)$ properly so as to yield the right initial conditions.

It is easily verified that

$$Z_{n-j}(t) = P_j(h)Z_n(t). \tag{61}$$

Evaluating this expression at the initial time we have

$$\sum_0^j a_{i,j}h^{j-i}Z_n(t_0) = \sum_0^j a_{i,j}b_{j-i} = Z_{n-j}(t_0).$$

$$(j = 0, 1, 2, \cdots, n - 1) \quad (62)$$

These are sufficient equations to determine the right-hand terms for a given set of b's.

To recapitulate our construction: find the roots of the polynomial P; by synthetic division or otherwise define the n new polynomials, P_i; evaluate $Z_j(t_0)$ in terms of the b's; by repeated use of the methods of the last section, equation (54), solve in turn for $Z_1(t), Z_2(t), \cdots, Z_n(t)$, using the initial conditions just determined; the resulting $Z_n(t)$ is the required solution. This proves the first part of our theorem.

To prove uniqueness, we shall assume that there are two distinct solutions and show that this leads to a contradiction. Clearly the difference between any two solutions of (56) will satisfy the reduced equation with initial conditions all equal to zero. We have only to show that the reduced equation with zero initial conditions cannot have a solution which is not identically zero. For the first order case our existence theorem insures that there can be no other solution than zero. We shall proceed by induction to show that if a reduced equation of order $(n - 1)$ has a unique zero solution for zero initial conditions, then so must an nth order equation.

Let us suppose that the $(n - 1)$th order equation has a unique vanishing solution and the nth order has a non-vanishing solution, $Y(t)$. Then

$$\{P(h)\,Y\} = (h - q_1)\{P_{n-1}(h)\,Y\} = (h - q_1)Z = 0, \qquad (63)$$

where

$$h^i Y(t_0) = 0, \qquad (i = 1, \cdots, n - 1)$$
$$Y(t) \neq 0,$$

and Z is defined by this equation. Our hypothesis on the $(n - 1)$th order equation's uniqueness tells us that Z must be nonvanishing, since otherwise our nonvanishing Y would satisfy the $(n - 1)$th order equation. On the other hand, the zero values of the n initial conditions of Y make $Z(t_0)$ be zero. With an initial value of zero, and satisfying a first order equation, Z must vanish identically. Thus, we have a contradiction, and our conclusion concerning the uniqueness of our solution is proved.

It is to be noted that the case of repeated roots in the characteristic polynomial P introduces no difficulties in the problem. Also, it is to be observed that the method of finding a solution outlined above is not necessarily a good one to follow in practical numerical computation. However, since it depends only upon repeated solution of first order equations, it can be readily mechanized or reduced to a routine if some suitable method of solving first order equations is at hand (e.g., differential analyzer, punch card equipment, etc.).

Exercises:

1. Write out the solution for a reduced second order differential equation with constant coefficients which has $y(0) = 1$, $y'(0) = 0$; which has $y(0) = 0$, $y'(0) = 1$.

2. Write out the solution of the unreduced equation with vanishing initial conditions.

3. Repeat (1) and (2) for any operator h, using the F function.

25. Having established the existence and uniqueness of the solution of the general operator equation of the nth order with prescribed initial conditions, we may explore better ways of arriving at its solution. Our work may be divided into two parts: finding a particular solution with vanishing initial conditions, and finding a solution of the reduced equation which satisfies the prescribed initial conditions. Clearly, there are other ways of splitting up the problem according to the properties the particular solution is to have. Thus, in many physics problems the right-hand function, $f(t)$, represents a periodic driving force, and the particular solution sought is the so-called steady state response of the system, while the reduced equation solution yields the "transient,' which dies out in a damped system.

The reduced equation involves no arbitrary functions and is simpler. We discuss it first. Its solution for the most general case can be built up out of first order solutions, $F(t, q, 1; 0)_h$. For brevity we shall write the latter as $F(t, q)$. Some of its properties may now be developed.

First, since

$$F(t_0, q) \equiv 1, \tag{64}$$

$$\frac{\partial^k}{\partial q^k} F(t_0, q) \equiv 0. \tag{65}$$

Also, by its definition as a solution of the reduced first order equation,

$$hF = qF,$$
$$h^2F = q^2F,$$
$$\cdot$$
$$\cdot$$
$$\cdot$$
$$h^nF = q^nF, \tag{66}$$

and

$$P(h)F = P(q)F. \tag{67}$$

Because of the linearity of our system, we have

$$P(h) \left[\frac{y(t, q_2) - y(t, q_1)}{q_2 - q_1} \right] = \frac{P(h)y(t, q_2) - P(h)y(t, q_1)}{q_2 - q_1}. \tag{68}$$

If y is a continuously differentiable function of the parameter q, we find in the limit

$$P(h) \frac{\partial y}{\partial q} = \frac{\partial}{\partial q} P(h)y. \tag{69}$$

For the moment we disregard all boundary conditions and seek solutions of the reduced equation

$$P(h)y = 0.$$

First we establish a lemma: If $\bar{q}$ is a root of multiplicity s of

$$P(q) = 0,$$

so that

$$\begin{array}{ll} P^i(\bar{q}) = 0, \\ P^s(\bar{q}) \neq 0, \end{array} \quad (i = 0, 1, \cdots, s-1) \tag{70}$$

then

$$P(h) \frac{\partial^k}{\partial q^k} F(t, \bar{q}) = 0. \quad (k = 0, 1, \cdots, s-1) \tag{71}$$

where the last expression is short for $\left[P(h) \dfrac{\partial^k}{\partial q^k} F(t, q) \right]_{q=\bar{q}}$

Actually

$$P(h) \frac{\partial^k}{\partial q^k} F = \frac{\partial^k}{\partial q^k} P(h) F(t, \bar{q}) = \frac{\partial^k}{\partial q^k} [P(\bar{q}) F(t, \bar{q})]$$

$$= P^k(\bar{q}) F(t, \bar{q}) + k P^{k-1}(\bar{q}) \frac{\partial}{\partial q} F(t, \bar{q}) + \cdots$$

$$+ P(\bar{q}) \frac{\partial^k}{\partial q^k} F(t, \bar{q})$$

$$= 0, \quad (k < s) \tag{72}$$

term for term because of (70).

Of course, any linear combinations of special solutions of this form are also solutions. Every polynomial has n roots, when repeated roots are counted according to their multiplicity; and every distinct root yields as many special solutions of the form given in (71) as the multiplicity of the root. It follows that we have

$$\sum_{1}^{r} m_i = n$$

special solutions, not yet shown to be all linearly independent. We take the most general linear combination of these

$$y = C_{10}F(t, q_1) + C_{11}\frac{\partial}{\partial q} F(t, q_1) + \cdots + C_{1,m_1-1}\frac{\partial^{m_1-1}}{\partial q^{m_1-1}} F(t, q_1) +$$

$$C_{20}F(t, q_2) + C_{21}\frac{\partial}{\partial q} F(t, q_2) + \cdots + C_{2,m_2-1}\frac{\partial^{m_2-1}}{\partial q^{m_2-1}} F(t, q_2) +$$

$$\cdots\cdots\cdots\cdots\cdots\cdots\cdots\cdots\cdots\cdots\cdots\cdots$$

$$\cdots\cdots\cdots\cdots\cdots\cdots\cdots\cdots\cdots\cdots\cdots\cdots$$

$$\cdots\cdots\cdots\cdots\cdots\cdots\cdots\cdots\cdots\cdots\cdots\cdots$$

$$C_{r0}F(t, q_r) + C_{r1}\frac{\partial}{\partial q} F(t, q_r) + \cdots + C_{r,m_r-1}\frac{\partial^{m_r-1}}{\partial q^{m_r-1}} F(t, q_r)$$

$$= \sum_{k=1}^{r} \sum_{j=0}^{m_k-1} C_{k,j}\frac{\partial^j}{\partial q^j} F(t, q_k), \tag{73}$$

where $(q_1, q_2, \cdots, q_r)$ are the distinct roots of P with respective multiplicities $(m_1, m_2, \cdots, m_r)$. This linear combination is a solution of the reduced equation. It remains to determine the n coefficients $(C_{10}, \cdots, C_{r,m-1})$ so as to satisfy the n arbitrary initial conditions in (56). Thus

$$h^i \sum_{k=1}^{r} \sum_{j=0}^{m_k-1} C_{kj}\frac{\partial^j}{\partial q^j} F(t, q_k) = b_i, \qquad (i = 0, 1, \cdots, n - 1) \tag{74}$$

or because of (66) and (69)

$$\sum_{k=1}^{r} \sum_{j=0}^{m_k-1} C_{kj}\frac{\partial^j}{\partial q^j} [q_k^i F(t_0, q_k)] = b_i. \qquad (i = 0, 1, \cdots, n - 1) \tag{75}$$

From (64), $F(t_0, q)$ is unity regardless of q, so we have

$$\sum_{k=1}^{r} \sum_{j=0}^{m_k-1} C_{kj}(q_k^i)^{(j)} = b_i, \qquad (i = 0, 1, \cdots, n - 1) \tag{76}$$

where

$$\left[\frac{d^j}{dq^j} q^i\right]_{q=q_k} = (q_k^i)^{(j)} = \frac{i!}{(i-j)!} q_k^{i-j}, \qquad (i \geqq j)$$
$$= 0. \qquad (i < j) \tag{77}$$

When all of the roots are distinct, the determinant of this system takes the familiar Vandermonde form

$$\begin{vmatrix} 1 & 1 & \cdots & 1 \\ q_1 & q_2 & \cdots & q_n \\ q_1^2 & q_2^2 & \cdots & q_n^2 \\ \cdot & \cdot & & \cdot \\ \cdot & \cdot & & \cdot \\ \cdot & \cdot & & \cdot \\ q_1^{n-1} & q_2^{n-1} & \cdots & q_n^{n-1} \end{vmatrix} = \prod_{i>j} (q_i - q_j), \qquad (78)$$

which does not vanish. Consequently the n equations can be solved to yield the n C's so as to satisfy the n initial conditions. The proof of the identity (78) follows from the fact that the determinant is a polynomial of the $(n - 1)$th degree in terms of any q_i, and vanishes for any q_j equal to q_i. This plus the essential symmetry in terms of the q's leads to the right-hand side of (78). An alternative proof would use induction.

In the general case of repeated roots, the determinant becomes

$$V = \begin{vmatrix} 1 & 0 & \cdots & 0 & 1 & \cdots & 0 & \cdots & 1 & \cdots & 0 \\ q_1 & 1 & \cdots & 0 & q_2 & \cdots & 0 & \cdots & q_r & \cdots & 0 \\ q_1^2 & 2q_1 & \cdots & 0 & q_2^2 & \cdots & 0 & \cdots & q_r^2 & \cdots & 0 \\ \cdot & \cdot & & \cdot & \cdot & & \cdot & & \cdot & & \cdot \\ q_1^i & (q_1^i)^{(\prime)} & \cdots & (q_1^i)^{(m_1-1)} & q_2^i & \cdots & (q_2^i)^{(m_2-1)} & \cdots & q_r^i & \cdots & (q_r^i)^{(m_r-1)} \\ \cdot & \cdot & & \cdot & \cdot & & \cdot & & \cdot & & \cdot \\ q_1^{n-1} & (n-1)q_1^{n-2} & \cdots & (q_1^{n-1})^{(m_1-1)} & q_2^{n-1} & \cdots & (q_2^{n-1})^{(m_2-1)} & \cdots & q_r^{n-1} & \cdots & (q_r^{n-1})^{(m_r-1)} \end{vmatrix} \quad (79)$$

no two q's being equal. This generalized Vandermonde determinant can be shown not to vanish.[10] This may be proved by induction, but for the present purpose we may omit the proof of this fact, and simply note its consequence: all of our constants can be uniquely determined.

Here I should like to point out that the inversion of a generalized Vandermonde matrix can be done once and for all, and the result is applicable against varying initial conditions. The exact form of the inversion is expedited by synthetic division and is closely related to contour integrations and the expansion of a poly-

[10] P. A. Samuelson, "A Simple Method of Interpolation," *Proceedings of the National Academy of Sciences*, XXIX (1943), 397–401. Also F. R. Moulton, *Differential Equations* (New York, 1930), chap. xv.

nomial in partial fractions, so that the classical and operational methods meet.[11]

26. I turn now to the problem of determining the unreduced special solutions with vanishing initial conditions. In the proof of our fundamental existence theorem we have seen one way that this can be built up out of the basic solution of the first order equation $F(t, q, 0; f)_h$. Once the latter is tabulated or catalogued for a great variety of the f's that arise in practice, the remaining work is simply that of calculating

$$F(t, q_1, 0; f)_h = Z_1,$$
$$F(t, q_1, q_2, 0; f)_h = F(t, q_2, 0; Z_1)_h = Z_2,$$
$$F(t, q_1, q_2, q_3, 0; f)_h = F(t, q_3, 0; Z_2)_h = Z_3$$

$$\cdot$$
$$\cdot$$
$$\cdot$$

$$F(t, q_1, q_2, \cdots, q_n, 0; f)_h = F(t, q_n, 0; Z_{n-1})_h = Z_n. \tag{80}$$

The last is the required solution.

In this section an alternative procedure is described whereby our special solution with vanishing initial conditions is built up out of the first order solution, $F(t, q, 0; f)_h$. First, let us recall the algebraic fact that any rational expression of the form

$$\frac{1}{P(x)} = \frac{1}{\prod\limits_{i=1}^{r} (x - q_i)^{m_i}} \qquad (\sum_1^r m_i = n) \tag{81}$$

can be split up into partial fractions of the form

$$\frac{1}{P(x)} = \frac{A_{11}}{(x - q_1)} + \frac{A_{12}}{(x - q_1)^2} + \cdots + \frac{A_{1m_1}}{(x - q_1)^{m_1}}$$
$$+ \frac{A_{21}}{(x - q_2)} + \cdots + \frac{A_{r1}}{(x - q_r)} + \cdots + \frac{A_{rm_r}}{(x - q_r)^{m_r}}. \tag{82}$$

In the usual case where all the roots are distinct, the coefficients are simply $1/P'(q_i)$, respectively. When we have a repeated root, the coefficients are given by

$$A_{ij} = \frac{1}{(m_i - j)!} \left[\frac{d^{m_i-j}}{dx^{m_i-j}} \frac{(x - q_i)^{m_i}}{P(x)} \right]_{x=q_i} \tag{83}$$

[11] P. A. Samuelson, "Efficient Computation of the Latent Vectors of a Matrix," *Proceedings of the National Academy of Sciences*, XXIX (1943). 393–397.

Numerically these can be evaluated fairly quickly by synthetic division.

The following important identity is an immediate consequence of (82).

$$1 \equiv \sum_{i=1}^{r} \sum_{j=1}^{m_i} A_{ij} \frac{P(x)}{(x - q_i)^j}. \tag{84}$$

Let us return now to the problem of finding a solution to the unreduced equation with vanishing initial conditions. In the first order case, the expression

$$y = \frac{1}{h - q} f(t) \tag{85}$$

has as yet no meaning. However, it looks like the solution to our equation, or would if operator expressions could be treated like any algebraic quantities. For the first time we are in a position to give a meaning to negative powers of h or rational expressions in h. We shall define the above expression to be

$$\frac{1}{h - q} f(t) = F(t, q, 0; f)_h. \tag{86}$$

Immediately $[1/P(h)]f(t)$ suggests itself as the solution to the nth order equation. But how is it to be interpreted? The use of partial fractions comes to mind, and so we may try for our solution in the case that all roots are simple

$$y = A_{11}F(t, q_1, 0; f)_h + A_{21}F(t, q_2, 0; f)_h + \cdots$$
$$+ A_{n1}F(t, q_n, 0; f)_h, \tag{87}$$

or in the general case

$$y = \sum_{i=1}^{r} \sum_{j=1}^{m_i} A_{ij}F_j(t, q_i, 0; f)_h, \tag{88}$$

where we define

$$\begin{array}{ll}
F_1(t, q_i, 0; f)_h = F(t, q_i, 0; f)_h, & (h - q_i)F_1 = f \\
F_2(t, q_i, 0; f)_h = F(t, q_i, 0; F_1)_h, & (h - q_i)^2 F_2 = f \\
\quad \cdot & \quad \cdot \\
\quad \cdot & \quad \cdot \\
\quad \cdot & \quad \cdot \\
F_s(t, q_i, 0; f)_h = F(t, q_i, 0; F_{s-1})_h. & (h - q_i)^s F_s = f
\end{array} \tag{89}$$

Clearly (88) satisfies the vanishing initial conditions of the problem. After substitution into the nth order equation we have

$$P(h)y = \sum_{i=1}^{r} \sum_{j=1}^{m_i} A_{ij} \left[\frac{P(h)}{(h - q_i)^j} \right] (h - q_i)^j F_j(t, q_i, 0; f)_h$$

$$= \sum_{i=1}^{r} \sum_{j=1}^{m_i} A_{ij} \left[\frac{P(h)}{(h - q_i)^j} \right] f \qquad (90)$$

$$= 1f(t)$$

by virtue of the identity (84).

Note that our discussion of negative operators was purely heuristic and not germane to our proof. The expression in brackets does *not* involve negative operators although notationally it appears to do so.

This completes our second construction of the unreduced equation with vanishing initial conditions.

27. The elementary mathematical literature on differential equations abounds with trick methods for arriving at particular solutions of the unreduced equation for special f's (e.g., polynomials, exponentials, trigonometric functions, etc.). At this point it is only necessary to discuss two such methods.

The first is a formal series expansion, of even greater importance in the field of difference equations than differential equations where convergence is not always certain. Let us write the formal expression

$$\frac{1}{P(x)} = \frac{1}{\alpha_0 + \alpha_1 x + \cdots + \alpha_n x^n} = \beta_0 + \beta_1 x + \beta_2 x^2 + \cdots.$$

$$(\alpha_0 \neq 0) \quad (91)$$

Multiply through by $P(x)$ and equate coefficients of like terms to get equations determining the infinite sequence of β's in terms of the α's.

$$\beta_0 = \frac{1}{\alpha_0},$$

$$\beta_1 = -\frac{(\alpha_1 \beta_0)}{\alpha_0},$$

$$\beta_2 = -\frac{(\alpha_1 \beta_1 + \alpha_2 \beta_0)}{\alpha_0}, \qquad (92)$$

$$\vdots$$

$$\beta_s = -\frac{(\alpha_1 \beta_{s-1} + \alpha_2 \beta_{s-2} + \cdots + \alpha_s \beta_0)}{\alpha_0}.$$

In practice there are a variety of ways of determining the β sequence from the α's (algebraic division, difference equations, Taylor's expansion of $1/P(x)$, determinants, etc.).

Formally, a particular solution of

$$P(h)y = f$$

is given by the infinite series

$$y = \frac{1}{P(h)}f = \sum_{j=0}^{\infty} \beta_j h^j f. \tag{93}$$

where $1/P$ is now defined differently from (86) and (87). Whether there is any meaning to the right-hand side, that is, whether the series is defined and convergent or not, depends upon the h, the f, and the α's. Thus,

$$(\alpha_1 D + 1)y = f \tag{94}$$

has a finite convergent solution for f equal to t^3 of the form

$$\begin{aligned} y &= 1f - \alpha_1 Df + \alpha_1{}^2 D^2 f - \alpha_1{}^3 D^3 f + \cdots + (-\alpha_1)^i h^i f \\ &= t^3 - \alpha_1 2t^2 + \alpha_1{}^2 4t - \alpha_1{}^3 4 + 0 - 0 + \cdots. \end{aligned} \tag{95}$$

While for f equal to $e^{\lambda t}$, we have a formal series

$$y = \sum_0^{\infty} (-\alpha_1)^i D^i e^{\lambda t}$$

$$= e^{\lambda t} \sum_0^{\infty} (-\alpha_1 \lambda)^i, \tag{96}$$

which converges for $|\alpha_1 \lambda|$ less than one, but seems to diverge otherwise. However, if we use the "formal" identity

$$\sum_0^{\infty} (-\alpha_1 \lambda)^i = \frac{1}{1 + \alpha_1 \lambda}, \tag{97}$$

we get the correct answer, $e^{\lambda t}(1 + \alpha_1 \lambda)^{-1}$, although not always by a legitimate path.

Let us write a difference equation in the form

$$\begin{aligned} \alpha_0 y(t) + \alpha_1 y(t-1) + \cdots + \alpha_n y(t-n) &= P(E^{-1})y(t) = f(t), \\ E^0 y(0) = y(0) &= 0, \\ E^{-1}y(0) &= 0, \\ E^{-(n-1)}y(0) &= 0, \\ f(t) &\equiv 0, \qquad (t < 1) \end{aligned} \tag{98}$$

Then

$$y(t) = \frac{1}{P(E^{-1})} f(t) = \sum_0^\infty \beta_j E^{-j} f(t). \tag{99}$$

This will always terminate after t terms, and will satisfy the equation and initial conditions.

Exercises:

1. Show that β_t is a solution of the equation

$$P(E^{-1})y = \alpha_0 y(t) + \alpha_1 y(t-1) + \cdots + \alpha_n y(t-n) = 0,$$
$$y(0) = 1,$$
$$y(-1) = 0,$$
$$\cdot$$
$$\cdot$$
$$\cdot$$
$$y(-n+1) = 0.$$

2. If $P(x)$ has n simple roots, q_i^{-1}, and $R(x) = \alpha_0^{-1} x^n P(x^{-1})$, show that

$$\beta_t = \sum_1^n \frac{1}{R'(q_i)} (q_i)^{t+1-n}.$$

3. If α_t equals $a^t/t!$, what is β_t? (Hint: Consider series expansion of e^a and $1/e^a$.)

4. Write β_t in determinantal form.

5. Write out the first three β's in terms of α's.

28. The second artifice for arriving at a particular solution comes into use when $f(t)$ is itself the solution of a reduced first order equation. That is

$$P(h)y = f$$

where

$$hf = \bar{q}f. \tag{100}$$

We try a solution in the form

$$y = cf, \tag{101}$$

where c is a constant. We have after substitution and cancellation of f

$$cP(\bar{q}) = 1. \tag{102}$$

If $\bar{q}$ is not a root of P, this has a solution,

$$c = \frac{1}{P(\bar{q})}. \tag{103}$$

In the important electrical engineering studies of frequency response, c is the *transfer function;* for $\bar{q}$ a pure imaginary, it is an impedance.

If $\bar{q}$ is a root of P, we have the phenomenon of resonance, and we must try for our solution

$$y = \frac{c\, \partial^m f(t)}{\partial q^m}, \tag{104}$$

where $m + 1$ is the multiplicity of the root $\bar{q}$. After substitution and cancellation we find

$$c = \frac{1}{P^m(\bar{q})}. \tag{105}$$

If f is composed of two or more components, $f_1, f_2, \cdots$, which are each solutions of the first order reduced equation with q equal to $q_1, q_2, \cdots$, by superposition we find a special solution of the unreduced equation to be

$$y = \frac{1}{P(q_1)} f_1 + \frac{1}{P(q_2)} f_2 + \cdots. \tag{106}$$

If any of the q's are roots of P, the modification given in (104) will of course be in order.

Important examples are provided by periodic driving forces in the field of differential or difference equations. Any well-behaved periodic function can be written as a Fourier series, of which each term satisfies a first order differential (difference) equation with pure imaginary (complex root of unit modulus) coefficient. Unless perfect resonance occurs, as it cannot in a damped system, our solution can be built up term by term of the same harmonic elements but with coefficients differing by the factor, $1/P(\dot{q}_i)$. The resulting solution (if it converges) will be a periodic function of time of the same period as the driving force.

Finally, if our $f(t)$ can be written as a general integral

$$f(t) = \int_c F(t, q) dW(q), \tag{107}$$

where

$$hF(t, q) = qF(t, q),$$

and c represents some contour in the complex plane, then we try the formal solution

$$y = \int_c F(t, q) \frac{1}{P(q)} dW(q). \tag{108}$$

In cases where $P(q)$ vanishes, this may be an improper integral whose limit nevertheless often provides a satisfactory solution.

The mathematician will recognize that in the field of differential equations, all the f's that are likely to arise in practice can be written in the form (107), by setting q equal to ia, and F equal to e^{iat}, and using Fourier's integral theorem.

29. The artifice of the Laplace transform will now be generalized to a wide class of simple operators other than D. The Laplace transform is defined as

$$\mathcal{L}(q; y) = \int_0^\infty e^{-qa} y(a) da, \tag{109}$$

which will be convergent for a wide class of y's, for the real part of q less than some constant.

The fundamental property of the Laplace transform which makes it a useful artifice in differential equations is as follows:

$$\mathcal{L}(q; Dy) = q\mathcal{L}(q; y) - y(0),$$
$$\mathcal{L}(q; D^2y) = q^2\mathcal{L}(q; y) - qy(0) - Dy(0),$$
$$\cdot$$
$$\cdot \tag{110}$$
$$\cdot$$
$$\mathcal{L}(q; D^ny) = q\mathcal{L}(q; D^{n-1}y) - D^ny(0)$$
$$= q^n\mathcal{L}(q; y) - q^{n-1}y(0) - q^{n-2}Dy(0) - \cdots$$
$$- qD^{n-1}y(0) - D^ny(0).$$

For then taking the Laplace transform of both sides of

$$P(D)y = \sum_0^n a_i D^{n-i} y = f(t), \tag{111}$$
$$D^k y(0) = b_k, \qquad (k = 0, 1, \cdots, n - 1)$$

we get

$$P(q)\mathcal{L}(q; y) = \mathcal{L}(q; f) + b_0(a_0q^{n-1} + a_1q^{n-2} + \cdots + a_{n-1})$$
$$+ b_1(a_0q^{n-2} + \cdots + a_{n-2}) + \cdots$$
$$+ b_{n-2}(a_0q + a_1) + b_{n-1}a_0. \tag{112}$$

This is an expression in q and involves no operators. Solving for the expression involving the unknown function, we have

$$\mathcal{L}(q;y) = \frac{R(q)}{P(q)} + \frac{\mathcal{L}(q;f)}{P(q)} = \bar{Y}(q), \tag{113}$$

where R is a polynomial involving the initial conditions, b_k, and is less than n in degree. Because f is known, the Laplace transform of our unknown function is determined. Under general mathematical conditions we can prove that our solution y is "essentially" unique once its Laplace transform is determined. One method of inversion is given by contour integration

$$y(t) = \frac{1}{2\pi i} \int_{c-i\infty}^{c+i\infty} \bar{Y}(q)e^{qt}dq, \tag{114}$$

where the contour is to the right of all poles of $\bar{Y}$.

In any case, once $\bar{Y}(q)$ is determined, the determination of $y(t)$ is a detail which need not concern us. Extensive tables are available to aid in inverting Laplace transforms involving a wide class of f's.

To extend the theory we need only seek a *functional* appropriate to any admissible h, with the fundamental property

$$\mathcal{L}(q;hy)_h = q\mathcal{L}(q;y)_h - y(t_0). \tag{115}$$

The following expression formally answers our problem

$$\mathcal{L}(q;f)_h = \lim_{t \to \infty} \frac{F(t, q, 0; f)_h}{F(t, q, 1; 0)_h}, \tag{116}$$

where q and f are such that

$$\lim_{t \to \infty} \frac{f(t)}{F(t, q, 1; 0)_h} = 0. \tag{117}$$

The proof that this is our generalized Laplace transform is given as follows:

$$\mathcal{L}(q;hf)_h = \lim_{t \to \infty} \frac{F(t, q, 0; hf)_h}{F(t, q, 1; 0)_h}. \tag{118}$$

By definition

$$\begin{array}{ll}
(h - q)F(t, q, 0; f)_h = f, & F(t_0, q, 0; f)_h = 0 \\
(h - q)F(t, q, 1; 0)_h = 0, & F(t_0, q, 1; 0)_h = 1 \qquad (119) \\
(h - q)F(t, q, 0; hf)_h = hf, & F(t_0, q, 0; hf)_h = 0,
\end{array}$$

and each of these systems has unique solutions. Now it can be verified that

$$F(t, q, 0; hf)_h \equiv hF(t, q, 0; f)_h - f(t_0)F(t, q, 1; 0)_h, \quad (120)$$

because

$$hF(t_0, q, 0; f)_h - f(t_0)F(t_0, q; 1; 0)_h \equiv f(t_0) - f(t_0) = 0, \quad (121)$$

and

$$(h - q)[hF(t, q, 0; f)_h - f(t_0)F(t, q, 1; 0)_h]$$
$$= h[(h - q)F(t, q, 0; f)_h] - f(t_0)(h - q)F(t, q, 1; 0)_h$$
$$= h[f] - 0. \quad (122)$$

Therefore,

$$\mathcal{L}(q; hf) = \lim_{t \to \infty} \left[\frac{hF(t, q, 0; f)_h}{F(t, q, 1; 0)_h} - f(t_0) \right]$$
$$= \lim_{t \to \infty} q \frac{F(t, q, 0; f)_h}{F(t, q, 1; 0)_h} + \lim_{t \to \infty} \frac{f(t)}{F(t, q, 1; 0)_h} - f(t_0) \quad (123)$$
$$= q\mathcal{L}(q; f)_h + 0 - f(t_0)$$

for q and f limited as in our hypotheses. Q. E. D.

Thus, the solution to the general nth order problem with prescribed boundary conditions is given by the inversion of

$$\mathcal{L}(q; y)_h = \frac{R(q)}{P(q)} + \frac{\mathcal{L}(q; f)_h}{P(q)} = \bar{Y}(q)_h, \quad (124)$$

or formally

$$y(t) = \mathcal{L}^{-1}\left[\frac{R(q)}{P(q)} \right] + \mathcal{L}^{-1}\left[\frac{\mathcal{L}(q; f)_h}{P(q)} \right]. \quad (125)$$

Moreover, even where there is no convergence of $\mathcal{L}$, "$\mathcal{L}$" can be "inverted" as the mathematically inclined reader may work out for himself. So long as $f(t)$ leads to a unique solution of the first order *operator* equation, its behavior at infinity is irrelevant.

Exercises:

1. Show that $\mathcal{L}(q; y)_E = \sum_0^\infty \frac{y(i)}{q^{i+1}} = \bar{Y}(q)_E$, where $t_0 = 0$.
2. What is $\mathcal{L}(q; y)_A$? What is $\mathcal{L}(q; y)_{iD}$?

3. Make and verify a table of transforms for E as follows:

$y(t)$	$\bar{Y}(q)_E$
$a^t = F(t, a, 1; 0)_h$	$\dfrac{1}{q - a}$
ta^{t-1}	$\left(\dfrac{1}{q - a}\right)^2$
$\dfrac{t(t - 1) \cdots (t - n + 1)a^{t-n}}{n!}$	$\left(\dfrac{1}{q - a}\right)^{n+1}$
$F(t, a, 0; y_1)_h$	$\dfrac{\bar{Y}_1(q)_h}{q - a}$
$\displaystyle\sum_0^{t-1} y_1(i)y_2(t - 1 - i)$	$\bar{Y}_1(q)_E \bar{Y}_2(q)_E$
$\dfrac{\partial^n y(t, a)}{\partial a^n}$	$\dfrac{\partial^n \bar{Y}(q, a)_h}{\partial a^n}$
$Ey(t)$	?

4. Trace the relationship between the "classical" and the generalized Laplace transform method.

Many Variable Systems

30. Let us return now to linear systems of many variables $(y_1, y_2, \cdots, y_m)$. For the dynamic system to be determinate, we must have at least m operator equations. These can, of course, be of high order, say n or less, and can be written as

$$
\begin{aligned}
a_{0,11}h^n y_1 + a_{0,12}h^n y_2 + \cdots + a_{1,11}h^{n-1}y_1 + \cdots \\
+ a_{n,1m}y_m = f_1(t), \\
a_{0,21}h^n y_1 + a_{0,22}h^n y_2 + \cdots + a_{1,21}h^{n-1}y_1 + \cdots \\
+ a_{n,2m}y_m = f_2(t),
\end{aligned}
\tag{126}
$$

$$
\begin{aligned}
\vdots \\
a_{0,m1}h^n y_1 + a_{0,m2}h^n y_2 + \cdots + a_{1,m1}h^{n-1}y_1 + \cdots \\
+ a_{n,mm}y_m = f_m(t),
\end{aligned}
$$

or as

$$
\begin{aligned}
P_{11}(h)y_1 + P_{12}(h)y_2 + \cdots + P_{1m}(h)y_m &= f_1(t), \\
P_{21}(h)y_1 + P_{22}(h)y_2 + \cdots + P_{2m}(h)y_m &= f_2(t), \\
\vdots \\
P_{m1}(h)y_1 + P_{m2}(h)y_2 + \cdots + P_{mm}(h)y_m &= f_m(t),
\end{aligned}
$$

where $P_{ij}(h)$ are polynomials in h of the nth degree or less; or in matrix notation as

$$a_0 h^n y + a_1 h^{n-1} y + \cdots a_{n-1} h y + a_n y = f(t)$$

and

$$Py = f,$$

where $(a_0, \cdots, a_n)$ are m^2 matrices, y and f column matrices of m elements. Of course, many of the elements in the a's may consist of zeros.

The maximum order of our system will be nm; but its *actual* order may well fall short of this. By the actual order of the system we mean the maximum number of initial conditions which can be arbitrarily imposed on the system.[12]

As an exercise in matrix notation the reader may work out the demonstration that by redefinition of variables [13] the system can be written as a first order one,

$$A_0 h Y + A_1 Y = F, \tag{127}$$

where

$$A_0 = \begin{bmatrix} I & 0 & \cdots & 0 & 0 \\ 0 & I & \cdots & 0 & 0 \\ \cdot & \cdot & \cdots & \cdot & \cdot \\ \cdot & \cdot & \cdots & \cdot & \cdot \\ \cdot & \cdot & \cdots & \cdot & \cdot \\ 0 & 0 & \cdots & 0 & I \\ 0 & 0 & \cdots & 0 & a_0 \end{bmatrix},$$

$$A_1 = \begin{bmatrix} 0 & -I & \cdots & 0 & 0 \\ 0 & 0 & \cdots & 0 & 0 \\ \cdot & \cdot & \cdots & \cdot & \cdot \\ \cdot & \cdot & \cdots & \cdot & \cdot \\ \cdot & \cdot & \cdots & \cdot & \cdot \\ 0 & 0 & \cdots & 0 & -I \\ a_n & a_{n-1} & \cdots & a_2 & a_1 \end{bmatrix}, \qquad F = \begin{bmatrix} 0 \\ 0 \\ \cdot \\ \cdot \\ f \end{bmatrix}.$$

[12] It can be shown that the order of the system, s, is equal to the degree in q of the determinant

$$\Delta(q) = |a_0 q^n + a_1 q^{n-1} + \cdots + a_n|.$$

See R. A. Frazer, W. J. Duncan, and A. R. Collar, *Elementary Matrices and Some Applications to Dynamics and Differential Equations* (Cambridge, 1938) for references. See par. 5.4.

[13] Frazer, Duncan, and Collar, *Elementary Matrices*, par. 5.5.

Although our system has been converted to a first order system, it is not yet in "normal" form with hY expressed explicitly in terms of Y and functions of time,

$$hY = AY + f. \tag{128}$$

If A_0 is non-singular, that is, if its determinant does not vanish, we can premultiply both sides of (127) by A_0^{-1} and immediately convert to normal form,

$$hY = -(A_0^{-1}A_1)Y + (A_0^{-1}F). \tag{129}$$

Similarly in (126) if a_0 is non-singular, our operators of highest order can be solved for in terms of those of lower order by the act of premultiplication with a_0^{-1}.

If a_0 *is* singular, our system is not well-specified. One of three situations must then prevail: (1) there exist purely *statical, algebraic relationships* between some of the variables. By means of these relations one or more variables can be eliminated, and the leading matrix of the resulting smaller system will then be non-singular; (2) the relationships are *not all independent* so that a unique solution does not exist. Arbitrary functions of time will enter into the solution. (Example: A system with two identical equations, permitting one variable to be chosen as an arbitrary function of time); (3) the system is inconsistent.

31. It is up to the economist to present a well-specified dynamical system. In what follows we shall assume that this task has been adequately performed so that whenever desirable our system can be written in the normal first order form of order s.

$$hy = Ay + f, \tag{130}$$

with initial conditions

$$y(t_0) = b.$$

As in previous sections we shall find our solution in two steps: first, the solution of the reduced or homogeneous system

$$hy = Ay, \tag{131}$$
$$y(t_0) = b;$$

and then the solution of the unreduced system

$$hy = Ay + f, \tag{132}$$
$$y(t_0) = 0.$$

The sum of these two solutions will be the solution to our general system (130).

32. Earlier we have seen that the solutions of the simple first order equation in one variable provided the building blocks for the solutions of more complicated cases. We try, therefore, a solution of the form

$$y_1 = c_1 F(t, q, 1; 0)_h = c_1 F(t, q),$$

$$\vdots \qquad\qquad\qquad\qquad (133)$$

$$y_s = c_s F(t, q, 1; 0)_h = c_s F(t, q),$$

where F is as defined in earlier sections, and the c's and q are unknown constants. After substituting into (131), we get by means of the fact that hF equals qF,

$$qc_1 F = A_{11}c_1 F + A_{12}c_2 F + \cdots + A_{1s}c_s F,$$
$$qc_2 F = A_{21}c_1 F + A_{22}c_2 F + \cdots + A_{2s}c_s F,$$
$$\vdots \qquad\qquad\qquad\qquad\qquad (134)$$
$$qc_s F = A_{s1}c_1 F + A_{s2}c_2 F + \cdots + A_{ss}c_s F.$$

The common factor F may be canceled from both sides of the equation, leaving us with s algebraic equations *which do not involve time.* If these equations can be satisfied, we shall have a solution of the operator equation, although not necessarily the solution with appropriate initial conditions.

Our linear equations involve known A's, undetermined c's and q. Our equations are homogeneous in the c's and may be written as

$$(A_{11} - q)c_1 + A_{12}c_2 + \cdots + A_{1s}c_s = 0,$$
$$A_{21}c_1 + (A_{22} - q)c_2 + \cdots + A_{2s}c_s = 0,$$
$$\vdots \qquad\qquad\qquad\qquad\qquad (135)$$
$$A_{s1}c_1 + A_{s2}c_2 + \cdots + (A_{ss} - q)c_s = 0.$$

If all the c's are zero, we have a trivial solution of the operator equation. When can we find a non-trivial solution? From the theory of ordinary linear equations (Cramer's rule, etc.), we know that a system of homogeneous linear equations has a non-trivial solution if, and only if, its determinant vanishes; in this case if

$$
\Delta(q) =
\begin{vmatrix}
A_{11} - q & A_{12} & \cdots & A_{1s} \\
A_{21} & A_{22} - q & \cdots & A_{2s} \\
\cdot & \cdot & \cdots & \cdot \\
\cdot & \cdot & \cdots & \cdot \\
\cdot & \cdot & \cdots & \cdot \\
A_{s1} & A_{s2} & \cdots & A_{ss} - q
\end{vmatrix}
$$
$$
= \pi_0 q^s + \pi_1 q^{s-1} + \cdots + \pi_{s-1} q + \pi_s = 0. \quad (136)
$$

For a q chosen at random the determinant will not vanish, and we shall have no non-trivial solution. But q is at our disposal; we select it to make the determinant vanish. The determinant is a polynomial of the sth degree in q, and is called the *characteristic equation* of the matrix (or secular equation). The roots of the characteristic equation must necessarily be s in number (counting multiplicities). They are called characteristic or latent roots of the matrix. If we designate them by $(q_1, \cdots, q_s)$, we can write

$$
\Delta(q) = (q_1 - q)(q_2 - q) \cdots (q_s - q) = 0. \quad (137)
$$

It is not easy in fact to find the characteristic roots of a matrix. From the definition of a determinant, the coefficients of the characteristic polynomial can be determined as the sums of principal minors of a given order (cf. Mathematical Appendix A, p. 374), and any of the customary methods for solving a polynomial for its roots may then be employed. Even with the best short cuts,[14] the computations are tedious. Fortunately, the economist does not always require the quantitative values of the roots.

Let us return to the problem of finding solutions to our reduced operator system. If we put a characteristic root, q_i, into the F in (133), and take for our c's a non-vanishing solution of (135), we shall have a solution which satisfies our reduced system. Note that our selection of c's is not unique; doubling each will also give us a solution.

A column of c's satisfying the homogeneous equations is called a *characteristic vector* or *latent vector* or sometimes a modal column or normal component. Some of the characteristic roots may be

---

[14] Frazer, Duncan, and Collar, *Elementary Matrices*, chaps. iv and v.

complex; the characteristic vectors will then be complex. Of course, conjugate complex magnitudes can always be combined so as to give only real quantities in the final answer.

If a root q_i is simple, then $\Delta'(q_i)$ is not equal to zero, and the rank of $[A - q_iI]$ is $(s - 1)$. Consequently, the latent vector corresponding to q_i is unique *except for scale factor*. We may dispose of this ambiguity by some normalization convention.

If all roots are distinct, the general solution can be simply written. Where roots are repeated, certain complications occur. However, these are not intrinsic and rarely concern the economist. Later, I show how these difficulties can be avoided. But for true mathematical insight the reader must be referred to the theory of elementary factors and divisors.[15]

If the s roots are simple, and the s latent vectors have been normalized, we have the following particular solutions of the reduced equation (131):

$$
\begin{array}{cccc}
c_{1,1}F(t, q_1); & c_{1,2}F(t, q_2); & \cdots & c_{1,s}F(t, q_s); \\
c_{2,1}F(t, q_1); & c_{2,2}F(t, q_2); & \cdots & c_{2,s}F(t, q_s); \\
\cdot & \cdot & & \cdot \\
\cdot & \cdot & & \cdot \\
\cdot & \cdot & & \cdot \\
c_{s,1}F(t, q_1); & c_{s,2}F(t, q_2); & \cdots & c_{s,s}F(t, q_s),
\end{array}
\tag{138}
$$

where $F(t, q)$ is an abbreviation for $F(t, q, 1; 0)_h$. Any linear combination of these is a solution, or

$$
y_j = K_1c_{j,1}F(t, q_1) + K_2c_{j,2}F(t, q_2) + \cdots + K_sc_{j,s}F(t, q_s).
$$
$$
(j = 1, \cdots, s) \tag{139}
$$

Note that the c's and q's depend only on the matrix and not on the initial conditions. But the K's must be determined by the s initial conditions. Thus,

$$
\begin{aligned}
y_1(0) &= K_1c_{1,1} + K_2c_{1,2} + \cdots + K_sc_{1,s} = b_1, \\
y_2(0) &= K_1c_{2,1} + K_2c_{2,2} + \cdots + K_sc_{2,s} = b_2, \\
&\quad\cdot \\
&\quad\cdot \\
&\quad\cdot \\
y_s(0) &= K_1c_{s,1} + K_2c_{s,2} + \cdots + K_sc_{s,s} = b_s,
\end{aligned}
\tag{140}
$$

[15] M. Bocher, *Introduction to Higher Algebra* (New York, 1933).

or
$$cK = b.$$

These equations are sufficient to solve for the K's in terms of the b's if the matrix c is non-singular. The reader may be referred to any mathematical text for the proof that c is non-singular, and that

$$c^{-1}Ac = [q_i\delta_{ij}].[16] \tag{141}$$

In the case of distinct roots, the solution to the reduced system (131) can be written in compact form as [17]

$$y = c[F(t, q_i)\delta_{ij}]c^{-1}b. \tag{142}$$

33. If b is the identity matrix, we have a fundamental *set* of solutions. This may be written formally as $F(t, A)$, either as an extension of Sylvester's Law of Latency mentioned in Mathematical Appendix A, footnote 13, or from the definition

$$F(t, A) = \sum_0^\infty m_i(t)A^i, \tag{143}$$

where the m's are defined by the formal identity

$$F(t, q) = \sum_0^\infty m_i(t)q^i. \tag{144}$$

Because of the property
$$hF = qF, \tag{145}$$

$$h \sum_0^\infty m_i(t)q^i = \sum_0^\infty m_i(t)q^{i+1}, \tag{146}$$

and we have the formal identities
$$hm_0(t) \equiv 0,$$
$$hm_i(t) = m_{i-1}(t), \qquad (i = 1, \cdots), \tag{147}$$
and hence

$$hF(t, A) \equiv AF(t, A). \tag{148}$$

Also

$$F(t_0, A) \equiv I. \tag{149}$$

Formally, these above relations hold even if there are equal roots. The formal solution given in this section is sometimes a

---

[16] In Mathematical Appendix A this fact is used in connection with symmetric matrices, for which c is orthogonal; i.e., $c^{-1} = c'$.

[17] Frazer, Duncan, and Collar, *Elementary Matrices*, chap. v.

very convenient one. For the differential equation system

$$Dy = Ay, \tag{150}$$

$F(t, A, 1; 0)_D$ takes the form

$$F_D = e^{At} = I + A\,\frac{t}{1!} + A^2\frac{t^2}{2!} + \cdots. \tag{151}$$

For the system

$$Ey = Ay, \tag{152}$$

we have

$$F(t, A, 1; 0)_E = A^t. \tag{153}$$

However, for stability investigations these solutions are not very convenient.

34. If instead of the roots all being simple, some are repeated, we may write

$$\Delta(q) = (q_1 - q)^{m_1}(q_2 - q)^{m_2} \cdots (q_r - q)^{m_r}, \tag{154}$$

where $(q_1, \cdots, q_r)$ are the r distinct roots with respective multiplicities $(m_1, \cdots, m_r)$.

As before, there are special solutions of the form, $c_i F(t, q_i)$, but the c's are no longer unique except for scale factor; in fact, even if the c's were uniquely defined, there would not be a sufficient number of particular solutions to combine to get a general solution for s arbitrary initial conditions.

Earlier, in the case of multiple roots we tried solutions of the form, $\dfrac{\partial F(t, q_i)}{\partial q}$, $\dfrac{\partial^2 F(t, q_i)}{\partial q^2}$, $\cdots$, $\dfrac{\partial^{m_i-1} F(t, q_i)}{\partial q^{m_i-1}}$, and so we shall here.

Let $R(q)$ be the *adjugate* of the q matrix,

$$P(q) = A - qI; \tag{155}$$

that is, $R(q)$ is the transpose of the matrix made up of the cofactors of $P(q)$.

By means of algebraic theory of no interest here, it could be shown [18] that from the columns of the matrix $\left[\dfrac{d^k R(q_i)}{dq^k}\right]$ can be selected vectors which when multiplied by the partial derivatives of F will give a complete solution. However, these difficulties can be

[18] Frazer, Duncan, and Collar, *Elementary Matrices*, par. 5.10.

side-stepped by the device of reducing the s first order equations in s different variables to single sth order equations in each variable.[19]

Thus if

$$hy = Ay, \tag{156}$$
$$y(t_0) = b,$$

then

$$hy(t_0) = Ab,$$
$$h^2y(t_0) = A^2b,$$
$$\cdot$$
$$\cdot \tag{157}$$
$$\cdot$$
$$h^{s-1}y(t_0) = A^{s-1}b.$$

Because of the Cayley-Hamilton Theorem that every matrix satisfies its own characteristic equation or

$$\Delta(A) \equiv 0, \tag{158}$$

we find from (156) that

$$\Delta(h)y = (\pi_0 h^s + \pi_1 h^{s-1} + \cdots + \pi_s)y = \Delta(A)y = 0. \tag{159}$$

Hence, each variable, say $y_j(t)$, satisfies an sth order equation. We also know from (157) the values of $[y_j(t_0), hy_j(t_0), \cdots, h^{s-1}y_j(t_0)]$. Hence, we have a well-determined system whose solution can be found by the methods of sections 24, 25, and 26. It is clear then that our final solutions take the form

$$y_j(t) = c_{j,11}F(t, q_1) + c_{j,12}\frac{\partial F(t, q_1) \cdot}{\partial q} + \cdots + c_{j,1m_1-1}\frac{\partial^{m_1-1}F(t, q_1)}{\partial q^{m_1-1}}$$

$$+ c_{j,21}F(t, q_2) + c_{j,22}\frac{\partial F(t, q_2)}{\partial q} + \cdots + c_{j,2m_2-1}\frac{\partial^{m_2-1}F(t, q_2)}{\partial q^{m_2-1}}$$

$$\cdot \qquad\qquad \cdot \qquad\qquad\qquad \cdot \tag{160}$$
$$\cdot \qquad\qquad \cdot \qquad\qquad\qquad \cdot$$
$$\cdot \qquad\qquad \cdot \qquad\qquad\qquad \cdot$$

$$+ c_{j,r1}F(t, q_r) + c_{j,r2}\frac{\partial F(t, q_r)}{\partial q} + \cdots + c_{j,rm_r-1}\frac{\partial^{m_r-1}F(t, q_r)}{\partial q^{m_r-1}},$$

$$(j = 1, \cdots, s)$$

[19] The method of attack suggested here is not only theoretically simple but is also computationally optimal. See P. A. Samuelson, "Efficient Computation of the Latent Vectors of a Matrix," *Proceedings of the National Academy of Sciences*, XXIX (1943), 393–397.

where the $s^2 c$'s are not all independent. All but s are determinable from the matrix above. The remaining s depend on the s initial conditions.

Thus, terms of the form $\partial F^k/\partial q^k$ may appear if there are multiple roots. But they *need not* appear even if there are multiple roots. That is, whatever the initial condition b, the coefficients $c_{j,ik}$ may be identically zero for $(1 < k < m_i)$. For example, in the matrix

$$A = [-3\delta_{ij}], \tag{161}$$

-3 is a repeated root of multiplicity s. $F(t, -3)$ appears in the final solutions, but not $\partial F(t, -3)/\partial q$, or any higher derivatives. The reader must again be referred to the theory of elementary divisors for insight into this possibility.

As far as stability is concerned, except for borderline cases (which we have excluded in our strong definition of stability), it is clear that

$$\lim_{t \to \infty} F(t, q) \equiv 0$$

implies

$$\lim_{t \to \infty} \frac{\partial F}{\partial q} = \lim_{t \to \infty} \lim_{\Delta q \to 0} \frac{F(t, q + \Delta q) - F(t, q)}{\Delta q} = \lim_{\Delta q \to 0} 0 = 0. \tag{162}$$

Therefore, it does not matter whether or not the partial derivatives of F are suppressed.[20]

35. We have now given the complete solution of the reduced equation. By the same method as the last section we may indicate the solution of the unreduced part.

$$hy = Ay + f, \tag{163}$$
$$y(t_0) = 0.$$

---

[20] A borderline case on the boundary between stability and instability is provided by a symmetrical conservative physical system. Here $F(t, iq)_D = e^{iqt}$ and is neither damped nor undamped. However, $\partial F/\partial q = ite^{iqt}$ is explosive, as is well known from the theory of resonance. But the autonomous reduced system $y = Ay$ will not have explosive solutions when there are multiple roots; for $A = A'$, the theory of elementary divisors assures the vanishing of coefficients of all terms of the form $(it)^k e^{iqt}$ so that only an external force can cause explosive resonance. [Added in 1951: L. J. Savage (*Journal of Political Economy*, LVI, 1948, p. 202) has correctly pointed out the invalidity of this double-limit argument, illustrating with $h = \frac{1}{2}(\exp - 2t) \times (D + 1)$ and $F(t,q) = \exp(-t + q \exp 2t)$ for imaginary q.]

We easily see that

$$h^0 y = y,$$
$$hy = Ay + f,$$
$$h^2 y = Ahy + hf = A^2 y + Af + hf,$$
$$h^3 y = A^3 y + A^2 f + Ahf + h^2 f,$$

$$\cdot$$
$$\cdot$$
$$\cdot$$

(164)

$$h^{s-1} y = A^{s-1} y + A^{s-2} f + A^{s-3} hf + \cdots + Ah^{s-3} f + h^{s-2} f,$$
$$h^s y = A^s y + A^{s-1} f + \cdots + Ah^{s-2} f + h^{s-1} f.$$

Multiplying the first line by π_s, the second by π_{s-1}, the last by π_0, and adding, we have

$$\Delta(h)y = \Delta(A)y + m_0 f + m_1 hf + \cdots m_{s-1} h^{s-1} f, \qquad (165)$$

where the first term on the right-hand side vanishes by the Cayley-Hamilton theorem, and where the m's are linear combinations of powers of A.

Each of the variables $(y_1, \cdots, y_m)$ must satisfy an unreduced sth order equation. The right-hand driving functions seem to depend upon hf, $h^2 f$ as well as f; and yet, we have nowhere made the assumption that expressions of the form $h^k f$ need even be defined. If we write out a typical equation, say in y_1, the paradox will be dispelled. We have

$$\Delta(h)y_1 = R_1(h)f, \qquad (166)$$

or

$$y_1 = \frac{R_1(h)f}{\Delta(h)}.$$

Because R_1 is of degree $(s - 1)$ at most, it will be clear that (by partial fraction expansion or otherwise) we can avoid all terms of the form $h^k f$. Only expressions of the type $F(t, q, b; f)_h$ will appear.

We have now only to specify the correct initial conditions. Because

$$A^k y(t_0) = 0, \qquad (k = 0, 1, \cdots)$$

our initial conditions should be

$$hy(t_0) = f(t_0),$$
$$h^2y(t_0) = Af(t_0) + hf(t_0),$$

$\cdot$

$\cdot$ (167)

$\cdot$

$$h^{s-1}y(t_0) = A^{s-2}f(t_0) + A^{s-3}hf(t_0) + \cdots$$
$$+ Ah^{s-3}f(t_0) + h^{s-2}f(t_0).$$

We now have an unreduced sth order equation with prescribed initial conditions which each variable must satisfy. Our problem has therefore been reduced to that of earlier sections, which has been completely solved.

Exercises:

1. Show that $\int_{t_0}^{t} e^{A(t-t_0-w)} f(w)dw$ upon proper definition becomes the solution of (132), when h is D.

2. Show that $\sum_{0}^{t-1} A^{(t-1-i)}f(i)$ performs the same role for h equal to E, $t_0 = 0$.

3. By using the generalized Laplace transform $\mathcal{L}(q; y)_h$, defined earlier, go from

$$hy = Ay + f,$$
$$y(t_0) = b$$

to

$$[\mathcal{L}(q; y)_h] = \left[\frac{T_{ij}(q)}{\Delta(q)}\right][\mathcal{L}(q; f)_h] + \left[\frac{T_{ij}(q)}{\Delta(q)}\right]b,$$

where $[T_{ij}(q)/\Delta(q)]$ equals $[qI - a]^{-1}$ and consists of rational functions whose numerator is of lower degree than denominator. Show that expressions of the form $h^k f(t)$ do not enter into the solution in an essential way.

36. We have already seen in Section 21 of this Appendix that it is necessary and sufficient for stability of a differential equation system with constant coefficients that the real parts of the roots of the characteristic polynomial should all be negative, i.e., the roots must all be in the left-hand half of the complex plane. Otherwise we should not have the required dampening factors in our exponential solutions.

Fortunately, it is not necessary to solve the characteristic equation for its roots to determine whether these stability conditions are satisfied. There exist known simple necessary and sufficient conditions on the coefficients of the polynomial which guarantee stability.   These are known as the Routh-Hurwitz conditions.[21]

Let our general polynomial of the nth degree be written as

$$f(X) = a_0 X^n + a_1 X^{n-1} + \cdots + a_{n-1} X + a_n = 0, \quad (168)$$

where a_0 can always be regarded as positive, and will often be taken to be unity for convenience.

If the a coefficients are all real, it is a familiar fact that such complex roots as occur will appear in conjugate pairs, $(u + iv)$ and $(u - iv)$.   If we write the polynomial as the product, $a_0 \prod_1^n (X - X_i)$, these complex roots will combine to form real quadratic factors. It follows, therefore, that every polynomial can be written as the product of quadratic factors and linear factors,

$$f(X) = a_0(X + m_1)(X + m_2) \cdots (X + m_r)$$
$$(X^2 + b_1 X + c_1)(X^2 + b_2 X + c_2) \cdots. \quad (169)$$

The linear factors can be grouped into quadratic factors except when n is odd; in which case f can be written as a product of quadratic factors and at most one linear factor.

Now the roots of f cannot be "stable," unless the roots of each linear and quadratic factor are stable.   We must investigate then these simple cases, which can fortunately be treated exhaustively in a simple way.   The linear factor

$$X + m_1 = 0$$

clearly has a Routhian root (one whose real part is negative) only if its coefficients are of the same sign.   For $-m_1$ is its root, and m_1 must hence be positive.

A quadratic factor of the form

$$X^2 + bX + c = 0$$

has roots which can be written as

$$X = \frac{-b \pm \sqrt{b^2 - 4c}}{2}. \quad (170)$$

[21] E. J. Routh, *Stability of Given State of Motion* (London, 1877), Adams Prize Essay; *Dynamics of a System of Rigid Bodies* (6th ed.; London, 1930), part II, chap. vi; A. Hurwitz, "Ueber die Bedingungen, unter welchen eine Gleichung nur Wurzeln mit negativen reellen Theilen besitzt," *Mathematische Annalen*, XLVI (1895), 273–284.

If $b^2 - 4c$ is greater than or equal to zero, the roots are real and the quadratic expression can be factored into the product of two linear expressions, $(X + m_1)(X + m_2)$. It is obviously necessary then that the coefficients b equal to $(m_1 + m_2)$ and c equal to $m_1 m_2$ should both be positive; for the sums and products of positive numbers must be positive.

We have so far proved only the necessity for the coefficients to be positive in the real root case. Are these conditions sufficient in the real root case? And what about the complex case? Leaving the latter aside, we easily deduce that positive coefficients are also sufficient to give negative roots. The first term in the numerator of (170) is clearly negative. If we choose the negative sign before the radical, we have one root which is clearly negative. But the other root will be positive only if the second term outweighs the first, i.e., depending upon whether b^2 is less than $b^2 - 4c$. By hypothesis, c is positive, and it follows that the second term cannot outweigh the first. Thus, *positive coefficients are both necessary and sufficient for negative roots of a quadratic*, when the roots are assumed to be real.

The complex case is even simpler. If we add the two roots, $(u + iv)$ and $(u - iv)$, the complex part cancels out, and $-b$ is twice the sum of the real parts. If these are negative, then b must be positive. In any case c is positive, or the roots would not be complex, i.e., $b^2 - 4c$ is less than zero only if c is greater than zero. Therefore, our coefficients must be positive if the roots are Routhian. This proves *necessity*. If both b and c are positive and the roots are complex, it follows immediately from (170) that u must be negative. This proves sufficiency.

Thus, from our treatment of the real and complex cases, we can enunciate the simple theorem: *a second degree polynomial has roots whose real parts are both negative if, and only if, its coefficients are both positive.*

Immediately we can deduce certain necessary (but not sufficient) conditions which must hold in the general case if the roots are all to be Routhian. Each linear and quadratic factor must have positive coefficients, and, therefore, *all the coefficients of our polynomial must be positive.* This necessary condition would also be sufficient if we dealt only with real roots by virtue of Descartes Rule of Signs discussed in every book on algebra.

But there is no reason in the general case to exclude complex roots.[22] What if some of the b's are zero or negative, but in combining to form the a coefficients the positive coefficients alway outweigh the negative ones? Then our a coefficients' all being positive would not be sufficient. A simple example establishes this possibility.

$$(X + 1)(X^2 - .001X + 1) = X^3$$
$$+ .999X^2 + .999X + 1 = 0. \quad (171)$$

Note that all the a's are positive even though the complex roots have real parts which are positive ($= + .0005$).

Now that we are warned, a number of possible modes of attack are open to us. We may tackle the third and fourth degree cases by themselves, knowing that but rarely will higher degree equations be involved. Or we may deduce further, stricter necessary conditions, hoping that when we have found enough of them they will be sufficient.

Thus, in the third degree case we have

$$X^3 + a_1X^2 + a_2X + a_3 = (X + m)(X^2 + bX + c)$$
$$= X^3 + (m + b)X^2 + (c + bm)X + mc. \quad (172)$$

We form the product—never mind why—

$$a_1a_2 - a_0a_3 = (m + b)(c + bm) - mc(1)$$
$$= b(c + mb + m^2) + 0. \quad (173)$$

If the roots are all Routhian, c, b, m are all positive, from which it follows our expression $a_1a_2 - a_0a_3$ is positive.

We now have a new necessary condition, or four in all,

$$a_1 > 0,$$
$$a_2 > 0, \quad (174)$$
$$a_3 > 0,$$
$$a_1a_2 - a_0a_3 > 0.$$

Are they sufficient? If we seek an example which satisfies them and yet yields non-Routhian roots, we shall be disappointed. Or so the author's experience suggests. But how can we be sure that

---

[22] If the polynomial in question is the characteristic equation of a symmetric matrix, the roots must all be real, and the simpler analysis can be applied.

a more clever, a more zealous investigation will not produce such an example? Only by a sufficiency proof.

As a matter of fact, these four conditions will be later shown to be both necessary and sufficient. But there is still one hitch. They are not all independent. The reader may verify that the condition $a_2 > 0$ can be deduced from the other three. (Can *any* one be deduced from the other three? Which can, and which cannot?) It was the great achievement of Routh to have derived an easily calculable set of independent necessary conditions.

As an introduction to what may be called Routh's test determinants, consider the 3×3 matrix

$$\begin{bmatrix} a_1 & a_3 & 0 \\ a_0 & a_2 & 0 \\ 0 & a_1 & a_3 \end{bmatrix}. \qquad (175)$$

Its three naturally ordered principal minors, Δ_1, Δ_2, Δ_3, are, respectively, a_1, $a_2 a_1 - a_3 a_0$, $a_3(a_1 a_2 - a_3 a_0)$, and if they are all positive, then the necessary and sufficient conditions for a cubic to be Routhian are realized. This suggests a general rule for a polynomial of the nth degree. List its odd coefficients in a row, treating all coefficients with subscripts greater than n as zero: $a_1 a_3 a_5 a_7 \cdots$. Let each of these elements head a column, whose subscripts decrease one at each step. Follow the convention that any negative subscript implies that the coefficient is zero. Thus we have a square array of numbers, of which only the first n rows and columns need concern us.

$$\begin{array}{ccccc} a_1 & a_3 & a_5 & a_7 & \cdots \\ a_0 & a_2 & a_4 & a_6 & \cdots \\ 0 & a_1 & a_3 & a_5 & \cdots \\ 0 & a_0 & a_2 & a_4 & \cdots \qquad (a_0 > 0) \\ \cdot & \cdot & \cdot & \cdot & \cdots \\ \cdot & \cdot & \cdot & \cdot & \cdots \\ \cdot & \cdot & \cdot & \cdot & \cdots \end{array} \qquad (176)$$

The reader should write out the matrix in full for an 8th and 9th degree polynomial, noting the difference between an odd and even n.

Routh's theorem states that *it is necessary and sufficient in order for the real parts of all roots to be negative that the principal minors of this matrix all be positive;* i.e.,

$$\Delta_1 = a_1 > 0,$$
$$\Delta_2 = a_1 a_2 - a_0 a_3 > 0,$$
$$\cdot$$
$$\cdot \qquad\qquad\qquad\qquad\qquad (177)$$
$$\cdot$$
$$\Delta_{n-1} > 0,$$
$$\Delta_n = a_n \Delta_{n-1} > 0.$$

The condition that all the a's are positive is contained within these conditions; but not vice versa (except if all roots are real).

The rigorous proof of this theorem cannot be given here. The reader must be referred to Routh's Adams Prize Essay. A brief sketch of the reasoning may, however, be indicated. Let X be any point in the complex plane, and $f(X)$ be a mapping into another complex plane. Consider any closed contour C in the X plane. The number of roots of $f(X)$ within this contour can be determined by an important theorem of Cauchy,[23] which is essentially topological in nature. Traverse the contour C in the positive sense (counter-clockwise) and consider the mapped contour of $f(X)$. The number of roots in C equals the number of times that $f(X)$ loops around the origin; or if we write $f(X)$ as $P + iQ$, the number of times that the ratio P/Q passes through zero from plus to minus in excess of the number of times that the ratio passes through zero from minus to plus.

Routh takes as his contour C the right half complex plane, or more rigorously a limitlessly large semicircle to the right of the origin and the imaginary axis. The changes in sign of P/Q on the semicircle are easily evaluated. Hence, if there are to be no roots in the right half plane, the number of changes in sign of P/Q on the imaginary axis are uniquely determined; and the polynomials $f_1(X)$ and $f_2(X)$ must have all real roots which separate each other, where

$$\pm f(iX) = f_1(X) + if_2(X). \qquad (178)$$

<hr/>

[23] See any textbook on complex variables.

By classical Sturmian theory this involves taking the greatest common divisor of $f_1(X)$ and $f_2(X)$ to get new functions $f_3(X)$, $f_4(X)$, $\cdots$. Finally, the conditions on these subsidiary functions can be shown to be equivalent to the Routh-Hurwitz test determinants given in (177).

Numerically, these determinants can be easily evaluated by various Gauss-Doolittle methods. As an exercise the reader may verify that the conditions for a fourth degree equation are as follows:

$$
\begin{aligned}
a_1 &> 0, \\
a_1 a_2 - a_0 a_3 &> 0, \\
a_1 a_2 a_3 - a_0 a_3{}^2 - a_1{}^2 a_4 &> 0, \\
a_4 &> 0.
\end{aligned}
\tag{179}
$$

It is worth noting that as we move continuously from a stable set of coefficients to an unstable set that a_n or Δ_{n-1} first change sign; also that a reverse numbering of the a's must satisfy the stability conditions.[24]

37. We have seen that for a difference equation system to be stable it is not necessary that the real parts of the roots of the characteristic equation be negative. Rather the roots must be less than unity in absolute value. Instead of all lying in the left half of the complex plane, they must all lie in the unit circle.

For first and second degree equations it is not hard to work out necessary and sufficient conditions by direct algebraic means. For higher degree equations such methods are tortuous. Fortunately, by a simple use of complex transformations we can reduce our problem to the Routhian problem already given a complete answer.[25] The complex transformation

$$
X = \frac{Z+1}{Z-1}, \qquad Z = \frac{X+1}{X-1}
\tag{180}
$$

converts the unit circle into the left half of the complex plane.

---

[24] In P. A. Samuelson, "Conditions that the Roots of a Polynomial be less than Unity in Absolute Value," *Annals of Mathematical Statistics*, XII (1941), 360–364, a numerical example is worked out and some further facts are noted. If a number of Δ's vanish, then a further test must be made.

[25] P. A. Samuelson, "Conditions that the Roots of a Polynomial be less than Unity in Absolute Value," *Annals of Mathematical Statistics*, XII (1941), 360–364.

Also

$$f(X) = f\left(\frac{Z+1}{Z-1}\right) = \frac{a_0(Z+1)^n + a_1(Z+1)^{n-1}(Z-1)}{(Z-1)^n} + \cdots$$

$$+ \frac{a_{n-1}(Z+1)(Z-1)^{n-1} + a_n(Z-1)^n}{(Z-1)^n}. \tag{181}$$

If the polynomial $f(X)$ is to have no roots in the unit circle, then the numerator of the right-hand side, regarded as a polynomial in Z, must satisfy the Routhian conditions. If we expand out this polynomial in the first degree case, we find as necessary and sufficient conditions that the root of $X + a_1 = 0$ be less than unity in absolute value;

$$\begin{matrix} 1 + a_1 > 0, \\ 1 - a_1 > 0, \end{matrix} \quad \text{or} \quad |a_1| < 1. \tag{182}$$

For the second degree polynomial, $X^2 + a_1 X + a_2 = 0$, the reader can show that the stability region of the (a_1, a_2) plane is a triangle defined by

$$\begin{matrix} 1 + a_1 + a_2 > 0, \\ 1 - a_2 > 0, \\ 1 - a_1 + a_2 > 0, \end{matrix} \tag{183}$$

It is to be noted that the conditions are always one greater in number than the degree of the equation. This is true in the general case of the nth degree equation.

$$f(X) = X^n + a_1 X^{n-1} + \cdots + a_{n-1} X + a_n = 0. \tag{184}$$

We form the equation in Z,

$$\bar{a}_0 Z^n + \bar{a}_1 Z^{n-1} + \cdots + \bar{a}_{n-1} Z + \bar{a}_n = \sum_{i=0}^{n} a_i(Z-1)^i(Z+1)^{n-i} \tag{185}$$

$$= \sum_{i=0}^{n} a_i \sum_{k=0}^{i} \sum_{j=0}^{n-i} \binom{i}{k} Z^{i-k}(-1)^k \binom{n-i}{j} Z^{n-i-j},$$

where

$$\begin{aligned} \binom{s}{t} &= \frac{s!}{t!(s-t)!}, & s \geq t; \quad t \geq 0 \\ &= 0, & s < t \\ &= 0. & t < 0 \end{aligned} \tag{186}$$

Collecting terms we find

$$\bar{a}_0 = \sum_{i=0}^{n} a_i,$$

$$\bar{a}_1 = \sum_{i=0}^{n} a_i(n - 2i),$$

.
.
. (187)

$$\bar{a}_r = \sum_{i=0}^{n} a_i \sum_{k=0}^{n} \binom{n-i}{r-k} (-1)^k \binom{i}{k},$$

.
.
.

$$\bar{a}_n = 1 - a_1 + a_2 - \cdots + (-1)^{n-1}a_{n-1} + (-1)^n a_n.$$

In addition to the condition,

$$\bar{a}_0 > 0,$$

we have the Routhian conditions

$$\Delta_1 > 0,$$
$$\Delta_2 > 0,$$
. (188)
.
.
$$\Delta_n > 0,$$

where these are naturally ordered principal minors of

$$\begin{bmatrix} \bar{a}_1 & \bar{a}_3 & \bar{a}_5 & \cdots \\ \bar{a}_0 & \bar{a}_2 & \bar{a}_4 & \cdots \\ 0 & \bar{a}_1 & \bar{a}_3 & \cdots \\ 0 & \bar{a}_0 & \bar{a}_2 & \cdots \\ \cdot & \cdot & \cdot & \cdots \\ \cdot & \cdot & \cdot & \cdots \\ \cdot & \cdot & \cdot & \cdots \end{bmatrix}$$ (189)

The reader may verify that for a cubic equation,

$$\bar{a}_0 = 1 + a_1 + a_2 + a_3,$$
$$\bar{a}_1 = 3 + a_1 - a_2 - 3a_3,$$
$$\bar{a}_2 = 3 - a_1 - a_2 + 3a_3,$$ (190)
$$\bar{a}_3 = 1 - a_1 + a_2 - a_3.$$

38. Formally, our stability criteria are complete. But for most theoretical purposes numerical values of the various coefficients are not at hand. It would be highly desirable to be able to infer from the qualitative properties of our dynamical matrices even before their characteristic determinants have been (laboriously) expanded out whether or not they are stable.

Unfortunately, this is rarely possible. Often, however, certain very general sufficient conditions can be indicated to guarantee that a differential equation is stable—or as I shall term it Routhian; or to indicate that a difference equation is stable with moduli less than unity—or as I shall term it Tinbergenian in honor of Professor Tinbergen's outstanding work with difference equations in economics.

The following theorems are listed more or less without proof:

Theorem 1: $\dot{x} = ax$ is stable, if the matrix a is symmetrical and negative definite; i.e., a is a Routhian matrix. (See Mathematical Appendix A, page 19 *passim* for this classical fact.)

Theorem 2: If a is quasi-definite, so that $\dfrac{a + a'}{2}$ is negative definite, then a is Routhian. $\left(\text{Hint: } \dfrac{d}{dt}(X'X) = X'aX \right.$

$= X'\left(\dfrac{a + a'}{2}\right)X < 0.$ Therefore, $\lim\limits_{t \to \infty} x_i(t) = 0$, and roots must

be damped. $\Big)$

Theorem 3: If $a'a - I$ is negative definite, then a is Tinbergenian; i.e., $X_{t+1} = aX_t$ is stable, and roots of $|a - \lambda I| = 0$ are all less than unity in absolute value. (Hint: $X_{t+1}'X_{t+1} = X_t'(a'a - I)X_t = \Delta(\sum x_t^2) < 0$ by hypothesis. Therefore, $\lim\limits_{t \to \infty} X_t = 0$.)

Theorem 4 (Metzler): If a is "Hicksian" as defined in chapter VI, with all its off-diagonal elements positive, then it is necessarily Tinbergenian.

Theorem 5 (Metzler): If $a_{ij} \geqq 0$ and $\sum\limits_{j=1}^{n} a_{ij} < 1$, then $(a - I)$ is Hicksian, and hence (by Theorem 4) is Tinbergenian.

Theorem 6 (Mosak): If a is Hicksian, and if the off-diagonal elements of a are all positive, then *all* of the elements of a^{-1} are negative.

Theorem 7 (Oppenheim-Yntema): If all the symbols are positive in

$$A = \left[\begin{array}{c|c} \dfrac{(v_i + \sum\limits_{j} a_{ij})\delta_{ij}}{b_{ks}} & a_{ij} \\ \hline b_{ks} & (w_k + \sum\limits_{s} b_{ks})\delta_{ks} \end{array} \right],$$

then the pattern of signs in A^{-1} is

$$\left[\begin{array}{ccc|ccc} + & \cdots & + & - & \cdots & - \\ \cdot & & \cdot & \cdot & & \cdot \\ \cdot & & \cdot & \cdot & & \cdot \\ \cdot & & \cdot & \cdot & & \cdot \\ + & \cdots & + & - & \cdots & - \\ \hline - & \cdots & - & + & \cdots & + \\ \cdot & & \cdot & \cdot & & \cdot \\ \cdot & & \cdot & \cdot & & \cdot \\ \cdot & & \cdot & \cdot & & \cdot \\ - & \cdots & - & + & \cdots & + \end{array} \right].$$

INDEX

ACCELERATION PRINCIPLE AND MULTIPLIER, interaction between, 341n.
"ACQUIRED CHARACTERISTICS", 211
ADVERTISING EXPENSE, 41
ALEXANDER, S. S., 155
ALLEN, R. G. D., 125n., 146, 180n., 196
  See also Hicks and Allen
"ALL OR NONE" PHENOMENA, 210, 241
ANALOGIES, BIOLOGICAL, 311
ANALYTIC FUNCTIONS AND HIGHER DERIVATIVES, 52ff.
"ANNALS OF MATHEMATICAL STATISTICS," 343n.
ANTI-TRUST, 203
ASYMMETRY AND INSTABILITY, 187
  See also Symmetry

BARONE, E., 212ff., 213, 245, 252
BASTIAT, F., 211n.
BATCHELDER, P. M., 380n.
BENEFIT FROM FREE TRADE, 204
BENNION, E. G., 341n. .
BENTHAM, J., 90
BERGSON (BURK), A., vii, 219 223, 225, 252
BERNOULLI'S LAW OF UTILITY, 227n.
BIOLOGICAL ANALOGIES, 311
BIRKHOFF, G. D., 54n., 262n., 300n., 319n., 334n., 339n.
BISHOP, R. L., 189n., 198
BOCHER, M., 137n., 423n.
BÖHM-BAWERK, E., 188, 233n.
BOOLE, G., 380n.
BORDERED DETERMINANT OR MATRIX, 37, 62, 101, 132, 167, 365, 377ff.
BORTKIEWICZ, L., 146
BOUNDARY OR CORNER MINIMA, 69ff.
BOWLEY, A. L. 146, 150
BROMWICH-WAGNER CONTOUR INTEGRALS, 398
BROWNIAN MOVEMENT, 268, 317n.
BUDGET EQUATION, 98, 166
BURK, A. See Bergson, A.

BUSCHEGUENNCE, S., 155
BUSINESS CYCLE, 350
  "billiard table" theories of, 340
  exogenous and endogenous theories of, 335ff.
  nature of the, 335ff.
  non-linearity and amplitude of, 337ff.

CANNAN, E., 223n.
CAPITALIZATION OF RESIDUAL PROFITS, 87
CARATHÉODORY, C., 363n.
CARDINAL UTILITY, 91ff., 135n., 172ff.
  and welfare economics, 196, 226ff.
CASSEL, G., 312n.
CASSELS, J. M., 210n.
CAUCHY THEOREM ON ROOTS OF AN EQUATION, 434
CAUSAL SYSTEMS, 285n., 315, 317ff.
CHAMBERLIN, E. H., 210n.
CHAMPERNOWNE, D. G., 125n.
CHANDRASEKHAR, S., 317n.
CHARACTERISTIC, equation, 271, 299, 371n., 422; mathematical theory of, 373ff.
  roots, 271, 299, 349, 371, 422
  vectors, 372, 422
CHARACTERISTIC EXPONENTS OR MULTIPLIERS, 339
CLARK, J. B., 35, 211n., 313
CLARK, J. M., 242, 313n.
COBWEB CYCLE PHENOMENON, 22, 265, 321, 339n., 390ff.
COLLAR, A. R. See Frazer
COMPENSATED CHANGE, 103
  under rationing, 168
COMPLEMENTARITY, 183ff.
COMPOSITE COMMODITIES, 141, 144
CONSTRAINED MAXIMA AND MINIMA, 60, 350, 362ff.
  See also Bordered Determinant
CONSUMER'S SURPLUS, 195ff., 206
  six versions of, 199

CONSUMPTION FUNCTION, 276
CONTRACT LOCUS, 238, 251
    generalized, 214, 233
CORN LAWS, 250
CORRESPONDENCE PRINCIPLE, 5, 258, 263, 284, 350
COST AND PRODUCTION THEORY OF THE FIRM, 57ff., 350
COURNOT, A. A., 141
COURT, L., 55n.
CRITERION FOR DISPLACEMENT OF EQUILIBRIUM, 39ff.

DAVIDSON, D., 328n.
DAVIS, H. T., 342n.
DECREASING COSTS, 210, 239, 242,312
DEDUCTIVE REASONING, 12
DEFICIT FINANCING, 354
DEMAND, for a group of commodities, 141ff.
    for consumers' goods, 96ff.
    for factors of production, 45, 55, 59
DESIGN, TELEOLOGICAL, 203
DETERMINANT. *See* Matrix
DETERMINANTAL EQUATION. *See* Characteristic equation
DETERMINATENESS OF EQUILIBRIUM, 62n., 75ff., 145, 351
DIFFERENCE EQUATIONS, 265, 282, 287, 302ff., 314, 380ff.
    types of stability points, 305
DIFFERENTIAL EQUATIONS, 263ff., 287, 288, 299, 314, 380ff.
DIMINISHING RETURNS, 12, 23, 62
DIRAC FUNCTION, 286, 333
DISCONTINUITIES, 70ff., 80
DISCRIMINATING MONOPOLY AND PRICE, 42, 247
DIVISIA, F., 150n.
DOETCH, G., 398n.
DRESCH, F., 268
DUNCAN, W. J. *See* Frazer
DUPUIT-MARSHALL, 218n.
DURAND, D., 124n.
DYNAMICS, 350
    and statics, six categories of, 315
    comparative, 351, 355
    definitions of, 284ff., 311ff.

ECONOMICS, boundaries of, 319
EDGEWORTH, F. Y., 90, 92, 93, 146, 183, 206, 225, 226n., 251
ELASTICITY COEFFICIENTS, 105, 125ff., 188n.
    dimensions of, 126n.
ELEMENTARY FACTORS AND DIVISORS, 373n., 423, 427
ELLIS, H. S., 117n.
ENDOGENOUS THEORIES. *See* Business Cycle
ENGEL'S LAWS, 193
EQUILIBRIA, MULTIPLE, 49, 240
    See also Determinateness
EQUILIBRIUM, 8
    absence of, 261n.
    and varying time periods, 330ff.
    external conditions, 81, 88
    receding, 326
    See also Determinateness
ETHICAL ASSUMPTIONS, 203ff
EULER'S THEOREM ON HOMOGENEOUS FUNCTIONS, 68, 83, 105
EVOLUTION AND ORGANIC GROWTH, 312
EXHAUSTION OF THE PRODUCT, 83, 88
EXOGENOUS THEORIES. *See* Business Cycle
EXTERNAL ECONOMIES OR DISECONOMIES, 208
    in consumption, 224

FACTOR OF PRODUCTION, 84
FELLER, W., 349n.
FINITE CHANGES, analysis of, 46, 109
FINITE DIFFERENCES, 381ff.
FISHER, I., 93n., 95, 139n., 146, 173n., 174n., 183, 228n.
FORCED MOTION, 325n., 335, 341
FRANCE, ANATOLE, 225n.
FRAZER, R. A., DUNCAN AND COLLAR, 419n., 422n., 424n., 425n.
FREE ENTRY, 87, 88
FREE TRADE, 204
FRICKEY, E., 146
FRIEDMAN, M., 180n., 181
FRISCH, R., 8n., 146, 174n., 196, 218, 228n., 261n., 284n., 285n., 314n., 317n., 328n., 342n.
    definition of normal equilibrium value, 327ff.

FRISCH-HOLME MIXED DIFFERENCE-DIFFERENTIAL EQUATION, 309
FUNCTIONAL EQUATIONS, 260, 286, 308ff., 380ff.

GAUSSIAN. *See* Normal
GENERAL EQUILIBRIUM, 8
GEORGESCU-ROEGEN,N., 139n., 182n., 351
GIBBS, J. W., 21n., 70n.
GIFFEN'S PARADOX, 115
and rationing, 169
GILBOY, E. W., 281n.
GOSSEN, H. H., 93
GRESHAM'S LAW, 170

HAAVELMO, T., 343n.
HABERLER, G., 146, 196
HANCOCK, H., 370n., 371n.
"HANDICAP SETTING" and Optimal Taxation, 247
HANSEN, A. H., 340n., 341n.
HARMONIC DIAL, 342n.
HARROD, R. F., 340n.
HART, A. G., 143n.
HAWTREY, R., 340
HAYEK, F. A., 214n.
HEAVISIDE, O., 401ff.
HEAVISIDE-CAUCHY OPERATIONAL CALCULUS, 397ff.
HENDERSON, A., 189n.
HENDERSON, L. J., 5n., 312
HERMITIAN MATRIX, 271, 371ff.
HERTZ-HERGLOTZ SOLUTION OF INTEGRAL EQUATIONS, 309
HESSIAN DETERMINANT OR MATRIX, 31, 49, 52, 67, 376n.
HICKS, J. R., vii, 18n., 86, 122, 123, 130, 133n., 143, 187, 189n., 208n., 219n., 252n., 269, 276n., 317n.
HICKS AND ALLEN, 95, 96, 139, 184, 351
HICKSIAN MATRIX, 133, 139, 141, 272, 438
HICKSIAN STABILITY AND TRUE DYNAMIC STABILITY, 273ff.
HISTORICAL SYSTEM, 316ff.
HOMOGENEITY of order one, 84n.
of order zero, 68, 105. *See also* Euler's Theorem

HOTELLING, H., 55n., 62n., 78n., 218n., 231, 252, 351
HURWITZ, A., 430n.

"IM KLEINEN" MAXIMUM, 206, 241
IMPLICIT FUNCTION THEOREM, 48, 145, 259n.
INDETERMINACY IN PUREST COMPETITION, 78ff.
INDEX NUMBER, best limits on, 149
economic, 111, 146ff.
Laspeyre formula, 155, 162
non-existence of perfect quantity indicator, 154
of price, 156
of quantity, 160
Paache formula, 162
INDIFFERENCE CURVE OR LOCUS, 94ff.
INDIVIDUALISTIC HYPOTHESIS, 223
INEQUALITY, 211, 225
INFANT INDUSTRY, 253
INFERIOR GOOD, 169, 201n.
INFINITE SUBSTITUTES IN WELFARE FUNCTION, 222
INITIAL CONDITIONS, change in, 352
INSTITUTIONAL ADVANTAGE, 87
INTEGRABILITY CONDITIONS, 54, 95, 107n., 179
INTEGRAL EQUATIONS, 286, 309, 314
INTEGRATING FACTOR, 95
INTEREST, lack of necessity for uniform real rate of, 233n.
INTERNATIONAL TRADE, 204
INTERPERSONAL additions of utility, 206
comparisons, 91, 205, 220, 245, 249. *See also* Welfare Economics
optimal welfare conditions, 243ff.

JACOBIAN DETERMINANT OR MATRIX, 127ff.
JEVONS, W. S., 90, 93, 146, 205
JOHNSON, W. E., 95, 115, 351

KAHN, R. F., 210n., 219n., 260n.
KALDOR, N., 219n., 252n., 260n.
KALECKI, M., 167n., 337n.
KÁRMÁN, T. VON, 339n.
KEYNES, J. M., 118, 122, 146

KEYNESIAN SYSTEM, 28, 276, 353
KNIGHT, F. H., 123, 196n., 208n.,
215n., 223, 226, 311
KÖNUS, A., 146, 155, 196
KONDRATIEFF LONG WAVES, 340

LAGRANGEAN MULTIPLIERS, 37, 60ff.,
98, 131, 166, 192, 231
See also Prices
LANGE, O., 127n., 173n., 219n., 232n.,
252, 274n., 276n., 354n., 239
LAPLACE TRANSFORM, 398
generalized for any operator,
415ff.
LASPEYRE. *See* Index Number
LATENT. *See* Characteristic
LAUNHARDT, W., 205
LE CHATELIER PRINCIPLE, 36, 38n.,
81, 168
LE CORBEILLER, Ph., 340n.
LEGENDRE TRANSFORMATION, 138n.
LEONTIEF, W., vii, 29n., 130, 146,
162n., 196, 339n., 390n.
LERNER, A. P., 146, 196, 217, 218n.,
245, 246, 252
LESER, C. E. V., 122n.
LEVINSON, N., 339n.
LEWIS, D. C., Jr. *See* Birkhoff, G. D.
LIMITATIONAL FACTORS, 71
LINEARITY AND NON-LINEARITY OF
SYSTEMS, 284, 288, 332, 391ff.
LIPPINCOTT, B. E., 232n.
LIQUIDITY PREFERENCE, 123, 276
LOCAL INDEPENDENCE CONDITIONS,
180
LOGISTIC LAW, 291
LOTKA, A. J., 292n., 309n., 323n.
LUMP-SUM TAXES OR BOUNTIES, 245,
247
LUNDBERG, E., 389n.
LUTZ, F. A., 124n.

MALTHUS, T. R., 203n.
MALTHUSIAN AND OPTIMUM POPULA-
TION THEORIES, 296
MANN, H. B., 343n.
MARGINAL COST, 65, 240ff.
MARGINAL EFFICIENCY OF CAPITAL,
276

MARGINAL PRODUCTIVITY, 58, 83
net, 75
of the last dollar, 60, 88
MARGINAL PROPENSITY TO CONSUME,
and stability, 279ff.
MARGINAL UTILITY OF INCOME, 99,
104, 135, 190
constancy of, 172ff., 189ff.
MARGINAL UTILITY OF MONEY, 190
MARKOFF CHAIN, 317n.
MARSCHAK, J., 121n.
MARSHALL, A., 6, 18n., 21n., 35n., 79,
93n., 141, 146, 173, 194n., 197, 198,
206, 207, 212, 242, 246, 264n., 311
MATHEMATICAL THEORY, of characteristic equation, 373ff.
of difference equations, 380ff.
of functional equations, 380ff.
of general operator equations,
396ff.
of generalized Laplace transform,
415ff.
of maxima, 357ff.
of maxima under constraints,
362ff. (*See also* Bordered
determinant)
of quadratic forms, 365ff. (*See
also* Transformation)
MATRIX, rank of, 132, 362ff.
"transpose" of, 132
See also Bordered determinant,
Hermitian, Hessian, Hicksian,
Jacobian, Quasi-definite, Routhian, Tinbergenian,
Symmetric and asymmetric
MAXIMIZATION of profit, 76ff.
of ordinal utility, 97ff.
MAXIMUM CONDITIONS, 29, 48, 258,
357ff., 362ff.
See also Quadratic forms
MAXIMUM PROBLEM, 15ff., 21, 98
convertibility into a, 52ff.
MAXIMUM UNDER CONSTRAINTS, 36ff.,
98, 131, 350
See also Bordered determinant
MEADE, J. E., 276n.
MEANINGFUL THEOREMS, 3, 4, 5,
46ff., 84, 91, 107, 172, 221, 257, 284,
350
three sources of, 21

MENGER, K., 90
METZLER, L. A., 273n., 438
MILL, J. S., 313
MILNE-THOMSON, L. M., 380n.
MINIMUM AVERAGE COST, 86, 88
MINIMUM TOTAL COST, 58, 59, 66, 73, 88
MITCHELL, W. C., 341n.
MONEY, demand for, 117ff.
MONOPOLISTIC COMPETITION, 210
MOORE, H. L., 315n., 321
MOSAK, J., 273n., 438
MOULTON, F. R., 388n., 408n.
MOVING EQUILIBRIUM, problem of definition of, 321ff.
  stability of, 329
MUTUAL INTERDEPENDENCE AND CAUSATION, 9

NEISSER, H., 167n., 170n.
NET AND GROSS REPRODUCTION RATES, 299
NEUMAN, J. VON, 170n.
NÖRLUND, N. E., 380n.
NON-COMPETING GROUPS, 211
NORMAL OR GAUSSIAN DISTRIBUTION OF PROBABILITIES, 343, 345, 349
"NUMERAIRE," 106, 117, 187, 190

OPERATIONAL SIGNIFICANCE. *See* Meaningful Theorems
OPPENHEIM-YNTEMA MATRIX, 439
OPPORTUNITY COST, 88n., 234n.
ORDINAL PREFERENCE, 22, 91, 94ff., 172ff., 221ff.

PAACHE. *See* Index Number
PALEY, W., 226
PARETO, V., 93, 96, 139n., 141, 183, 191, 212n., 213, 236, 245, 249, 252, 351
PERIODOGRAM AND FOURIER ANALYSIS, 342
PERIOD OF PRODUCTION, 188ff.
PERPETUAL STEW, 188n.
PERSONS, W., 146
PFAFFIAN, 95, 139
PICARD, E., 289n., 300n., 334n.
PIGOU, A. C., 146, 182n., 196n., 207, 215, 245, 246, 249

PLANNING, optimum economic, 203ff.
POSSIBILITY FUNCTION OF SOCIETY, 236, 244, 250, 251n.
PRICE DISCRIMINATION, 197
PRICES AS LAGRANGEAN MULTIPLIERS, 216, 231, 235, 247
PRODUCERS' SURPLUS, 208
PRODUCTION FUNCTION, 57, 230
  homogeneous, 83
  See also Euler's Theorem
  See also Homogeneity
PROFITS, 85ff.
PURE COMPETITION, 78, 82
  as a norm, 204

QUADRATIC FORM, definite, 30n., 55, 68, 77, 126, 140, 366ff. (*See also* Maximum conditions)
  definite under constraint, 62, 376ff. (*See also* Bordered Determinant)
  definition of, 30, 365ff.
  semi-definite, 113, 366ff., 379
QUALITATIVE RELATIONS, a calculus of, 23ff.
QUALITATIVE RESTRICTIONS, 20
QUASI-DEFINITE, property of a matrix, 140, 438

RATIONAL BEHAVIOR, 90, 98
RATIONING, 167n.
  "point," 165
  simple, 163
RAYLEIGH, LORD, 194
REAL COST, 211, 234n.
RECIPROCAL RELATIONS, 89, 103, 107
  See also Integrability Conditions
REDER, M, W., 143n.
REGULAR MAXIMUM OR MINIMUM, 30, 55, 358ff.
RELAXATION OSCILLATIONS and non-linear systems, 338ff.
RENT, 87, 208
RESIDUAL THEORIES, 87
RICARDO, D., 35
ROBBINS, L., 219n., 220, 223, 249, 313
ROBERTSON, D. H., 208n.
ROBERTSONIAN IDENTITIES, 278
ROBIN HOOD, 206

ROBINSON, G.   *See* Whittaker
ROBINSON, JOAN, 75n.
ROUTH, E. J., 430n.
ROUTH-HURWITZ CONDITIONS FOR STABLE ROOTS, 430
ROUTHIAN MATRIX, 431, 438
SAMUELSON, P. A., 111n., 123n., 139n., 189n., 219n., 234n., 252n., 273n., 311n., 341n., 388n., 408n., 409n., 426n.. 435n.
SAVAGE, L. J., 427n.
SCARCITY, natural and contrived, 87
SCHLESINGER, K., 170n.
SCHULTZ, H., 104n., 128n., 155n., 184n.
SCHUMPETER, J. A., vii, 117, 312n., 316n., 320n., 341n.
SCITOVSKY, T., 167n., 219n., 251n.
SECONDARY EXTREMUM CONDITIONS. *See* Maximum and Quadratic Form
SECULAR EQUATION, *See* Characteristic Equation
SELF-EVIDENT TRUTHS, 84
SELF-GENERATING CYCLE and circular reasoning, 336
SENIOR, N., 211
SIDGWICK, H., 90, 226
SLUTSKY, E., 4n., 102, 103n., 115, 167, 180n., 182, 184n., 317n., 343, 351
SMITH, ADAM, 203, 313
SMITH, OLIVER K., 339n.
SOCIAL WELFARE FUNCTION, 219ff., 226ff., 248
    eight assumptions about, 221ff.
SOCIOLOGY, 90
STABILITY conditions, 5, 258ff., 350.
    (*See also* Correspondence Principle)
    and maximum conditions, 301
    danger of assuming non-dampening, 268, 336
    different concepts of, 261ff., 272, 290, 300, 312, 333ff.
    higher-order, 294
    of multiple markets, 269
    of single market, 18, 263
    Walrasian and Marshallian, 264n.
STACKELBERG, H. VON, 170n.
STAEHLE, H., 146, 196
STAMP, Sir J., 223n.
STATICAL VS. STATIONARY, 313

STATICS, COMPARATIVE, 8, 258ff., 350
STIGLER, G. J., 252n.
STOCHASTICAL SYSTEM, 316ff.
    non-linear, 344ff.
STOLPER, W. F., 234n.
SUPERPOSITION THEOREM AND LINEARITY, 352
SUPPLY AND DEMAND, 257
SUPPLY CURVE, 41, 51, 77n., 260, 264
SWEEZY, A. R., 91n.
SYLVESTER'S LAW of Inertia, 369ff.
    of latency, 375n., 424
SYMMETRY AND ASYMMETRY, 140n., 141, 187, 272n., 438
SYMMETRY OF PERSONS, 224

TAX, direct vs. indirect, 197
    doctrine of equal or minimum sacrifice, 226, 227n.
    formula, "curvature" and risks, 248n.
    problem, 14, 39
TEMPORARY NATIONAL ECONOMIC COMMITTEE (TNEC), 203
THERMODYNAMICS, 21n., 36
THRIFTINESS and capital formation, 353
THÜNEN, J. H. 211
TINBERGEN, J., 8n., 340n.
TINBERGENIAN MATRIX, 438
TRANSFORMATION, cogredient, 133
    congruent, 133, 138
    contragredient, 137, 274
    curve of society, 230, 234
    logarithmic, 125
    of commodities and prices, 135
    of dependent variable, 133
    of independent variables, 129
    of time, 318
    of utility, 94, 175, 376n.
"'TWERE BETTER" PROPOSITIONS, 250, 251

UNCERTAINTY, 117
U-SHAPED COST CURVES, 85
UTILITARIANISM, 206
UTILITY, evolution of concept, 90ff.
    independence of, 174ff.
    index, 94

invariance of, 95, 99, 104, 183, 193. (*See also* Transformation) mathematical aspects of, 92ff. *See also* Marginal utility of income

VALUE JUDGMENTS, 220
VAN DER POL, B., 339n.
VEBLEN, T., 119, 224
VERHULST-PEARL-REED. *See* Logistic Law
VINER, J., 34, 35, 66n., 197n., 208, 219n., 260n., 312n.
"VIX MEDICATRIX NATURAE," 312

WALD, A., 146, 150, 170n., 196, 343n.
WALRAS, L., 8, 79, 86, 90, 93n., 118, 141, 204, 205n., 260, 264, 351
three theorems of, 87
WELFARE ECONOMICS, vii, 52, 173, 203ff., 220
and cardinal utility, 196n.
and rationing, 171
modifications introduced by dynamical considerations, 253
new and old, 212, 249

optimum conditions between persons, 245ff.; in exchange, 212, 218, 236ff.; in production, 217, 218, 230ff.; of degree of product differentiation, 197, 232n., 241; of saving, 253n.
WELFARE FUNCTION. *See* Social welfare function
WESTERN MAN, 226
WHITTAKER, E. T., 381n.
WICKSELL, K., 86, 146, 204n., 205n., 206, 212, 215n., 328n.
WIENER, N., 342n.
WILSON, E. B., vii, 81
WINTNER, A., 138n.
WOLD, H., 317n., 342n.
WONG, Y. K., 34, 66n.
WONG-VINER-HARROD ENVELOPE THEOREM, 243

YNTEMA, T. O., 439
YOUNG, ALLYN, 146, 208n.
YULE, G. U., 317n.

ZONE OF INDIFFERENCE AND INTERNAL MARGIN, 212

PAUL ANTHONY SAMUELSON, born at Gary, Indiana, in 1915, was educated at the University of Chicago and Harvard. Professor of Economics at the Massachusetts Institute of Technology since 1940, President of the American Economic Association in 1961, he is a Fellow of the British Academy. He has served as consultant to the National Resources Planning Board, to the War Production Board, to the United States Treasury, and to the Rand Corporation. For the *Foundations of Economic Analysis,* he was awarded the John Bates Clark Medal of the American Economic Association. His other books include *Economics, an Introductory Analysis; Readings in Economics; Linear Programming and Economic Analysis.*

Atheneum Paperbacks

HISTORY–AMERICAN–BEFORE 1900
6 ROGER WILLIAMS *by Perry Miller*
17 MYTHS AND REALITIES *by Carl Bridenbaugh*
32 STRANGERS IN THE LAND *by John Higham*
40 THE UNITED STATES AND MEXICO *by Howard F. Cline*
51 TURMOIL AND TRADITION *by Elting E. Morison*
70 THE CHINA TANGLE *by Herbert Feis*
84 THE DIMENSIONS OF LIBERTY *by Oscar and Mary Handlin*
86 THE CORPORATION IN MODERN SOCIETY *edited by Edward S. Mason*
110 DRED SCOTT'S CASE *by Vincent C. Hopkins, S.J.*
111 THE DECLINE OF AMERICAN LIBERALISM *by Arthur A. Ekirch, Jr.*
113 HARVARD GUIDE TO AMERICAN HISTORY *edited by Oscar Handlin,
    Arthur Meier Schlesinger, Samuel Eliot Morison, Frederick Merk,
    Arthur Meier Schlesinger, Jr., Paul Herman Buck*
115 THE ROOTS OF AMERICAN LOYALTY *by Merle Curti*
116 THE POLITICS OF PREJUDICE *by Roger Daniels*
117 CENTURY OF STRUGGLE *by Eleanor Flexner*
118 BOSTON'S IMMIGRANTS *by Oscar Handlin*
123 THE AMERICAN APPROACH TO FOREIGN POLICY *by Dexter Perkins*
125 THE EIGHTEENTH-CENTURY COMMONWEALTHMAN *by Caroline Robbins*
126 THE AMERICAN AS REFORMER *by Arthur M. Schlesinger*
132 ASA GRAY *by A. Hunter Dupree*
134 THE COLONIAL MERCHANTS AND THE AMERICAN REVOLUTION–
    1763–1776 *by Arthur M. Schlesinger*
136 THE ROAD TO APPOMATTOX *by Bell Irvin Wiley*
137 FREE SPEECH IN THE UNITED STATES *by Zechariah Chafee, Jr.*
139 CONSERVATION AND THE GOSPEL OF EFFICIENCY *by Samuel P. Hays*
142 THE PROFESSIONAL ALTRUIST *by Roy Lubove*
144 POVERTY AND PROGRESS *by Stephan Thernstrom*
145 STREETCAR SUBURBS *by Sam B. Warner*
150 THE DECLINE OF AGRARIAN DEMOCRACY *by Grant McConnell*
151 POLITICS AND POWER *by David J. Rothman*
161 QUANTIFICATION IN AMERICAN HISTORY *by Robert P. Swierenga*
166 THE CATTLE TOWNS *by Robert R. Dykstra*
169 POLICING THE CITY: BOSTON: 1822-1885 *by Roger Lane*

Atheneum Paperbacks

HISTORY—AMERICAN—1900 TO THE PRESENT

2 POWER AND DIPLOMACY *by Dean Acheson*

7 THE REPUBLICAN ROOSEVELT *by John Morton Blum*

40 THE UNITED STATES AND MEXICO *by Howard F. Cline*

43 HOLMES-LASKI LETTERS: THE CORRESPONDENCE OF JUSTICE OLIVER
A&B WENDELL HOLMES AND HAROLD J. LASKI *1916—1935 edited by Mark De Wolfe Howe, abridged by Alger Hiss, 2 vols.*

51 TURMOIL AND TRADITION *by Elting E. Morison*

70 THE CHINA TANGLE *by Herbert Feis*

86 THE CORPORATION IN MODERN SOCIETY *edited by Edward S. Mason*

111 THE DECLINE OF AMERICAN LIBERALISM *by Arthur A. Ekirch, Jr.*

113 HARVARD GUIDE TO AMERICAN HISTORY *edited by Oscar Handlin, Arthur Meier Schlesinger, Samuel Eliot Morison, Frederick Merk, Arthur Meier Schlesinger, Jr., Paul Herman Buck*

115 THE ROOTS OF AMERICAN LOYALTY *by Merle Curti*

116 THE POLITICS OF PREJUDICE *by Roger Daniels*

117 CENTURY OF STRUGGLE *by Eleanor Flexner*

123 THE AMERICAN APPROACH TO FOREIGN POLICY *by Dexter Perkins*

126 THE AMERICAN AS REFORMER *by Arthur M. Schlesinger*

129 THE LEGEND OF HENRY FORD *by Keith Sward*

137 FREE SPEECH IN THE UNITED STATES *by Zechariah Chafee, Jr.*

140 MASSACHUSETTS PEOPLE AND POLITICS, 1919—1933 *by J. Joseph Huthmacher*

142 THE PROFESSIONAL ALTRUIST *by Roy Lubove*

149 THE COMMUNIST CONTROVERSY IN WASHINGTON *by Earl Latham*

150 THE DECLINE OF AGRARIAN DEMOCRACY *by Grant McConnell*

151 POLITICS AND POWER *by David J. Rothman*

160 UP AGAINST THE IVY WALL *by Jerry Avorn and members of the staff of the* Columbia Daily Spectator

161 QUANTIFICATION IN AMERICAN HISTORY *by Robert P. Swierenga*

162 PROHIBITION AND THE PROGRESSIVE MOVEMENT *by James H. Timberlake*

163 FARM POLICIES AND POLITICS IN THE TRUMAN YEARS *by Allen J. Matusow*

167 SENATOR ROBERT F. WAGNER AND THE RISE OF URBAN LIBERALISM *by J. Joseph Huthmacher*

173 THE IMAGE *by Daniel J. Boorstin*

175 SECOND CHANCE *by Robert A. Divine*

178 THE END OF THE AMERICAN ERA *by Andrew Hacker*

Atheneum Paperbacks

STUDIES IN AMERICAN NEGRO LIFE

NL1 THE NEGRO IN COLONIAL NEW ENGLAND *by Lorenzo Johnston Greene*
NL2 SEPARATE AND UNEQUAL *by Louis R. Harlan*
NL3 AFTER FREEDOM *by Hortense Powdermaker*
NL4 FREDERICK DOUGLASS *by Benjamin Quarles*
NL5 PREFACE TO PEASANTRY *by Arthur F. Raper*
NL6 W.E.B. DU BOIS: PROPAGANDIST OF THE NEGRO PROTEST
   by Elliott Rudwick
NL7 THE BLACK WORKER *by Sterling D. Spero and Abram L. Harris*
NL8 THE MAKING OF BLACK AMERICA *edited*
A&B *by August Meier and Elliott Rudwick, 2 vols.*
NL9 BLACK MANHATTAN *by James Weldon Johnson*
NL10 THE NEW NEGRO *edited by Alain Locke*
NL11 THE NEGRO'S GOD AS REFLECTED IN HIS LITERATURE
   by Benjamin Mays
NL12 NEGRO POETRY AND DRAMA AND THE NEGRO IN AMERICAN FICTION
   by Sterling Brown
NL13 WHEN NEGROES MARCH *by Harbert Garfinkel*
NL14 PHILOSOPHY AND OPINIONS OF MARCUS GARVEY *by Marcus Garvey,*
   edited by Amy Jacques-Garvey
NL15 FREE NEGRO LABOR AND PROPERTY HOLDING IN VIRGINIA, 1830—1860
   by Luther Porter Jackson
NL16 SEA ISLAND TO CITY *by Clyde Vernon Kiser*
NL17 NEGRO EDUCATION IN ALABAMA *by Horace Mann Bond*
NL18 POLITICS, PRINCIPLE AND PREJUDICE, 1865—1866
   by LaWanda and John H. Cox
NL19 NEGRO POLITICAL LEADERSHIP IN THE SOUTH *by Everett Carll Ladd, Jr.*
NL20 BLACK RECONSTRUCTION IN AMERICA, 1860—1880 *by W. E. B. Du Bois*
NL21 NEGROES IN CITIES *by Karl E. and Alma F. Taeuber*
NL22 TWO JAMAICAS *by Philip De Armond Curtin*
NL23 VASSOURASS: A BRAZILIAN COFFEE COUNTY, 1850—1900 *by Stanley J. Stein*
NL24 THE ROYAL AFRICAN COMPANY *by K. G. Davies*
NL25 STRANGE ENTHUSIASM: A LIFE OF THOMAS WENTWORTH HIGGINSON
   by Tilden G. Edelstein
NL26 THE *Guardian* OF BOSTON: WILLIAM MONROE TROTTER
   by Stephen R. Fox
NL27 LEWIS TAPPAN AND THE EVANGELICAL WAR AGAINST SLAVERY
   by Bertram Wyatt-Brown
NL28 THE NEGRO IN BRAZILIAN SOCIETY *by Florestan Fernandes*
NL29 THE NEGRO AND THE COMMUNIST PARTY *by Wilson Record*

Atheneum Paperbacks

HISTORY

3   SIX MEDIEVAL MEN AND WOMEN *by H. S. Bennett*
10   TRAVEL AND DISCOVERY IN THE RENAISSANCE *by Boies Penrose*
30   GHANA IN TRANSITION *by David E. Apter*
58   TROTSKY'S DIARY IN EXILE—1935 *translated by Elena Zarudnaya*
63   THE SINO-SOVIET CONFLICT 1956–1961 *by Donald S. Zagoria*
83   KARAMZIN'S MEMOIR ON ANCIENT AND MODERN RUSSIA
      by Richard Pipes
97   THE EIGHTEENTH CENTURY CONFRONTS THE GODS *by Frank E. Manuel*
103   JACOBEAN PAGEANT *by G. P. V. Akrigg*
104   THE MAKING OF VICTORIAN ENGLAND *by G. Kitson Clark*
107   RUSSIA LEAVES THE WAR *by George F. Kennan*
108   THE DECISION TO INTERVENE *by George F. Kennan*
121   DRIVING FORCES IN HISTORY *by Halvdan Koht*
124   THE FORMATION OF THE SOVIET UNION *by Richard Pipes*
127   THE THREE LIVES OF CHARLES DE GAULLE *by David Schoenbrun*
128   AS FRANCE GOES *by David Schoenbrun*
141   SERGEI WITTE AND THE INDUSTRIALIZATION OF RUSSIA
      by Theodore Von Laue
152   A HISTORY OF THE WEIMAR REPUBLIC *by Erich Eyck,*
A&B   *2 vols.*
161   QUANTIFICATION IN AMERICAN HISTORY *by Robert P. Swierenga*
181   THE COURT AND THE COUNTRY *by Perez Zagorin*

HISTORY—ASIA

44   CHINA'S RESPONSE TO THE WEST *by Ssu-Yü Teng and John K. Fairbank*
63   THE SINO-SOVIET CONFLICT 1956–1961 *by Donald S. Zagoria*
70   THE CHINA TANGLE *by Herbert Feis*
87   A DOCUMENTARY HISTORY OF CHINESE COMMUNISM
      by Conrad Brandt, Benjamin Schwartz and John K. Fairbank
92   THE LAST STAND OF CHINESE CONSERVATISM *by Mary Clabaugh Wright*
93   THE TRAGEDY OF THE CHINESE REVOLUTION *by Harold R. Isaacs*
147   AFTER IMPERIALISM *by Akira Iriye*
153   CHINA'S EARLY INDUSTRIALIZATION *by Albert Feuerwerker*
154   LI TA-CHAO AND THE ORIGINS OF CHINESE MARXISM *by Maurice Meisner*
164   COMMUNISM AND CHINA: IDEOLOGY IN FLUX *by Benjamin I. Schwartz*
168   LITERARY DISSENT IN COMMUNIST CHINA *by Merle Goldman*
176   THE COMMUNISTS AND THE CHINESE PEASANT REBELLIONS *by*
      James P. Harrison

Atheneum Paperbacks

THE NEW YORK TIMES BYLINE BOOKS

CHINA by *Harry Schwartz*
RUSSIA by *Harrison E. Salisbury*
THE MIDDLE EAST by *Jay Walz*
AFRICA by *Waldemar A. Nielsen*
LATIN AMERICA by *Tad Szulc*
SOUTHEAST ASIA by *Tillman Durdin*

THE ADAMS PAPERS

TAP THE ADAMS PAPERS: DIARY AND AUTOBIOGRAPHY OF JOHN ADAMS
1,2,3,4 *edited by L. H. Butterfield, 4 vols.*
TAP THE ADAMS PAPERS: ADAMS FAMILY CORRESPONDENCE *edited by*
5,6 *L. H. Butterfield, 2 vols.*
TAP THE ADAMS PAPERS: DIARY OF CHARLES FRANCIS ADAMS *edited by*
7,8 *L. H. Butterfield, 2 vols.*
TAP THE ADAMS PAPERS: LEGAL PAPERS OF JOHN ADAMS *edited by*
9,10,11 *L. H. Butterfield, 3 vols.*

ECONOMICS AND BUSINESS

21 BIG BUSINESS LEADERS IN AMERICA by *W. Lloyd Warner and
James Abegglen*
24 PROSPERITY AND DEPRESSION by *Gottfried Haberler*
34 THE DIPLOMACY OF ECONOMIC DEVELOPMENT by *Eugene R. Black*
47 ECONOMIC CONCENTRATION AND THE MONOPOLY PROBLEM
by *Edward S. Mason*
78 THE ECONOMICS OF DEFENSE IN THE NUCLEAR AGE by *Charles J. Hitch
and Roland N. McKean*
80 FOUNDATIONS OF ECONOMIC ANALYSIS by *Paul Anthony Samuelson*
86 THE CORPORATION IN MODERN SOCIETY *edited by Edward S. Mason*
174 BLACK CAPITALISM by *Theodore L. Cross*

PHYSICAL SCIENCES AND MATHEMATICS

13 THE AIM AND STRUCTURE OF PHYSICAL THEORY by *Pierre Duhem*
31 PHILOSOPHY OF MATHEMATICS AND NATURAL SCIENCE
by *Hermann Weyl*
56 THE EARTH BENEATH THE SEA by *Francis P. Shepard*
57 SATELLITE OF THE SUN by *Athelstan Spilhaus*
59 PLAYING WITH INFINITY by *Rózsa Péter*
100 GALAXIES by *Harlow Shapley*

Atheneum Paperbacks

LAW AND GOVERNMENT

20 DOCUMENTS ON FUNDAMENTAL HUMAN RIGHTS *edited by Zechariah*
A&B *Chafee, Jr., 2 vols.*

23 THE CONSTITUTION AND WHAT IT MEANS TODAY *by Edward S. Corwin*

27 COURTS ON TRIAL *by Jerome Frank*

30 GHANA IN TRANSITION *by David E. Apter*

46 THE FUTURE OF FEDERALISM *by Nelson A. Rockefeller*

53 THE BILL OF RIGHTS *by Learned Hand*

72 MR. JUSTICE HOLMES AND THE SUPREME COURT *by Felix Frankfurter*

84 THE DIMENSIONS OF LIBERTY *by Oscar and Mary Handlin*

89 MAKERS OF MODERN STRATEGY *edited by Edward M. Earle*

105 DILEMMAS OF URBAN AMERICA *by Robert C. Weaver*

110 DRED SCOTT'S CASE *by Vincent C. Hopkins, S.J.*

130 THE REVOLUTION OF THE SAINTS *by Michael Walzer*

138 OF LAW AND LIFE AND OTHER THINGS THAT MATTER *by Felix
     Frankfurter, edited by Philip B. Kurland*

148 POLITICAL CHANGE IN A WEST AFRICAN STATE *by Martin Kilson*

149 THE COMMUNIST CONTROVERSY IN WASHINGTON *by Earl Latham*

150 THE DECLINE OF AGRARIAN DEMOCRACY *by Grant McConnell*

156 VARIETIES OF POLICE BEHAVIOR *by James Q. Wilson*

157 AFRICA: FROM INDEPENDENCE TO TOMORROW *by David Hapgood*

160 UP AGAINST THE IVY WALL *by Jerry Avorn and members of the staff of
     the* Columbia Daily Spectator

178 THE END OF THE AMERICAN ERA *by Andrew Hacker*

179 CONGRESS AND THE PUBLIC TRUST *by James C. Kirby, Jr.*

DIPLOMACY AND INTERNATIONAL RELATIONS

2 POWER AND DIPLOMACY *by Dean Acheson*

4 THE ROAD TO PEARL HARBOR *by Herbert Feis*

15 CALL TO GREATNESS *by Adlai E. Stevenson*

34 THE DIPLOMACY OF ECONOMIC DEVELOPMENT *by Eugene B. Black*

40 THE UNITED STATES AND MEXICO *by Howard F. Cline*

41 THE DIPLOMATS 1919–1939 *by Gordon A. Craig and*
A&B *Felix Gilbert*

44 CHINA'S RESPONSE TO THE WEST *by Ssu-Yü Teng and John K. Fairbank*

54 STRATEGIC SURRENDER *by Paul Kecskemeti*

63 THE SINO-SOVIET CONFLICT 1956–1961 *by Donald S. Zagoria*

70 THE CHINA TANGLE *by Herbert Feis*

74 STALIN'S FOREIGN POLICY REAPPRAISED *by Marshall Shulman*

89 MAKERS OF MODERN STRATEGY *edited by Edward M. Earle*

107 RUSSIA LEAVES THE WAR *by George F. Kennan*

108 THE DECISION TO INTERVENE *by George F. Kennan*

147 AFTER IMPERIALISM *by Akira Iriye*

175 SECOND CHANCE *by Robert A. Divine*

Atheneum Paperbacks

TEMPLE BOOKS—*The Jewish Publication Society*
T1 JEWISH LIFE IN THE MIDDLE AGES *by Israel Abrahams*
T2 FOR THE SAKE OF HEAVEN *by Martin Buber*
T3 A HISTORY OF THE CONTEMPORARY JEWS *by Solomon Grayzel*
T4 THE ZIONIST IDEA *edited by Arthur Hertzberg*
T5 A HISTORY OF MEDIAEVAL JEWISH PHILOSOPHY *by Isaac Husik*
T6 THREE JEWISH PHILOSOPHERS *edited by Hans Lewy,*
Alexander Altmann and Isaak Heinemann
T7 THE JEW IN THE MEDIEVAL WORLD *by Jacob R. Marcus*
T8 A HISTORY OF THE JEWISH PEOPLE *by Max L. Margolis and*
Alexander Marx
T9 THE CONFLICT OF THE CHURCH AND THE SYNAGOGUE *by James Parkes*
T10 INTRODUCTION TO THE TALMUD AND MIDRASH *by Hermann L. Strack*
T11 AKIBA: SCHOLAR, SAINT AND MARTYR *by Louis Finkelstein*
T12 OF JEWISH LAW AND LORE *by Louis Ginzberg*
T13 JUDAISM AND MODERN MAN *by William Herberg*
T14 STUDIES IN JUDAISM *by Solomon Schechter*
T15 JEWISH MAGIC AND SUPERSTITION *by Joshua Trachtenberg*
T16 THE WILD GOATS OF EIN GEDI *by Herbert Weiner*
T17 JUDAISM AND CHRISTIANITY *by Leo Baeck*
T18 THEODORE HERZL *by Alex Bein*
T19 AMERICAN JEWRY AND THE CIVIL WAR *by Bertram W. Korn*
T20 SELECTED ESSAYS OF AHAD HA-'AM *by Leon Simon*
T21 NATIONALISM AND HISTORY *by Simon Dubnow*
T22 HELLENISTIC CIVILIZATION AND THE JEWS *by Victor Tcherikover*

PHILOSOPHY AND RELIGION
6 ROGER WILLIAMS *by Perry Miller*
9 MATTER, MIND AND MAN *by Edmund W. Sinnott*
19 BUDDHISM IN TRANSLATIONS *by Henry Clarke Warren*
31 PHILOSOPHY OF MATHEMATICS AND NATURAL SCIENCE
by Hermann Weyl
38 TOWARD REUNION IN PHILOSOPHY *by Morton White*
52 RELIGION IN TWENTIETH CENTURY AMERICA *by Herbert W. Schneider*
60 HERACLITUS *by Philip Wheelwright*
69 ON THE USE OF PHILOSOPHY *by Jacques Maritain*
75 RELIGIOUS PHILOSOPHY *by Harry Austryn Wolfson*
97 THE EIGHTEENTH CENTURY CONFRONTS THE GODS *by Frank E. Manuel*
183 GENERALIZATION IN ETHICS *by Marcus Singer*

Atheneum Paperbacks

PSYCHOLOGY AND SOCIOLOGY

21 BIG BUSINESS LEADERS IN AMERICA *by W. Lloyd Warner and James Abegglen*

67 ON KNOWING *by Jerome S. Bruner*

100 AFRICAN HOMICIDE AND SUICIDE *edited by Paul Bohannan*

119 THE LAW OF PRIMITIVE MAN *by E. Adamson Hoebel*

120 THE SOVIET CITIZEN *by Alex Inkeles and Raymond Bauer*

133 THE FAMILY REVOLUTION IN MODERN CHINA *by Marion J. Levy, Jr.*

165 MOVIES: A PSYCHOLOGICAL STUDY *by Martha Wolfenstein and Nathan Leites*

182 THE CONSPIRACY AGAINST CHILDHOOD *by Eda J. LeShan*

LIFE SCIENCES AND ANTHROPOLOGY

9 MATTER, MIND AND MAN *by Edmund W. Sinnott*

16 THE HORMONES IN HUMAN REPRODUCTION *by George W. Corner*

26 THE OLD STONE AGE *by Miles C. Burkitt*

28 MORPHOGENESIS *by John Tyler Bonner*

33 LOST CITY OF THE INCAS *by Hiram Bingham*

35 GENETICS, PALEONTOLOGY, AND EVOLUTION *edited by Glenn L. Jepsen, Ernst Mayr and George Gaylord Simpson*

45 THE SEA SHORE *by C. M. Yonge*

48 TRISTES TROPIQUES *by Claude Lévi-Strauss*

62 TERRITORY IN BIRD LIFE *by Eliot Howard*

71 HEREDITY AND EVOLUTION IN HUMAN POPULATIONS *by L. C. Dunn*

85 THE INTEGRITY OF THE BODY *by F. M. Burnet, F.R.S.*

88 SPEECH AND BRAIN-MECHANISMS *by Wilder Penfield and Lamar Roberts*

91 CELLS AND SOCIETIES *by John Tyler Bonner*

95 THE FIRMAMENT OF TIME *by Loren Eiseley*

98 IDEAS ON HUMAN EVOLUTION *edited by William Howells*

101 COMMUNICATION AMONG SOCIAL BEES *by Martin Lindauer*

106 ON THE ORIGIN OF SPECIES *by Charles Darwin, a Facsimile of the First Edition, edited by Ernst Mayr*

109 AFRICAN HOMICIDE AND SUICIDE *edited by Paul Bohannon*

155 PEOPLE OF RIMROCK *edited by Evon Z. Vogt and Ethel M. Albert*

STUDIES IN HUMAN BEHAVIOR

Alfred M. Freedman, M.D., and Harold I. Kaplan, M.D., General Editors

HB1 DIAGNOSING MENTAL ILLNESS

HB2 INTERPRETING PERSONALITY

HB3 HUMAN BEHAVIOR

HB4 TREATING MENTAL ILLNESS

HB5 THE CHILD: NORMAL DEVELOPMENT AND PSYCHOLOGICAL ASSESSMENT, *Vol. 1*

HB6 THE CHILD: THE MAJOR PSYCHOLOGICAL DISORDERS AND THEIR TREATMENT, *Vol. 2*